Donated by
The Chester Garden Club
2004

# ENCYCLOPEDIA OF WATER GARDEN PLANTS

# Encyclopedia of

# WATER GARDEN PLANTS

Greg Speichert & Sue Speichert

Foreword by Ann Lovejoy

TIMBER PRESS

Portland • Cambridge

Half-title page: *Nymphaea* 'Queen of Whites' set off by *Myriophyllum aquaticum* among the rocks, *Hedera* beside the birds, and *Weigela* in the background

Frontispiece: Waterfall framed by *Hydrocotyle verticillata* 'Little Umbrellas', left, and *Eichhornia crassipes*, *Hibiscus*, *Lobelia cardinalis*, and *Ruellia brittoniana*, back to front on the right

Published in 2004 by

Timber Press, Inc.
The Haseltine Building
133 S.W. Second Avenue, Suite 450
Portland, Oregon 97204 U.S.A.

Timber Press
2 Station Road
Swavesey
Cambridge CB4 5QJ, U.K.

Printed through Colorcraft Ltd., Hong Kong

Library of Congress Cataloging-in-Publication Data

Speichert, C. Greg.
  Encyclopedia of water garden plants / by Greg Speichert and Sue
Speichert.
    p. cm.
  ISBN 0-88192-625-6 (hardcover)
  1. Aquatic plants. 2. Water gardens. I. Speichert, Sue. II. Title.
  SB423 .S62 2004
  581.7'6--dc22                                    2003016619

A Catalogue record for this book is also available from the British Library.

# Contents

# Foreword

I first met Greg Speichert many years ago, at a symposium in Chicago where we were both presenting. I was immediately impressed by Greg's enthusiasm, experience, and knowledge, as well as his obvious passion for water plants. The talk he gave that day and the slides that accompanied it led me to explore the rich world of hardy marginals and streamside dwellers with new interest. Again and again in the years that followed, I used Greg and Sue's enticing Crystal Palace Perennials catalog as a resource to help design clients choose just the right plant for a challenging situation.

Through their catalog and their *Water Gardening* magazine, Greg and Sue have introduced me to a terrific range of plants that thrive in heavy clay soils and tolerate winter immersion (common problems here in the maritime Northwest). Thousands of home gardeners and professionals have come to rely on Greg and Sue for news about the latest trends in water gardening, hot new plants, cool new fish, and a whole lot more.

As I have good reason to know, Greg and Sue are both solid, reliable, and efficient problem-solvers with a remarkable range and depth of experience. The Speicherts' new *Encyclopedia of Water Garden Plants* already has a place waiting for it on my reference shelf, and I am certainly not alone in this anticipation. This rich new resource will replace a whole boxful of old Speichert catalogs and article clippings in a much handier format, and I can't wait to get my hands on it.

ANN LOVEJOY
*Bainbridge Island*

# CHAPTER 1

# INTRODUCTION TO WATER PLANTS

## WHAT IS A WATER PLANT?

In most ways, water plants are just like any other kind of plant. They have roots, leaves, stems, and usually flowers. Like all plants, they need sunlight and food in order to grow. They need air to breathe and water to drink.

What makes water plants, or aquatics, different is their ability to grow in a wet, watery environment. Most terrestrial plants cannot tolerate having their roots submerged in wet soil or in water. They are even less tolerant of having their foliage submerged. For water plants, these conditions are beneficial, even vital, to their survival. Their roots, stems, and leaves have adapted so that they require increased water levels in order to survive and grow. They are not hydroponic, which involves growing terrestrial plants in an inert medium, periodically applying a nutrient solution to keep the plants moist. Water plants need water-soaked soil in order to grow and thrive.

### How Are the Roots Different?

The roots of most water plants lack the root hairs that terrestrial plants have. Root hairs function to pull water from the soil. Not having these hairs means that water plants are unable to pull water from the soil. They rely on the water being so freely available that they can simply take it up without search or strain or effort. Some water plants use water pressure to force the water up into the plant. For example, the leaves of pickerel plant (*Pontederia cordata*) act as water towers, signaling the plant to grow shorter in shallow water and taller in deeper water.

### How Are the Leaves and Stems Different?

The leaves of water plants are generally more waxy and have the stomata on the surface of the leaf rather than underneath, or at least they have a reduced number on the bottom. Stom-

With *Lysimachia nummularia* in the foreground and *Colocasia esculenta* 'Violet Stem' and *Cyperus longus* in the back of the pond, an abundant stand of *Pontederia* is surrounded by, clockwise from the top right, *Canna* 'Pretoria', a Louisiana iris, *Saururus cernuus*, and a waterlily

*Cyperus textilis*, front left, *Canna* 'Erebus', *Thalia geniculata*, *Ludwigia, Echinodorus palaefolius*, and *Zephyranthes*

*Ranunculus aquatilis* grows submerged and can send up emergent leaves and flowers

ata are the pores in the epidermis of the leaf where oxygen is exchanged. If they were on the bottom, the plants would be more open to pathogens in the water, and being on the surface, they are more available to the exchange of oxygen and carbon dioxide. Most terrestrial plants have their stomata on the bottom of the leaf to help protect the plant from losing too much moisture. This is not a problem for water plants.

The stems of water plants are often similar to those of terrestrial plants, though they rely on the water to support them. The leaves and stems are often somewhat spongy, having minuscule air holes that buoy them up in water. Several, like lotus, have hollow, inflated air vacuoles. They have adapted by creating larger air chambers that take in oxygen up top to pump to the roots. In trees and terrestrial plants, the oxygen comes both from the soil through the roots and from the air through the leaves. In water plants, the leaves act

like snorkels for the whole plant, drawing in oxygen that is transported to the roots.

These adaptions to the watery world have given many water plants the ability to float on the water surface. They take in air, holding it in pockets in their leaves, so that the plant becomes buoyant. Consider the leaf of water hyacinth (*Eichhornia crassipes*), for example.

## How Are the Blooms Different?

Flowers on water plants have structure and function similar to blooms of terrestrial plants. They tend to be more water resistant, though, with a waxier coating to protect them from splashing and wave action. Otherwise, they are just like other types of flowers.

Water lettuce, in this case *Pistia stratiotes* 'Aqua Velvet', floats on the water

*Peltandra* and other marginals filling in the edge of the pond

*Ranunculus flammula* and *Myosotis scorpioides* in front of *Lobelia fulgens*

## CLASSIFYING WATER PLANTS

Water plants are most commonly classified by their position in the landscape. Plants that grow in wet or moist soil, or that grow in a few inches to a few feet of water, are called "water plants." They are then classified by how much water they need, or tolerate, in order to grow. This is the most common method of grouping water plants for hobby gardeners and the one that is used in this book.

### Submerged Water Plants

Plants that grow entirely underwater are called submerged water plants. They are also called oxygenators for their ability to add oxygen to the water column during daylight hours. Aquatics include the familiar aquarium plants that

Hardy waterlily *Nymphaea* 'Cherokee'

Tropical waterlily *Nymphaea* 'Bluebird'

are grown in children's goldfish bowls. They also encompass the many underwater plants that provide cover and spawning ground for fish in natural lakes, rivers, and streams. Do not underrate the beauty of submerged plants in the water garden. Many have colorful foliage that glistens underwater, and several even have flowers that float on the water surface during the summer. They are very easy to grow and need very little care to make their important contribution to the ecology and life of the pond.

## Floating Water Plants

Plants that sit on the water surface with no need of pot or soil are called floating water plants. Floaters are extremely easy to grow and some even flower, with bright blue blooms that start when the weather warms and continue until fall. All they need is a container that holds water, and they will grow right on the deck or patio. Their roots dangle down in the water, drawing nutrients that could otherwise cause an algae bloom. Among the least expensive of all water plants, they are usually bought fresh each year by most water gardeners. In the winter, simply add them to the compost pile or use them to mulch around perennials—because of their high nitrogen content, they add nutrients to the soil even after being removed from the pond.

## Marginal Water Plants

At the edge of the pond are the "marginals." These plants grow with their roots in the soil but with most of their foliage above the soil and out of the water. They are also referred to as "emergent" because their leaves emerge above the soil and water. Some grow in soil that is only moist or wet, while others like to be in soil that is a few inches under the water. Marginals can be more than 6 feet or less than 2 inches tall. Some are clump forming and stay where they are put. Others are rambling types that come up all over the pond edge. Both flowers and foliage can range from red to pink, from white to yellow or orange, and even from purple to blue. Fans of variegated foliage will not be disappointed with the selection of striped, blotched, streaked, or margined foliage among the marginal water plants.

## Waterlilies

Another classification of water plants is those that grow with their roots and stems below water and their foliage floating on the water surface, right out in the middle of the pond. The best known members of this group are the waterlilies, of course. Their leaves are round and look like floating green pads on the water. Waterlily flowers are many petaled and vary in shape from round to stellate. Some float on the water, and others are held on stems several inches out of the water.

Waterlilies are classified into two broad groups. Hardy waterlilies survive winters in colder climates. Tropical waterlilies cannot withstand a winter freeze and need special care during colder months. To tell if a waterlily is hardy or tropical, look at the edge of its rounded leaves. If the edge is smooth, then the lily is hardy. If the edge is crinkled, wavy, or toothed, then the lily is tropical.

Hardy waterlily flowers come in many colors—white, red, pink, yellow, even orange and changeable. No one has been able, so far, to grow a hardy waterlily with blue or purple blooms. Leaves may be light or dark green, sometimes edged in red or maroon. The undersides of the leaves may be green, maroon, or splotched in dark red. One cultivar, *Nymphaea* 'Arc en Ciel', has foliage that is streaked in pink, red, white, and green. Hardy waterlilies flower during the day—none open at night.

Flowers of tropical waterlilies, on the other hand, may open in the evening. These cultivars, called night-blooming tropicals, range from red to pink to white. No night-blooming tropical waterlilies are blue. Day-blooming tropicals are similar to hardy waterlilies and can be found in a wide range of colors, from deep blue and vivid purple to orange, pink, yellow, and white. One cultivar even is a green-yellow called *Nymphaea* 'Green Smoke'.

Tropical waterlilies have a distinct, enticing fragrance that floats out over the wind. Often you can tell from several feet away that the flowers are open, even when you are not looking at them. Hardy waterlilies, although having some scent, are not nearly as perfumed as tropical waterlilies.

## Waterlily-like Plants

Plants that are not waterlilies but that do grow in soil several inches below the water surface and hold their leaves and flowers on top of the water are grouped together as waterlily-like plants. Some, such as the water snowflakes (*Nymphoides*), have dainty, star-shaped flowers and rounded leaves. Others, such as the water poppies (*Hydrocleys*), have creamy yellow flowers that resemble single roses. Some are very winter hardy, like water hawthorne (*Aponogeton distachyus*), which prefers the cool waters of spring and fall and may go completely dormant in the heat of summer. All make excellent contributions to container water gardens as well as in-ground ponds.

## Lotus

Lotus are similar to waterlilies but hold their leaves and flowers well above the water. Many varieties that are commercially available originated in the Orient. Lotus have bowl-shaped, highly fragrant blossoms with delicate colors. Pink and white are most common, but yellow and a dark pink that is almost red are also available. Lotus leaves are very round and stand out of the water like inverted parasols. They are covered with a velvety wax that makes raindrops roll around like little balls of mercury. Lotus cultivars grow anywhere from 6 inches to 6 feet in height. Smaller selections, called bowl lotus, thrive in containers that are less than a foot wide and in just a few inches of soil and water. Lotus also grow well in bogs with a few inches of standing water.

Lotus in the landscape

# CHAPTER 2

# POTS AND SOIL

Water plants are not fussy or particular about what they are planted in, although they do have a few basic requirements. Like other plants, they need above all the right amount of moisture, sunlight, and food to grow and flower well. As long as these needs are met, water plants grow well, usually with little additional care or attention.

## POTS

Gardeners who have rubber, concrete, or fiberglass ponds often grow their water plants in pots. Pots are also good to use in earth-bottom ponds to contain running plants and to make them look more full. The selection is as wide and varied as that of overall pond designs.

The purpose of a pot is to keep plant and the soil together in the pond, where you want them to be, without dirtying the water or damaging the pond. Many different types of pots are available, and most serve their essential function well. Being informed of their relative benefits and drawbacks is important so that pondkeepers are able to pick the ones that are right for their particular growing plans and water feature designs.

Open weave and fabric baskets are favored by water gardeners because they allow the water to diffuse through all the pot surfaces, enabling the plant to pull more nutrients from the water. This is especially important for plants grown for their filtration qualities, because the pots allow the roots to grow through the weave or holes to filter the water more effectively.

Just be aware that plants growing in open weave or fabric baskets may need transplanting more frequently. As plants mature, their roots will naturally seek the open water, and over time they will break through a basket that has holes or one that is made of a lightweight fabric. Once they look like they are outgrowing their pot, once the pot is no longer visible, the plants must be quickly transplanted to another pot. If the pond includes large, hungry fish, they will look upon the roots as a new treat in the pond. Besides, waiting too long to transplant will require near surgical technique to extricate the plant from its pot, since the

A tub garden displays, left to right, *Peltandra virginica*, a dwarf hardy waterlily, and *Equisetum hyemale*

roots will become highly entangled in the plastic or fabric of the basket.

Hard-sided plastic pots may have one, none, or several bottom holes. Holes can be a problem with deep rooted plants with long root systems—they will quickly find the holes and grow out through them. A coffee filter or piece of newspaper will usually hold soil in the pot, but not roots. For this reason, water gardeners sometimes use no-hole pots, so that neither roots nor soil can escape. No-hole containers are excellent for making into miniature patio or table-top ponds. When they are part of a larger pond, be careful that the lip of the container stays below the pond's water surface. If the water level dips in the pond, the edge of the container may rise above the water surface. The plant will suddenly be in its own desert even though it is completely surrounded by water. It is easier to simply pot the plants in a plastic pot with a single hole in the bottom so that water can enter but the plant's roots will not be able to grow out of the sides of the pot.

In large, natural ponds, water plants are often planted without any pots at all. Burlap bags with soil are useful to hold waterlilies on the soil below the water surface. As the lily grows, the burlap disintegrates and the plant moves into the soil on its own. Some submerged plants are simply placed in a bunch, weighted, and tossed to the bottom of the pond, even when the pond is lined in rubber or concrete. The muck that builds on the pond's floor is often enough for the plants to root into for the growing season.

# SOIL

Ask ten water gardeners what they use to plant their waterlilies and you will probably get ten different answers. Clay soil, sand, even cat litter, all have their proponents in the great debate over the "perfect" water plant potting mix. No one potting medium is right for all water plants. Certain types are better than others for different kinds of plants. Plants generally need a potting medium for three things: anchorage, fertilization, and moisture retention. Soil keeps plants standing up straight and prevents them from falling over, it holds the nutrients that the plants need to grow and bloom, and it holds the water that the plants also need to flourish.

Besides being good for the plants, the potting mix must also suit the needs of the plant keeper. Growers want a potting mix that is easy to use, will not smell, and will not make the pond look dirty or muddy. We also want something that is economical and readily available.

## Clay Garden Soil

The most obvious choice for potting a water plant is garden soil, but it turns out there are several different kinds of soil. Two of the most common are clay soil and sandy soil.

Water plants grow best in clay soil—a higher amount of clay is a good thing for a water plant. Clay holds more water and nutrients for the plant to absorb. It also holds the plants in place better than sandy soil. Clay loam is sticky, though, so your hands get pretty dirty from it. And it is very, very heavy. Cleaning plants' rhizomes, tubers, or roots for transplanting is not too difficult as long as the hose can give out a strong jet of water. When a pot full of clay soil falls over in the pond, it can get the water pretty dirty.

Clay soil is ideal for all water plants. It is acceptable for pondkeepers who have strong muscles, do not mind getting their hands dirty, and will not get upset when something causes a little dirt to spill into the pond.

## Sandy Garden Soil

Sandy soil, or even pure sand, is good for plants that are shorter and have a mounded or creeping habit. Tall plants have problems in sand, because they may topple over in a strong wind or a strong water current. Sand does not hold fertilizer as well as clay soil, but it does hold some nutrients. Plants growing in sand must be fertilized regularly. Sand will not get the grower's hands as dirty as clay, and transplanting is a snap.

Sand is acceptable for shorter plants, especially those in a quiet pond protected from strong winds. It is very good for water gardeners who consistently fertilize their plants and do not mind that the pots are heavy once the sand gets wet.

## Potting Soil

Then, soils are available in bags under the labels "potting soil" and "garden soil." Neither is suitable for water plants. They usually contain a high degree of organic matter, such as peat moss and manure. These are wonderful for geraniums and rose bushes, but they can be harmful, even deadly, for water plants. Organic matter starts to rot and decay once it gets wet. Put it under water and it breaks down very quickly. As the organic material decomposes, it releases salts and other chemicals that can burn the plant's roots. In severe cases, this can cause the water plant's total demise. As if this were not bad enough, bagged soil often contains vermiculite and perlite, which float right to the water surface once they enter the pond! They are unsightly and a dickens to try to skim out of the pond. If you are shopping for potting soil for water plants, keep walking right past those bags of commercial soil mixes. They are intended strictly for plants in the rest of the yard, not in the pond.

## Pebbles and Pea Gravel

Pea gravel and small pebbles are ideal for potting filtration plants, ones whose roots can catch nutrients as they pass through the crevices created by the small stones. Pea gravel is not very good at holding and storing nutrients for the plants to absorb, but as long as the plants can absorb nutrients directly from the water, this is not critical. The plants are better able to work as biological filters to clean the water.

Do not bother to fertilize water plants potted in pea gravel. Pushing a fertilizer tablet into a pot of pea gravel is hard, especially one that is tight with plant roots. Even if the tablet is successfully lodged in the pot, the fertilizer is likely to dissolve into the water rather than being absorbed by the plant's roots, which can lead to an algae bloom. If the plants are adequately nourished directly from the water, then fertilizer is of little use. If the pond water is very clear, though, the plants may go undernourished.

Transplanting something that has been growing in pea gravel can be tricky. The roots get tangled in the small rocks and sometimes the only way to separate root from pea gravel is to trim the roots away. Pea gravel is a good potting mix for plants that are especially adept at drawing nutrients directly from the water, such as rushes (*Scirpus*), reeds (*Phragmites*), and pickerel plant (*Pontederia*). Make sure to plant them in a large pot so they will not need transplanting very often, and put them somewhere in the pond where they will not have to be moved.

## Cat Litter

Cat litter is one material that was never intended for water plants, yet it works well as a potting medium. The right kind of cat litter says "calcified clay" on the label, not shredded paper or something else. It is the generic form that has not been chemically treated or deodorized, which could harm the pond. Calcified clay has been mined from the earth, cleaned, baked, and pulverized.

Cat litter has about the same good nutrient and moisture-retention qualities as clay soil. It is heavy but is not dirty like clay soil. It does not float (although you would think it would) and it does not clump together into a brick once it gets wet (although you would think it would do that, too). It can have some dust to it when it comes out of the bag, but do not rinse it off before use as it will dissolve. If it spills into the

Cat litter, soil, and pea gravel

pond, it is not as dirty looking as clay soil, since it is usually tan or gray instead of black. And transplanting from cat litter is just as easy as it is from clay soil or sand.

## Rockwool

Rockwool is another potting medium that has been around for a long time. It is the backbone of hydroponics—the concept of growing regular plants, like tomatoes, directly in water and with no soil whatsoever.

Rockwool is excellent for growing shorter water plants with a mounded or creeping growth habit. Plants stand up straight in it and will not shift around in the pot. Rockwool is clean and sterile and certainly less dirty looking than clay soil, sand, or pea gravel. It contains fine fibers and some recommend wearing a mask when using it. It is extremely lightweight, though, so pots can have a tendency to float around the pond. Add a top layer of rock, such as pea gravel, to give the pot weight. Do not use it for tall marginals like cannas or cattails (*Typha*), which would be more prone to topple in a strong wind. For growers willing to do a little extra work to keep pots from bobbing up in the water, rockwool is very clean and effective for water plants. It can be a little difficult, however, to extricate a plant's roots for transplanting if the plant is overgrown. Rockwool is also difficult to fertilize because it is like a block of felt.

## Cocoa Fiber

Cocoa fiber is a potting medium that some manufacturers have been touting of late. It looks like brown strands of straw that have been woven together. Filtration plants love to be potted in cocoa fiber. The material acts like pea gravel because it allows water to flow over the plants' roots. Fertilizing with tablets is unnecessary, since the fertilizer would simply dissolve directly into the water long before the plant could absorb it.

Shorter filtration plants are better suited for cocoa fiber. It is lightweight, which makes it easier to move in the pond but prone to floating around if not somehow weighted down. It certainly will not get the pond water dirty if a pot tips over. Like rockwool, separating a plant's roots from the cocoa fiber for transplanting may be difficult if the plant is overgrown.

## CHARACTERISTICS OF POTTING MEDIA

| Medium | Anchorage | Nutrient Retention | Weight | Dirtiness | Transplantability | Comment |
|---|---|---|---|---|---|---|
| **Clay soil** | good | good | heavy | high | easy | good for all water plants |
| **Sand** | poor | poor | heavy | low | easy | good for shorter plants; fertilize consistently |
| **Pea gravel** | good | poor | heavy | low | some difficulty | good for filtration plants |
| **Rockwool** | poor | poor | light | low | some difficulty | good for shorter plants; very clean |
| **Cocoa fiber** | good | poor | light | low | some difficulty | good for filtration plants |
| **Cat litter** (calicified clay) | good | good | heavy | high | easy | good for all water plants |
| **Potting soil** | good | very bad | heavy | yes | easy | unsuitable for water plants |

Such a variety of potting media explains why the subject creates such controversy among water gardeners. Each has its virtues and drawbacks. Each is suitable for growing healthy water plants, given the right set of circumstances and conditions in the pond. The right choice depends largely on your own personal preferences and the extent to which one medium or another is economical and easily available in the area. Here is a table to help water gardeners compare the pros and cons of the different potting media.

## TOPPINGS

Like a bowl of ice cream at a sundae bar, water plants need a topping over their soil. Toppings help prevent fish from digging the soil out of the pot, and they reduce the amount of weeds that can grow in the soil. And, a pot of soil dressed with a topping looks prettier, turning a ho-hum "swamp weed" into a water garden knockout.

Pea gravel, sand, and stones are used to top off the soil, with pea gravel generally being the most popular. Sand is the nicest to use on oxygenating, or submerged, plants and tropical lilies because it is softer and lessens the possibility of damaging the crown of the plant. Toppings should be dark colored, making the plants look greener. Light colors will make the plants look more yellow. Larger stones are generally used where large koi or goldfish live in the pond, because they are so adept at sucking smaller ones out of the pot. Some water gardeners have even used slabs of black slate to keep lilies in their containers.

Back to front, *Canna* 'Pretoria' and *Canna* 'Phasion', *Cyperus alternifolius* 'Nanus', repeated at front, *Colocasia esculenta* 'Black Magic', and *Oenanthe sarmentosa*. *Arundo donax* 'Variegata', left

# CHAPTER 3

# FERTILIZERS FOR POND PLANTS

Like vitamins for humans, fertilizer provides the necessary building blocks for plants to live and grow. Fertilizer works by manipulating three basic ingredients—nitrogen, phosphorus, and potassium (N-P-K)—the three numbers that appear on all fertilizer packages. Depending on the amounts of each of these ingredients, fertilizers can cause plants to grow more leaves, set more fruit, or produce more flowers.

Although water plants are a lot like perennials, their watery growing conditions can impact the way they take in, process, and use fertilizer. Certain fertilizer components, and certain types of fertilizers, are less effective when used in the pond. Knowing these important distinctions will help water gardeners grow better, stronger, and healthier pond plants.

## COMPONENTS OF FERTILIZER

### Nitrogen

The first ingredient listed on bags of fertilizer is N, which stands for nitrogen. Nitrogen is used by plants to produce green growth and healthy foliage. Summer grass food always has a high concentration of nitrogen, in order to promote lush, full, green lawns.

Nitrogen is produced in ponds as part of the natural nitrogen cycle, in which ammonia from fish waste breaks down into nitrite, which is converted to nitrate, which plants absorb. Generally, water plants grow better if their fertilizer contains a certain amount of nitrogen, even though they may also find nitrogen in the water. Plants are usually better able to take up the form of nitrogen found in the soil than that found in pond water.

*Zantedeschia* blooms in the center, with *Caltha* and *Iris* in front

## Phosphorous

The second ingredient listed for fertilizer is P, which stands for phosphorus and is found in phosphate. This is the ingredient that plants need most to bloom. Miracle-Gro Bloom Booster is listed as 10-52-10. The 52 means that it is high in phosphorous so plants produce lots of flowers.

The amounts of phosphorous and nitrogen are related. Plants need one phosphorus atom to use seven nitrogen atoms. Without enough phosphorus, they are unable to assimilate and use nitrogen. Not having enough phosphorus can slow a plant's growth.

Although phosphorus occurs naturally in most waters in the United States, new evidence shows that much of it is in a form that plants cannot absorb. Moreover, a form of phosphorous called calcium phosphate—which some municipalities add to buffer their water in order to protect pipes—may promote dreaded string algae. What is worse, calcium phosphate is absorbed and converted more efficiently by string algae than it is by pond plants, meaning it will help string algae grow but do little for pond plants.

## Potassium

The third ingredient listed on a box of fertilizer is K, which stands for potassium and is found in potash. It is the all-around food necessary for plant fitness and strength. It is the "Special K"—the stuff that makes a plant body strong. Plants use potassium to develop roots, store energy, and build cells.

Pond water naturally contains a certain amount of potassium. Many creatures in the pond, both single cell and multicell, use potassium to live and grow. Although plants may be able to absorb potassium directly from the water, they will get a big boost from having it in their fertilizer, too.

## Micronutrients

Besides the three main building blocks for good plant health, micronutrients also play an important role. Called "trace elements" because plants need them only in small amounts, they include calcium, magnesium, and sulfur, as well as iron, manganese, copper, zinc, and boron. These trace elements aid plants with photosynthesis, chlorophyll production, vitamin production, and many other important functions.

Most plants, including water plants, require their soil and water pH to range between 6.5 and 8.5 in order to be able to absorb micronutrients properly. For water plants, the pH level of the water can drastically impact the pH value of the soil in which plants are potted. Water that is very acid or alkaline can change the pH reading of soil in the water. For example, water that has a pH of 9 can cause neutral soil (7 pH) to increase its pH value. Similarly, water that has a pH of 6 can cause neutral soil to lower its pH value. Consider both the soil and water when determining the pH level of a pond. A few plants need to be in soil that is slightly more acidic (pH 6.5), such as pitcher plants (*Sarracenia*), but most water plants are highly adaptable and are able to absorb fertilizer in a wide range of pH levels.

Average garden soil often contains the trace elements needed for good terrestrial perennial plant growth. For water plants, the soil in which they are planted may not have the trace minerals they require. Heavy clay soil often contains the essential trace minerals, but cat litter does not. Some of the soilless aquatic media, such as coconut fiber or rockwool, lack any micronutrients whatsoever. Plants potted in these media benefit from regular fertilization.

Pond water usually contains many of the micronutrients that water plants need and relish, but may not have all of them. Having micronutrients included in the fertilizer is always helpful. If you think your water may be high in a certain ingredient, have the local water authorities check it.

# KINDS OF FERTILIZER

Whatever the kind of fertilizer, make sure to check the label. Pay attention to the ratio of N, P, and K that it contains. Whether a fertilizer is for perennials or specially designed for water plants, using a lower ratio, such as 6-6-6, more often is always better than using a higher ratio, such as 20-20-20, less often. A higher ratio can burn a plant's roots, causing it more harm than good. A fertilizer that has a roughly equivalent ratio of nitrogen, phosphorous, and potassium is usually best for feeding plants from spring through fall.

Organic forms of fertilizer should be used for water plants with great caution, or better yet, not at all. When mixed into the soil for perennial growth, organic fertilizers such as bone meal, dried blood, and the like release their compounds gradually and interact with the soil and moisture around them. Their compounds may respond quite differently when submerged in water or kept continuously moist in the bog or water garden. Some organic materials create salts as a by-product of decomposition. In the perennial garden, these salts take longer to develop and are washed away from the plants without ill effects. In the pond, though, they develop more quickly and remain in the soil longer, and

A Louisiana iris backs *Cyperus alternifolius* 'Nanus' and *Cyperus isocladus* to the left of *Nymphaea* 'Sunrise'

Algae in the pond

can burn plants' roots, ultimately causing their death. Manure, for example, is often suggested as a fertilizer for pond plants. If it is not very, very well aged and fully composted, however, manure will continue to rot while underwater and will inhibit plants' growth and health. If you have lots of manure, use it for your vegetables and roses rather than your pond plants. Leaves, hay, and plant debris should never be mixed with soil for potting pond plants. These, too, will decompose in the pond and harm the plants with which they are planted.

Often pond owners use fertilizers for perennials, trees, or shrubs instead of fertilizer made specially for aquatics. Although they are not likely to be harmful to fish or other wildlife, be sure to pay attention to the list and amounts of ingredients. Aquatic plant fertilizers have been designed, studied, and tested to be effective for the special circumstances of the water garden. Fertilizers for perennials, trees, and shrubs have been made for very different conditions and may not respond the same when placed in water. Some may break down too quickly and over-fertilize the plants. Ammonia levels can peak, killing fish. Pond owners should be care-

ful when using fertilizers not designed for ponds. The best course is to use some on a few plants to see how the fertilizer works before applying it to every plant in the water garden.

One good rule of thumb, regardless of the type of fertilizer, is to alternate feedings to lessen the effect of any fertilizer leaching into the pond. Fertilize half the plants one week, and then the rest of the plants a week or so later. In the spring, we fertilize half the plants first, then wait two weeks before fertilizing the others. In the summer, we wait a week rather than two before fertilizing the second half of plants. Always, always follow the manufacturer's directions when fertilizing any plants.

## Liquid

Fertilizers that are already in liquid form are a big boon for gardeners who grow houseplants. Just add a teaspoon to a gallon of water and use it to water all the plants in the house. Liquid fertilizers can be a big problem for water gardeners. The liquid can quickly leach into the pond, feeding an algae bloom instead of a waterlily bloom. After all, algae is a plant,

Granular fertilizer

to water, it becomes a liquid fertilizer that will promote algae growth more than any water plant growth. My best advice is to avoid using it to fertilize water plants.

Muriate of potash in its pure form is a water-soluble salt. Since it contains mostly potassium, it helps promote overall health and vitality but does not aid in a plant's foliar growth or flowering. It is highly concentrated and you do not need much to fertilize. For commercial greenhouse applications, growers mix 50 grams of muriate of potash in 500 milliliters of water. They then take 300 milliliters of this mixture and add it to 800 gallons of water in order to fertilize their plants. Hardly a tablespoon or so is enough to feed most of the water plants in a backyard pond. Be careful to use it in small amounts, so that it will not harm the plants—it can be too much of a good thing.

too, and it appreciates a fertilizer boost just as much as the water plants. Using a liquid fertilizer in the pond to feed *only* the plants and not the algae is virtually impossible. For container ponds, however, where plants like papyrus (*Cyperus papyrus*) or lotus are the only inhabitants of a crock or tub, liquid fertilizer is great.

If you do decide to use a liquid fertilizer, check its list of ingredients to be sure it has all three nutrients, N, P, and K. Some liquid fertilizer contains mostly potassium (K) and maybe some iron, but little else. Take the water plants out of the pond and keep them in a separate container of water. Treat them with the liquid fertilizer in this separate holding tank. Follow the directions so as not to over fertilize the plants. Once they have had a day or two to take up the nutrients in the fertilized water, rinse them and return them to the pond. This method is very useful for feeding water hyacinth (*Eichhornia crassipes*) and water lettuce (*Pistia stratiotes*) without affecting the pond water. If your water hyacinths never bloom, this will give them the extra lift they need to flower.

## Granular

Fertilizer in granular form has the consistency of sugar. In chemical terms, granulated fertilizer is made up of nitrogen, phosphorous, and potash in salt form. These salts are mixed with a carrier so that they form little tiny pearls. The carrier is an inert ingredient that holds the fertilizer until it is released for the plants' use. Gypsum is the most common carrier but clay is also used.

One way to use granulated fertilizer is to measure it out and mix it with the soil when the plants are potted. After several weeks, more fertilizer can be added in small doses. It can also be wrapped into a piece of paper and then pushed into the soil, much like a tablet of fertilizer. To avoid worrying about dissolving paper in the soil, simply make a hole in the soil with your finger, pour in a few tablespoons of the fertilizer, and push the soil back over to cover the hole, but you need to lift the pots out of the pond to do this.

## Water Soluble

Some fertilizers look like they are granular but are classified as water soluble. They are often applied as foliar fertilizers—after being mixed with water, they are sprayed onto the leaves where they are absorbed directly. Foliar fertilizers are wonderful for rose beds or vegetable gardens. They can be disastrous on a water garden. A water-soluble fertilizer is simply a dehydrated form of liquid fertilizer (like gelatin in a box before you add water to make Jell-O). Once you add it

## Tablets

A very popular form of fertilizer for water plants is a tablet that can be pushed into the soil. Like granulated fertilizer, these tablets are made up of fertilizer salts that are bound onto a carrier.

Tablets are useful because they afford water gardeners more control over the amount and frequency

Fertilizer tablets

of the fertilizer. You can feed certain plants but not others, or feed less often in the spring and fall and more often in the heat of summer. If you have a section of the pond with plants grown especially to filter water, denying them fertilizer can "force" them to rely on the nitrogen and other nutrients in the water. Some brands of tablet fertilizer dissolve quickly in water. Pondtabbs, for example, uses bentonite clay as a carrier, which dissolves in water almost instantly.

Tablet forms of fertilizer that are intended for use in the perennial garden may not be suitable for the water garden. Some use a carrier that can leave behind a residue in the soil. This is not so much of a problem when the fertilizer is used for a terrestrial plant, like a rose or a geranium, but when the fertilizer is used for a water plant, the carrier may not break down completely. We have had some fertilizers leave behind a carrier that made a hard rock-like ball in the soil. As we added more of the fertilizer, we got more little rocks in the soil. Perhaps it was a function of our local water, which is very alkaline. For us, tree spikes and other tablet forms of perennial fertilizer seem more prone to leave behind hard rock-like pieces of carrier in the soil.

## Time-Release Fertilizer

Some fertilizers are designed to release gradually over a period of several weeks and are called "time-release." For perennials, trees, and shrubs, these fertilizers are often activated by moisture and release their fertilizer in small doses every time it rains or you turn on your sprinkler. For water plants, these types of time-release fertilizers will not be effective at all—put them in water and they release all their fertilizer in just a few days. Like with other kinds of fertilizers, first test it on just one or two plants. If you notice that the test plants have started to wane or slow down, then you know that the time-release fertilizer has been used up too soon and you need to fertilize again.

## FERTILIZING WITH GREEN WATER

Although most people probably do not care for a pond full of green water, water plants see it differently. That bright green means that pea-soup algae is busy munching away at the nitrogen in the water, and the water plants will not waste any time joining in the banquet. They may have to work hard to convert the nitrogen, though. Studies appear to show that water plants need more energy to convert nitrogen directly from the water than they do to use nitrogen found in the soil. Some exceptional plants have adapted to taking nitrogen directly from the water. Floating water plants such as water hyacinth (*Eichhornia crassipes*) and water lettuce (*Pistia stratiotes*) are adept at absorbing nitrogen as their roots dangle in the water. Submerged water plants absorb nitrogen directly through their leaves as well as their roots. Letting the pond water turn green is not the best way to promote healthy water plant growth. Algae acts much like weeds in a garden. It ties up the nutrients and shades the pond, and the shade can kill submerged plants.

The same caution applies to the adage that you can "let your fish feed your plants." It is true that fish produce nitrogen in the ammonia ($NH_4$) that they excrete. In fact, the higher the protein content of their food, the more ammonia they add to the pond, which is why cheaper fish food and bulk "trout chow," both of which are high in protein, increase the ammonia load in the pond. Beneficial bacteria break down the ammonia to nitrite, and still more beneficial bacteria convert the nitrite to nitrate, turning one form of nitrogen into another. Plants are then able to convert the nitrate to help them grow. It is not a one-for-one equation, though—one fish does not feed one lily. For the fish to feed the plants, the pond would need an awful lot of fish. And an awful lot of very green water. Meanwhile, the risk of ammonia toxicity to the fish would be infinitely greater than any benefit to the pond plants. The water would be too green to ever allow sight of the fish anyway. Better to invest a few dollars in a good plant fertilizer and keep the water clean and clear for the fish.

Clockwise from lower left, *Myosotis scorpioides* and *Ranunculus flammula*, *Glyceria*, *Pontederia*, *Lythrum* and *Thalia*, *Cyperus longus*, *Baldellia ranunculoides* f. *repens*, *Alisma*, and *Phragmites australis*

# CHAPTER 4

# HARDY WATERLILIES

Hardy waterlilies are the sturdy souls that can survive a cold winter climate. Their one requirement is that they be protected from a hard freeze during winter. Compared to terrestrial perennials, they are just as easy to grow and need little care or attention. For the effort of an hour or so a week during the summer, waterlily gardeners are rewarded with many weeks of flowers and lush, green growth.

All hardy waterlilies are day blooming. Their flowers open in the morning, the precise hour depending upon the climate, season, and cultivar, and then close in mid to late afternoon. Growing hardy waterlilies is not the best endeavor for those who work every day and are home only in the evenings—they will see the blooms only on the weekends.

Hardy waterlilies belong to the genus *Nymphaea*. The hardy species—*N. alba*, *N. candida*, *N. caroliniana*, *N. odorata*, *N. tetragona*, and *N. tuberosa*—have been found growing wild in the coldest waters of the Scandinavian countries, in ponds and lakes of the North American continent, and in the warm waters of Central America. Native species are still extant in lakes across the world, including those of the British Isles, Scandinavia, the United States, Europe, and Asia. *Nymphaea tetragona* is found in northern Australia and possibly New Zealand, but this is debated. Wild species of hardy waterlilies do not always flower well or reliably. Most are white or light pink, though a few are more reddish in color. Certain species are very small, miniature even. Others are large and can be so rampant as to overtake a natural pond in only a few years.

New colors in hardy waterlilies were largely unexplored until Joseph Bory Latour-Marliac took up hardy waterlily hybridization in the late 1800s. In the 40 years or so that he hybridized his lilies in central France, he introduced more than 100 cultivars. He developed superior waterlilies that grew well and produced more flowers with better color. They were not as likely to spread rapidly in the earth-bottom ponds common during his time. Many had low seed fertility, a fortunate trait for growers wanting to avoid having tons of seedlings sprouting in the pond. Many of Marliac's selections are still available today, and most have become the basis for later efforts to produce new waterlily cultivars. Marliac is, truly, the father of the hardy waterlily.

Hardy waterlilies float with *Stratiotes aloides* while *Lythrum* blooms behind the bridge and *Filipendula* rises in the background

Rhizomes of hardy waterlilies

*Nymphaea* 'Pink Heaven' shows the sometimes overlapping sinus of hardy waterlily leaves

Today, the colors on hardy waterlilies range from very dark garnet-red to clear pristine white. Yellows were introduced in 1887. Some hardies even change color as the flower ages. Most of these blossoms start light yellow, mature to a reddish-orange over the next few days, and finally reach a darker red for the last day or so before fading completely. These are called "changeable" hardy waterlilies, and they are among the most captivating for the pond or water garden. New peach colors are also being developed, and soon we may even see a bright orange cultivar. The only colors not found in hardy waterlilies are blues and purples.

## PLANT PARTS AND HABIT

Hardy waterlilies grow from underground swollen stems called rhizomes. Some leaf growth will always be present, even when the plant is completely dormant. As the rhizome grows, new leaves and flowers sprout from the tip. Roots, often thick and fleshy, also grow from the rhizome. The larger retractor roots hold the plant in place, and the thinner ones absorb nutrients from the soil and water.

The leaves rather than the roots are the primary oxygen absorbers. The stomata, which take in oxygen, are located almost exclusively on the upper, floating portion of the leaf rather than on its underside. The leaf grows from the underwater rhizome and uses a long "stem," actually a petiole, to reach and float on the water surface. A very few hardy cultivars have foliage that stands up slightly out of the water; more often this is caused by the leaves becoming crowded

on the surface rather than any inherent plant trait or characteristic. The leaves are glossy and leathery on top and of a green shade. Most hardy lilies have leaves of a solid hue, although a few are green with brown or dark purple markings. The leaves' undersides are often slightly hairy and may be green, reddish, brown, or slightly purplish. The underside coloring is thought to be intended to block sunlight so that it may be captured and absorbed for photosynthesis.

Leaves of hardy waterlilies are roundish and smooth-edged and may be 1–12 inches wide, depending upon the species or cultivar. All have a single split, called a sinus, which runs from the outer edge to the middle of the leaf, where it joins the petiole. In some selections this cleft is straight and matches exactly, so that it seals precisely. In other cultivars, though, the cleft can be concave, convex, or overlapping. These distinctions are important because they aid in the proper identification of the more than 400 cultivars, which can sometimes depend upon subtle differences.

Waterlilies have a habit of creating a wide circle of foliage that can spread over several feet in larger cultivars. As each leaf grows, its petiole elongates and it gradually reaches the outer edge of the circle. As it ages, the leaf yellows and is replaced by new growth that stretches farther away from the crown of the plant. In certain selections this process creates a hollow, empty zone between the outer ring of foliage and the center bouquet of flowers. Improved cultivars are purposely selected because the maturing foliage does not drift so far away from the center crown of blossoms.

Flowers tend to stem straight upward from the crown of the plant, not straying outward as do the leaves of most selections. The blossoms usually float on the water surface,

Waterlilies in a canal

*Iris, Typha, Lobelia, Pontederia, Thalia,* and hardy *Nymphaea* transform a drainage ditch

although some hardy lilies, especially those with parentage of *Nymphaea mexicana*, may stand above the water surface. Older cultivars, as well as the species, generally have only one flower in bloom on any given day. More recent selections may have up to six or seven flowers open at one time.

Hardy waterlily flowers are generally classified as stellate, or star-shaped, rounded, peony-shaped, or some variation of these. Petal count may range from 12 or so to more than 100. Anatomically, the blooms are composed of outer sepals that are usually green in color. In succeeding inward rows these change color gradually and transform from green sepals to colored petals. These petals themselves also gradually alter in structure, taking on the characteristics of anthers with stamens and pollen. In the center, one finds the stigmatic disk. In first-day flowers, this center is open and often holds stigmatic fluid, or nectar. On the second day, the stamens begin to shed pollen and fold over the center. By the third day, the stamens have completely encased the center

of the flower. Nevertheless, waterlily flowers are unable to self-pollinate—the pollen needs nectar in order to pollinate, but the first-day flowers with the nectar have no pollen. On the second day, when pollen is produced, the nectar has disappeared. This makes waterlilies easier to hybridize by controlled crosses.

## IN THE LANDSCAPE

Waterlilies are the color palette of the pond. Though they lack much textural variety, they provide lots of color choices and the look of disks of color on a flat surface. They grow in the deeper water and in the main body of the pond, but can also be used along the edge of earth-bottom ponds beyond the marginal zone. In this position they can alter the shape of the open water, changing a flat edge into an undulating landscape. Waterlilies are best used in water 3–6 feet deep in natural ponds and 6 inches to 3 feet deep in lined ponds.

## SUN, WIND, AND WATER DEPTH

Most hardy waterlilies need more than six hours of direct sunlight in order to grow and bloom consistently. Nevertheless some cultivars, many of them quite attractive, will still flower in part shade, between four and six hours of sunlight daily. No hardy waterlily cultivar will flower reliably if it is grown in dense shade with less than three hours of sunlight every day. Under these conditions, some cultivars will not only refuse to flower, but may even die altogether. It is not surprising that most hardy waterlilies do best in full sun; after all, how many trees grow in the middle of a lake?

Although hardy waterlilies usually prefer full sun, a few cultivars do appreciate some afternoon shade, especially the burgundy selections which, by virtue of their deep red pigmentation, have a tendency to "melt" in full sun. Deep red cultivars, such as 'Black Princess' or 'Atropurpurea', growing in full sun will show petal wilt and discoloration on even newly-opened blossoms. These selections grow best in part shade, where they are protected from the hot midday sun.

Mild winds will not damage or harm hardy waterlilies. Wind can be a problem, though, if it reaches a strength sufficient to cause large ripples on the water—it is the water movement that creates a problem. Wave action can pull the leaves away from their stems, stretching the petioles to their limit. The result is the same as planting the lily in too much water—the plant perceives that it is growing in water too deep and starts to fail. The waves may also pull the leaves completely free from the plant, ripping the petioles away from the plant's rhizome. This, too, interferes with the lily's proper

Hardy waterlilies fill a planter in a shady pond to help them bloom more. Along the back edge of the pond, left to right, are *Cyperus alternifolius*, *Carex elata* 'Knightshayes', *Saururus cernuus*, *Carex muskingumensis*, and *Myriophyllum aquaticum*

growth. In large ponds and lakes with considerable wave action, hardy waterlilies often suffer, wither, and die. They do best in areas where the water will remain still and calm.

They also must be planted well clear of the spray of fountains, waterfalls, or streams. Because waterlilies breathe through the stomata on top of their leaves, the splash from waterfalls and fountains can be fatal. As the leaves become coated with water, the plants effectively drown and die. Even if the amount of water on the leaves is not sufficient to drown the plants, water carries pathogens that will flow into the open stomata and cause disease. If the process continues, the entire plant will succumb.

As a general rule, hardy waterlilies grow best in still water that is approximately 18–30 inches deep. Smaller cultivars, such as the miniatures and dwarfs, grow well in water that is only 6 inches deep. Even larger selections will grow in shallow water, although they may not flower as much as they would in deeper waters. Very large cultivars grow well in water that is considerably deeper, up to 4 feet or more.

Regardless of the cultivar, the adult leaves of hardy waterlilies are able to adapt to variations in water depth and are capable of stretching longer in order to extend themselves by a few inches over several days. The stems of flower buds also stretch themselves if the blossom has not yet opened. Once it has started to open or is showing color, however, the stem is unlikely to stretch itself to overcome deeper water. The importance of this feat is that plants may be taken from a shallower pond and placed in deeper waters without drowning the foliage or the plant itself. Lilies already in active growth may be placed with their foliage below the surface, and they will stretch in a few days to accommodate their new depth. Heavy rainfall may cause a pond to increase in depth by several inches, and the lilies will simply raise their heads until they can once again see above the waters. Moving a waterlily from deeper to more shallow water is no problem; the leaves will just be rather farther away from the central crown of the plant.

## SOIL AND WATER CHEMISTRY

For optimum growth, hardy waterlilies should be planted in soil that has a neutral or slightly alkaline pH. The pond water, too, should have a pH in the range of 7 to 8 or so. Water and soil that are alkaline, above 7, are more readily tolerated than ranges below 7. Whether the conditions are too alkaline or too acidic, the plant's reaction is the same—its growth is weakened because it is unable to absorb nutrients. As the conditions continue, the lily will fade away completely.

Hardy waterlilies and *Pontederia* at the foot of *Thuja*

Waterlilies generally tolerate only a very, very low level of salt concentration in the pond. The salt changes the osmotic potential of the lily, causing it to develop black spots on its leaves. Over time, the foliage will become oily and mushy, and then die away. This affects new and old foliage alike and is akin to herbicide damage. It is best to plant waterlilies in ponds that will not hold salted water. In koi ponds, where salt is used as a prophylactic measure to treat diseases, the lilies should be removed to holding tanks until the salt treatment is ended. Ponds in areas with naturally occurring salt water, such as the Southwest or coastal areas, should be rinsed out periodically to ensure that the salt levels remain at a minimum. Otherwise, as the pond water evaporates, the salt level in the pond will increase.

Hardy waterlilies often enjoy very warm weather and enjoy warm waters as well. Exceptions are those whose native range is naturally cooler, such as *Nymphaea tetrag-*

*ona* and cultivars of that parentage, as well as *N. rubra* and its offspring. Both of these species lilies prefer cooler temperatures and may go summer dormant in very warm water. Those that have *N. mexicana* as a parent, however, come from semitropical conditions for which hot temperatures are the norm. By growing a combination of cultivars with a range of heat tolerances, you can have flowers early in the cool waters of spring and yet others that flourish in the heat of summer.

## SEASONAL CARE

Hardy waterlilies are primarily day-length dependent, relying on the number of hours of sunlight to tell them when they should start growing in the spring or stop growing in the fall. In the fall, some develop "indicator leaves" that remain underwater at the base of the plant throughout the winter. They are thin and transparent, not unlike little leaves of bib lettuce. These leaves let the plant know that the days are getting longer and signal when new growth should begin. In the fall, these indicator leaves should be left untouched, while other foliage may be trimmed away. Once trimmed of old foliage, submerge the lilies to a depth in the pond where they will not freeze. If ice forms in the dormant rhizomes, they will turn soft and rot, as do frozen potatoes. Another option is to remove them from the water garden and keep them cool, dark, and damp. In the South where the lilies will not be subjected to freezing water, simply let the pots stay in the pond. Allow the lilies to go dormant for the winter so that they will return well rested in the spring.

These methods apply uniformly for all the cultivars of hardy waterlilies. It is not generally advisable to force hardy waterlilies to continue growing through the winter, since they need a period of winter dormancy in order to resume proper growth in the spring. If they are required to grow during the winter, they are unlikely to prosper or grow for many seasons thereafter. The hybrids of *Nymphaea mexicana* tolerate winter forcing more readily, since they are of semitropical stock.

Although they rely on the hours of sunlight as a signal of spring, hardy waterlilies nonetheless benefit from the warmth of the sun after their long winter sleep. The pond itself is driven by water temperature in spring and summer. In the spring, bring the lilies up to the warmer water at the surface. Fertilize them when they start to show some floating leaves and the water temperature is above 65°F. Hardy waterlilies are not able to absorb fertilizer well in cool water; therefore, feeding the lilies too soon will simply contribute

*Nymphaea 'Hermine' going dormant with submerged leaves*

to an algae bloom without prompting any growth in the lilies themselves.

In the summer, feed the plants regularly, generally about once a month, so that they will grow well and bloom often. As the flowers fade after about three to five days, they become soaked with water and sink out of sight beneath the surface. Leaves last a few weeks, and then yellow and fade away. Both spent flowers and aging leaves can be removed, and indeed should be discarded so they do not add to the nutrient load in the pond as they decompose.

## PLANTING

Waterlilies are really quite easy to pot up. How you plant them depends upon whether they are still dormant or actively growing. Hardy waterlilies may be planted dormant when they have little or no leaves or roots, or they may be planted when in active growth with leaves and roots that have already sprouted.

To plant a hardy lily, fill the pot about two-thirds full of potting soil. Make a mound in the middle of the pot with a handful of soil. Place the rhizome on the mound in the middle of the pot. Spread out any roots so that they are on top of the soil and out from under the rhizome. Sprinkle soil over the roots and around the rhizome, and then add more soil so that the rhizome is just covered with soil. Try to bury the entire rhizome under just less than 1 inch or so of soil, since more soil will make sprouting new leaves more difficult. Water the pot thoroughly, and then add pea gravel around the rhizome, just enough to cover it.

Planting a hardy waterlily

Waterlilies are extremely buoyant when in leaf, but even dormant rhizomes have been known to suddenly pop out of the soil and float on the water surface. If planting the lilies when they are actively growing, try to retain as many roots as possible and anchor them firmly in the soil. Larger lilies may need to be helped for the first week or so, by placing a smooth rock on top of the soil over the rhizome.

## DIVISION

Dividing a hardy waterlily is essential for its health and vitality. Waterlilies are not like trees, they do not grow larger rings around the previous year's growth. Instead, they grow by adding onto last years' rhizome, much like new layers of tree branches at the top of an evergreen. As it gets older, a waterlily can grow over and out of its pot. Even if it does not escape from the pot, it still may fill the container with roots and rhizomes, displacing soil and leaving no room for fertilizer. Dividing a waterlily is a way to discard old roots and rhizomes that would otherwise rot and decompose in the pot, giving the lily new room to grow, making space for the plant as well as soil and fertilizer. The waterlily will have renewed strength to keep growing and flowering well.

Not all waterlilies need to be divided every year. Some need division only every few years. Others may need to be divided more than once a year, especially in warmer, southern climates of the United States. It depends upon the plant, its container, and how well it is growing.

A lily needs to be divided if it shows signs of "crowding," including foliage that is mounded up and standing out of the water, fewer flowers, or blossoms that are hidden among the leaves. All are tell-tale signs that the plant is crowded and needs more room to grow. Crowding can sometimes cause the lily to lose its vigor, so that its leaves become smaller and more sparse and its flowers less frequent.

Sometimes lilies need to be repotted simply because they have overgrown their pots. These may root into muck in the bottom of the pond or grow into a neighbor's container. Although the lily may grow as though it is perfectly happy, its rambunctious nature needs to be restrained through prudent division and repotting.

As a general rule, the best time of year to divide a hardy waterlily is in the early spring, just before it has started to actively grow. By dividing the lily early in the growing season, it has ample time to put on new roots and become established. If the lily is divided later in the year, it still needs at least six weeks of good growing weather before it must prepare for the winter chill ahead. If cool weather is bound

Hardy waterlily ready for division

To divide a hardy waterlily, take the entire plant out of the pot and loosen it

Wash away soil with a strong jet from the garden hose

Find the main growing tip of the rhizome

Identify new side-eyes and cut them away

The "new rhizomes" produced from dividing one plant

Potting up the new rhizomes

to begin in fewer than six weeks, wait until the following spring to divide the plant.

To divide a hardy waterlily, take the entire plant out of the pot, soil and all. Use a strong spray of water from a garden hose to wash the soil away from the rhizome. Do not be shy or bashful, the lily can withstand a pretty fair amount of water pressure from the hose. Rinse as much of the soil away from the roots and rhizome as you can, then examine the rhizome closely. Waterlilies have several different types of rhizomes, which call for somewhat specialized methods of division (see the following paragraphs for more specific instructions). Generally, make sure the rhizome has a main growing tip. On most waterlilies, only the newest 4–5 inches of rhizome need to be retained with the growing tip. Smaller waterlilies need only the newest 2–3 inches. The old growth from prior years will not grow but will only rot in the pot—cut it away from the rhizome. If it has no new side-eyes on it, throw it away. If the roots are very long on the remaining rhizome, trim them back to 4–5 inches in length. They will resprout quickly and grow anew. Their purpose is first and foremost to anchor the plant in the soil. Trimming them back will not diminish the plant's ability to put on new growth.

Inspect the entire rhizome for side-eyes. A sharp knife is usually best used to separate the new side-growing rhizomes from the mother rhizome. Pot up the new rhizomes in their own containers. This will give the new side-eyes as well as the mother plant more room to live and grow. New growth should appear soon, as the weather warms and spring begins in earnest.

## Waterlily Rhizome Types

Not all hardy waterlily rhizomes are the same shape or size. Growers have developed guidelines for dividing and planting based on the following general classifications. Determining what type of rhizome a lily most resembles helps in gauging how best to divide and repot it. Some lilies defy classification of course, having rhizomes that share characteristics of more than one type. Sometimes these are simply unique lilies, but more commonly a mix of characteristics is owed to the lily's parentage. When classification becomes difficult, find the closest match based on the size and shape of the rhizomes and side-eyes, then just divide the lily when the side-eyes are large enough to support their own growth, and plant the lily in a large pot with suitable soil and fertilizer. Beyond that, it will not matter whether the lily is an odorata-type, a pineapple-type, or somewhere in between.

Odorata-type rhizome

## Odorata-type

Odorata-types are the oldest cultivated and most common of the hardy waterlilies. They are named for the botanical species *Nymphaea odorata*. Odorata-types are characterized by thick, fleshy rootstock that grows horizontally across the width of the pot. Odoratas run freely and get very large in a short period of time. They grow from a stout tip that will often have six or more leaf and bud sprouts. As the leaves and flowers develop, the growing tip elongates. Leaves and flower joints on the rhizome that were once close together become more spaced apart—they are commonly an inch or more away from each other on an odorata-type rhizome. In the parlance of water plant growers, the leaves and flower stems are said to be less compact on odorata-type rhizomes than on other types of waterlily rhizomes.

Because of their horizontal growing habit, odorata-type rhizomes are best potted with the blunt end of the rhizome at the outer edge of the container and the growing tip pointed toward the center of the pot. Keep the rhizome at a 45 degree angle with the growing tip exposed above the soil surface. Since they are often very vigorous growers, most odorata-type waterlilies need to be divided and repotted every spring.

Odorata-type rhizomes form growing eyes that quickly develop their own roots and tips. These side-eyes can become large over time and easily fill the container, to the detriment of the main rhizome. Use a sharp knife to divide the side-eyes away from the mother plant once the new growth has sprouted a few leaves and several roots.

Tuberosa-type rhizome

Marliac-type rhizome

## Tuberosa-type

Tuberosa-type waterlilies earn their name from the way their side-eyes develop. In tuberosas, the main rhizome can be literally almost covered by new side-eyes that are very round with ends that are narrower and more pinched where they join to the mother plant. This new growth is easily snapped away from the main plant. In fact, the new rhizomes can even break away on their own if the pot is jarred or if pressure is placed on the soil. To divide a tuberosa-type rhizome, simply snap the new growth away from the mother plant. New tubers can be planted in their own pots before they have roots. Often these new tubers will only develop roots after they have been divided away from the mother plant.

Because tuberosa-type rhizomes have a horizontal growing habit, like odoratas, the rhizome should be planted with its blunt end near the edge of the pot and the growing tip pointed toward the center. Place the rhizome at a roughly 45 degree angle beneath the soil. Make sure the growing tip is exposed above the soil level and any pea gravel placed over the soil. Many tuberosa-type lilies grow several inches in a single year, and often require annual division and replanting to maintain health and vigor. Like odoratas, the main rhizome can be large and stout, with leaf and flower stems only slightly closer together along the rhizome. A tuberosa's growth habit is usually a bit more compact than an odorata's, but not appreciably so.

## Marliac-type

This type of rhizome is named for waterlily hybridizer Joseph Bory Latour-Marliac, who developed many hardy cultivars in the early 1900s. Marliac contributed much to modern hardy waterlilies—one significant achievement was to develop rhizomes that did not need the large pots or annual division that were customary with odoratas and tuberosas. A Marliac-type rhizome is noted for its compact habit. Although it grows horizontally across the width of the pot, its leaf and flower stems remain more close together on the rhizome, even as it matures. The growing tip of a Marliac-type rhizome is crammed with the scars of leaves and flower buds.

Marliac rhizomes should be planted horizontally with the growing tip above the soil line. Because their growth is more compact, they may be planted more toward the center of the pot. They often grow well in the same container for a year or more, and only need to be divided and repotted when they are outgrowing their pot or when their flowering and growth have started to wane.

Marliac-type rhizomes form side-eyes that are stout, just as odoratas, and do not have the characteristic pinch at their base like tuberosas. These are forked and branch away from the main plant. Use a sharp knife to divide the side-eyes, removing them from the mother plant when they have sprouted new growth and their own roots.

Mexicana-type rhizome

Pineapple-type rhizome

## Mexicana-type

One unique type of rhizome is the mexicana type, named after the species *Nymphaea mexicana*. Mexicanas have small rhizomes that resemble little pineapples. However, instead of growing side-eyes, mexicanas have long, fleshy runners that produce, at their ends, entirely new tubers. These new tubers may take one of two different shapes. Sometimes they are shaped like small pineapples, just like the mother plant. Sometimes, though, the new tubers will look like little fingers joined together at one end, so that they look like a bunch of bananas. In the fall, mexicanas often produce these banana-like rhizomes at the bottom of the pot. These can be overwintered in damp sand or sphagnum moss, and then planted up in the spring.

Because of its odd running habit, a mexicana-type rhizome is best potted in the middle of its container. Mexicanas should be divided and repotted every year to prevent the container from being over-crowded with small plants. Rhizomes can be divided from their fleshy runners any time during the spring or summer, provided the new plants will have enough time to establish themselves before winter.

## Pineapple-type

The pineapple-type rhizome is so named because it grows vertically rather than horizontally, with its growing tip on top of the rhizome. Leaf and flower stem joints are close together along the rhizome. Although they are sometimes also called mexicana-type, these rhizomes do not produce the fleshy runners that are characteristic of mexicanas. Many pineapple-type waterlilies do have *Nymphaea mexicana* parentage that contributes to the characteristic pineapple shape of their rhizomes.

Side-eyes of a pineapple-type rhizome appear as branches along the side of the tuber. They can be removed easily with a sharp knife once they have sprouted a few leaves and their own roots. Plant them in the middle of the pot, with the growing tip slightly below the soil surface, making sure that the tip is only slightly covered by pea gravel. Pineapple-type rhizomes should be divided and repotted when they begin to mound up above the soil surface or when the side-eyes become more vigorous than the mother plant.

# PROPAGATION

A few hardy waterlilies are viviparous. Unlike tropical waterlilies, hardies do not produce viviparous growth from their leaves, but instead sprout new plantlets from their flowers. These new plants may be detached from the dying flower and potted up once they have sprouted their own roots or the main stem has rotted away.

The primary method for propagating hardy waterlilies, however, is by dividing off and planting up the side-eyes. Sometimes it is necessary to promote the growth of new side-eyes by making a slit in the rhizome just in front of a leaf node. The slit need be only ½ inch or so deep and just 1–2 inches wide. It need not be deep into the rhizome—the purpose is simply to interfere with the plant's normal growth habit of "apical dominance," the habit of growing from the apex, or end, of the rhizome rather than from side-eyes. This apical dominance is the same habit that causes trees to grow from a central stem rather than from side branches. In hardy waterlilies, the rhizome's natural habit is to grow from a terminal sprout of leaves and flower buds. Once a slit is made in the rhizome, the plant is less able to tell where the terminal growth should occur. As a result, it starts to grow side-eyes that will quickly develop into full-fledged plants. These may be divided from the main rhizome and potted up once they have established their own root and stem growth. This method is particularly useful in varieties that are slow to propagate. A lily may not necessarily produce more side-eyes through this method, but it will produce them sooner.

## Hybridizing

Marliac never divulged his techniques for hybridizing hardy waterlilies, nor did his family after his death, but there is no great mystery to it. The procedure itself is simple—take the pollen from one flower (the pollen parent) and place it in the center of another flower (the seed parent, which is the plant that will produce the seed). Then, place a nylon sock or muslin sack over the flower of the seed parent so that it will not be pollinated by insects. In a few days, the flower will sink and begin to set seed. Watch carefully for seed set, and remove the seed as soon as it is mature, when it splits.

As a very general rule, the hybrid lily will bear the flower shape and size of the seed parent. Its other traits, including color, will derive from the pollen parent.

To obtain pollen, many hybridizers remove the entire stamen with its pollen. Tweezers or scissors are appropriate. Store the pollen in small, clean containers in the refrigerator. It often lasts for several days, even weeks, when maintained properly. To make the cross, the entire stamen may be placed in the fluid-filled disk of a first-day flower of the seed parent. Make sure to emasculate the flower of the seed parent before attempting the cross, removing all the stamens, preferably before the flower has opened. Though hardy waterlilies are unable to self-pollinate, breeders generally like to ensure that the cross is pure. Once the pollen has been placed in the seed parent flower, cover it with nylon, muslin, or some other material that will hold the flower and yet allow moisture to pass through to the plant. A plastic bag will cook the flower and destroy the cross.

Although hardy waterlily cultivars such as those from Marliac were once thought to be completely infertile, more recent efforts dispute this conclusion. The problem is not with the lilies' fertility or lack of it, but with the high variability of chromosome counts, or ploidy, in their pollen. Each plant will have a definite and stable chromosome or

Collect pollen for hybridizing by using a tweezers to remove entire stamens

ploidy count, but its pollen will not. Pollen and eggs in hardy lilies can have anywhere from twice as many to as little as half as many chromosomes as the plants themselves. For a cross to be successful, the pollen and eggs must either have the same chromosome count, or they must have a chromosome count that totals an even number. If at least one of these conditions is not satisfied, the cross may not be successful and the flower may not set seed. This is a very simplified explanation of a very complicated subject.

Whether a lily produces many flowers is no indication of its fertility. In fact, a lily that flowers more may actually be less fertile, because the lily expends its energy flowering, not setting seed. In hybridizing, making as many crosses as possible is essential for increasing the chances that the cross will take and that the plant will set viable seed.

Hybridizers have learned certain techniques to help along the process of fertilization and seed set, which are easily adapted by novice or more accomplished lily growers. Make the same cross at different times of the day—morning, afternoon, and evening. Use pollen of varying ages—one day, two days, or even several days old. Experiment with doing the same cross at different times of the year. Another "trick" is to remove the fluid in the flower of the seed parent and replace it with the fluid of the pollen parent. The fluid in the seed parent may be antagonistic to fertilization, or it may be missing an essential enzyme that would trigger pollen growth or fertilization. By replacing it with the fluid of the pollen parent, the odds of fertilization may be increased dramatically.

Seed pod of a hardy waterlily

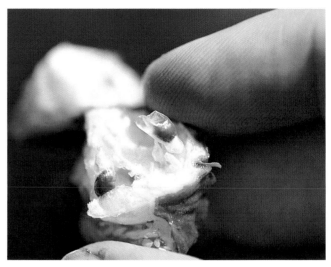

Fertile waterlily seed inside the seed pod

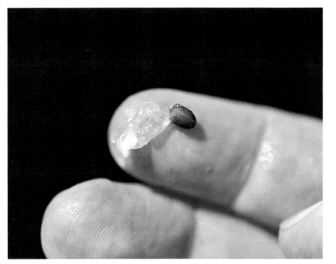

Remove the jelly from around the seed

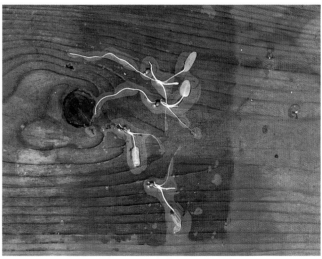

Hardy waterlily seedlings

## Starting from Seed

Once a cross has been made and seed set accomplished, the lily will often (but not always) form a tight coil with its stem as it pulls the seed head beneath the water surface. The seed pod sometimes becomes very enlarged and inflated, although this is less likely to happen when only a few seed are viable in the entire pod. Seed may take anywhere from three to eight weeks to mature. Individual seed that is fertile generally will be hard and black. Those that remain green are infertile and may be discarded. All seed, fertile or infertile, are surrounded by a jelly-like substance resembling orange juice pulp that helps the seed float on the water. The seed pod may hold one or two fertile seed or several hundred. When mature, the seed pod splits, releasing all the seed, which float to the water surface. After a few days, the fertile seed begin to sink.

To start hardy waterlily seed, remove the jelly from around the seed by simply wiping it away or by letting the seed sit in water until the jelly dissolves. Some hybridizers simply let the seed float in distilled water until they sprout. Others plant the seed by spreading them over soil, covering them lightly with sand, and submerging them in a few inches of water. Give them indirect sunlight, or direct morning sun, until they sprout.

Once the seed sprout, they are very delicate and are easily overcome by string algae, the archenemy of all waterlily seed growers. They must be moved to clean, distilled water so that they may continue growing unimpeded by the algae. The seed's first leaves are juvenile and will remain submerged if the seed have been planted in soil. The second set of leaves are adult and will, with time, mature and reach the water surface. Once these second leaves have reached the surface, the plantlets may be transplanted to larger quarters. Here they need as much sunlight, especially direct sunlight, as possible.

Some seed will grow quickly, while some may take up to a year to grow their second set of leaves. The key is to be patient and use clean, distilled water. Fertilize the soil, not the water, taking care to add fertilizer tablets that will not leach into the water. Change the water often, to keep algae to a minimum. For the first year, waterlily seedlings may be kept actively growing in an aquarium with artificial light during the lean winter months. Thereafter, though, hardy waterlilies must have a rest of three or four months during winter, returning them to active growth in the spring. We put our seedlings in the bottom of the pond in a plastic container with a lid punched with several holes. This protects the plant from fish and other pond creatures, but allows it to overwinter as part of the pond. Often we start seedlings in the same type of container.

# PLANT PROFILES

Waterlily pond backed by *Epilobium*, left, and *Eupatorium purpureum*, and front, left to right, *Hosta*, *Primula japonica*, *Lysichiton*, and *Rorippa nasturtium-aquaticum*

Not unlike roses, hostas, and daylilies, waterlilies have been extensively hybridized across, between, and among the various species of *Nymphaea* so that it is no longer feasible, or possible, to trace their precise heritage. Very few of the species waterlilies are available for purchase, although some can be found in the United States and elsewhere; botanists may dispute, sometimes with good reason, whether those labeled as a certain species are indeed true to that identity.

In his detailed *Waterlilies* (1983, Timber Press: Portland, Ore.), Philip Swindells lists more than eight species of *Nymphaea* that are considered hardy in colder climates. Perry Slocum, Peter Robinson, and Frances Perry list more than six (*Water Gardening, Water Lilies and Lotuses*, 1996, Timber Press: Portland, Ore.). Many of these survive only in the water gardens of collectors or in the wild; only a few are commonly sold in commerce. Those that are often available to hobby pond owners are listed in this chapter.

Virtually all the waterlilies currently sold are hybridized cultivars for which no species name is generally provided. The International Waterlily and Water Gardening Society (IWGS) has been chosen by the Royal Horticultural Society to officially identify and register named cultivars of all waterlilies, hardy and tropical. This prodigious task is already underway with the hope that it will dispel some of the confusion surrounding certain cultivars already in commercial production, preventing usage of the identical name for two different selections, as well as the usage of different names for the same cultivar.

More than 400 cultivars of hardy waterlilies have been mentioned in books or gardening catalogs since the middle of the twentieth century. Many of these have fallen out of cultivation and are very difficult, or almost impossible, to find in the trade. Others have been surpassed by more recent, and superior, introductions. Discussed in this chapter are the newer named cultivars from the United States, the U.K., and Australia that are generally available for sale today.

Hardy waterlilies are evaluated based on the color, size, and shape of their flowers and foliage. How well they flower, whether they tolerate especially warm or cool conditions, and the extent to which they will grow well in deep waters are also taken into account. Like other plants, many of these attributes can vary depending upon climate, humidity, sometimes even elevation above sea level. Included here are the averages for each cultivar as we have found them to be, derived from our own experiences as well as discussions with other water gardeners and waterlily growers.

Red waterlily petals melted by too much hot sun

## Red

Red hardy waterlilies include some of my all-time favorites. There are reds as bright and juicy as watermelon and as dark as burgundy Depression glass. With fiery orange or sunshine-yellow centers, red waterlilies look ablaze on the water surface. Blooming from early summer through late fall, they include some of the longest-flowering cultivars available.

Many red cultivars of hardy waterlilies have their ancestral roots in the species *Nymphaea rubra*, or *N. alba* var. *rubra*, of which Marliac was especially fond in his breeding efforts. Because *N. rubra* harkens from the very cold waters of Scandinavia, it performs best in water that never warms above 75–80°F, roughly USDA Zone 7 and northward in North America. In warmer waters, these cold-loving cultivars will stop flowering or producing foliage and even may go completely dormant. Day length seems to make no difference—simply the rise in water temperature affects them. Older red cultivars, such as those produced by Marliac, tend to act this way. 'Atropurpurea' is a prime example. Even in our rather cool Zone 5 ponds, it will cease to flower or produce leaves when the water warms appreciably in late July and August. Once the water cools in September, it resumes its growth and blooming. Fortunately, since it prefers cool waters, it will continue to flower until the end of September or so.

More recent hybrids, which are third and fourth generation offspring with more complicated parentage, do not suffer from summer heat doldrums. Cultivars such as 'Mary', 'Perry's Baby Red', 'Perry's Red Dwarf', and 'Red Spider' flower better and more reliably in warmer climates and so fare better in the ponds of gardeners in Zone 8 and southward. If you live in a warmer-water environment, look for more recent introductions, especially those from Perry

Slocum and Kirk Strawn, who spent years hybridizing in North Carolina and Texas respectively, and so have created red hardy cultivars that are more tolerant of warm-water ponds.

Besides a potential problem with warm water temperatures, some red cultivars are especially sensitive to direct sunlight. The flowers of these cultivars have a tendency to "melt" in full sun. The issue is not water temperature, but light intensity. The blooms will appear to disintegrate in full sun even when the water temperature remains cool. The problem arises in cultivars with very deep, dark red flowers. Their summer meltdown occurs because their petals are so dark they absorb too much sunlight, causing the petals to overheat and dissolve.

Dark burgundy cultivars, such as 'Almost Black', 'Black Princess', and 'Burgundy Princess', have exclusively red pigment in their petals and are prone to melt in full sun in summer. In more northern areas, these will grow and bloom reliably despite the summer melting. They generally struggle more in the South. Other red cultivars, such as 'Wucai', have some white in their pigment and are not likely to fall apart in full sun. In a sunny environment, grow dark red cultivars where they will receive afternoon shade or filtered sun. The other alternative, of course, is to grow a red-blooming tropical waterlily, which is better adapted to warmer water and higher light intensities.

## Seasonal Characteristics

In spring, red hardy waterlilies generally show their foliage and flowers sooner than other colors, often because of their parentage—*Nymphaea rubra* is an early growing species. In our USDA Zone 5 ponds, reds usually flower about two weeks earlier than other cultivars, sometimes as early as May. They produce their foliage earlier as well, often in April, making them important allies in combating spring algae growth. Because they are among the first to grow in the spring, red hardy waterlilies benefit from an early feeding. They should be divided sooner in the spring, as well, and potted up earlier than cultivars of other colors.

In the cool waters of both spring and fall, red hardies have an attractive deep red foliage, making them very ornamental even when they are not in flower. Sometimes foliage will appear as soon as the marsh marigolds (*Caltha*) are in bloom, creating a pond with coppery waterlily foliage and yellow-marigold flowers along the shoreline. We have found that 'Laydekeri Rubra' is an especially early riser in the spring. During the summer also a certain red cast appears on the new growth of red waterlily cultivars.

## White

Because many white species of hardy waterlilies, such as *Nymphaea tuberosa* and *N. odorata*, are large-flowering, many older, named cultivars are selections from the species rather than specially hybridized cultivars. Newer cultivars are more complicated in their parentage, with shorter rhizomes and more doubled flowers. Often the newer cultivars bloom more reliably than older selections.

Many white waterlilies are prized by pondkeepers because they tolerate shade, and flower well with only four or five hours of daily sunlight, even less than the reds need. If they receive too little light, though, they have a tendency to grow foliage and no flowers. Just the same, white hardy waterlilies will often survive where other lilies might fail altogether.

## Seasonal Characteristics

White hardy waterlilies start to grow rather early in the spring, just after red-blooming varieties. They also begin to bloom rather early. One of the first to appear is *Nymphaea tetragona*, which is not surprising since it is native as far north as USDA Zone 3. Begin feeding in the spring just as first growth appears. I have found that white hardy waterlilies grow well but may need extra food to keep them flowering well. Fertilize every few weeks instead of every month, and make sure to use well-rounded food. Because they grow earlier in the spring, they can be divided and potted up sooner without going into transplant shock. 'Denver' is an exception. Since its parentage includes *N. mexicana*, an almost tropical lily, it starts growing and flowers with the yellows, about two weeks later than the other whites.

Unlike red-blooming waterlilies, hardy white waterlilies do not go dormant or melt in the hot summer sun. Their foliage is usually green from spring through fall, without tints, flecks, or marbling. Some very pale yellows are occasionally listed as white (such as 'Denver') and these may have flecked or slightly mottled foliage. 'Marliac Albida' has white flowers but with red-tinged leaves owing to its complex parentage, which may include *N. rubra*.

In our ponds, white cultivars are usually the first to stop flowering in fall as the water starts to cool. Their foliage begins to yellow, and they are the first to go dormant. They often have winter indicator leaves, common for the species *Nymphaea odorata* and *N. tuberosa*.

## Pink

Hardy waterlilies with pink flowers are both species and hybridized cultivars. *Nymphaea caroliniana* produces pink flowers, as do pink-flowering forms of *N. tuberosa* and *N. odorata*. Newer cultivars are crosses with these and other named selections, producing a wide range of colors, from almost white to deep rose and almost red. Most pink hardy waterlilies have a red or burgundy flush to their leaves, especially on spring foliage, adding to their ornamental value in the water garden. Few pink waterlilies tolerate shade.

### Seasonal Characteristics

Pink selections of hardy waterlilies usually appear later in the spring than other colors. They have no special seasonal needs, and require nothing more than the occasional clean-up and regular fertilization. They have no changeable colors in flower or foliage during the seasons, and generally go dormant in our ponds about the same time as white waterlilies.

## Yellow

Many yellow forms of hardy waterlilies have *Nymphaea mexicana* in their parentage, which is itself only a semihardy waterlily. Because of this, yellow-flowering waterlilies often need warmer water than other hardy waterlilies. Many yellow cultivars now available to homeowners are introductions from Perry Slocum, who worked extensively with them for years in order to create yellow hardies that bloom well and tolerate cooler waters. In our ponds, yellow waterlilies do not begin to flower until the water temperature reaches above 75°F.

One exception to this, though, is the cultivar 'Colonel AJ Welch', which is now thought to be, perhaps, a species from Victoria Falls in Zimbabwe, since its rhizome type is different from that of other yellow waterlilies. More importantly, 'Colonel AJ Welch' is able to bloom well in cool water. Also, its flowers are not stellate—other yellows are because of their *Nymphaea mexicana* parentage. In our ponds, 'Colonel AJ Welch' is among the first waterlilies to appear, and often it is up as early as the first reds in the spring. It blooms as early as the first red hardy waterlilies, too. In June as the water warms, 'Colonel AJ Welch' stops flowering, waiting for the cooler waters of fall to start blooming again. I would not recommend 'Colonel AJ Welch' for southern climates, but it is a beauty for ponds in Zones 3 and 4, especially those that are spring-fed with water that never reaches above 75°F.

Another yellow that grows well in cooler waters is 'Chromatella', a Marliac hybrid. It also comes up early in spring, although not as early as 'Colonel AJ Welch'. It flowers reliably in cool weather and is good for northern climates. 'Chromatella' does not go summer dormant and keeps going into fall.

### Seasonal Characteristics

Most yellow hardy waterlilies begin to grow in mid-May in our Zone 5 ponds and do not start flowering until early June. 'Joey Tomocik', a hybrid of *Nymphaea mexicana* and *N. odorata*, is one of the first to flower. Once the yellow lilies start, they continue flowering until fall, often staying open later in the season than the pinks and whites, and almost as late as the red waterlilies.

Many yellow cultivars will tolerate some shade, because of their more tropical heritage. 'Texas Dawn' is one yellow hardy waterlily that blooms reliably with only four or five hours of direct sunlight.

## Peach

Perhaps the most important color break in hardy waterlilies was the introduction of true peach-colored selections. Unlike changeable waterlilies, which may have a peach hue for a few hours or a day, truly peach-flowering hardy waterlilies retain a consistent color throughout the life of each blossom.

We have found, though, that some peach cultivars change color depending on the water temperature of the pond. Of the peach selections available, only 'Clyde Ikins' stays peach from spring through fall. 'Pink Grapefruit' comes close, with peach-pink flowers all through the season. 'Peaches and Cream' and 'Carolina Sunset' start out peach in the spring and return to that color in the fall, but have yellow flowers in the summer when the water temperature rises above 70–75°F. 'Colorado' begins in the spring with pink and yellow flowers, then in summer as the water warms, it turns a rich cantaloupe or smoked-salmon color. 'Barbara Davies' and 'Barbara Dobbins' are pink-yellow in spring and fall, but in summer they both send up pink blooms, those of 'Barbara Davies' a more peach-pink.

Also in the peach-colored family is an orange-flowering cultivar named 'Berit Strawn'. Perry Slocum has introduced other selections that have an orangey cast to their flowers.

### Seasonal Characteristics

Peach-flowering waterlilies generally start growing in late spring, about the same time as their yellow counterparts. They also remain in flower until late in the fall, just as the yellow hardy waterlilies. In fact, 'Colorado' stays in flower longer than any other waterlily in our ponds, continuing to flower even after all its foliage has died back for winter.

## Changeable

A special group of hardy waterlilies has flowers that change color from day to day. This group is called "changeable" for their habit of opening in one shade and then maturing or fading to another. Roughly a dozen hardy waterlilies are usually called changeables. Before the introduction of peach-flowering hardy waterlilies, ponds could have an orange-flowering lily only by growing a changeable.

Some cultivars open yellow on the first day, fading to red by the third day. Others open red on the first day and slowly fade to yellow by their third day. 'Indiana' and 'Little Sue', for example, undergo a remarkable transformation, from orange sorbet to maraschino red in just three days. 'Cherokee' starts orange and turns brilliant red.

Those that begin as yellow-blooming lilies often have parentage that includes *Nymphaea mexicana*, and so may be only semihardy in cold climates. Those with red pigment do not usually melt or fade in the heat of summer, since those available today are not of the deeply red-colored varieties, though they have *N. rubra* in their parentage. Most tolerate some shade, especially 'Little Sue'.

Most changeable waterlilies are suitable for small or medium ponds and grow well in tub or container gardens. Many have a spread of less than 4 feet, again owing to their heritage with *Nymphaea mexicana* or *N. rubra*. Both 'Sioux' and 'JCN Forestier', however, are full-sized lilies for large ponds. Both have yellow flowers flushed with orange, which only slightly fade toward yellow from day to day.

### Seasonal Characteristics
Changeable waterlilies have color-changing flowers regardless of the season. Their foliage is also generally consistent from spring through fall. They start to sprout in midspring but do not stop flowering until late in the fall, roughly the same time as red waterlilies.

### Cultivars and Species

The cultivars in the following list are all hybrids in the genus *Nymphaea*. The "*N.*" that should begin each name has been omitted for brevity. Measurements for the pond sizes suggested in the following descriptions are small (4–6 feet across), medium (7–9 feet), and large (more than 10 feet). Tub and container water gardens are considered to be up to 3 feet across.

*Nymphaea 'Almost Black'*

### 'Alba plenissima'

Creamy white. Marliac-type rhizome. Peony-shaped blooms of 4–6 inches. Green leaves. Grows 5–7 feet high in full sun in 2–4 feet of water. Good for medium to large ponds. Marliac.

### 'Almost Black'

Black, cherry-soda red. Marliac-type rhizome. Peony-shaped blooms of 8–9 inches. Dark green leaves. Grows 6–12 feet wide in full sun in 6 inches to 4 feet of water. Good for medium to large ponds. Slocum.

### 'Amabilis' (syn. 'Pink Marvel')

Rich, soft pink. Marliac-type rhizome. Stellate blooms of 6–7½ inches. Green leaves, reddish purple when new. Grows 5–7½ feet wide in full sun in 6–36 inches of water. Description varies slightly based on location and cultural conditions. Good for medium to large ponds. Marliac, 1921.

### 'American Star'

Bright silvery pink. Odorata-type rhizome. Star-like blooms of 6–7 inches, with very long, narrow petals. Green leaves, purple-green when new. Grows to 4–5 feet in full sun in 6 inches to 6 feet of water. Good for medium to large ponds. Slocum, 1985. A chance seedling of 'Rose Arey' named and introduced by Stapeley Water Gardens in the U.K.

### 'Andreana' (syn. *N.* ×*andreana*)

Changeable reddish orange fading to rusty orange. Cuplike blooms of 5–7 inches. Green leaves with dark reddish brown

*Nymphaea* 'Anna Epple'

*Nymphaea* 'Arc en Ciel'

*Nymphaea* 'Atropurpurea'

*Nymphaea* 'Atropurpurea'

blotches. Grows to 3–4 feet wide in full sun in 6–36 inches of water. Looks much like 'Aurora' but has larger flowers and is larger plant overall. Upright rhizome. Good for ponds of any size. Marliac, 1895. Parentage is *N. alba* var. *rubra* × *N. mexicana*.

### 'Anna Epple'

Baby pink. Cup- or peony-shaped blooms of 4 inches. A good bloomer. Green leaves with red tint at edges. Grows to 2–6 feet wide in full sun in 6–24 inches of water. Odorata-type rhizome. Good for medium ponds. Epple, 1970.

### 'Appleblossom'

Blushed pink. Cup-shaped blooms of 4–6 inches. Green leaves. Grows to 2–6 feet wide in full sun in 6–36 inches of water. Compact odorata-type rhizome. Good for medium or large ponds.

### 'Arc en Ciel'

White with a hint of pink. Cactus stellate blooms of 5–6 inches. Highly mottled leaves. Grows to 4–5 feet wide in full sun to shade in 6–24 inches of water. Odorata-type rhizome. Good for medium or large ponds. Marliac, 1901.

### 'Atropurpurea'

Deep red. Bowl-shaped blooms of 7–8 inches. Purple new leaves that age to green. Grows to more than 4 feet wide in full sun in 6–36 inches of water. Marliac-type rhizome. Good for medium or large ponds. Marliac, 1901. Earned the Royal Horticultural Society Award of Garden Merit in 1906.

*Nymphaea* 'Arc en Ciel'

*Nymphaea* 'Attraction'

*Nymphaea* 'Attraction 3'

*Nymphaea* 'Aurora'

## 'Attraction'

Dark watermelon-red. Goblet-shaped blooms of 10–12 inches. Green leaves. Grows to 4–5 feet wide in full sun in 6–48 inches of water. Marliac-type rhizome. Good for large ponds. Marliac, 1910. Many forms of 'Attraction' are now sold. Some are close to the original description and some are not.

## 'Aurora'

Changeable creamy yellow, orange, dark red. Cup-shaped blooms of 4–4½ inches. Green leaves blotched purple or maroon. Grows to 3 feet wide in full sun in 6–24 inches of water. Small pineapple-type rhizome. Good for tub or small ponds. Marliac, 1895.

*Nymphaea* 'Barbara Dobbins'

*Nymphaea* 'Betsy Sakata'

### 'Barbara Davies'

Peach from pale yellow with a pink blush. Goblet-shaped blooms of 3–5 inches. Green leaves with faint purple blotches most noticeable on new foliage. Grows to 2–5 feet wide in full sun in 6–36 inches of water. Mexicana–tuberosa-type rhizome. Good for medium to large ponds. Strawn, 1992.

### 'Barbara Dobbins'

Peach from pale yellow with deeper pink blush. Goblet-shaped blooms of 4–8 inches. Mottled leaves. Grows to 6–8 feet wide in full sun in 6–24 inches of water. Mexicana–tuberosa-type rhizome. Good for medium or large ponds. Strawn, 1996.

### 'Berit Strawn'

Orange with maraschino-red flecks. Cup- or ball-shaped blooms of 3–5 inches. Leaves peppered with maroon. Grows to 3–5 feet wide in full sun to part shade in 6–20 inches of water. Pineapple-type rhizome. Good for small or medium ponds. Strawn, 1993.

### 'Betsy Sakata'

Soft lemon-yellow. Goblet-shaped blooms of 4–6 inches. Green leaves with small purple flecks. Grows to 3–5 feet wide in full sun in 6–36 inches of water. Mexicana–Marliac-type rhizome. Good for medium or large ponds. Strawn, 1997.

*Nymphaea* 'Black Opal'

*Nymphaea* 'Bleeding Heart'

### 'Black Opal'

Deep red. Goblet-shaped blooms of 3–5 inches. Burgundy foliage fades to a deep maroon-green. Grows to 3–5 feet wide in full sun to part shade in 6–30 inches of water. Odorata-type rhizome. Good for small to medium ponds.

### 'Black Princess'

Red-black. Goblet- or peony-shaped blooms of 4–6 inches. Green leaves; new growth is flushed red. Grows to 3–5 feet wide in full sun in 6–36 inches of water. Marliac-type rhizome. Good for medium to large ponds. Slocum, 1996. Plant patent 09,662.

### 'Bleeding Heart'

Very, very pink that is almost red. Goblet- or peony-shaped blooms of 4–6 inches. Bright green leaves. Grows 3–5 feet wide in full sun in 6–36 inches of water. Odorata-type rhizome. Good for medium to large ponds. Slocum, 1995.

### 'Bory de St-Vincent'

Red-pink or burgundy. Peony-shaped blooms of 4–6 inches. Deep green leaves. Grows to 3–5 feet wide in full sun in 6–36 inches of water. Compact odorata-type rhizome. Good for medium or large ponds. Marliac, 1937.

### 'Burgundy Princess'

Bing-cherry-red. Goblet- or peony-shaped blooms of 6–8 inches. Dark green leaves. Grows to 4–8 feet wide in full sun in 6–24 inches of water. Odorata-type rhizome. Good for medium or large ponds. Strawn, 1993.

### 'Candida' (syn. 'Candidissima')

White. Peony-shaped blooms of 4 inches. Bright green leaves. Grows to 2–4 feet wide in full sun to part shade in 6–24 inches of water. Odorata-type rhizome. Good for small or medium ponds. A naturally occurring hybrid between *N. alba* and *N. candida.*

### 'Carolina Sunset'

Yellow with a hint of peach. Goblet-shaped blooms of 4–8 inches. Mottled leaves. Grows to 6–8 feet wide in full sun to part shade in 6–40 inches of water. Marliac-type rhizome. Good for medium to large ponds. Slocum, 1991.

*Nymphaea* 'Celebration'

### 'Celebration'

Very intense rose-pink. Peony-shaped blooms of 5–6 inches. Deep green leaves. Grows to 6–12 feet wide in full sun in 6–24 inches of water. Compact odorata-type rhizome. Good for medium or large ponds. Strawn, 1994.

### 'Charles de Meurville'

Wine red. Peony-shaped blooms of 4–7 inches. Dark green leaves. Grows to 4–8 feet wide in full sun in 6–48 inches of water. Marliac-type rhizome. Good for medium or large ponds. Marliac, circa 1931. In an earth-bottom pond, blooms reach 8–9 inches across, deepening in color, and leaves are 18 inches wide.

### 'Charlie's Choice'

Red on white. Flat, peony-shaped blooms of 3–5 inches. Green leaves with faint mottling. Grows to 2–3 feet wide in full sun in 6–24 inches of water. Mexicana–Marliac-type rhizome. Good for small to medium ponds. Strawn, 1995.

### 'Cherokee'

Changeable. Blooms of 3–5 inches open orange, turning redder each day until they become a glassy, candy-apple-red. Green leaves brushed in purple. Grows 3–4 feet wide in 6–30 inches of water. Good for containers and small to medium ponds. Slocum, 1989.

*Nymphaea* 'Cherokee'

*Nymphaea* 'Chromatella'

*Nymphaea* 'Chrysantha'

*Nymphaea* 'Chrysantha'

### 'Chromatella'

Canary-yellow. Goblet-shaped blooms of 4–6 inches. Olive-green leaves with bronze markings. Grows to 6–12 feet wide in full sun to part shade in 6–48 inches of water. Marliac-type to pineapple-type rhizome. Good for any size pond, from small to earth bottom. Marliac, 1887. Earned Royal Horticultural Society Award of Garden Merit in 1895.

### 'Chrysantha'

Chrome-yellow. Star-shaped blooms of 5–6 inches. Green leaves with purple flecks. Grows to 6–24 inches wide in full sun in 6–24 inches of water. Pineapple-type rhizome. Good for small or medium ponds and containers. Beldt.

*Nymphaea* 'Chubby'

### 'Chubby'

Creamy white. Peony-shaped blooms of 4 inches. Green leaves with red tint at edges. Grows to 2–6 feet wide in full sun in 6–24 inches of water. Odorata-type rhizome. Good for medium ponds. Strawn, 1993.

### 'Clyde Ikins'

Peach, even on the golden side of cantaloupe. Ball- or goblet-shaped blooms of 8–9 inches. Green, flecked leaves. Grows to 6–12 feet wide in full sun in 6–24 inches or more of water. Slow to spread or increase. Marliac-type rhizome. Good for medium or large ponds. Strawn.

### 'Colonel AJ Welch'

Canary-yellow. Star-shaped blooms of 4–6 inches. Green leaves lightly marbled in maroon. Grows to 4–6 feet wide in full sun in 6–48 inches or more of water. Performs well in cool water. Marliac-type rhizome. Good for medium to large ponds. Marliac, 1929.

*Nymphaea* 'Clyde Ikins'

*Nymphaea* 'Colorado'

*Nymphaea* 'Colorado'

*Nymphaea* 'Comanche', day one

*Nymphaea* 'Conqueror'

### 'Colorado'

Peach, starting yellow with pink in spring, then smoked salmon in summer. Cactus-shaped blooms of 4–6 inches. New leaves are mottled in burgundy, maturing to green. Grows to 4–6 feet wide in full sun to part shade in 6–36 inches of water. Congested mexicana- or tuberosa-type rhizome. Good for medium ponds. Strawn, 1994.

### 'Colossea'

Off-white. Cup-shaped blooms of 4–10 inches. Deep green leaves. Grows to 6–12 feet or more wide in full sun in 6–24 inches of water. Marliac-type rhizome. Good for medium or large ponds. Marliac, 1901.

### 'Comanche'

Changeable, from pale yellow to pale orange. Peony-shaped blooms of 3–5 inches. Freckled leaves. Grows to 3–5 feet wide in full sun in 6–20 inches of water. Marliac-type rhizome. Good for small or medium ponds. Marliac, 1908.

### 'Conqueror'

Watermelon-red on white. Goblet-shaped blooms of 6–8 inches. Grows to 6–8 feet wide in full sun in 6–48 inches of water. Marliac-type rhizome. Good for medium or large ponds. Marliac.

*Nymphaea* 'Denver'

*Nymphaea* 'Denver'

*Nymphaea* 'Escarboucle'

### 'Cynthia Ann'

Peach or yellow-pink. Goblet-shaped blooms of 4–6 inches. Dark green leaves. Grows to 3–5 feet wide in full sun in 6–30 inches of water. Compact odorata–mexicana-type rhizome. Good for any size pond. Strawn, 2001.

### 'Dallas'

Soft, pale rose-pink. Peony-shaped blooms of 5–6 inches with big, round petals. Green leaves. Grows to 6–12 feet wide in full sun in 6–24 inches of water. Odorata-type rhizome. Good for medium to large ponds. Strawn, 1991.

### 'Denver'

White-yellow. Peony-shaped blooms of 4 inches. Green leaves with red tint at edges. Grows to 2–6 feet wide in full sun in 6–24 inches of water. Marliac-type rhizome. Good for medium ponds. Strawn, 1997.

### 'Doll House'

Creamy off-white. Cup-shaped blooms of 2–3 inches. Green leaves. Grows to 2–3 feet wide in full sun in 6–24 inches of water. Odorata-type rhizome. Good for small or medium ponds. Strawn.

### 'Ellisiana'

Glassy red. Cup-shaped blooms of 3–4 inches. Green leaves with a red cast. Grows to 2–3 feet wide in full sun in 6–24 inches of water. Marliac-type rhizome. Good for small or medium ponds. Marliac.

### 'Escarboucle'

Deep cherry-red. Cup-shaped blooms of 6–7 inches. Green leaves. Grows to 4–5 feet wide in full sun in 6–48 inches of water. Marliac-type rhizome. Good for medium or large ponds. Marliac, 1909.

*Nymphaea* 'Fabiola'

*Nymphaea* 'Florida Sunset'

*Nymphaea* 'Formosa'

### 'Fabiola' (syn. 'Pink Beauty')

Bubblegum-pink. Cactus blooms of 4 inches. Red-bottomed green leaves. Grows to 6–12 feet wide in full sun in 6–24 inches of water. Odorata-type rhizome. Good for medium or large ponds. Marliac, 1913.

### 'Fireball'

Rose-red. Peony-shaped blooms of 4 inches or more. Deep green leaves. Grows to 3–4 feet wide in full sun in 6–36 inches of water. Marliac-type rhizome. Good for medium ponds. Slocum.

### 'Firecrest'

Hot pink with orange stamens. Cactus or cup-shaped blooms of 3–5 inches. Deep green leaves. Grows to 2–6 feet wide in full sun in 6–24 inches of water. Odorata-type rhizome. Good for any size pond.

### 'Florida Sunset'

Peach or yellow with pink and orange. Ball- or goblet-shaped blooms of 8–9 inches. Green leaves flecked with brown. Grows to 6–12 feet wide in full sun in 6–48 inches of water. Marliac–odorata-type rhizome. Good for medium or large ponds. Slocum, 1995.

### 'Formosa'

Pale, chiffon-pink. Open, cup-shaped blooms of 3–5 inches. Green leaves. Grows to 3–5 feet wide in full sun in 6–36 inches of water. Odorata-type rhizome. Good for medium or large ponds. Marliac, 1909.

*Nymphaea* 'Gladstone'

*Nymphaea* 'Gloire du Temple-sur-Lot'

### 'Froebelii'

Dark wine-red. Cup-shaped blooms of 3–5 inches. Marbled green leaves with red edges. Grows to 2–3 feet wide in full sun in 6–24 inches of water. Tuberosa-type rhizome. Good for small ponds. Froebel, 1898.

### 'Georgia Peach'

Peach or orange-yellow. Cup- or peony-shaped blooms of 6 inches or more. Green leaves with moderate burgundy mottling. Grows to 3–6 feet wide in full sun in 6–48 inches of water. Marliac-type rhizome. Good for medium or large ponds. Strawn, 1998.

### 'Gladstone'

Snow-white. Goblet- or cup-shaped blooms of 4–6 inches. Dark green leaves. Grows to 6–12 feet or more wide in full sun in 6–48 inches or more of water. Marliac-type rhizome. Good for medium or large ponds.

### 'Gloire du Temple-sur-Lot'

Pale but very pink. Ball- or peony-shaped blooms of 6 inches. Green leaves. Grows to 6–12 feet wide in full sun in 6–24 inches of water. Marliac- or odorata-type rhizome. Good for medium or large ponds. Marliac, 1913.

### 'Gloriosa'

Bright candy-apple-red. Cup-shaped blooms of 6 inches. Bronze-green leaves. Grows to 3–5 feet wide in full sun to part shade in 6–20 inches of water. Tuberosa-type rhizome. Good for small or medium ponds. Marliac, 1896.

*Nymphaea* 'Gold Medal'

### 'Gold Medal'

Strong golden yellow. Goblet-shaped blooms of 6–8 inches. Green leaves. Grows to 4–6 feet wide in full sun in 6–48 inches or more of water. Marliac-type rhizome. Good for large ponds. Slocum, 1991.

*Nymphaea* 'Gonnère'

*Nymphaea* 'Helvola'

### 'Gonnère' (syn. 'Snowball', 'Crystal White')

Snow-white. Ball- or peony-shaped blooms of 4–6 inches. Pea-green leaves. Grows to 4–6 feet wide in full sun in 6–30 inches of water. Marliac-type rhizome. Good for medium or large ponds. Marliac, 1914.

### 'Gypsy'

Red-orange. Cup-shaped blooms of 3–5 inches. Green leaves with faint mottling. Grows to 2–3 feet wide in full sun in 6–24 inches of water. Mexicana–Marliac-type rhizome. Good for small or medium ponds or containers. Strawn, 1998.

### 'Hal Miller'

Eggshell-white. Cup-shaped blooms of 4 inches. Green leaves. Grows to 2–6 feet wide in full sun in 6–24 inches of water. Tuberosa-type rhizome. Good for small or medium ponds. Miller, 1940.

### 'Helvola'

Light lemon-yellow. Small, star-shaped bloom or 1–2 inches. Burgundy-freckled leaves. Grows to 1–3 feet wide in full sun in 1–12 inches of water. Pineapple-type rhizome. Good for containers or small ponds. Marliac.

### 'Hermine' (syn. 'Hermione')

Paper-white. Cup-shaped blooms of 3–5 inches. Dark green leaves. Grows to 2–4 feet wide in full sun to part shade in 6–24 inches of water. Marliac–tuberosa-type rhizome. Good for small or medium ponds. Marliac, 1910.

### 'Highlight'

Pale, pale yellow with a hint of pink. Cactus or peony-shaped blooms of 4–6 inches or more. Green leaves with very faint marbling. Grows to 3–5 feet wide in full sun in 6–36 inches of water. Mexicana- or tuberosa-type rhizome. Good for medium or large ponds. Strawn 1998.

### 'Hollandia' (syn. 'Darwin')

White with red dots for a pink look. Peony-shaped blooms of 5–6 inches. Grows to 6–12 feet wide in full sun in 6–24 inches of water. Marliac-type rhizome. Good for medium or large ponds. Marliac.

### 'Improved Firecrest'

Rich pink with orange stamens. Cup-shaped blooms of 3–5 inches. Green leaves with red edges. Grows to 2–4 feet wide in full sun to part shade in 6–36 inches of water. Odorata-type rhizome. Good for medium or large ponds. Slocum. This form has more flowers and more compact foliage.

*Nymphaea* 'Indiana'

*Nymphaea* 'Indiana', day three

*Nymphaea* 'Hollandia'

*Nymphaea* 'James Brydon'

### 'Indiana'

Changeable red, yellow, and orange. Cup-shaped blooms of 2–3 inches. Green leaves with red spots. Grows to 1–3 feet wide in full sun in 6–24 inches of water. Pineapple-type rhizome. Good for small ponds or containers.

### 'James Brydon'

Unique red-rose-pink. Ball or peony-shaped blooms of 4–6 inches. Green leaves. Grows to 4–12 feet wide in full sun to part shade in 6–48 inches of water. Tolerates more shade than most. Marliac-type rhizome. Good for small to large ponds. Dreer, 1899.

*Nymphaea* 'JCN Forestier'

*Nymphaea* 'Joey Tomocik'

## 'JCN Forestier'

Creamy yellow with red and orange highlights. Cup-shaped blooms of 4–8 inches. Peppered leaves. Grows to 6–12 feet wide in full sun in 6–48 inches of water. Marliac- or odorata-type rhizome. Good for medium or large ponds. Marliac, 1893.

## 'Joanne Pring'

Very washed-out red. Open cup-shaped blooms of 2–3 inches. Green leaves with deep edges. Grows 1–3 feet wide in full sun in 1–12 inches of water. Small Marliac-type rhizome. Good for very small to small ponds. Pring, 1942. A sport of 'Helvola'. Also sold as *N. tetragona* 'Johann Pring' or 'Tetragona Joanne Pring', or 'Pygmaea Joanne Pring'.

## 'Joey Tomocik'

Canary-yellow. Loose cactus blooms of 4–6 inches. Speckled leaves. Grows 6–10 feet in full sun to part shade in 6–40 inches of water. Marliac-type rhizome. Good for medium or large ponds. Strawn, 1993.

## 'Laura Strawn'

Creamy off-white. Very cup- and almost mug-shaped blooms of 6–8 inches. Grows to 6–12 feet wide in full sun in 6–48 inches of water. Marliac-type rhizome. Good for medium or large ponds. Strawn, 1997.

*Nymphaea* 'Laura Strawn'

## 'Laydekeri Alba'

Snow-white. Cup- or star-shaped blooms of 2–3 inches. Green leaves. Grows to 1–3 feet wide in full sun in 6–24 inches of water. Tuberosa-type rhizome. Good for small ponds and containers. Marliac.

## 'Laydekeri Fulgens' (syn. 'Laydekeri Red')

Deep red. Cup-shaped blooms of 6–10 inches. Dark green leaves. Grows to 6–12 feet wide in full sun in 6–30 inches of water. Pineapple–tuberosa-type rhizome. Good for medium or large ponds. Marliac, 1893.

*Nymphaea* 'Laydekeri Rosea'

*Nymphaea* 'Laydekeri Rosea'

*Nymphaea* 'Lily Pons'

### 'Laydekeri Purpurata'

Deep red on white. Cup-shaped blooms of 2–3 inches. Dark green leaves with a red overcast. Grows to 1–3 feet wide in full sun in 6–24 inches of water. Small Marliac-type rhizome. Good for small ponds and containers. Marliac.

### 'Laydekeri Rosea'

Washed-out red. Open, cup-shaped blooms of 2–4 inches. Green leaves with red edges. Grows to 1–3 feet wide in full sun in 6–24 inches of water. Small Marliac-type rhizome. Good for small ponds or containers. Marliac, 1892.

### 'Lemon Chiffon'
Lemon-sherbet-yellow. Ball- or peony-shaped blooms of 4–6 inches. Freckled leaves. Grows to 4–8 feet wide in full sun to part shade in 6–36 inches of water. Marliac-type rhizome. Good for medium or large ponds. Strawn.

### 'Lemon Mist'

Lemon-sherbet-yellow. Goblet-shaped blooms of 4–6 inches. Green, mottled leaves. Grows to 3–5 feet wide in full sun in 6–36 inches of water. Mexicana- or Marliac-type rhizome. Good for small or medium ponds. Strawn, 1997.

### 'Lily Pons'

Bubblegum-pink. Ball- or peony-shaped blooms of 6–8 inches. Green leaves. Grows to 4–6 feet wide in full sun in 6–48 inches of water. Odorata-type rhizome. Good for medium or large ponds. Slocum, 1996.

### 'Little Sue'

Changeable orange with red streaking. Peony-shaped blooms of 3–4 inches. Freckled leaves. Grows to 3–5 feet wide in full sun in 6–24 inches of water. Marliac- or mexicana-type rhizome. Good for small or medium ponds. Strawn, 1993.

### 'Little Champion'

Very intense red-orange. Ball- or peony-shaped blooms of 3–5 inches. Green leaves with faint mottling. Grows to 1–3 feet wide in full sun in 6–24 inches of water. Odorata-type rhizome. Good for small or medium ponds. Slocum.

*Nymphaea* 'Louise Villemarette'

*Nymphaea* 'Marliacea Carnea'

## 'Louise Villemarette'

Soft pink. Cup-shaped blooms of 3–5 inches. Green leaves. Grows to 4–6 feet wide in full sun in 6–48 inches of water. Odorata-type rhizome. Good for medium or large ponds. Thomas, 1962.

## 'Low Country'

Light red. Cup- or star-shaped blooms of 3–5 inches. Green leaves. Grows to 3–5 feet wide in full sun in 6–48 inches of water. Odorata-type rhizome. Good for medium or large ponds.

## 'Lucida'

Glassy red. Cup-shaped blooms of 6–8 inches. Flecked green leaves. Grows to 6–12 feet wide in full sun in 6–48 inches of water. Tuberosa- or Marliac-type rhizome. Good for medium or large ponds. Marliac, 1894.

## 'Marliacea Carnea'

White with red flares. Cup-shaped blooms of 4–6 inches. Green leaves. Grows to 6–8 feet wide in full sun to part shade in 6–48 inches of water. Marliac-type rhizome. Good for medium or large ponds. Marliac, 1887.

## 'Martha'

Washed-out red. Peony-shaped blooms of 4–6 inches. Green leaves. Grows to 4–6 feet wide in full sun in 6–36 inches of water. Marliac- or odorata-type rhizome. Good for medium or large ponds. Strawn, 1993.

## 'Mary'

Very rosy, almost red. Peony- or cup-shaped blooms of 4–6 inches. Green leaves. Grows to 3–6 feet wide in full sun in 6–36 inches of water. Marliac-type rhizome. Good for small or medium ponds. Strawn, 1993.

*Nymphaea* 'Mary'

*Nymphaea* 'Mayla'

### 'Masaniello'

Pink with lighter tips. Peony-shaped blooms of 4–6 inches. Green leaves. Grows to 4–6 feet wide in full sun in 6–48 inches of water. Marliac-type rhizome. Good for medium or large ponds. Marliac, 1908.

### 'Mayla'

Deep rose-pink. Peony-shaped blooms of 5–6 inches. Deep green leaves. Grows to 6–12 feet wide in full sun in 6–24 inches of water. Marliac- or odorata-type rhizome. Good for medium or large ponds. Strawn, 1993.

### 'Météor'

Red. Flat, peony-shaped blooms of 5–6 inches. Green leaves flecked and shaded with red and with red undersides. Grows to 4–6 feet wide in full sun in 6–36 inches of water. Marliac-type rhizome. Good for medium or large ponds. Marliac, 1909.

### *N. mexicana* (syn. 'Mexicana')

Yellow that varies from pale to canary. Star-shaped blooms of 3–5 inches. Tropical-looking green leaves with purple mottling. Grows to 3–5 feet wide in full sun to part shade in 6–48 inches of water. Mexicana-type rhizome. Good for any size pond. Native to North America.

### 'Moon Dance'

Pale blue-white with a hint of yellow. Peony-shaped blooms of 4–6 inches or more. Green, mottled leaves. Grows to 3–5 feet wide in full sun in 6–36 inches of water. Mexicana- or Marliac-type rhizome. Good for small, medium, or large ponds. Florida Aquatic Nurseries.

*Nymphaea* 'Météor'

*Nymphaea* 'Moorei'

*Nymphaea* 'Newton'

### 'Moorei' (syn. 'Mooreana')

Yellow. Goblet-shaped blooms of 3–5 inches. Green leaves. Grows to 3–5 feet in full sun in 6–24 inches of water. Marliac–pineapple-type rhizome. Good for small or medium ponds. Adelaide Botanic Garden, 1896.

### 'Mrs CW Thomas'

Soft baby-pink. Peony- or goblet-shaped blooms of 4–6 inches. Green leaves. Grows to 3–5 feet wide in full sun in 6–24 inches of water. Marliac- or odorata-type rhizome. Good for medium or large ponds. Thomas, 1930.

### 'Mrs. Richmond'

Washed-out red with pink, like pink sand on white paper. Flat, peony-shaped blooms of 4–6 inches. Green leaves. Grows to 3–6 feet wide in full sun in 6–36 inches of water. Odorata-type rhizome. Good for medium or large ponds. Marliac, 1910.

### 'Mt Shasta'

Snow-white. Cactus or ball-shaped blooms of 6–8 inches. Green leaves. Grows to 4–6 feet wide in full sun in 6–48 inches of water. Odorata-type rhizome. Good for medium or large ponds. Slocum, 1996.

### 'Newton'

Red with a hint of orange. Cactus or cup-shaped blooms of 4–6 inches. Green leaves with purple mottling. Grows to 3–5 feet wide in full sun in 6–36 inches of water. Marliac-type rhizome. Good for medium ponds. Marliac, 1910.

### 'Norma Gedye'

Pink edged with diamond dust. Cup- or peony-shaped blooms of 3–5 inches. Green leaves. Grows to 3–5 feet wide in full sun in 6–36 inches of water. Marliac-type rhizome. Good for medium ponds. Gedye, 1972.

### 'Odorata Dwarf'

White. Small cup-shaped blooms. Green leaves. Grows to 1–3 feet wide in full sun to part shade in 6–24 inches of water. Odorata-type rhizome. Good for small or medium ponds.

*Nymphaea* 'Odorata Gigantea'

### 'Odorata Gigantea' (syn. *N. odorata* 'Aiton')

Snow-white to creamy. Cup- or goblet-shaped blooms of 4–8 inches. Green leaves. Grows to 4–6 feet in full sun to part shade in 6–72 inches of water. Odorata-type rhizome. Good for medium or large ponds.

### 'Patio Joe'

Pinky peach. Cup-shaped blooms of 3–5 inches. Green leaves with slight mottling. Grows to 3-5 feet wide in full sun in 6–24 inches of water. Marliac- or mexicana-type rhizome. Good for any size pond. Strawn.

### 'Paul Hariot'

Changeable orange and red. Cup-shaped blooms of 2–3 inches. Green leaves. Grows to 1–3 feet wide in full sun in 6–24 inches of water. Pineapple-type rhizome. Good for small ponds and containers. Marliac, 1905.

*Nymphaea* 'Paul Hariot'

### 'Peace Lily'

Pink, white, and yellow. Cactus blooms of 3–5 inches. Green leaves with slight mottling. Grows to 3–5 feet wide in full sun in 6–36 inches of water. Mexicana- or odorata-type rhizome. Good for any size pond. Strawn, 1999.

### 'Peaches and Cream'

Peach or yellow and deep pink. Peony-shaped blooms of 6–8 inches. Green leaves, purple-speckled when young. Grows to 4–6 feet wide in full sun in 6–48 inches of water. Congested tuberosa-type rhizome. Good for medium or large ponds. Slocum, 1996. Plant patent 09,676.

*Nymphaea* 'Peaches and Cream'

*Nymphaea* 'Peach Glow'

*Nymphaea* 'Perry's Baby Red'

### 'Peach Glow'

Peach or orangey pink. Goblet-shaped blooms of 6 inches or more. Green leaves with faint mottling. Grows to 3–5 feet wide in full sun in 6–36 inches of water. Marliac-type rhizome. Good for medium or large ponds. Strawn, 1997.

### 'Pearl of the Pool'

Very pink. Flat, peony-shaped blooms of 4–6 inches. Green leaves. Grows to 4–6 feet wide in full sun in 6–48 inches of water. Odorata-type rhizome. Good for medium or large ponds. Slocum, 1946.

### 'Perry's Baby Red'

Deep red. Cup- or ball-shaped blooms of 2–4 inches. Medium to dark green leaves. Grows to 2–4 feet wide in full sun to part shade in 4–12 inches of water. Compact tuberosa-type rhizome. Good for small ponds. Slocum, 1983.

### 'Perry's Black Opal'

Black cherry-soda-red. Peony- or ball-shaped blooms of 4–6 inches. Dark green leaves with purple-flushed new growth Grows 3–5 feet wide in full sun in 6–24 inches of water. Tuberosa-type rhizome. Good for medium ponds. Slocum, 1990.

### 'Perry's Crinkled Pink'

Bubblegum-pink. Cactus blooms of 3–5 inches. Green leaves. Grows to 3–5 feet wide in full sun in 6–36 inches of water. Odorata-type rhizome. Slocum, 1989.

### 'Perry's Double White'

Off-white. Peony-shaped blooms of 4–6 inches. Green leaves. Grows to 1–3 feet wide in full sun in 6–24 inches of water. Compact odorata-type rhizome. Good for any size pond. Slocum, 1990.

### 'Perry's Dwarf Red'

Very Kool-Aid-red. Ball-shaped blooms of 3–5 inches. Green leaves. Grows to 1–3 feet wide in full sun in 6–24 inches of water. Compact odorata-type rhizome. Good for any size pond. Slocum.

### 'Perry's Fire Opal'

Strong pink with orange stamens. Cactus or cup-shaped blooms of 3–5 inches. Green leaves. Grows to 2–4 feet wide in full sun in 6–24 inches of water. Odorata-type rhizome. Good for any size pond. Slocum, 1987.

### 'Perry's Red Sensation'

Glassy red. Cup-shaped blooms of 4–6 inches. Green leaves with red-flushed new growth. Grows to 3–5 feet wide in full sun in 6–24 inches of water. Marliac-type rhizome. Good for medium ponds. Slocum.

### 'Perry's Rich Rose'

Very solid pink, almost red. Peony-shaped blooms of 4–6 inches. Green leaves with red edges. Grows to 3–5 feet wide in full sun in 6–36 inches of water. Odorata-type rhizome. Good for medium to large ponds. Slocum, 1990.

### 'Perry's Vivid Rose'

Very rich, rosy pink. Peony-shaped blooms of 3–5 inches. Green leaves. Grows to 3–5 feet wide in full sun in 6–36 inches of water. Odorata-type rhizome. Good for medium or large ponds. Slocum, 1990.

### 'Perry's White Wonder'

Creamy white. Flat, peony-shaped blooms of 3–5 inches. Green leaves. Grows to 1–3 feet wide in full sun in 6–24 inches of water. Marliac-type rhizome. Good for any size pond. Slocum.

### 'Pink Grapefruit'

Grapefruit-pink. Flat, peony-shaped blooms of 6–8 inches. Green leaves with slightly mottled new growth. Grows to 4–8 feet wide in full sun in 6–48 inches of water. Marliac- or mexicana-type rhizome. Good for medium or large ponds. Strawn.

*Nymphaea* 'Pink Sparkle'

### 'Pink Opal'

Pale pink. Cactus or cup-shaped blooms of 4–6 inches. Green leaves with red-edged new growth. Grows to 2–4 feet wide in full sun in 6–24 inches of water. Odorata-type rhizome. Good for any size pond. Fowler, 1915.

### 'Pink Pumpkin'

Pale balloon-pink. Ball-shaped blooms, like a pumpkin, of 4–6 inches. Green leaves. Grows to 4–12 feet wide in full sun in 6–36 inches of water. Odorata-type rhizome. Good for medium or large ponds. Strawn, 1994.

### 'Pink Sensation'

Rosy pink. Cactus or cup-shaped blooms of 4–6 inches. Green leaves. Grows to 3–5 feet wide in full sun in 6–24 inches of water. Marliac-type rhizome. Good for medium ponds. Slocum, 1947.

*Nymphaea* 'Pink Sunrise'

### 'Pink Sparkle'

Silvery pink. Cup-shaped blooms of 4–6 inches. Green leaves reach 10–12 inches across. Grows to 3–5 feet wide in full sun in 6–24 inches of water. Odorata-type rhizome. Good for medium ponds. Strawn, 1998.

### 'Pink Sunrise'

Grapefruit-pink. Peony-shaped blooms of 5–8 inches. Flecked, green leaves. Grows to 6–12 feet wide in full sun in 6–24 inches or more of water. Marliac- or mexicana-type rhizome. Good for medium or large ponds. Strawn, 1993.

*Nymphaea* 'Pink Sensation'

*Nymphaea* 'Pöstlingberg'

*Nymphaea* 'Ray Davies'

### 'Pöstlingberg'

Off-white. Cup-shaped blooms of 6–7 inches. Green leaves. Grows to 6 feet wide in full sun in 6–48 inches of water. Odorata-type rhizome. Good for large ponds. Buggele.

### 'Queen of Whites'

Clean, crisp white. Goblet-shaped blooms of 4–6 inches. Green leaves. Grows to 4–8 feet wide in full sun to part shade in 6–48 inches or more of water. Marliac-type rhizome. Good for medium or large ponds. Gedye, 1970.

### 'Ray Davies'

Rose-pink. Goblet-shaped blooms of 4–6 inches. Green leaves. Grows to 4–8 feet wide in full sun in 6–36 inches of water. Compact odorata-type rhizome. Good for medium or large ponds. Slocum.

### 'Red Queen'

Bright candy-apple-red. Goblet-shaped blooms of 4–6 inches. Deep green leaves. Grows to 3–5 feet wide in full sun in 6–48 inches of water. Marliac-type rhizome. Good for medium or large ponds. Slocum.

*Nymphaea* 'Queen of Whites'

*Nymphaea* 'Ray Davies'

*Nymphaea* 'Reflected Flame'

*Nymphaea* 'Reflected Flame'

### 'Reflected Flame'

Cream with a pinky peach blush. Cactus stellate blooms of 4–6 inches. Green leaves with faint mottling. Grows to 4–6 feet wide in full sun in 6–48 inches of water. Tuberosa-type rhizome. Good for medium or large ponds. Strawn, 1998.

### 'Rembrandt'

Antique red. Goblet-shaped blooms of 4–6 inches. Green leaves. Grows to 6–8 feet wide in full sun to part shade in 6–24 inches of water. Marliac-type rhizome. Good for medium or large ponds. Debate exists as to this plant's real name—some experts say it is 'Météor' renamed.

### 'René Gérard'

Rosy red. Peony-shaped blooms of 6–9 inches. Green leaves. Grows to 5 feet wide in full sun in 6–36 inches of water. Marliac-type rhizome. Good for medium or large ponds. Marliac, 1914.

### 'Robinsonii'

Changeable mix of reds and pale orange. Cup-shaped blooms of 2–3 inches. Green leaves with red blotches. Grows to 1–3 feet wide in full sun in 6–24 inches of water. Upright pineapple-type rhizome. Good for small ponds and containers. Marliac, 1895.

*Nymphaea* 'Robinsonii'

*Nymphaea* 'Rose Arey'

*Nymphaea* 'Sioux'

### 'Rose Arey'

Soft baby-pink. Cactus or cup-shaped blooms of 4–6 inches. Green leaves with a purple cast. Grows to 4–5 feet wide in full sun in 6–36 inches of water. Tuberosa-type rhizome. Good for medium or large ponds. Fowler, 1913.

### 'Rosennymphe'

Pale pink or very washed-out red. Cactus or cup-shaped blooms of 4–6 inches. Green leaves. Grows to 3–5 feet wide in full sun in 6–36 inches of water. Tuberosa-type rhizome. Good for small or medium ponds. Junge.

### 'Rosey Morn'

Soft, tissue-paper pink. Peony-shaped blooms of 3–5 inches. Green leaves with red-flushed new growth. Grows to 3–5 feet wide in full sun in 6–36 inches of water. Compact odorata-type rhizome. Good for any size pond. Johnson, 1932.

### 'Sioux'

Changeable creamy yellow with red and orange blushing. Cup-shaped blooms of 3–4 inches. Mottled leaves. Grows to 3–5 feet wide in full sun in 6–20 inches of water. Marliac-type rhizome. Good for small or medium ponds. Marliac, 1908.

### 'Sirius'

Glassy red. Cactus or cup-shaped blooms of 3–5 inches. Green leaves. Grows to 3–5 feet wide in full sun in 6–24 inches of water. Marliac-type rhizome. Good for medium ponds. Marliac, 1913.

### 'Solfatare'

Changeable pale yellow with soft red flare. Cactus blooms of 3–5 inches. Green leaves with light purple marking. Grows to 4–6 feet wide in full sun in 6–24 inches of water. Marliac- or ordorata-type rhizome. Good for medium or large ponds. Marliac, 1906.

### 'Somptuosa'

Pink. Cactus or cup-shaped blooms of 3–5 inches. Green leaves. Grows to 4–6 feet wide in full sun in 6–36 inches of water. Compact odorata-type rhizome. Good for medium or large ponds. Marliac, 1909.

### 'Splendida'

Pale pink, like a pink marshmallow Peeps. Cactus or cup-shaped blooms of 4–6 inches. Green leaves. Grows to 4–6 feet wide in full sun in 6–24 inches of water. Compact odorata-type rhizome. Good for medium or large ponds. Marliac, 1909.

*Nymphaea* 'Starbright'

### 'Starbright'

White with yellow and pink at the base. Thin petals on a peony-shaped bloom of 4–6 inches. Green leaves with faint mottling. Grows to 3–5 feet wide in full sun in 6–24 inches of water. Mexicana-type rhizome. Good for medium ponds. Strawn, 1997.

### 'Starburst'

White with yellow. Cactus blooms of 4–6 inches. Green, mottled leaves. Grows to 3–6 feet wide in full sun in 6–24 inches of water. Tuberosa-type rhizome. Good for medium ponds. Strawn, 1997.

### 'Steven Strawn'

Bright red. Cup-shaped blooms of 3–5 inches. Deep green leaves. Grows to 3–5 feet wide in full sun in 6–36 inches of water. Marliac-type rhizome. Good for medium or large ponds. Strawn, 1999.

### 'Strawberry Pink'

Pale pink tips and a deep, almost red center. Star-shaped blooms of 3–5 inches. Green leaves. Grows to 3–5 feet wide in full sun in 6–36 inches of water. Odorata-type rhizome. Good for medium or large ponds. Slocum.

### 'Sulphurea'

Canary-yellow. Star-shaped blooms of 4 inches. Leaves heavily mottled in purple. Grows to 4–6 feet or more wide in full sun in 6–36 inches of water. Mexicana-type rhizome. Good for medium or large ponds. Marliac.

### 'Sulphurea Okeechobee'

Banana-yellow. Cactus blooms of 4–6 inches or more. Green, purple-splashed leaves. Grows to 4–6 feet or more wide in full sun in 6 inches to 6 feet of water. Mexicana-type rhizome. Good for medium or large ponds.

### 'Sultan'

Red. Cup-shaped blooms of 4–6 inches. Green leaves. Grows to 4–8 feet or more wide in full sun in 6–48 inches of water. Marliac-type rhizome. Good for medium or large ponds. Marliac.

### 'Sunny Pink'

Peach or a pink-grapefruit color. Peony-shaped blooms of 6–10 inches. Flecked, green leaves. Grows to 6–12 feet wide in full sun in 6–40 inches of water. Tuberosa- or mexicana-type rhizome. Good for medium or large ponds. Strawn, 1997.

### 'Sunrise'

White-yellow. Goblet- or peony-shaped blooms of 6–8 inches. Green, speckled leaves. Grows to 4–8 feet wide in full sun in 6–36 inches of water. Marliac-type rhizome. Good for medium or large ponds. Marliac.

### *N. tetragona*

Creamy white. Small, thimble-like blooms of 1–2 inches. Freckled leaves. Grows to 1–3 feet wide in full sun in 1–12 inches of water. Tetragona-type rhizome. Good for very small or small ponds.

*Nymphaea* 'Texas Dawn'

*Nymphaea* 'Virginalis'

*Nymphaea* 'Venus'

### 'Texas Dawn'

Strong yellow. Peony-shaped blooms of 6–10 inches. Freckled leaves. Grows to 6–12 feet wide in full sun in 6–40 inches of water. Marliac-type rhizome. Good for medium or large ponds. Landon, 1990.

### 'Thomas O'Brien'

Warm peach sherbet. Goblet-shaped blooms of 6–8 inches. Green leaves with faint mottling. Grows to 4–8 feet wide in full sun in 6–36 inches of water. Compact tuberosa-type rhizome. Good for medium or large ponds. Strawn.

### 'Venus'

Whitest white. Cactus blooms of 4–6 inches. Deep green leaves. Grows to 4–8 feet wide in full sun in 6–36 inches of water. Odorata-type rhizome. Good for medium ponds. Slocum, 1985.

### 'Vésuve'

Bright red. Cactus blooms of 3–5 inches. Green leaves. Grows to 4–6 feet wide in full sun in 6–36 inches of water. Odorata-type rhizome. Good for medium ponds. Marliac, 1906.

### 'Virginalis'

Paper-white. Goblet-shaped flowers of 4–5 inches. Green leaves with a purple cast. Grows to 4–8 feet wide in full sun in 6–48 inches of water. Marliac-type rhizome. Good for any size pond. Marliac, 1910.

### 'Virginia'

Paper-white. Peony-shaped blooms of 6–10 inches. Dark green leaves. Grows to 6–12 feet wide in full sun to part shade in 6–48 inches of water. Marliac-type rhizome. Good for medium or large ponds. Thomas, 1962. Plant patent 2172.

*Nymphaea* 'Walter Pagels'

*Nymphaea* 'Wow'

### 'Walter Pagels'

Creamy white with pink. Cup-shaped blooms of 2–4 inches–the classic waterlily shape. Army-green leaves. Grows to 1–3 feet wide in full sun to part shade in 6–20 inches of water. Compact tuberosa-type rhizome. Good for small or medium ponds. Strawn, 1993.

### 'White 1000 Petals'

Off-white. Ball- or peony-shaped blooms of 6–8 inches. Green leaves. Grows to 4–8 feet wide in full sun in 6–36 inches of water. Compact odorata-type rhizome. Good for medium or large ponds. Slocum.

### 'White Sensation'

Paper-white. Goblet-shaped blooms of 4–6 inches. Green leaves. Grows to 3–5 feet wide in full sun in 6–24 inches of water. Marliac-type rhizome. Slocum, 1999.

### 'White Sultan'

Eggshell-white. Goblet-shaped blooms of 8 inches or more. Green leaves. Grows to 4–8 feet wide in full sun in 6–48 inches of water. Marliac-type rhizome. Good for medium or large ponds. This form is a sport of 'Sultan'.

### 'Wildfire'

Pinky red. Goblet-shaped blooms of 4 inches. Green leaves with a red cast. Grows to 3–5 feet wide in full sun in 6–24 inches of water. Compact odorata-type rhizome. Slocum.

### 'Wow'

Deep rose sometimes considered red. Flat, peony-shaped blooms of 4–6 inches. Green leaves with red-flushed new growth. Grows to 4–6 feet wide in full sun in 6–36 inches of water. Compact odorata-type rhizome. Good for medium or large ponds. Slocum, 1990.

*Nymphaea* 'Wucai'

### 'Wucai'

Watermelon-red that is more red in summer than spring. Cup-shaped blooms of 4–6 inches. Green leaves with a red flush. Grows to 6–8 feet wide in full sun in 6–24 inches of water. Marliac-type rhizome. Good for medium or large ponds.

### 'Yogiji'

Paper-white. Cup-shaped blooms of 3–5 inches. Green leaves. Grows to 2–4 feet wide in full sun in 6–24 inches of water. Tuberosa-type rhizome. Good for small or medium ponds. Strawn.

### 'Yuh Ling'

Pale pink. Cactus or cup-shaped blooms of 4–6 inches. Dark green leaves. Grows to 2–6 feet wide in full sun in 6–24 inches of water. Marliac- or odorata-type rhizome. Good for medium ponds. Strawn, 1992.

### 'Ziyu'

Watermelon-red. Cup-shaped blooms of 4–6 inches. Green leaves. Grows to 6–8 feet wide in full sun in 6–24 inches of water. Marliac-type rhizome. Good for medium or large ponds. Chinese origin.

*Nymphaea* 'Yuh Ling'

*Nymphaea* 'Ziyu' backed by *Orontium aquaticum*

# CHAPTER 5

# TROPICAL WATERLILIES

Tropical waterlilies are exotic, intoxicating creatures sure to captivate the hearts of gardeners of all ages and experience. Pondkeepers in warmer climates make their first water features big enough to hold at least one of these hot-blooded beauties. Gardeners in colder climates may at first hesitate to grow them, since they cannot overwinter in the outdoor pond. Once they have a glance at the tropical lily's enchanting color, and then a whiff of its heady fragrance, they are quick to change their minds.

Tropical waterlilies are the true "blue lotus of the Nile" so revered in ancient Egypt. They have played a part in the history of many different cultures. Besides their ornamental uses, they were important in religious ceremonies, and their nectar is reputed to have narcotic or euphoric effect when ingested.

Flowers of tropical waterlilies are magnificent and huge, reaching more than 12 inches in diameter. They often have seven or more blooms open at a time. Their fragrance can be anything from soft vanilla to spicy ginger or fruity citrus. Even their foliage adds color and sparkle to the pond. Leaves are often speckled or streaked in brown, maroon, or purple. Most cultivars now sold flower during daylight hours, but some only come out at night. One night-blooming species, *Victoria amazonica*, commonly called the Victoria waterlily, has spiny leaves and enormous, night-blooming flowers that emit a fragrance reminiscent of pineapple.

Many of the tropical waterlilies available today are cultivars, hybrids, and crosses of the well more than 100 species of tropical waterlilies. The overall native range of the species places them on virtually every continent. Some of these species lilies are still available in the trade, but others can only be found in specialized collections and are not usually sold commercially. For a detailed examination of the species of tropical waterlilies, consult *Water Gardening, Water Lilies and Lotuses* by Perry Slocum, Peter Robinson, and Frances Perry (1996, Timber Press: Portland, Ore.).

Not until the middle of the twentieth century was consistent hybridization of tropical waterlilies undertaken when George Pring, at the Missouri Botanical Garden in St. Louis, began his three decades of work to study and develop tropical waterlilies. Newer ones are

A tropical waterlily blooms in the center of the pond with, counterclockwise from lower left, *Aeschynomene fluitans*, *Menyanthes trifoliata*, *Cyperus alternifolius* 'Nanus', and a lotus in the background

The toothed edges of tropical waterlily leaves on *Nymphaea* 'Wood's White Night'

now being introduced by hybridizers in the United States and Australia, including Perry Slocum, Kirk Strawn, Kenneth Landon, Lee Anne Connelly, Jack Wood, Brad and Bruce McLane, and others.

## PLANT PARTS AND HABIT

Tropical waterlilies resemble their hardy cousins in their overall plant habit, with leaves and flowers that float on the water surface while the crown of the plant remains several inches beneath, rooted into the soil well below the waterline. The foliage of tropicals, like that of hardies, is rounded or oblong, and split with a sinus that runs to the center of the leaf where it joins with the stem. This sinus may be convex, concave, or even. Veining is often more prominent in tropical than in hardy waterlilies, and the leaves more oval than round.

Unlike hardy waterlily leaves, though, those of tropicals are not smooth at their edges. Instead, tropical waterlily leaves are highly toothed, looking as though their edges have been cut with scalloped scissors. This distinction is often the best way to tell whether a lily is hardy or tropical. The foliage of a tropical is often, although not always, more heavily marked or mottled than that of a hardy waterlily, and often much larger in size.

Like hardy waterlily leaves, those of tropicals have stomata on the leaf surface through which they take in oxygen. Their undersides are often a dark red or lavender color, trapping sunlight so that it may be used in photosynthesis. They are heavily veined underneath as well.

A dwarf waterlily fills a tub garden along with *Typha laxmannii*, *Eichhornia crassipes*, *Juncus effusus* 'Spiralis', *Hydrocharis morsus-ranae*, and *Iris pseudacorus*

Some tropical waterlilies bloom in colors ranging from white to red, with shades of pink and even maroon. Some of these open their flowers during the daytime, from morning to late afternoon. Others, the night-blooming tropicals, open only in the evening and close the following morning. Still other tropicals, although only day-blooming, come in yellows that may be as light as cream or as gold as butter. There are even day-blooming tropicals with blue, lavender, and even purple flowers. New spotted flower forms are becoming available, as are new multi- or double-flowered forms. More colorful foliage is also being developed.

## IN THE LANDSCAPE

Tropical waterlilies often have a wide leaf spread, making them suitable for large ponds that are 8 feet or more in diameter and at least 6 inches deep. Because they will not overwinter in colder climates, they can be grown in shallower water that tends to heat up sooner. One or two in a wide open pond makes a truly stunning display for weeks on end. Few if any additional water plants are needed to complete the scene.

Fortunately some cultivars are suitable for smaller water gardens, and a few will even grow well in a container pond that is only a few feet wide. These grow away quite happily when nestled alongside and among marginal water plants. Placed near a doorway or the outside patio table, their sweet fragrance is carried along on the slightest breeze to be enjoyed effortlessly—one never needs to bend down or lean over in order to appreciate their smell. Tropical waterlilies also respond well to the higher water temperatures in container and tub gardens; they seem not only to thrive in such conditions but to reward us with more blooms.

I prefer to grow smaller day-bloomers and night-bloomers in small to medium ponds, those with up to 4,000 gallons water capacity. Larger cultivars I grow as annuals in lakes and very large lined ponds.

## SUN, WIND, AND WATER DEPTH

Like their hardy relatives, tropical waterlilies usually require full sunlight, at least eight hours every day, in order to grow and flower well. If some shade will occur, it is best for the lilies in the morning, so the stronger afternoon sun still reaches the plant. In warmer climates, where daytime temperatures reach or exceed 100°F for 10 days or more, most tropical waterlilies appreciate a few hours of morning shade. Despite this general rule, many of the blue-flowering cultivars of tropical waterlilies grow and flower well even when they have not received a full day's sunlight. Those that perform well in part shade are noted below in the cultivar descriptions.

Just like hardy waterlilies, tropical forms suffer under continuous wave action or heavy wind. Likewise, they will drown if subjected to water splashing on their leaves from waterfalls, fountains, and the like. A leaf will turn brown or black, slowly dissolving, and then will disappear altogether. If continued for too long, the splashing water will so completely damage the leaves, and weaken new ones beginning

to develop, that the entire plant will succumb. Tropical waterlilies are best kept in mostly calm, still waters to keep them fit, trim, and in peak condition.

Most cultivars grow best in water that is between 6 inches and 4 feet in depth. A few varieties can grow in more than 6 feet of water. Tropicals perform poorly in ponds with substantial changes in water depth, such as irrigation ponds. I have found that they grow best in water ranging from 12 to 24 inches deep. Just the same, I have seen tropical waterlilies growing in containers with no free water over their crown, just very moist soil, and the plants were still in bloom nonetheless.

## SOIL AND WATER CHEMISTRY

Although tropical waterlilies tolerate a wide range in soil and water pH, they do best in neutral to slightly acidic conditions. They also prefer hot water temperatures reaching above 80°F. Most are not tolerant of salt. The leaves turn black and mushy and the whole plant becomes soft. New foliage turns weak and brittle.

## SEASONAL CARE

Tropical waterlilies may be safely placed in the outdoor pond when the water reaches a consistent temperature of about 70°F. Placing a growing tropical into a cold pond can stunt or even kill it. Being placed outside too soon will send the plants into shock, triggering them to return to dormancy. Once a tropical waterlily starts to grow, it resents cooling down. Some may take weeks or even months to recover.

Once the lilies are safely outside, begin to fertilize them every two or three weeks according to the manufacturer's directions. Remove old flowers and leaves that are turning yellow or looking faded. When the weather is very warm and the plant is blooming heavily, it may need fertilizer more often.

In warmer climates, tropical waterlilies can stay in the pond throughout the winter. Even where the weather cools, the lilies are fine outdoors so long as the water temperature does not fall below 60°F.

In colder areas where frost is an issue, tropical waterlilies will have to be brought indoors in order to survive the winter. Some cultivars, especially those prone to viviparous growth, are not likely to form dormant tubers and so must be overwintered using the aquarium method. Other selections may be dried down and stored as dormant tubers. The following paragraphs detail the various techniques for overwintering tropical waterlilies.

## The Aquarium Method

One way to carry a tropical over the winter is to keep it in an aquarium. Take the plant out of the pond before the first frost. Cut off excess foliage and roots and replant the tuber in a smaller pot. Place the pot in an aquarium with more than 2 inches of water over the crown of the plant. Next, put a heater in the water and keep the water warmed to 70–75°F. Put lights over the aquarium to give the lily 14 hours of daylight. I have found four cool white fluorescent bulbs to be sufficient for supplying the necessary 1500 or more footcandles. Then, wait for spring. Do not fertilize the lily while it is in the aquarium.

This overwintering technique may be adapted to a large tub or whiskey barrel liner instead of an aquarium—water, heat, and light needs are the same. Covering the tub with plastic or glass helps retain heat and humidity.

In its temporary aquarium-pond, the lily will grow small leaves that float to the water surface, and it may flower. When spring returns and the pond temperature reaches 70°F, replant the lily in a larger pot and put it back in the pond. Make sure to fertilize it and it will quickly grow and flower as it did in prior years.

We have found that the aquarium method is best suited to pondkeepers who already have the right equipment. To be successful, the water temperature and daylight requirements must be met consistently. For some gardeners, this method may be cost prohibitive, given the price of the aquarium, the heater, and the lighting. Pondkeepers who do not have the necessary supplies would probably prefer to use a different overwintering method, or to simply buy a new plant every year, which in areas of high energy costs may be a cheaper alternative.

## The Distilled Water Method

Another way to overwinter a tropical waterlily calls for a jar and some distilled water. Again, remove the lily from the pond before the first frost. Gradually let the lily go dry in a cool, dark place over the course of a few weeks. Cut off dead or dying foliage and flowers. Once the soil is somewhat dry, remove the pot and break apart the soil to reveal the nut-like tuber in which the lily has gone dormant. Wash the tuber free of soil and cut back remnant stems and roots. Place the tuber in a quart jar of distilled water and close the jar with a tight-fitting lid. Make sure to mark the container with the name of the lily to avoid confusion in the spring. Keep it in a cool, dark place for the winter. Check the water periodically to make sure that it has not fouled, and replace the water when it becomes discolored.

We have had some success with the distilled water method, but have found that a lily may be prone to mold or rot if it is not very well cleaned before it is placed in the jar of distilled water. Also, keeping the jar at 55–60°F during the entire period of overwintering is very important. A significant increase in water temperature may foul the water and cause the lily to rot. It also appears that certain lilies may have a tendency to resprout if the water temperature rises above 60°F. Although a small amount of growth is no cause for alarm, substantial growth can deplete the tuber's energy reserve and destroy the plant. Too much growth may leave the tender new shoots open to fungal or bacterial attack. The distilled water method is best for those who can store the jars of water at the proper temperature. Checking the water weekly to make sure that the lily is faring well is very important.

## The Damp Sand or Peat Moss Method (Nature's Way)

The third method for overwintering a tropical waterlily also relies upon drying down the lily for the winter. Bring the lily inside to a cool, dark place before the first frost. Let it go dry gradually over a few weeks. Remove spent flowers and foliage. When the lily is dormant, remove the pot and find the nut-like tuber in the soil. Wash it so that it is free of soil and cut off any remnant roots to the base of the tuber. If desired, treat it with fungicide. Place the tuber in damp—not wet—sand or peat moss in a plastic container with a lid. Poke a few holes in the lid to allow for air circulation. The sand or peat moss should be only barely damp, enough to prevent the tuber from drying and shriveling. To make sure the sand or peat moss is not too wet, squeeze it until it holds a shape but no longer drips water.

Keep the container in a cool, dark place, such as an unheated garage or basement, where the temperature will remain at 55–60°F. Make sure to mark the container with the name of the lily. Check the tuber often for softness or discoloration and ensure that the sand or peat moss has not dried out completely. When spring returns and brings water temperatures up to 70°F, repot the lily and return it to the pool. The renewed moisture, along with the warmth and sunlight, quickly prompt the lily to start growing.

The lack of moisture in this method is similar to the natural condition in which lilies go dormant because the lake has gone dry during the winter season. We have had the most success of all the methods when we store our lily tubers in damp peat moss. Because the tuber is stored in peat moss instead of water, it is less likely to think that it is time to start growing again, even if the temperature temporarily climbs above 60°F. At high temperatures the relative dryness of the environment convinces the lily that it should remain dormant.

These drying methods seem best suited for tropical night-blooming lilies, less so for day-blooming ones. Also, smaller tubers store better than larger ones. While the lily is growing in the summer, however, it should be as large as possible to produce larger flowers and more of them. This will result in larger tubers, which do not store as well. Winter storage and growing large ornamental lilies are diametrically opposed for those who live in colder climates and do not have the benefit of an aquarium or a heated greenhouse.

Our primary problem with this method of winter storage has been the ubiquitous field mouse. It has an unnerving talent for breaking into our containers and nibbling away at our stored tubers, which we keep in a cool greenhouse. For the homeowner, the solution is obvious: store the plastic containers where they will be out of reach to animals that may find them a tasty meal.

## PLANTING

Tropical waterlilies generally grow from a central crown. Unlike many hardy waterlilies, which grow from creeping rhizomes that crawl across the width of the pot, tropicals grow in an upright position, looking much like a pineapple. As a result, a dormant tuber can be simply planted in the middle of a pot filled about two-thirds full with cat litter or heavy clay soil—nothing with added organic matter—that has been mixed with a granular fertilizer. I use Landon fertilizer from Pondtabbs. Plant the tuber about 1–3 inches below the soil surface. The tuber sends sprouts up to the surface, as many as 18 in some tubers, resulting in 18 plants.

We start our small waterlilies in quart or 4-inch pots. When they have filled that out, or if they have larger crowns, we use a 7-gallon pot. I try to grow them in the largest pot possible. Tropical waterlilies are heavy feeders and those for larger ponds appreciate a lot of room.

Tropical waterlilies that are shipped in active growth do not have a well defined tuber. Instead, their roots and crown look more like a bare-root impatiens plant. To plant the lily, fill the pot about two-thirds full of soil, making a slight

Tropical waterlily tubers

The larger tropical waterlily in active growth compared to a hardy waterlily

To pot up a tropical waterlily, place the lily on top of the soil and spread out the roots

Include granular or tablet fertilizer in the pot

Match previous soil depth where light-colored stems change to dark

mound in the middle. Place the lily on top of the mound, spreading out its roots across the soil. The stems of the lily leaves will generally be light colored where they emerge from the base of the plant, and then a darker color a few inches away from the base. The point at which light changes to dark shows the soil line where the leaves of the lily were planted below the soil surface. Try to match that depth, or plant them at a more shallow depth, when potting up tropical waterlilies.

Tropical waterlilies, whether planted as dormant tubers or in active growth, float very easily when they have started to sprout roots and leaves. It is not uncommon for us to plant several and suddenly see them pop out of the soil and float around on the water surface. To keep them in their pots, do not cut away all the roots—leave some so they can help anchor the plant in the soil. Place a smooth rock on top of the soil over the roots for the first week or so to keep larger lilies in place. Or, use string to criss-cross the crown and foliage in order to anchor the plant in the pot. New roots grow quickly once the lily is in warm water, often rooting into the pot in about a week.

## DIVISION

Tropical waterlilies demonstrate their need for larger quarters by displaying flowers and leaves that are smaller than normal, as well as producing fewer blooms or foliage. It is better not to divide them, however. Instead, simply transplant the lily to a larger pot.

## PROPAGATION

A method of propagating tropical waterlilies takes advantage of their habit of resprouting to form new plants when the main growing crown of the plant is placed below the soil level. Night-blooming tropical waterlilies are particularly prone to resprouting many new plants when they have been planted too deeply. The disadvantage is that this sacrifices the main, large crown which will stop growing in order to produce new plantlets. Eventually new plants will form, but they will all be smaller. By the time they reach the size to bloom well, it may be too late in the season to enjoy them. Take extra special care with the soil depth when potting up tropical night-blooming waterlilies.

As an alternative method, the side-eyes on main tubers can be removed and planted in the spring, placing them 1–2 inches below the soil surface. They will sprout new plantlets that can be divided and grown on. We have also propagated tropical waterlilies by placing dormant tubers in a Ziploc bag filled with water. We then placed the bags in a warm pond or fish tank. The tubers sprouted new plantlets, which we separated from the main plant once the plantlets had formed their own roots.

During the summer, viviparous waterlilies produce new plants in the sinus of the leaf. These can be removed and potted up once they have developed roots. Some plantlets will even flower while still attached to the mother plant.

Both hybridizing tropical waterlilies and starting them from seed are done in much the same manner as for hardy waterlilies. See Chapter 4 for details.

New plantlet sprouting from the leaf sinus of a tropical waterlily

Hardy and tropical waterlilies and lotus, far left, share the water while in the margin stand, right to left, *Thalia, Lythrum, Colocasia, Colocasia esculenta* 'Metallica', *Scirpus albescens, Cyperus longus, Typha laxmannii*, and *Cyperus alternifolius* 'Nanus'

The many cultivars of tropical waterlilies have suffered the same inconsistencies of naming as have beset the hardy lilies. Many seed strains have developed, too, since tropical waterlilies are notoriously fertile at setting seed. As official registrar authority of all *Nymphaea*, hardy and tropical, the International Waterlily and Water Gardening Society (IWGS) has undertaken to sort them all out. A provisional checklist includes more than 500 cultivars of tropical waterlilies. Several of these are now lost to cultivation, but many still remain available, and new ones are introduced every year.

## Cultivars and Species

The cultivars in the following list are all hybrids in the genus *Nymphaea*. The "*N.*" that should begin each name has been omitted for brevity. Measurements for the pond sizes suggested in the following descriptions are small (4–6 feet across), medium (7–9 feet), and large (more than 10 feet). Tub and container water gardens are considered to be up to 3 feet across.

*Nymphaea* 'Albert Greenburg'

*Nymphaea* 'Albert Greenburg'

*Nymphaea* 'Afterglow'

### 'Afterglow'

Day-blooming in peachy pink autumn shades. Stellate of 6–10 inches. Green leaves. Large spread. Good for medium to large ponds. Randig, 1946.

### 'Albert Greenburg'

Day-blooming in a mix of pink, yellow, and orange. Cup-shaped flowers of 8 inches. Mottled green leaves. Spread 6½ feet. Good for medium to large ponds. Will tolerate just four hours of sun and still bloom. Birdsey.

### 'Alice Tricker'

Day-blooming in eggshell-white. Platter-shaped flowers of 4–8 inches. Green leaves with red flecks. Medium spread. Good for medium to large ponds. Tricker, 1937.

### 'Anne Emmet'

Day-blooming in purple over yellow for a smoky green effect. Platter-shaped flowers of 4–6 inches. Green leaves. Medium spread. Good for medium to large ponds. Winch.

### 'Antares'

Night-blooming in intense crimson. Cup-shaped blooms of 5–6 inches. Bronze leaves. Spread of 6 feet. Good for medium to large ponds. Stands up well under artificial light. Longwood Gardens.

### 'August Koch'

Day-blooming in medium blue. Platter-shaped, fragrant blooms of 8–10 inches. Good for cutting, and will bloom in winter if kept warm. Green leaves. Spread of 4–6 feet. Good for medium to large ponds. Koch, 1922.

### 'Aviator Pring'

Day-blooming in golden yellow. Cup-shaped blooms of 6 inches held well above the water. Mottled green leaves. Spread of 6½ feet. Good for medium ponds. Pring.

### 'Bagdad'

Day-blooming in blue with gold centers and yellow stamens. Broad, flat blooms of 6–8 inches. Light green leaves mottled with red and brown. Spread of 7 feet. Good for medium to large ponds. Pring, 1941.

### 'Barbara Barnette'

Day-blooming in autumn shades of peach, pink, and yellow. Cup-shaped blooms of 4–6 inches. Mottled leaves. Medium to large spread. Good for medium to large ponds. Florida Aquatic Nurseries, 1998.

*Nymphaea* 'Blue Beauty'

### 'Blue Beauty'

Day-blooming in lilac-blue. Cup-shaped blooms of 8–10 inches with a spicy perfume. Dark green leaves speckled with brown. Spread of 6½ feet. Good for large ponds or containers. Tricker, 1897.

### 'Blue Spider'

Day-blooming in true blue. Star-shaped blooms of 4–6 inches. Leaves variegated in a spiderweb. Medium to large spread. Good for medium to large ponds. Florida Aquatic Nurseries, 1995.

### 'Blue Star'

Day-blooming in bright violet-blue. Star-shaped blooms of 4–6 inches. Green leaves. Medium spread. Good for medium ponds.

### 'Bob Tricker'

Day-blooming in light blue with gold stamens. Cup-shaped blooms of 6–8 inches. Green leaves with red and green veins on the undersides. Spread of 6½ feet. Good for medium to large ponds. Pring.

### 'Brazo's White'

Night-blooming in moonlight-white. Blooms of 4–6 inches. Copperish leaves. Medium to large spread. Good for medium to large ponds. Strawn.

### *N. caerulea*

Day-blooming in light but intense blue. Star-shaped blooms of 4–6 inches. Green leaves. Spread of 6–10 feet. Good for medium to large ponds.

### *N. capensis*

Day-blooming in shades of purple. Platter-shaped blooms of 6–10 inches. Mottled leaves. Medium to large spread. Good for medium to large ponds. Three selections are sold as 'Blue Capensis', 'Pink Capensis', and 'White Capensis'.

*Nymphaea colorata*

*Nymphaea* 'Dauben'

### 'Catherine Marie'

Night-blooming in intense pink. Cup-shaped blooms of 6–7 inches. Coppery green leaves. Spread of 6–7 feet. Good for medium to large ponds. Landon.

### 'Charles Thomas'

Day-blooming in periwinkle-blue. Long narrow petals on blooms of 6 inches. Green, mottled leaves. Spread of 6½ feet. Good for medium to large ponds. Tolerates partial shade. Wood.

### 'Clint Bryant'

Day-blooming in deep blue-violet-purple. Platter-shaped blooms of 6 inches. Emerald-green leaves. Medium spread. Good for medium ponds. Tolerates some shade. Van Ness.

### N. colorata

Day-blooming in purple-blue-violet. Pinwheel-shaped blooms of 3–4 inches. Green leaves. Spread of 2–3 feet. Good for small to medium ponds and containers.

### 'Crystal'

Day-blooming in pure white. Star-shaped blooms of 4–6 inches. Green leaves with maroon streaks. Medium to large spread. Good for medium to large ponds. Viviparous. Bryne.

### 'Dauben' (syn. 'Daubeniana')

Day-blooming in creamy white with lavender tips. Star-shaped, fragrant blooms of 2–4 inches. Green leaves. Spread of 1–8 feet. Good for small to medium ponds and containers. Highly viviparous. Daubeny.

### 'Dir. Geo. T. Moore'

Day-blooming in intense violet-blue with gold centers. Cup-shaped blooms of 8 inches. Dark green leaves mottled with purple. Spread of 6½ feet. Good for any size pond. Pring, 1941.

### 'Edward D. Uber'

Day-blooming in electric purple with pink centers. Platter-shaped blooms of 4–6 inches. Jade-green leaves. Medium to large spread. Good for medium to large ponds. Viviparous and tolerant of 60 percent shade. Van Ness, 1985.

### 'El Dorado'

Day-blooming in lemony yellow. Star- or platter-shaped blooms of 6–8 inches. Mottled leaves. Spread of 5–6 feet. Good for small to medium ponds. Tolerates cold better than most. Randig.

### 'Electra'

Day-blooming in light blue. Stellate blooms of 4 inches. Almost black speckles on green leaves. Spread of 4–6 feet. Good for small to medium ponds. Frase.

### N. elegans

Day-blooming in blue. Star-shaped blooms of 4–6 inches. Green leaves. Medium to large spread. Good for medium to large ponds.

*Nymphaea* 'Emily Grant Hutchings'

*Nymphaea* 'General Pershing'

### 'Emily Grant Hutchings'

Night-blooming in rose-pink. Cup-shaped blooms of 10 inches. Bronze leaves. Spread of 6½ feet. Good for medium to large ponds. Pring, 1922.

### 'Enchantment'

Day-blooming in salmon-rose with orange centers. Star-shaped blooms of 6 inches. Speckled green leaves. Spread of 5–6 feet. Good for small to medium ponds. Randig.

### 'Evelyn Randig'

Day-blooming in hot pink. Cup-shaped blooms of 6 inches. Leaves boldly splashed with purple. Spread of 6–10 feet. Good for medium to large ponds. Randig, 1931.

### 'Florida Star'

Day-blooming in white. Star-shaped blooms of 4–6 inches. Green leaves with purple mottling. Medium to large spread. Good for medium to large ponds. Florida Aquatic Nurseries.

### 'General Pershing'

Day-blooming in orchid-pink, opening early and closing late. Deeply fragrant, double, platter-shaped blooms of 8–10 inches. Dark green leaves mottled with purple. Spread of 6½ feet. Good for medium to large ponds. Pring, 1920.

### N. gigantea

Day-blooming in pale lavender-blue. Peony-shaped blooms of 8–10 inches that sometimes last up to seven days. Green leaves. Spread of 7 feet. Good for medium to large ponds.

*Nymphaea* 'Green Smoke'

*Nymphaea* 'Hilary'

*Nymphaea* 'Jack Wood'

### 'Golden West'

Day-blooming in autumn shades of peachy pink. Platter-shaped, very fragrant blooms of 6–10 inches held high out of the water. Highly mottled leaves. Large spread. Good for medium to large ponds. Randig.

### 'Green Smoke'

Day-blooming in chartreuse with smoky blue tips. Platter-shaped blooms of 6–8 inches. Lightly speckled, bronze-green leaves. Spread of 5–6 feet. Good for small to medium ponds. Randig, 1965.

### 'Hilary'

Day-blooming in pale lavender. Cup- or star-shaped blooms of 4–6 inches. Green leaves. Medium spread. Good for medium ponds. Viviparous. Wood.

### 'Hudsonia'

Day-blooming in translucent white. Cup-shaped blooms, looking like orange segments, of 8–12 inches. Green leaves. Medium to large spread. Good for large ponds. Hudson, 1893.

### 'Isabella Pring'

Day-blooming in white with yellow stamens. Platter-shaped blooms of 6–8 inches. Light green leaves. Spread of 5–6 feet. Good for small to medium ponds. Viviparous. Pring, 1941.

### 'Islamorada'

Day-blooming in pale purple with light freckles. Platter-shaped blooms of 6 inches. Green leaves. Spread of 6 feet. Good for medium ponds. Florida Aquatic Nurseries.

### 'Jack Wood'

Day-blooming in raspberry-red. Platter-shaped, abundant blooms of 6–8 inches. Purple-mottled leaves. Spread of 5–6 feet. Good for small to medium ponds. Wood.

### 'James Gurney'

Night-blooming in deep rose-pink. Fragrant blooms of 8–10 inches. Reddish green leaves. Spread of 6–7 feet. Good for medium to large ponds. Pring, 1948.

### 'Jamie Lu Skare'

Day-blooming in butter-yellow. Cup-shaped, fragrant blooms of 4–6 inches. Green leaves. Medium spread. Good for small, medium, or large ponds. Van Ness.

*Nymphaea* 'Juno'

### 'Janice Wood'

Day-blooming in white. Star-shaped blooms of 4–6 inches. Green leaves with purple spots and a red cast around the edges. Medium to large spread. Good for medium to large ponds. Wood.

### 'Jennifer Rebecca'

Night-blooming in crimson. Sunflower- or platter-shaped blooms of 6–8 inches. Bronze leaves. Spread of 6–7 feet. Good for medium to large ponds. Tolerates heat well. Landon, 1990.

### 'JoAnn'

Day-blooming in raspberry-red. Platter-shaped, very fragrant blooms of 6 inches. Deep green leaves. Medium to large spread. Good for medium to large ponds. Van Ness, 1981.

### 'Josephine'

Day-blooming in white. Cup-shaped blooms of 3–5 inches. Green leaves with purple mottling. Small to medium spread.

Good for small to medium ponds. Viviparous. Florida Aquatic Nurseries.

### 'Judge Hitchcock'

Day-blooming in purplish blue with deep violet tips. Cup-shaped blooms of 6–8 inches. Dark green leaves flecked with brown. Large spread. Good for large ponds. Pring, 1941.

### 'Juno'

Night-blooming in creamy white. Star-shaped blooms of 4–6 inches. Green leaves. Medium to large spread. Good for large ponds. Pring.

### 'Key Lime'

Day-blooming in yellow. Star-shaped blooms of 3–5 inches. Green leaves with purple mottling. Medium spread. Good for small to medium ponds. Florida Aquatic Nurseries.

### 'Laura Frase'

Day-blooming in blue. Cup-shaped blooms of 4–6 inches. Green leaves with purple spots. Medium to large spread. Good for medium to large ponds. Frase.

*Nymphaea* 'Leopardess'

*Nymphaea* 'Lindsey Woods'

### 'Leopardess'

Day-blooming in cobalt blue. Platter-shaped, highly fragrant blooms of 6–8 inches. Green leaves heavily mottled with maroon. Spread of 5½ feet. Good for small, medium, or large ponds. Randig, 1931.

### 'Lindsey Woods'

Day-blooming in deep purple. Platter-shaped blooms of 4–6 inches. Green leaves with purple spots. Medium to large spread. Good for medium to large ponds. Nelson.

### 'Louella G. Uber'

Day-blooming in snowy white. Cup-shaped, double blooms of 4–6 inches that stay open later than other day bloomers. Green leaves. Medium spread. Good for medium ponds. Van Ness.

### 'Margaret Mary'

Day-blooming in pale blue. Very small star- or cup-shaped blooms of 1–3 inches. Green leaves. Spread of 5½ feet. Good for small to medium ponds and containers. Tolerates light shade. Thomas, 1964.

### 'Margaret Randig'

Day-blooming in sky blue with yellow centers. Cup-shaped blooms of 6–8 inches. Deeply mottled leaves. Spread of 5½ inches good for small, medium, or large ponds. Viviparous. Randig.

*Nymphaea* 'Marion Strawn'

*Nymphaea* 'Marion Strawn'

*Nymphaea* 'Midnight'

## 'Marion Strawn'

Day-blooming in snow-white that is slightly gray. Stellate blooms of 6 inches. Slightly mottled leaves. Spread of 6 feet. Good for medium to large ponds. Strawn.

## 'Maroon Beauty'

Night-blooming in deep maroon with dark centers. Very free-flowering with star-shaped blooms of 8–10 inches. Red-bronze leaves. Spread of 4–6 feet. Good for medium to large ponds. Slocum, 1950.

## 'Miami Rose'

Day-blooming in fuchsia-raspberry, almost red. Cup-shaped blooms of 4–6 inches. Green leaves. Small to medium spread. Good for small, medium, or large ponds and containers. Florida Aquatic Nurseries.

## 'Midnight'

Day-blooming in purple with gold centers. Free-flowering with star-shaped, double, fragrant blooms of 6 inches. Dark green, red-flecked leaves. Spread of 4–5 feet. Good for small, medium, or large ponds. Pring, 1941.

## 'Missouri'

Night-blooming in creamy white. Star-shaped blooms of 12 inches with broad petals. Green leaves with copper-brown new growth. Spread of 6–7 feet. Good for large ponds—it gets huge. Pring, 1932.

## 'Mme. Ganna Walska'

Day-blooming in dramatic lipstick-pink-lavender. Abundant platter-shaped blooms of 6 inches. Heavily mottled leaves. Spread of 4½ feet. Good for small, medium, or large ponds. Viviparous. Wood.

## 'Moon Shadow'

Day-blooming in green created by yellow tips over blue. Cup-shaped blooms of 6–8 inches. Green leaves. Medium spread. Good for medium ponds. Florida Aquatic Nurseries, 1999.

## 'Mr. Martin E. Randig'

Day-blooming in lavender-blue, maturing to blue-purple. Cup-shaped, very fragrant blooms of 6 inches. Mottled green leaves. Spread of 4½ inches. Good for small, medium, or large ponds. Viviparous. Randig, 1939.

*Nymphaea* 'Mrs. Geo. Hitchcock'

*Nymphaea* 'Missouri'

### 'Mrs. Geo. Hitchcock'

Night-blooming in orchid-pink, continuing into the fall. Blooms of 12 inches. Bronze leaves. Spread of 6–7 feet. Good for medium to large ponds. Pring, 1926.

### 'Mrs. Geo. H. Pring'

Day-blooming in creamy white. Star-shaped blooms of 13 inches. Green leaves lightly mottled with red. Spread of 6½ feet. Good for medium to large ponds. Pring, 1932.

### 'Mrs. John Wood'

Night-blooming in red. Platter-shaped blooms of 4–8 inches. Bronze leaves. Medium to large spread. Good for medium or large ponds. Van Ness.

### 'Mrs. Martin E. Randig'

Day-blooming in lavender-blue. Platter-shaped, fragrant blooms of 6–10 inches. Green leaves. Spread of 4½ feet. Good for medium to large ponds. Highly viviparous. Randig, 1938.

### 'Nolene'

Day-blooming in bright, vibrant pink. Star-shaped, fragrant blooms of 4–6 inches. Green leaves. Small to medium spread. Good for small, medium, or large ponds and containers. Winch, 1972.

### 'Nora'

Day-blooming in blue-violet. Platter-shaped blooms of 4–6 inches. Heavily mottled green leaves. Medium to large spread. Good for medium to large ponds. Viviparous. Tolman.

### 'Pamela'

Day-blooming in sky-blue. Saucer-shaped blooms of 10–12 inches held high above the water. Green leaves marbled with chestnut. Spread of 5½ feet. Good for medium to large ponds. Koch, 1931.

### 'Panama Pacific'

Day-blooming in deep plum with yellow stamens. Platter-shaped blooms of 6–12 inches. Bronze-green leaves with reddish spots. Spread of 6½ feet. Good for any size pond. Viviparous. Tricker, 1914.

### 'Patricia Eileen'

Night-blooming in pale pink. Star-shaped blooms of 4–8 inches. Green leaves flushed with bronze. Medium spread. Good for medium to large ponds. Stetson.

### 'Paul Stetson'

Day-blooming in porcelain-blue. Platter-shaped blooms of 6–10 inches. Mottled leaves. Medium spread. Good for medium to large ponds. Wood, 1984.

*Nymphaea* 'Peach Blow'

### 'Peach Blow'

Day-blooming in pink with peach centers. Platter-shaped blooms of 6–10 inches. Light green leaves with lots of tiny red flecks. Spread of 6½ feet. Good for medium to large ponds. Highly viviparous. Pring, 1941.

### 'Perry's Blue Heaven'

Day-blooming in pale silver-blue. Star-shaped blooms of 4–6 inches. Green leaves. Medium spread. Good for small, medium, or large ponds and containers. Slocum.

### 'Pink Champagne'

Day-blooming in a rosy bubblegum-pink. Cup-shaped blooms of 4–6 inches. Green and mottled leaves. Medium spread. Good for medium to large ponds. Florida Aquatic Nurseries, 1998.

### 'Pink Indian Goddess'

Day-blooming in deep pink with large, speckled sepals. Cup-shaped blooms of 4–6 inches. Green leaves mottled with red. Small to large spread. Good for small, medium, or large ponds. Asian origin.

### 'Pink Passion'

Day-blooming in rich, medium pink. Platter-shaped blooms of 3–5 inches. Green leaves slightly flecked with purple. Medium spread. Florida Aquatic Nurseries.

### 'Pink Perfection'

Day-blooming in bubblegum-pink. Platter-shaped, very fragrant blooms of 6 inches. Heavily variegated leaves. Large spread. Good for medium to large ponds. Lingg.

### 'Pink Platter'

Day-blooming in pink with gold-tipped stamens. Platter-shaped blooms of 6–10 inches. Light green leaves flecked with red. Spread of 5–6 feet. Good for medium to large ponds. Pring, 1934.

### 'Pink Star'

Day-blooming in bright baby-pink. Star-shaped blooms of 4–6 inches. Green leaves. Medium to large spread. Good for small to medium ponds. Beldt.

### 'Purple Indian Goddess'

Day-blooming in deep purple. Cup-shaped blooms of 4–6 inches with elongated sepals that stretch above the petals. Green, mottled leaves. Small to medium spread. Good for small, medium, or large ponds. Asian origin.

### 'Purple Zanzibar'

Day-blooming in very deep purple—the deepest to date. Star-shaped blooms of 4–6 inches. Green leaves. Medium to large spread. Good for medium to large ponds. Florida Aquatic Nurseries, 1997.

### 'Queen of Siam'

Day-blooming in pink with green in the outer petals. Double, star-shaped blooms of 6–8 inches. Highly mottled leaves. Medium to large spread. Good for medium to large ponds. Viviparous. Asian origin.

### 'Red Beauty'

Day-blooming in fuchsia-raspberry-red. Cup-shaped blooms of 4–6 inches. Green leaves with blotches. Medium to large spread. Good for medium to large ponds. Slocum, 1966.

### 'Red Cup'

Night-blooming in strong red-rose. Star-shaped blooms of 4–6 inches. Red leaves. Medium spread. Good for medium to large ponds. Strawn, 1986.

*Nymphaea* 'Pink Perfection'

### 'Red Flare'

Night-blooming in deep red. Star-shaped blooms of 6–10 inches. Maroon leaves. Spread of 6½ feet. Good for medium to large ponds. A strong performer. Randig, 1938.

### 'Rhonda Kay'

Day-blooming in violet-blue with gold stamens. Tons of star-shaped blooms of 6 inches—up to 22 at a time. Green leaves. Spread of 6½ feet and tall—has been known to rise out of the water as high as 18 inches. Good for medium to large ponds. Landon.

### 'Robert Strawn'

Day-blooming in light lavender. Platter-shaped blooms of 4–6 inches. Green leaves. Spread of 6 feet. Good for medium to large ponds. Strawn.

### 'Rosa de Noche'

Night-blooming in pale pink or flushed white. Star-shaped blooms of 6–8 inches. Green leaves. Medium spread. Good for medium to large ponds. Van Ness.

### 'Rose Bowl'

Night-blooming in pink. Platter-shaped blooms of 4–6 inches. Green leaves with a bronze cast. Medium to large spread. Good for medium to large ponds. Florida Aquatic Nurseries.

### 'Ruby'

Day-blooming in dark raspberry-pink. Platter-shaped blooms of 4–6 inches. Green leaves. Spread of 2–4 feet. Good for small to medium ponds. Viviparous. Suwannee Labs, 1994.

### 'Shirley Ann'

Day-blooming in pale blue. Star- or cup-shaped blooms of 4–6 inches. Green leaves. Medium to large spread. Good for medium to large ponds. Strawn.

### 'Shirley Bryne'

Day-blooming in deep pink with yellow centers. Cup-shaped blooms of 4–6 inches. A strong bloomer. Green leaves. Spread of 5½ feet. Good for medium ponds. Highly viviparous. Suwannee Labs, 1990.

*Nymphaea* 'Sturtevantii'

*Nymphaea* 'Sturtevantii'

### 'Silvermist'

Day-blooming in pale blue tipped with dark blue. Star- or cup-shaped blooms of 4–6 inches. Green leaves. Medium spread. Good for small, medium or large ponds and containers. Viviparous. Van Ness.

### 'Sir Galahad'

Night-blooming in pure white. Abundant star-shaped blooms of 6 inches. Green leaves. Spread of 6½–7½ feet. Good for large ponds. Randig.

### 'Star of Siam'

Day-blooming in vibrant blue. Star- or cup-shaped blooms of 4–6 inches. Mottled leaves. Medium to large spread. Good for medium to large ponds. Sacher.

### 'Star of Zanzibar'

Day-blooming in blue. Star-shaped blooms. Green leaves heavily mottled in purple. Medium to large spread. Good for medium to large ponds. Sacher.

### 'St. Louis Gold'

Day-blooming in deep yellow. Platter-shaped blooms of 7 inches. Green leaves. Spread of 6½ inches. Good for small ponds and containers. Pring.

### 'Sturtevantii'

Night-blooming in strong pink-edged blooms with pale centers. Heavily scented, star-shaped blooms of 6–10 inches. Bronze leaves. Medium to large spread. Good for medium ponds. Sturtevant, 1884.

### 'Tammy Sue'

Day-blooming in hot fuchsia-pink. Star-shaped blooms of 4–8 inches. Mottled leaves. Medium spread. Good for small to large ponds and containers. Van Ness.

### 'Ted Uber'

Day-blooming in cloud-white. Semidouble, platter-shaped blooms of 4–6 inches. Green leaves. Medium to large spread. Good for small to large ponds. Randig.

### 'Terri Dunn'

Day-blooming in deep purple. Cup-shaped blooms of 4–6 inches. Green leaves. Medium spread. Good for medium to large ponds. Viviparous and tolerant of cooler water. Frase.

### 'Texas Shell Pink'

Night-blooming in pale pink. Enticingly fragrant, star-shaped blooms of 6–10 inches. Bronze leaves. Spread of 6½ feet. Good for medium to large ponds. Nelson.

### 'Tina'

Day-blooming in blue and pink with yellow centers. Star-shaped blooms of 4–6 inches. Green leaves. Spread of 6½ feet. Good for small to medium ponds and containers. Viviparous. Van Ness.

*Nymphaea* 'Wood's Blue Goddess'

*Nymphaea* 'Yellow Dazzler'

### 'Trail Blazer'

Day-blooming in pale butter-yellow. Star- or cup-shaped blooms of 4–6 inches. Green leaves. Medium to large spread. Good for small to large ponds.

### 'Trudy Slocum'

Night-blooming in snow-white. Platter-shaped blooms of 4–8 inches. Green leaves. Spread of 6–10 feet. Good for medium to large ponds. Slocum. This is a large form of 'Wood's White Knight', but with fewer flowers.

### 'White Delight'

Day-blooming in snowy white. Cactus blooms of 6 inches. Green leaves with faint mottling. Spread of 6–10 feet. Good for medium to large ponds. Winch.

### 'White Fleck'

Day-blooming in snowy white. Cactus blooms of 4–6 inches—a good bloomer. Green leaves with flecks. Medium spread. Good for medium to large ponds.

### 'White Lightning'

Day-blooming in white. Platter-shaped blooms of 8–12 inches. Green leaves neatly splotched in black. Medium spread. Good for medium to large ponds. Florida Aquatic Nurseries.

### 'William McLane'

Day-blooming in purple. Platter-shaped blooms of 4–6 inches or more. Mostly purple leaves with green inclusions. Medium spread. Good for medium to large ponds. Florida Aquatic Nurseries.

### 'Wood's Blue Goddess'

Day-blooming in powder blue edged in purple. Blooms of 6–8 inches. Green leaves. Foliage and flowers are odd, similar to those of night bloomers. Medium to large spread. Good for medium to large ponds. Wood.

### 'Wood's White Knight'

Night-blooming in white with yellow stamens. Prolific, reliable, star-shaped, fragrant blooms of 6–8 inches. Green leaves. Spread of 6½ feet. Good for medium to large ponds. Wood.

### 'Yellow Dazzler'

Day-blooming in bright yellow. Abundant, fragrant, star-shaped blooms of 6 inches. Deeply speckled green leaves. Spread of 6½–10 feet. Good for small to medium ponds. Randig, 1938.

# CHAPTER 6

# LOTUS

Lotus have enchanted the Orient and Asia for more than 3,000 years. Grown for food and flower, revered as a symbol of spiritual perfection, they are deeply rooted in Far Eastern cultures. In the Americas, native lotus were used for food and medicine. In more modern times, they are exotic beauties that grace many water gardens, both public and private.

The two species of lotus are *Nelumbo lutea*, the native American lotus, and *N. nucifera*, the Asian lotus. The American lotus has creamy yellow flowers that are usually single but sometimes semidouble. The Asian lotus has white or pink blossoms and may be single, semidouble, or fully double. The American lotus grows wild in North America, extending southward into Central America. The native range of the Asian lotus spreads from China into India, the Philippines, and even Australia, reaching eastward to Japan.

Many selections and hybrids have been developed in the Asian lotus, and more than 600 varieties are recorded. Few have made selections or developed hybrids of the American native lotus. One hybridizer in the U.S., Perry Slocum, has crossed the American *Nelumbo lutea* with the Asian *N. nucifera* to make selections that are free-flowering and with rich colors not previously known. Slocum's additional contribution has been the introduction of lotus with blossoms that consistently rise above the foliage—an important trait, since many forms of lotus have flowers that appear among or remain completely hidden underneath the large, parasol leaves.

## LOTUS IN THE LANDSCAPE

Spectacular leaves of lotus growing at Chicago Botanic Garden

When grown in a pond, whether lined or earth bottom, lotus are best contained in pots that prevent their tubers from running rampant throughout the water garden. Left unchecked, the lotus will overtake the entire water feature, crowding out waterlilies, submerged plants, and even floating water plants. A bog or pond filled with lotus is a spectacular sight, but quite ghastly if other plants were intended to grow there as well.

A field of lotus

Making a bog specifically for a lotus, however, is a great idea for anywhere in the garden. Simply dig a hole 2 feet deep and 3–4 feet across, line with 45 ml EPDM liner, refill with soil, and plant the lotus tuber. The plant will grow roots that retract it into the soil and by late summer will shower itself in flowers. Kept in this fashion, the lotus growing in our bogs have surpassed our pot-grown lotus both in flower, foliage, and ease of care. They have overwintered outdoors in our Zone 5 gardens without any need for further attention.

Lotus are ideal candidates for containerized water gardens, however. In fact, for centuries they have been planted in bowls and pots of all shapes and sizes in Eastern cultures. All sizes of lotus are grown in pots, even the largest that reach taller than 5 feet with leaves more than 2 feet in diameter. The most enormous and stunning are placed outside temples, sometimes in containers that are more than 6 feet in diameter. Smaller tub gardens are grown for personal enjoyment in the home or office. Tub gardens filled with lotus are a perfect accent to an entryway and quickly liven up a drab corner of a backyard patio. Containerized lotus look tropical and exotic, despite their winter hardiness.

Taking the container to its smallest extreme are bowl lotus. An Oriental innovation, bowl lotus are diminutive siblings to their larger, standard-sized brethren. They grow to no more than 2 feet in height. Some, in fact, grow as small as 4 inches tall. They are perfectly happy in a 6-inch pot and need only a few inches of water over their crown. Often they are grown in rice bowls in China. They are ideally suited for a pot on the patio table or in a sunny window. Virtually any decorative houseplant container can be waterproofed and used to grow bowl lotus. Such a miniature lotus garden needs little more than full sunlight and constant moisture.

Bowl lotus are lotus in all respects, taking virtually as many forms as full-sized lotus do. Also called teacup lotus, some are single-petaled and others are double or almost so. Colors range from rosy red to white, with shades of pink and rose in between. Foliage is a characteristic gray-green, held in velvety circles above the water surface. Tubers are slender and grow a few inches below the soil.

Lotus growing in their own bog, in this case for production purposes, *Nelumbo* 'First Lady' in front

Lotus growing in containers

## PLANT PARTS AND HABIT

Lotus cultivars are available in a wide range of sizes and colors. Some selections are truly miniature, growing no more than a foot or so in height and having flowers no larger than a tennis ball. Others are huge, stately additions to the water garden, reaching over 6 feet in height, with leaves more than 2 feet in diameter and flowers as large as a basketball. Fragrance varies from heady and fruity to mild, not unlike baby powder. Colors range from the deepest rosy pink—none are truly red—to the cleanest white. Some are also bicolors, changeables, or tones that blush or fade. By the addition of the yellow of *Nelumbo lutea* to the white and pink of *N. nucifera*, we can now grow lotus that have soft, pastel-yellow flowers with a pink blush.

Lotus flowers are composed of outer sepals and either single or multiple rows of petals. These are thick and may be deeply veined. Blossoms may be no larger than an orange on the smallest cultivars, to those that are larger than a basketball on large selections. The center, or heart of the flower, is a disk-shaped cone that holds the seed and pistils. This heart is usually yellow, occasionally green in some selections. The anthers and stamens stand around the center cone-like structure. Once the flower is spent, the cone gradually changes color, turning a light, tawny brown. Seed that are fertile become enlarged and black, while those that did not fertilize shrivel into the seed head. If some seed are fertile, the entire seed head will often tilt to the water, so the seed will fall and disperse on the open water.

Lotus begin to flower several weeks later than waterlilies, often not until July and August in Zone 5. Bowl lotus begin to bloom about a month earlier, starting their show in June rather than July. Flowering continues until frost, into September and October depending upon the climate. Lotus flowers open at different times, depending upon

Characteristic lotus flower on *Nelumbo* 'Momo Botan'

Lotus seed head

attaching to the leaf's center so that it resembles an inverted parasol. The texture is fine, and slightly waxy; droplets of water roll on the leaf's surface like beads of liquid mercury. The color is usually bright green or slightly bluish green, highlighting the often lavender undertones of white or pink blossoms. Leaf and flower stems are hairy, almost prickly, and hollow. They exude a white, milky, gooey substance when bent or broken.

Lotus grow from underground stems that are properly called tubers. They resemble elongated potatoes, each tuber section connected to the next section at a twisted joint. One leaf and one flower stem grow from each of these joints, as well as hairy roots that hold the plant tightly in the ground. Cutting into a tuber reveals that it is full of small, hollow channels like a honeycomb. By this unique design, lotus pump oxygen into their root system and through their leaves and flowers. If the tuber is damaged and the air channel exposed or compromised, the plant has little ability to prevent the entry of water and can essentially drown because it is unable to breathe. Also, damage to the air channels can facilitate the entry of pathogens that may weaken and destroy the plant. Pathogens are most prevalent when water and soil have low levels of dissolved oxygen. Damaged tubers are most susceptible to these pathogens in the spring, before they have started growing to heal off damaged areas. If the water is too cold or deep and the plant cannot send leaves to the surface for oxygen, it may not survive. This can also happen in the summer with severe defoliation from animals or hail. On the positive side, this is a great way to control unwanted plants.

## SUN, WIND, AND WATER DEPTH

Lotus grow best in full sun, since they are warm-loving plants. Sunlight is especially critical when the plant is first emerging from winter dormancy and starting its spring growth. A few cultivars grow and flower in partial shade where they receive five or six hours of sunlight, but these are exceptions to the rule.

Day-length requirements vary greatly from cultivar to cultivar. Further research is needed to determine the day-length needs of the smaller-sized cultivars so that they may be forced indoors and produced for midwinter sales. A few lotus are even day neutral—they never seem to go dormant or produce overwintering tubers. These "tropical lotus" grow and flower constantly, making them excellent candidates for large interior landscapes.

their age. One must often rise early to appreciate the lotus blossom in full flush. First-day blooms usually open around 4 or 5 in the morning, staying open for just three or four hours, and then closing around 8 a.m. On the second day, the flower begins to open just after midnight, at about 1 a.m. By 7 or 8 in the morning, the flower will be fully open. Again it stays open for only a short time, closing around noon that same day. On the third day, the flower again opens in the dark, around 1 a.m. It opens fully by 9 a.m. By noon, it will close, but may not close fully or completely. On the fourth and final day, the flower opens during the morning or afternoon. It will be faded and tattered and will begin to shed its petals.

The foliage of a lotus is a spectacular sight, especially in larger selections. Each leaf is round and wavy, with the stem

Lotus tuber

Lotus are susceptible to high winds, which can tatter or break off leaves. Leaf damage below the water surface allows water to enter the lotus "root," or submerged stem, and can lead to fungal or bacterial infections. Lotus generally can tolerate wave action, such as that from a fountain, as long as the leaves are not constantly being wetted once the foliage is up off the water.

Lotus, even larger cultivars that reach several feet, grow well in water that is no more than a few inches over the crown. Shallow water is a good thing in cooler climates, because it allows the sunlight to penetrate and warm the soil, and the lotus like this warmth. In warmer areas, more water over the soil surface will reduce the need later to replace water that has been lost to evaporation. Lotus will grow well in water that is more than 6–8 inches deep. Large selections tolerate very deep water more than 12 inches, or even up to 6 feet, over the soil.

## SOIL AND WATER CHEMISTRY

Lotus grow best in an organic, rich, clay-like soil and prefer an acid or neutral pH. Optimum water and soil acidity is 6.5 pH, and may range from 5.6 to 7.5 pH. Lotus are very susceptible to disease when they are grown in hard water that has a high pH. The combination of the high pH with increased calcium content inhibits the plant from taking up nutrients. I have seen plants that quickly withered, blackened, and died in our nursery water, which has a very high pH (9+) and is also very hard (total calcium 600 parts per

million). When water has a high pH, add buffering agents so the lotus in the pond will not be damaged by the quality of the water. And lotus are intolerant of any amount of salt in the water.

Lotus prefer warm, humid summers where the water and soil are between 70°F and 86°F. These temperatures encourage rampant growth. Even temperatures are the best—wide fluctuations in water temperature will delay flowering and in extreme instances may send the plants back into early dormancy. In areas where the days are warm but the nights are cool, lotus grown in a free-standing pot can be covered with a plastic canopy to retain warmth overnight. Air temperatures, however, above 104°F can cause growth to slow or stop completely. Lotus also suffer in cool weather. Reduced temperatures can slow growth to such an extent that soil-borne pathogens such as fusarium or water molds can kill the plant.

## SEASONAL CARE

### Spring and Summer

Lotus are late sleepers in the spring and often will not begin to sprout and grow until the water temperature warms appreciably in the pond. In colder areas where a lotus has been overwintered at the bottom of the pond, raise the pot so that it is just a few inches below the water surface, so that the lotus can be warmed by the spring sunlight. If the lotus has been kept as a dormant bare-root tuber, it can be potted up in the spring but should not be put outside until the pond is warmer, about 65°F. If the tuber has been kept in a pot in a cooler, as soon as the risk of freezing is past, bring it outside and return it to pond or container.

For lotus that have been grown under cover with plans to move them outside, good ventilation is important in hardening off the foliage. Without proper ventilation, the leaves completely dessicate when removed from the greenhouse.

Lotus are heavy feeders and should be fertilized regularly throughout the summer—once a month at least, and follow the fertilizer's directions—especially when they are in flower. Push the fertilizer tablets as far as possible into the soil, so the fertilizer reaches the tubers at the bottom of the pot. Make sure to firm up the soil over the fertilizer tab, so it does not dissolve back into the water and promote algae instead of the lotus.

For the most part, lotus that are suitable for smaller growing quarters have the same cultural requirements as their larger relatives. Bowl lotus are more sensitive to pH and can be burned by hard tap water. Use distilled water, or rain water may be suitable depending upon how acid it is in the area. Be especially careful with the amount of fertilizer added during the growing season. Miniature lotus burn more easily from fertilizer than standard lotus, because of the smaller roots and soil volume. Fertilize once a month, using one tablet in a 10-inch pot. Other growers have reported different results with fertilizer use—such as the plants not burning or needing less frequent feedings—which may be a peculiarity reflecting the particular soil and water conditions in which the bowl lotus are grown.

Keep the pot in full sun for best growth and most blooms. Remove spent leaves and flowers by cutting the stem just above the water surface.

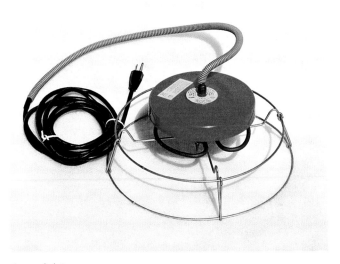

A pond deicer

## Fall and Winter

Trim back the foliage after it has died and turned brown. If leaves are cut while still green, the plant is susceptible to diseases entering though the hollow stems, leading to fungal or bacterial infections in the underground tuber and killing the plant. If stems must be cut while still green, make sure to trim them above the waterline, so that water does not enter the stems and essentially drown the plant.

Lotus are generally hardy water plants that grow from Zone 4 to 11. In colder climates, lotus tubers must not be allowed to freeze in the winter, and containers should be moved to a cool but frost-free area, such as the bottom of a pond that is deep enough to keep the tubers from freezing. As an alternative, a pond deicer may be used to keep a small ornamental pond from freezing. Also, the container may be buried in the ground under a mound of soil or mulch to protect the lotus from the frost. In warmer climates, lotus may slow in growth as day length wanes, but need not go dormant to ensure vitality and renewed growth in following months.

Fall and winter care of bowl lotus is minimal. You can leave the pot and plant outside in the pond during the first few hard frosts. Then, bring the pot indoors and keep it in a cool, dark place. Check the plant every so often to make sure that the soil stays moist. In the spring, add water to the pot and bring it to a warm, sunny spot indoors, moving it outdoors when the days are especially warm and sunny. Or, place it outside after all danger of frost has passed and let it resume growing on its own.

## PLANTING

Lotus grow best in pots that are rounded rather than square or rectangular. Because their tubers grow end to end, they can become stunted once they encounter a corner, or may crawl up and out of the pot. Smaller, bowl lotus grow well in pots that are only 8–10 inches wide, though slightly larger, 10–14 inches across, is better. Larger cultivars prefer more spacious quarters, and can be potted in containers that are 24 inches or more in width. I have observed them in 60-inch pots.

Some cultivars of bowl lotus are simply dwarf, free-flowering lotus that are willing to grow and flower in a very small pot. When planted in larger pots they will grow much larger, although never reaching the giant size. Some of these will change flower size and shape—by adding petals—so much so that they almost seem to be two completely different cultivars.

The best time of year to pot up lotus is in early spring, when the tubers are dormant or have barely sprouted new growth. At this time of the year, the growing tip, although fragile, is less likely to break easily. Once broken, the tuber is less apt to sprout and grow. Also avoid bruising the tuber. Although a slight amount of bruising is not usually fatal in and of itself, the damage may allow water molds to break down the sugar-rich tuber.

If the growing tip does become damaged, or if the tuber is bruised, do not give up all hope and throw the tuber away. Instead, float it in warm, well-aerated water to protect it from infections. If the plant does grow, it will do so rapidly and quickly outgrow the old, damaged tuber.

Most sources recommend planting bare-root lotus tubers in soil, with the growing tip exposed above the soil surface. We have found this method to be only moderately successful; a good portion of our spring crop planted in this fashion either never sprouted, or grew just a few leaves and then withered away.

We learned that the Chinese float bare-root lotus tubers in their planting pots, allowing the plant to sprout and grow before it is put into the soil. We now have much better success with this planting method. Fill each pot roughly half full with soil, and then add a few inches of water to the pot. Float a single tuber in the water and keep it warm, between 75°F and 86°F, and place the pot in a sunny location. Change the water every few days to prevent it from fouling and infecting the lotus tuber. Once the plant has sprouted three or four leaves, gently place the tuber on the soil, holding it in place with a flat, smooth rock. As the tuber grows, it develops retractor roots that pull the tuber down into the soil. After the first few floating "coin leaves" are produced, the plant develops aerial leaves on its own (no extra support or decrease in water level is needed). Add more water to the pot as the plant matures. After it has grown six or seven aerial leaves, place the plant in the pond, increasing its depth only gradually.

Lotus leaves are not able to stretch to reach above the water surface. If a tuber has already started to sprout a few leaves, do not submerge them in the water. Simply add as much water as will permit the leaves to float on the surface. The plant will sprout more leaves that will be able to stand above the water. The amount of water in the pot may then be increased accordingly. We have found that bowl lotus grow well with just 3–4 inches of soil in the pot and 2–3 inches of water.

# DIVISION

Lotus need to be divided every few years in order to remove old tuber growth from the pot. This old growth will simply rot in the bottom of the pot. Lotus signal their need for division by producing smaller foliage and fewer or smaller flowers. Judging containerized lotus is even easier—just flip the plant over and check the tubers. If the tubers look crowded, the plant needs division.

Wait until spring to divide. Do not do it in the fall—the plant will have to stay dormant and may bruise if handled. Also, be sure to repot lotus early in the spring, before they have a chance to sprout and grow. Once a lotus has grown a

Lotus tubers ready for division

few leaves, it is probably too brittle to survive being split apart and moved to new pots.

Transplanting a lotus in the spring is easy—you just have to know what you are looking for. First gently turn the pot upside down on an even, flat surface, leaving the soil from the bottom of the pot at the top of the pile, since the lotus tubers are probably deep in the soil. Gently push your fingers around to find the lotus tubers. As you lift the tubers away, find the joints where the tuber sections join together, and the terminal growing tips. Wash the soil away very gently with a stream of water from the hose, until all the lotus tubers are free.

The easiest way to distinguish new growth from old is to start at the growing tip and work backward. Each new division must include a growing tip plus at least one or two sections behind it—everything else is garbage. Cut the tuber *after* the joint, not in the joint, using a scissors or sharp knife. The tuber with the exposed flesh may rot, but because of the joint, the infection will not be able to spread into the rest of the plant. Take special care not to break off the growing tip, since the plant has a difficult time sprouting without it.

Tubers may be straight or curved, long or short. The number of growing tips is more important than the size or shape of the tuber. Healthy lotus can produce anywhere from two to 50 divisions, depending upon the cultivar and climate. A bowl lotus tuber may be no longer than your index finger, while a tuber of 'Alba Grandiflora' can measure almost 2 feet in length.

## PROPAGATION

Division is the best way to propagate lotus, but they also can be started from seed. The first step is to break through the hard outer seed coat that seals the seed from the elements. Use a file to scrape through the seed coat just slightly, until the white of the seed is visible. Be careful not to cut into the seed, which can damage it and prevent it from sprouting. Soak the seed for a day or so in a bowl of 75–80°F, distilled water. The water must be chlorine-free since chlorine will damage the seed, and later, the roots. Change the water daily. After a day or so, the seed coat becomes soft, developing a texture similar to a grape skin. The seed starts to expand and tear away the seed coat.

Once the seed coat is softened, carefully remove it and discard it. Inside you will find the swollen seed with a green shoot. Keep the seed in 1–2 inches of distilled water. To keep the seed underwater, I lay each seed on clay soil suitable for water plants and gently push a loop of wire over the seed and into the soil so that it holds the seed on the soil surface. I use a plastic cat litter tray that is 4 inches or so deep. Change the water daily and keep it warm, about 75–85°F. Indoors, keep the seed in very strong light, such as a south window or under fluorescent lights. Outside give them a half-day of sun from an eastern exposure. Check the water often for fouling, and if needed, change it.

During this process and throughout seed growing I prefer to keep the water well aerated with an aquarium bubbler. Aeration is important because it reduces the chances that the plant will become infected with fusarium or similar diseases.

The first leaves to form are called "coin leaves." They are smaller, about ½–1 inch in size, and float on the water surface. Handle them with caution, for they are thin and papery and tear easily. After three leaves have formed, you can move the seedling to its own pot. Use a 4-inch pot about 2 inches deep, or a 4-inch deep bowl about 4–6 inches across. Put 2 inches of fertile soil—stick to clay with fertilizer or garden soil—in the bottom and 1–2 inches of water over the soil so that the leaves will not be submerged. Place the new seedling in the pot but do not bury it. Simply weigh it down on the surface of the soil with a nickel, a small piece of broken pottery, or a rock. Be careful not to damage any leaves or stems, as they are very brittle at this stage. Keep the plant warm (75–80°F) and in as much sun as possible, and it will grow into the soil. Although the seedling will grow rapidly, do not expect a bloom the first year. Whether it will flower the first year or not depends upon the cultivar and the length of the season.

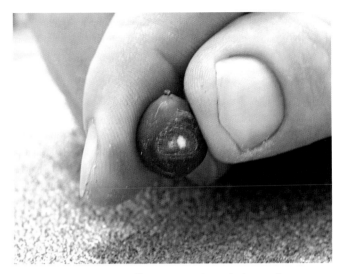

To start lotus seed, use a file to scrape through the seed coat

Fertilizing can begin once the plants have sprouted their three coin leaves. I use Miracle-Gro, one teaspoon per gallon of water all the time. If you transplant at this point, include fertilizer in the soil of the new pot. Once the plants are big enough to move to the pond, switch to regular fertilizer tablets.

Growing lotus from seed is not the first choice among propagation methods. Nevertheless it can be a relatively easy way to produce stock for mitigation sites or to increase non-cultivar stock forms. For some landscape uses, growing from seed is quite satisfactory and cost effective. I do not recommend it for those who sell lotus for retail, because it takes too long to produce a flowering-sized plant, and the seedling may be of unknown parentage, quality, and characteristic.

## HYBRIDIZING

Lotus flower parts mature on different days, with the female parts first and the male parts on the following day. Consequently, the flowers are essentially self sterile. This also makes creating new cultivars easy. The flowers do not need to be emasculated.

To hybridize, choose a first-day flower as the female or seed parent and a second-day flower as the male or pollen parent. Isolate the flower of the pollen parent by bagging it in cheesecloth to prevent insects from bringing in other pollen. Perform the cross early in the morning, generally before 8 a.m. to make sure the stigmas are still receptive—the stigmas should be moist and shiny. Seed will set in just

New lotus shoots

6–8 hours after pollination. The seed should be ready to harvest 30 days later.

## PESTS AND DISEASES

Aphids are the only real problem, which attack in late summer. Use a strong spray of water to eliminate them, or use diatomaceous earth for plants in the pond, Sevin dust for plants growing in separate containers.

According to Peter Robinson, lotus suffer from two kinds of blight, fungal and bacterial. In both, the leaves develop brown edges that overtake the entire leaf, causing it to disintegrate. Robinson recommends treating the fungal form by covering the growing bed with a powdered form of fungicide. The bacterial form is harder to treat because it is more resistant to chemicals. Remove all infected plant material immediately. Lotus blight seems to be rare in the U.S.; I have never had it on my plants.

At our nursery, we noticed that the standard-sized and smaller lotus, not bowl lotus, were also experiencing inhibited growth and leaf scorch. Suspecting that our 9.1 pH well water was the culprit, we now use rain water instead. The plants have shown dramatic improvements in growth.

Lotus leaves may also develop a necrotic condition in which they yellow and develop gray or black interveinal spots. Foliage looks as though it has been damaged by a blow torch. We have seen this occur almost overnight and for no apparent reason. Subsequent growth is further debilitated, and the plant may eventually wither and die. After some experimentation, we have concluded that improper pH and over-fertilization were the probable causes of this condition. Sensitivity to pH appears especially pronounced in the smaller bowl lotus.

# PLANT PROFILES

Since lotus are used so diversely in China, Japan, and other parts of the Orient, it is no surprise that many cultivars are available. In his book *Lotus of China* (1987), Ni Xueming of the Wuhan Botanical Garden recounts that the garden alone has more than 150 selections of lotus. Many of these are ornamental varieties, and others are grown for seed or tuber crops. Similarly, Satomi Watanabe of Tokyo University describes more than 50 cultivars of Japanese lotus in *The Fascinating World of Lotus* (1990).

Until the early 1990s, none of the lotus mentioned in these books could be found in the U.S. Only a handful of any Oriental lotus were available, brought back by collectors who had traveled to the Far East. Two Chinese or Japanese cultivars, 'Momo Botan' and 'Chawan Basu', are commercially available and are suited for tub gardens. Other, newer selections of Japanese lotus also adapt well to containers, but they are not yet readily available in the U.S. Chinese selections are becoming more accessible, including such cultivars as 'Autumn Sky' and 'Little Green'.

A special Japanese seed introduction is 'Ohga', a full-sized, single, dark pink variety that looks almost red when the blooms first open. It also can be grown in containers, but only large, 7–15 gallon tubs. In the years after World War II, a Japanese gentleman by the name of Ohga attempted in vain to grow ancient lotus seeds excavated from a site near the Namegawa River in Japan. After his attempts failed, he recalled that ancient lotus seed had also been discovered at a site near the Kemigawa River. In March 1951, Ohga traveled to the area and enlisted help from local residents to find the lotus seed. The volunteer crew, aided by children from the local elementary and high schools, dug for almost a month. At last they found the ancient lotus seed, estimated to be more than 2,000 years old. Ohga set the seed in water, and amazingly, they sprouted and grew. The resulting lotus cultivar now bears Ohga's name. It is a beautiful example of what lotus must have looked like centuries ago.

American pondkeepers may look closer to home in order to find lotus suitable for growing in tub gardens. American grower Perry Slocum persevered during the hiatus in lotus popularity, and since about 1975, he has hybridized a number of cultivars that are now commercially available. His selections are noteworthy because they bloom well above the foliage, they bloom more reliably, and they flower longer over the season. Five Slocum cultivars are particularly suitable for container water gardening: 'Angel Wings', which performs well in only a few inches of water, 'Baby Doll', 'Ben Gibson', 'Charles Thomas', and 'Sharon'.

*Nelumbo* 'Alba Plena'

Another excellent cultivar for tub growing is 'Perry's Super Star', a seedling of 'Mrs. Perry D. Slocum' that opens a pale cream and yellow, taking on pink tones as it ages.

Ni Xueming lists approximately 45 selections of Chinese bowl lotus, some of which are now being introduced in the United States. 'Chong Shui Hua' has dainty double flowers. 'Xiamen Bowl' is a clear, single or semidouble white and needs no more than a few inches of water over its crown. An intermediate-sized bowl lotus is 'Wan-er Hong'. Rose forms are also available, such as 'Table Lotus' and 'Welcoming', and pink cultivars include 'Yangzhou Bowl' and 'Shining Sunglow'.

## Cultivars and Species

The cultivars in the following list are all hybrids in the genus *Nelumbo*. The "*N.*" that should begin each name has been omitted for brevity. Lotus cultivar names can be quite a mess. Many were brought from China or Japan and over the years have been renamed.

Measurements for the pond sizes suggested in the following descriptions are small (4–6 feet across), medium (7–9 feet), and large (more than 10 feet). Tub and container water gardens are considered to be up to 3 feet across. The spread stated for each plant is based on its performance in a 7-gallon pot. Lotus will spread indefinitely if allowed.

### 'Alba Plena'

Snow-white, double blooms of 8–10 inches. Height 4–6 feet. Medium to large spread. Good for medium to large ponds with water up to 4 feet deep. This may be the same as 'Shiroman'.

### 'Alba Striata'

White with red streaks. Single blooms of 6–10 inches. Height 4–6 feet. Medium to large spread. Good for medium to large ponds with water up to 4 feet deep. This may be the same as 'Empress'.

### 'Angel Wings'

Snow-white, single blooms of 4–6 inches. Height 2–4 feet. Dwarf to medium spread. Good for containers and small to medium ponds with water less than 2 feet deep. Slocum.

### 'Antique Pink'

Pink, single blooms of 10–12 inches with yellow centers. Height 4–6 feet. Medium to large spread. Good for medium to large ponds with water up to 4 feet deep. Chinese origin.

### 'Asiatica' (syn. 'Alba Grandiflora')

Snow-white, single blooms of 8–10 inches. Height 4–6 feet. Medium to large spread. Good for medium to large ponds with water up to 2 feet deep.

### 'Autumn Sky'

Pink, yellow, and white, semidouble blooms of up to 4 inches. Height 2–3 feet. Dwarf to small spread. Good for containers and small to medium ponds with water up to 6 inches deep. Chinese origin.

### 'Baby Doll'

Very white, paper-white, single blooms of 4–6 inches. Height 2–3 feet. Dwarf to small spread. Good for containers and small to medium ponds with water up to 6 inches deep. Slocum.

### 'Bai Mudan'

White, double blooms of up to 4 inches. Height 2–3 feet. Dwarf to small spread. Good for containers and small to medium ponds with water up to 6 inches deep. Chinese origin.

### 'Baiyun Wanlian'

White with pale pink tips. Semidouble blooms of up to 4 inches. A very cactus-like flower. Height 2–3 feet. Dwarf to small spread. Good for containers and small to medium ponds with water up to 6 inches deep. Chinese origin.

*Nelumbo* 'Baiyun Wanlian'

### 'Beauty'

Pink-lavender, double or semidouble blooms of 4–6 inches. Height 3–5 feet. Medium to large spread. Good for medium to large ponds with water up to 2 feet deep. Chinese origin.

### 'Ben Gibson'

Rosy pink, double blooms of 4–6 inches. Height 2–3 feet. Small to medium spread. Looks very much like 'Momo Botan'. Good for containers and small to medium ponds with water up to 2 feet deep. Slocum.

### 'Betsy'

Pink, single blooms of 4–6 inches. Height 3–5 feet. Small to medium spread. Good for small to medium ponds with water up to 3 feet deep. Slocum. This looks like 'Charles Thomas'.

### 'Big Green'

White with lots of green petals. Semidouble blooms of 4–6 inches. Height 3–5 inches. Medium to large spread. Good for medium to large ponds with water up to 2 feet deep. Chinese origin.

### 'Big Versicolor'

White with red and pink streaks. Double or semidouble blooms of 4–6 inches. Height 4–6 feet. Medium to large spread. Good for medium to large ponds. Chinese origin.

*Nelumbo* 'Carolina Queen'

*Nelumbo* 'Charles Thomas'

### 'Carolina Queen'

Deep pink with yellow centers. Single blooms of 8–12 inches. Height 4–6 feet. Medium to large spread. Good for medium to large ponds with water up to 4 feet or more deep. Slocum.

### 'Carolina Snow'

White blooms of 4–8 inches. Height 3–5 feet. Medium to large spread. Good for medium to large ponds with water up to 3 feet deep. Slocum.

### 'Caspicum' (syn. 'Volga')

Red-rose, single or semidouble blooms of 8–12 inches. Height 4–6 feet. Large spread. Good for medium to large ponds with water up to to 6 feet deep. Creech.

### 'Charles Thomas'

Lavender-pink, single, fragrant blooms of 6–8 inches. Height 3–4 feet. Dwarf to small spread. Good for containers and small to medium ponds with water less than 2 feet deep. Slocum.

### 'Charming Pink Cups'

Pale pink on white. Semidouble blooms of up to 4 inches. Height 2–3 feet. Dwarf to small spread. Very much like 'Biayun Wanlian'. Good for containers and small to medium ponds with water up to 6 inches deep. Chinese origin.

### 'Bird in Spring Water'

Pale yellow, single or semidouble blooms of up to 4 inches. Height 2–3 feet. Dwarf to small spread. Good for containers and small to medium ponds with water up to 6 inches deep. Chinese origin.

### 'Birthday Peach'

Silky pink-lavender, semidouble blooms of 4–6 inches. Height 3–4 feet. Medium spread. Good for small to medium ponds with water less than 2 feet deep. Chinese origin.

### 'Blue Girl'

Not blue, just pink with a hint of lavender. Semidouble blooms of 4–6 inches. Height 3–5 feet. Medium to large spread. Good for medium to large ponds with water up to 2 feet deep. Chinese origin.

*Nelumbo* 'Chawan Basu'

*Nelumbo* 'Chong Shui Hua'

### 'Chawan Basu'

Pink edges that slowly mature through crystal-white petals. Single blooms of 4–6 inches. Height 2–3 feet. Dwarf to medium spread. Good for containers and small to medium ponds with water less than 2 feet deep. Chinese or Japanese origin.

### 'Children'

Eggshell-white, semidouble blooms of 4 inches. Height 2–3 feet. Dwarf to small spread. Good for containers and small to medium ponds with water less than 12 inches deep. Chinese origin.

### 'Chinese Pink'

Pink tips and edges with pale white centers. Double blooms of 4–6 inches. Height 2–3 feet. Dwarf to small spread. Good for small to medium ponds with water less than 2 feet deep. Chinese origin.

### 'Chong Shui Hua'

Red-rose, double blooms of up to 4 inches. It flowers well. Height 2–3 feet. Dwarf to small spread. Good for containers and small to medium ponds with water up to 6 inches deep. Chinese origin.

### 'Crane Head Red'

White with red-pink tips. Semidouble blooms of up to 4 inches. Height 2–3 feet. Dwarf to small spread. Good for containers and small to medium ponds with water up to 6 inches deep. Chinese origin.

*Nelumbo* 'Debbie Gibson'

### 'Debbie Gibson'

Cream, semidouble blooms of 6–10 inches. Height 5–6 feet. Large spread. Good for medium to large ponds with water up to 4 feet deep. Slocum.

### 'Desk Spring'

White flushed with rosy red. Semidouble blooms, like tulips, of 4 inches or more. Height 2–3 feet. Dwarf to small spread. Good for containers and small to medium ponds with water less than 12 inches deep. Chinese origin.

*Nelumbo* 'Double Pink'

### 'Double Pink'

Rose-pink with pale centers. Double blooms of 6–8 inches. Height 4–5 feet. Medium to large spread. Good for medium to large ponds with water to 2 feet deep or more. Chinese origin.

### 'Drunkard on a Jade Tower'

White with pale rose edges. Flat, semidouble blooms of up to 4 inches. The most un-lotus-like blossom–resembles a tropical night-blooming waterlily. Height 1–2 feet. Dwarf to small spread. Good for containers and small to medium ponds with water up to 6 inches deep. Chinese origin.

### 'Empress'

White with red streaks. Semidouble or single blooms of 8–10 inches. Height 4–5 feet. Medium to large spread. Good for medium to large ponds with water up to 2 feet deep. Chinese or Japanese origin.

### 'First Lady'

Lavender-red or pink, single blooms of 6–8 inches. Height 4–5 feet. Medium to large spread. Good for small to large ponds with water up to 2 feet deep or more. Slocum.

### 'Giant Sunburst'

Bright lemon-yellow, single blooms of 8–12 inches. Considered the best yellow to date. Height 4–5 feet. Medium to large spread. Good for medium to large ponds with water up to 4 feet deep. Slocum.

### 'Glen Gibson'

Pink-yellow, semidouble blooms of 4–8 inches. Height 3–5 feet. Small to medium spread. Good for containers or any size pond with water up to 2 feet deep. Slocum.

### 'Goliath'

Creamy to eggshell-white, single blooms of 8–10 inches. Height 4–6 feet. Large spread. Good for medium to large ponds with water up to 4 feet deep. Slocum.

### 'Greg Gibson'

Silvery lavender pink that fades. Semidouble blooms of 6–8 inches. Height 2–3 feet. Dwarf to small spread. Good for containers and small to medium ponds with water less than 2 feet deep. Slocum.

### 'Hindu' (syn. 'Egyptian')

Deep pink with lighter centers. Single blooms of 8–12 inches. Height 4–6 feet. Medium to large spread. Good for medium to large ponds with water up to 6 feet deep.

### 'Jade Bowl'

White with green tips. Double or semidouble blooms of up to 4 inches. Height 2–3 feet. Dwarf to small spread. Good for containers and small to medium ponds with water up to 6 inches deep. Chinese origin.

### 'Lavender Lady'

Silvery lavender with slightly darker veins. Single blooms of 6–10 inches. Height 4–5 feet. Medium to large spread. Good for medium to large ponds with water up to 2 feet deep. Slocum.

### 'Linda'

Deep pink throat on the outside, yellow inside, much like 'Carolina Queen' in color. Double blooms of 6–10 inches. Height 4–5 feet. Medium to large spread. Good for medium to large ponds with water up to 4 feet deep. Slocum.

### 'Little Chris'

White, single blooms. Height up to 3 feet. Small spread. Good for containers or small ponds with water 6–12 inches deep. Slocum.

### 'Little Green'

Snow-white, double or semidouble, abundant blooms of 4 inches or more. Height 2–3 feet. Dwarf to small spread. Good for containers and small to medium ponds with water less than 6 inches deep. Chinese origin.

### 'Little Tom Thumb'

Pink, single blooms of 4–6 inches. Height up to 3 feet. Small spread. Good for tubs or small ponds with water 6–12 inches deep. Slocum.

### 'Lushan'

White petals with pink-rose-edged tips. Double blooms of 4–6 inches. Height 2–4 feet. Medium to large spread. Good for medium to large ponds with water up to 2 feet deep. Chinese origin. Introduced to Western cultivation by Charleston Aquatic Nurseries.

### *N. lutea*

Variable yellow, single blooms of 4–12 inches. Height 3–5 feet. Medium to large spread. Good for medium to large ponds with water up to 4 feet deep. U.S. native.

### 'Maggie Bell Slocum'

Soft lavender-pink, single blooms of 8–12 inches. Considered the best lavender. Height 4–5 feet. Large spread. Good for medium to large ponds with water up to 4 feet deep. Slocum.

### 'Manjiang Hong'

White petals edged and flushed with deep rose. Double or semidouble blooms of 4 inches or more. Height 2–3 feet. Dwarf to small spread. Good for containers and small to medium ponds with water less than 12 inches deep. Chinese origin.

### 'Momo Botan'

Rosy pink, double blooms of 4–6 inches. Height 2–3 feet. Small to medium spread. Good for containers and small to medium ponds with water up to 2 feet deep. Chinese or Japanese origin.

### 'Mrs. Perry D. Slocum'

Rosy pink and yellow, turning more pink each day it opens. Semidouble blooms of 8–12 inches. Height 4–6 feet.

*Nelumbo* 'Momo Botan'

Medium to large spread. Good for medium to large ponds with water up to 4 feet deep. Slocum.

### 'Nikki Gibson'

Pink-yellow blooms of 4–10 inches. Height 3–5 feet. Good for medium to large ponds with water 6–12 inches deep. This is a smaller version of 'Mrs. Perry D. Slocum'.

### 'Ohga'

Pink with rosy tips. Single blooms of 6–10 inches. Height 4–6 feet. Medium to large spread. Good for medium to large ponds with water less than 4 feet deep. Japanese origin. Started from seed found in 2,000-year-old peat bed.

### 'Patricia Garrett'

Pink-edged yellow. Single blooms of 6–10 inches. Height 4–5 feet. Large spread. Good for medium to large ponds with water up to 2 feet deep. Slocum.

*Nelumbo* 'Pekinensis Rubra'

*Nelumbo* 'Perry's Super Star'

*Nelumbo* 'Perry's Super Star'

### 'Pekinensis Rubra'

Deep rose-red, single blooms of 8–12 inches. Height 4–6 feet. Large spread. Good for medium to large ponds with water up to 6 feet deep. Unknown origin.

### 'Perry's Super Star'

Pink and yellow-green, semidouble blooms of 6–8 inches. Height 3–5 feet. Dwarf to medium spread. Good for small to large ponds with water up to 2 feet deep. Slocum. This is my favorite lotus–if you can have only one, choose this.

### 'Pink Bowl'

Silvery pink, semidouble blooms of 4–6 inches. Height 2–3 feet. Small to medium spread. Good for containers and small to medium ponds with water less than 2 feet deep. Slocum.

### 'Pink Crane'

Rosy pink, double blooms of 4–6 inches. Height 2–4 feet. Medium to large spread. Good for medium to large ponds with water up to 2 feet deep. Chinese origin. Introduced to Western cultivation by Charleston Aquatic Nurseries.

### 'Pink N Yellow'

Yellow-green with pink edges. Single blooms of 6–10 inches. Height 4–5 feet. Medium to large spread. Good for medium to large ponds with water up to 4 feet deep. Slocum.

### 'Purple Gold'

White petals edged in bright pink with orange centers. Single or semidouble blooms of 8–10 inches. Height 3–4 feet. Medium to large spread. Good for medium to large ponds with water up to 2 feet deep. Chinese origin.

*Nelumbo* 'Rose'

### 'Red Bowl'

Red-rose, double blooms of up to 4 inches. Height 2–3 feet. Dwarf to small spread. Good for containers and small to medium ponds with water up to 6 inches deep. Chinese origin.

### 'Red Camellia'

Red, double blooms of up to 4 inches. It flowers well. Height 2–3 feet. Dwarf to small spread. Good for containers and small to medium ponds with water up to 6 inches deep. Chinese origin.

### 'Red Children'

Red-pink with pale centers. Double blooms of 4–6 inches. Height 2 feet. Dwarf to medium spread. Good for containers and small to medium ponds with water up to 2 feet deep. Chinese origin.

### 'Red Friendship'

Rosy red with white flush. Semidouble blooms of 4–6 inches. Height 2–3 feet. Small to medium spread. Good for small to medium ponds with water less than 2 feet deep. Chinese origin.

### 'Red Scarf'

Red with white centers. Single blooms of 4–6 inches. Height 2 feet. Dwarf to medium spread. Good for containers and small to medium ponds with water up to 2 feet deep. Chinese origin.

### 'Rose'

Deep rose-pink with pale centers. Semidouble blooms of 8–12 inches. Height 3–5 feet. Medium to large spread. Good for medium to large ponds with water up to 4 feet deep or more. Chinese origin.

### 'Rosea Plena'

Rosy pink-red, double blooms of 6–10 inches, much like a pale 'Momo Botan'. Height 4–5 feet. Medium to large spread. Good for medium to large ponds with water up to 4 feet deep. Chinese or Japanese origin.

### 'Rosy Clouds'

Rosy red, single blooms of 6–8 inches. Height 2–4 feet. Medium to large spread. Good for medium to large ponds with water up to 2 feet deep. Much like a small 'Pekinensis Rubra'. Chinese origin. Introduced to Western cultivation by Charleston Aquatic Nurseries.

### 'Sharon'

Pale, silvery pink with deeper veins. Semidouble to double blooms of 6–8 inches. Height 3–4 feet. Medium to large spread. Good for medium to large ponds with water up to 2 feet deep. Slocum.

### 'Shining Sunglow'

Pink with yellow in base of petals. Single or semidouble blooms of up to 4 inches. Height 2–3 feet. Small spread. Good for containers and small to medium ponds with water up to 6 inches deep. Chinese origin.

*Nelumbo* 'Shirokunshi'

### 'Shirokunshi'

Very snow-white, single blooms of 4–8 inches. Height 2–3 feet. Dwarf to medium spread. Good for containers and small to medium ponds with water less than 2 feet deep. Chinese or Japanese origin.

### 'Shiroman'

Snow-white, double blooms of 8–10 inches with small outer petals. Height 4–6 feet. Medium to large spread. Good for medium to large ponds with water up to 4 feet deep. Chinese origin. This may be the same as 'Alba Plena'.

### 'Snow Green'

Snow-white with green centers. Single blooms up to 4 inches. Height 2–3 feet. Dwarf to small spread. Good for containers and small to medium ponds with water up to 6 inches deep. Chinese origin.

### 'Song Bird'

Creamy white, double blooms of 4–6 inches. Height 2–3 feet. Dwarf spread. Good for small to large ponds with water less than 2 feet deep. Chinese origin.

### 'Sparks'

Red with white centers. Very showy single blooms of 4 inches or more. Height 2–3 feet. Dwarf to small spread. Good for containers and small to medium ponds with water up to 6 inches deep. Chinese origin.

### 'Spring Water'

White with a hint of pink. Single blooms of up to 4 inches. Height 2–3 feet. Dwarf to small spread. Good for containers and small to medium ponds with water up to 6 inches deep. Chinese origin.

### 'Sunflower'

Rosy pink, single blooms of 4–6 inches. Height 2–4 feet. Medium to large spread. Good for medium to large ponds with water up to 2 feet deep. Chinese origin. Introduced to Western cultivation by Charleston Aquatic Nurseries.

### 'Suzanne'

Medium pink with dark pink veins. Semidouble blooms of 6–8 inches. Height 4–5 feet. Medium to large spread. Good for small to large ponds with water up to 2 feet deep. Slocum.

### 'Table Lotus'

Pink-rose, abundant, single blooms of 4–6 inches, very wide and flaring. Height 2–3 feet. Dwarf to small spread. Good for containers and small to medium ponds with water up to 6 inches deep. Chinese origin. One of my favorites.

### 'The President'

Deep rose-pink or -red, single blooms of 6–10 inches. Height 3–5 feet. Medium to large spread. Good for medium to large ponds with water up to 4 feet deep. Slocum.

### 'The Queen'

Cream and green, semidouble blooms of 8–10 inches. Height 4–5 feet. Medium to large spread. Good for medium to large ponds with water up to 4 feet deep. Slocum.

### 'Thousand Petal'

Crepe-paper-pink, double blooms of 4–8 inches. The most double lotus flower. It is so double that the bloom has no room for a center cone–the petals go all the way to the stem. Height 3–5 feet. Medium to large spread. Good for medium to large ponds with water up to 2 feet deep or more. Chinese origin.

### 'Tulip'

Paper-white, single blooms of 4–6 inches. Height 2–4 feet. Dwarf to small spread. Good for small to large ponds with water less than 2 feet deep. Chinese origin.

### 'Twinkling Star'

White tinged with pink. Semidouble blooms of 4–6 inches. Height 2–3 feet. Dwarf to medium spread. Good for small to medium ponds with water less than 2 feet deep. Chinese origin.

### 'Versicolor Edge'

White with pink stripes. Semidouble or double blooms of 4–6 inches. Height 2–3 feet. Medium spread. Good for containers and small to medium ponds with water up to 6 inches deep. Chinese origin.

### 'Wan-er Hong'

Rose-pink-red, double blooms of up to 4 inches. Height 2–3 feet. Dwarf to small spread. Good for containers and small to medium ponds with water up to 6 inches deep. Chinese origin.

### 'Welcoming'

Rosy pink, semidouble or double blooms of up to 4 inches. Height 2–3 feet. Dwarf to small spread. Good for containers and small to medium ponds with water up to 6 inches deep. Chinese origin.

### 'Xiamen Bowl' (syn. 'Rice Paper')

Snow-white and green, single or semidouble blooms of up to 4 inches. Height 2–3 feet. Dwarf to small spread. Good for containers and small to medium ponds with water up to 6 inches deep. Chinese origin.

*Nelumbo 'Xiamen Bowl'*

### 'Xiao Zuixian'

White with a pink flush and pink tips. Semidouble blooms of 4–8 inches. Height 2–3 feet. Medium spread. Good for small to medium ponds with water less than 2 feet deep. Chinese origin.

### 'Yangzhou Bowl'

Pale pink, double blooms of up to 4 inches with lots of small petals. Height 2–3 feet. Dwarf to small spread. Good for containers and small to medium ponds with water up to 6 inches deep. Chinese origin.

### 'Yellow Bird'

Pale yellow, single blooms of 4–6 inches. Height 3–5 feet. Medium spread. Good for small to medium ponds with water 6–24 inches deep. Lilypons, 1975.

# CHAPTER 7

# MARGINALS

Marginal water plants, those growing at the edge of the pond, are the most misunderstood and underrated components of the aquatic landscape. Like the plight of poor Cinderella, held in reproach by her sisters before she was found by her prince, marginal water plants are thought of only after all preoccupations with waterlilies and lotus have passed. This is unfortunate. A pond design that overlooks the complex beauty of marginal water plants is sure to be trite and superficial. Marginal aquatics deserve to be given first consideration in any landscape design involving water. Besides their aesthetic softening of the edge between rock and water, they are often vital in maintaining proper water quality, to say nothing of their value in attracting wildlife to the pond.

Marginal water plants as a group earn their name from their position in the landscape: they grow and thrive at the edge, or margin, of the pond. They prefer to have their roots or their crown in water, but their foliage for the most part emerges above soil and water. Some marginals grow best only in soil that is wet, but not submerged. Others prefer water-logged soil and perhaps a slight amount of water over the top. Still others will thrive if their roots and growing crown are a few inches, or even a foot or more, below the water surface. The listings that follow include advice on the amount of water each particular plant will tolerate over its growing crown.

## SOIL CHEMISTRY

Plants that grow at the edge of the pond are not usually fussy or hard to maintain as long as their soil is roughly neutral in pH. Many will tolerate soils that are slightly acidic or slightly alkaline. A few, such as *Calla palustris* (northern calla lily) and *Sarracenia* (pitcher plants), require soil that is acidic and will languish if this condition is not met. Such particularity is rare and is noted, when necessary, in the plant descriptions given in this chapter. Like all plants, marginals perform best when they are adequately fertilized during spring and summer.

## PLANTING

Pondside plants grow in a wide variety of ways. Some grow from a central crown, others grow from underground rhizomes, and still others crawl across the soil surface. Most marginals grow perfectly well in plastic or mesh pots, but many are highly suitable for the bog garden, where they are freed from such restraints. If using a pot, be sensitive to the plant's natural growth habit. For example, those that grow from roots that run across the top of the soil, such as pennywort (*Hydrocotyle*) or water clovers (*Marsilea*), should be grown without a topping of pea gravel so the roots can spread across the surface. Following are the basic categories of growth habits for marginal plants and the corresponding ways to plant them.

### Marginals That Grow from a Rhizome (water iris)

The most commonly grown marginals that fall into this category are sweet flag (*Acorus calamus*) and variegated sweet flag (*A. calamus* 'Variegatus'). They are potted the same way as water iris, by dividing the rhizome and placing it on the soil surface, and then covering the rhizome with only a slight amount of soil.

Planting *Acorus calamus*, which grows from a rhizome

Planting *Saururus cernuus*, which grows from a single stem

## Marginals That Grow from a Single Stem (lizard tail)

Lizard tail (*Saururus cernuus*) forms a colony of individual stems, much like obedient plant (*Physostegia virginiana*), *Lysimachia*, *Houttuynia*, and water willow (*Justicia americana*). All these are planted in the same fashion. Fill the pot about two-thirds full with soil. Select several stems to pot together. Make a hole in the soil in the center of the pot, and place the stems in the hole. Move the soil back around the stems, adding more soil to fill the pot. These plants root from their stems, so their roots may be placed well below the soil surface. If you only plant one stem in a pot, you will have a single, solitary stick for the entire year. When it comes to these plants, plant more rather than less.

The potting requirements of Japanese sweet flag (*Acorus gramineus*) fall somewhere between water iris and lizard tail. Multiple fans need to be planted in one pot to be effective, since only one fan will look far too sparse. Fill the pot two-thirds full of soil, and place the rhizomes in the center of the pot. Face the fans outward in a roughly triangular fashion to allow them to branch and fill out the pot while forming a cluster in the center. Finally fill the pot with soil, using enough to anchor the fans firmly in place.

## Marginals That Grow from a Central Crown or Cluster of Stems (umbrella grass)

All members of the family Cyperaceae, including umbrella grasses (*Cyperus* spp.), sedges (*Carex* spp.), and rushes (*Eleocharis*, *Juncus*, and *Scirpus* spp.), all grow in essentially the same manner. They branch from a central crown or cluster of stems. Umbrella grasses and sedges generally sprout in

Planting *Juncus*, which grows from a central cluster of stems

groups of three, while rushes sprout in any number from the outside edge of the crown or rhizome.

Fill the pot two-thirds full with soil. Place the plant in the center, spreading the roots around the pot. Then fill the pot with soil. Generally, the crown or rhizome can be covered with about 1 inch of soil, to help it anchor into the soil. Do not submerge the pots for at least a week after they have been potted. Instead, keep the water at the crown level to prevent the plants from floating up out of the pot or tipping over, because the stems are so buoyant.

## Marginals That Grow from a Single Crown (pickerel plant)

Many water plants grow from a single crown or tuber, such as pickerel plant (*Pontederia cordata*), water plantain (*Alisma*), lobelias, monkey flower (*Mimulus*), bog arum

Planting turions of *Sagittaria*

(*Peltandra virginica*), and gold club (*Orontium aquaticum*). All are potted in much the same fashion. Simply fill the pot about two-thirds full of soil, place the plant in the center of the pot with the roots spread out over the soil, and cover the roots with soil. The crown of the plant, which is the "union" between the roots and stems, can usually be about 1 inch below the soil surface.

When potted as an already growing plant with a central crown, arrowhead (*Sagittaria*) is also placed in the middle of the pot and its crown submerged about 1 inch under the soil level. In the fall, arrowhead forms a tuber-like part called a "turion," the reason arrowhead is commonly called duck potato. The turion resembles a small potato and is a favorite food of water fowl. In the spring, the turion will sprout and send a runner toward the soil surface. Once it reaches the surface, the runner sprouts a single plant with a central crown. If potting up turions, plant them well toward the bottom of the pot. Fill the pot one-fourth full with soil, place the turions on the soil, then fill the pot with soil. Each turion will elongate and place a new plantlet at the top of the soil.

## Marginals That Grow from Running Stems (parrot feather)

Parrot feather (*Myriophyllum aquaticum*) and water clover (*Marsilea*) are potted in the same manner. First, fill a pot with soil and top off with sand or pea gravel. Water the soil thoroughly. Put a hole in the center of the pot about 1½–2 inches deep and insert five to ten stem cuttings. Push the soil back around the stems, and submerge the pots in the pond.

Planting stem cuttings of *Myriophyllum aquaticum*

Comparison of *Acorus* foliage and flowers

Fall clean-up of *Acorus*

## Acorus
## sweet flag
## Araceae

Sweet flags are an invaluable addition to the water garden for their neat, clean appearance. Hardy and foolproof, they add great textural interest to the pond. Taller forms provide an upright, architectural accent, and smaller selections have a graceful, arching appearance. The smaller Japanese sweet flag (*Acorus gramineus*) is generally evergreen even in colder climates. The larger sweet flag (*A. calamus*), on the other hand, loses its foliage during winter. The flowers on sweet flags are cone-like and inconspicuous on the smaller forms. They are borne on hook-like clubs that appear in summertime about one-third to halfway up from the base of the foliage. These clubs turn brown when mature. On some selections, the clubs are very difficult to find and often go completely unnoticed.

All sweet flags grow well in sun to shade and require soil that is constantly moist. Underwatering causes the leaf tips to burn. Seasonal flooding does no harm, but the different species and cultivars vary in the amount of water they will tolerate over their crowns.

Sweet flags are most easily propagated by dividing the rootstock, which can be done anytime from spring through fall. They may also be propagated from seed, but this does not ensure that the offspring will be true to type. Sprinkle seed over the soil in the spring and cover lightly with a fine amount of soil. It does not seem to matter whether they are sown dry or stratified for three weeks or three months, they sprout at 60 percent.

All sweet flags tolerate freezing temperatures and can freeze solid provided they remain in water while frozen. If they are removed from the water garden, they may be over-wintered by mulching them into the perennial border. Care should be taken that they do not dry out during winter, or they will become parched and die. Sweet flag is hardy in

Acorus calamus

Acorus calamus

Zones 4–11. Japanese sweet flag and its cultivars are slightly more tender, classified hardy in Zones 5–11.

Sweet flags are generally easy to grow and pest-free. Smaller forms are prone to spider mites. Larger selections may develop a fungus that causes black spots that can kill all the foliage. Clean up dead foliage in the fall, or as the black spots appear.

Sweet flags earned their common name from their ability to release a sweet fruity fragrance when bruised or crushed. Because of this, *Acorus calamus* was used as a strewing herb and potpourri in colonial times. Its foliage and rootstock were also used to flavor candy, gin, and beer. Native Americans used the plant medicinally to treat stomach ailments as well as coughs and colds, and even as a dentifrice.

## Acorus calamus

A decorative, hardy pond plant that is sometimes mistaken for water iris because of its leaf shape. *Acorus calamus* is native to North America and can be found growing wild in marshy areas from Nova Scotia to Texas and westward to the Oregon coast. This species grows from roots that run freely. It is not invasive, but the plant's best ornamental value is achieved by keeping it in a pot, even in an earth-bottom pond. Confining it to a container will bring out the full effect that makes sweet flag showy. Leaves reach 36 inches high. Tolerates water depths up to 6 inches.

Acorus gramineus

Acorus calamus 'Variegatus'

Acorus gramineus 'Hangzhou'

### Acorus calamus 'Variegatus'
**variegated sweet flag**

Beautiful green and white foliage that blends well with the blue flowers of irises, pickerel plant (*Pontederia cordata*), and water forget-me-nots (*Myosotis scorpioides*). This cultivar also tolerates up to 6 inches of water over the crown, though just moist soil is best. It has the same running habit as the species. Height is 24–36 inches.

### Acorus gramineus
Japanese sweet flag

The Japanese sweet flag, native to Japan, China, Korea, and southeast Asia, is more restrained and will not run rampant throughout the pond as the larger sweet flag (*Acorus calamus*) is prone to do. Instead, the Japanese selections form small clumps, like hostas. They are especially attractive at the edge of the pond or stream in only 1–2 inches of water, or in just damp soil, as they do best. Japanese sweet flag reaches 8–12 inches high and will spread 12 inches across.

### Acorus gramineus 'Barry Yinger'

A green selection of Japanese sweet flag, this cultivar is larger than the standard yet not so tall as *Acorus calamus*. It grows 18 inches high and wide. A bright green, it is excellent in medium-sized ponds and valuable for its non-running, clumping habit. It can take water over its crown at a depth of 1 inch.

### Acorus gramineus 'Hangzhou'

This selection is the most shade tolerant of the *Acorus gramineus* group, thriving in even deep shade. It also takes the deepest water—I have seen it growing in water as deep as

*Acorus gramineus* 'Licorice'

*Acorus gramineus* 'Ogon'

10 inches, almost fully submerged. It has the same look as *A. gramineus* 'Licorice'.

### Acorus gramineus 'Licorice'

Identical in size and habit to the standard Japanese sweet flag, 'Licorice' has darker green foliage that smells remarkably like licorice, or anise, when bruised or crushed. Plant at a water depth of 1 inch and it will grow a foot high and wide.

### Acorus gramineus 'Oborozuki'

A smaller Japanese sweet flag with yellow-striped foliage, this cultivar grows to about 8 inches in height and spread. The variegation is subtle, and it is sometimes difficult to distinguish this cultivar from other Japanese sweet flags—-it is often confused in the nursery trade. It will grow well in moist soil or with up to 1 inch of water over its crown.

### Acorus gramineus 'Ogon'
**golden Japanese sweet flag**

'Ogon' has light green foliage accented with bright yellow stripes. It tolerates shade better than other sweet flags and is evergreen in many climates, generally Zone 6 and above. This cultivar is great for keeping color all winter in the water garden. Give it moist soil or up to 2 inches of water. It grows 8–12 inches high and spreads 12 inches.

### Acorus gramineus 'Pusillus'

A dwarf form of Japanese sweet flag that has dark green grass-like foliage, growing to only 4–5 inches in height. The spread is also 4–5 inches. 'Pusillus' is ideal for the edge of the pond where people may tread, since it tolerates light foot traffic. Give it sun to shade exposure and moist soil.

### Acorus gramineus 'Pusillus Minimus'
**miniature Japanese sweet flag**

A rare form of 'Pusillus', this cultivar grows to only about 2½ inches in height, with a 2½-inch spread. It is sometimes used in bonsai but is nice as an evergreen pond edging. It does best in moist soil but can take up to ½ inch of standing water.

### Acorus gramineus 'Pusillus Minimus Aurea'
**miniature golden Japanese sweet flag**

A rare cultivar, this miniature form is golden yellow and reaches a height of only 2 inches, spreading 2 inches as well. It does best in just moist soil but can take water ½ inch deep.

*Acorus gramineus* 'Pusillus Minimus Aurea'

*Acorus gramineus 'Variegatus'*

*Acrostichum danaeifolium*

*Acorus gramineus 'Yodo-no-yuki'*

### *Acorus gramineus* 'Variegatus'
**variegated Japanese sweet flag**

White-striped cousin to 'Ogon', this cultivar is excellent in the margin of the pond or in the perennial border. Good for keeping winter color in the water garden in Zone 6 and up. Spreads to 12 inches and reaches a height of 8–10 inches. Will take moist soil or up to 1 inch of water.

### *Acorus gramineus* 'Yodo-no-yuki'

The green leaves of this cultivar are streaked in yellow along the midrib. It reaches about 8 inches in height and width and is sometimes confused with 'Ogon' in the trade. Plant at a water depth of 1 inch. This cultivar is more troubled by grasshoppers and rust than most sweet flags are.

### *Acrostichum danaeifolium*
**water leather fern**
Pteridaceae

A true fern, water leather fern is noted for its large fern-shaped leaves that take on a shiny, leathery texture. It makes

*Acrostichum danaeifolium*

Leaves of *Alisma* species compared to one of *Echinodorus*, far left

a bold statement in larger ponds and is a wonderful accent plant. The leaves appear almost plastic and assume a cinnamon shade due to the great number of spores they produce on the backs of the leaves. Native to southern Florida, two forms are listed, an inland and a coastal. We have obtained many specimens from both areas and have found that under good conditions all have grown to enormous proportions. After only a few months of the warm climate they prefer, they grew to 9–11 feet. Listed stature is 1–12 feet high and wide. Recommended water depth is moist to 3 inches, but mature plants can tolerate up to 18 inches. If the water level is kept constant, the plant has a tendency to form a thick mound of rootstock. Does best in shade and can do quite well in interior waterscapes in relatively poor light. In full sun they take on a yellow cast. Zones 9–11.

Multiple shoots rise above the water and can be removed to increase stocks. It is not unheard of to have large plants produce 25 or more offshoots. Because it is a true fern, water leather fern may be propagated from spores that

are sown fresh on wet compost. It may also be divided by cutting the mounded trunk, which will sprout new plantlets.

Water leather fern will safely overwinter in a greenhouse where the water and air temperature do not fall below 45°F. No special pruning is required. Cut back dead or dying leaves. We have not yet experienced pests with water leather fern.

## *Alisma*
### water plantain
### Alismataceae

*Alisma* grows in many parts of the temperate world. Many species are native to North America, and others may also be found in Europe and North Africa. *Alisma*, commonly known as water plantain, is a genus of herbaceous perennials characterized by foliage that is spoon- or lance-shaped, deeply veined, and somewhat spongy. When growing along the edge of a pond or stream, the leaves stand erect above the water. Though bearing a close resemblance to the leaves of melon sword (*Echinodorus*), these are more supple and pliable. When growing submerged, water plantain leaves become long and ribbon-like and are difficult to distinguish from submerged arrowhead (*Sagittaria*) or *Vallisneria*.

The flower heads, which appear in summer and continue through fall, are arranged in whorls that form large clouds of white, pink, or lavender. Blooms form a pyramid-like shape that is larger at the bottom and tapered to a point at the top. The flower arrangements last long into the winter and provide a focal point that gives the pond depth and interest even during this otherwise drab time of year.

Water plantains are suitable for medium to large ponds. Situate them in sun to part shade and they will reach a height of 12–36 inches and spread of 18 inches, except for the small *Alisma gramineum*. They self-seed freely if not deadheaded on a regular basis and can become well established in a short period of time in an earth-bottom pond. They generally prefer soil that is moist or up to 3 inches under water, though there are a few exceptions that grow well deeper. They are not a pest in areas where water levels stay constant. In ponds or streams with fluctuating water levels where there is a period of little or no water along the bank or shoreline, *Alisma* seed are prone to sprout in large numbers and can become a nuisance.

Seed heads and corms of *Alisma* provide nourishment to wildlife, including ducks and geese. Native Americans used the foliage in teas to relieve kidney and lung ailments. It was once used to treat rabies and was known as the mad-dog weed.

All *Alisma* species overwinter in colder climates. They are hardy in Zones 3–11. They may remain in the pond to freeze solid, provided they stay in the water. A period of winter chilling is essential to the plant's growth and flowering in subsequent seasons. To survive the winter, the plants form bulb-like corms at the base of the plant, while the leaves and roots die off completely. These corms are easily overlooked and thrown away during spring cleaning.

Propagation is most common by sowing seed early in the spring on wet soil and leaving them out to the fluctuating temperatures and depths of spring. I sow mine in trays that have no holes and leave them outside all winter, letting them thaw in the spring and sprout. Another method of propagation is by dividing the corms in early spring.

Water plantains are occasionally bothered by black aphids but otherwise are unscathed by insects or other pests or diseases. They sometimes get a black spot, but it is not lethal as the plants seem to make a full recovery once fertilized.

Nomenclature of particular species of *Alisma* is open to some dispute. Some authorities list separate species. Others list only one species (*A. subcordatum* or *A. plantago-aquatica*) and consider others (*A. parviflorum*, *A. gramineum*, *A. lanceolatum*) to be subspecies. To the homeowner and hobby grower, the main differences are the color and size of the flowers, the shape and size of the leaves, and the overall size of the plant. *Alisma plantago-aquatica* is the standard species most commonly sold in the trade.

*Alisma gramineum*

### Alisma gramineum
**narrow-leafed water plantain**

A diminutive form, growing just 5–6 inches high and wide, particularly suited to container water gardens and small ponds or streams. Small leaves are variable: spoon-shaped, pointed, thumb-shaped, teardrop-shaped. White to pinkish blooms look like twinkling dots. Keep water level no more than 1 inch deep. Native to the U.S. and throughout the northern hemisphere. Grows wild in Europe and into northern Africa and southern Asia.

### Alisma lanceolatum
**lance-leafed water plantain**

As its Latin name implies, this form has longer, narrower leaves than *Alisma plantago-aquatica*. Foliage is slightly more blue-green and heavier textured, and the lavender flowers have a pink blush. I have grown this in 24 inches of water and it makes it to the surface and flowers. Grows wild in Europe and into northern Africa and southern Asia.

*Alisma lanceolatum*

*Alisma plantago-aquatica*

## Alisma parviflorum
**round-leafed water plantain**

Foliage is very round, like a wooden spoon, and heavily veined. Flowers are pinkish and larger than *Alisma plantago-aquatica*. Native to North America. Species is sometimes listed as a variety of *A. subcordatum* or *A. plantago-aquatica*.

## Alisma plantago-aquatica (syn. *A. subcordatum*)
**water baby's breath**

Tapered leaves 4 inches wide and 6–8 inches long. Flowers are white to pink. Tolerates seasonal flooding, and I have grown it in 12–24 inches of water with no ill effects. Foliage can be pure green to red-backed with red stems. The most commonly available alisma, this species is a robust water plant that flowers well. Native to the northern hemisphere, and in North America primarily in the East and Midwest. It grows wild in marshy areas from Quebec to Wisconsin. Some authorities separate the two species *Alisma plantago-aquatica* and *A. subcordatum*, but all the specimens I've seen, from around the world, look exactly the same to me.

*Alisma parviflorum*

*Alisma plantago-aquatica*

*Alisma triviale* (syn. *A. plantago-aquatica* var. *americanum*)
**northern water plantain**

This species is grown for its white flowers that are reputedly one-third larger than the standard water plantain. Foliage is rounded and also larger than *Alisma plantago-aquatica*. Will tolerate seasonal flooding. Native to the eastern U.S., mostly around the Great Lakes, but is also found in California and northern Mexico.

*Alternanthera*
Amaranthaceae

A low-growing plant that often trails out on the water surface, *Alternanthera* is a genus of tropical marginals that provide cover and shade for fish in ponds, streams, and waterfalls. They are also suitable for growing in hanging baskets. In the water garden, they clamber at the base of taller marginals, such as *Canna*, *Thalia*, or *Cyperus* (umbrella grass), weaving together larger plantings and hiding the edges of pots or stones. All the alternantheras grow equally well above or at the waterline. When grown submerged, they must have crystal-clear water or will be prone to rot away and die. When grown as marginals with fully moist soil, they provide color and interest and are very carefree. Many selections that are currently available for the aquarium may also be grown in sun to shade at the edge of the pond or water garden.

Alternantheras produce white flowers at any time, and generally more under short days. Most will grow to less than 6 inches high and will spread 12 inches or more. They are native to the tropical areas of South America and are hardy in Zones 9–11. Frost will kill them. To overwinter, keep them in temperatures above 50°F and supply extra light to make 12-hour days, so they will not flower themselves to death. They propagate easily from stem cuttings, which root in water in a few days' time. They may also be grown from seed, although these may not grow true from parentage. Mealybugs, spider mites, and aphids can be a threat, especially in indoor environments, but simply submerging the plant in water for a day or two will take care of the problem.

*Alternanthera cardinalis* (syn. *A. reineckii* 'Cardinalis')
**cardinal leaf**

Often found as an aquarium plant, this species is easily distinguished for the undersides of its leaves, which are a bright crimson. Leaves are broader than in some of the other

*Alternanthera cardinalis*

species and are often slightly ruffled at the edges. This species may grow slightly taller, up to 8 inches, performing best when grown at just the surface of the water. Native to southern Brazil.

*Alternanthera lilacina* (syn. *A. reineckii* 'Lilacina')
**lilac-leafed alternanthera**

More commonly available for the aquarium, this alternanthera has leaves that are green on top, lilac colored underneath. It will have best color when given a sunny exposure and a place on the margin of a stream where the soil is just wet. This species may grow taller yet, up to 10 inches, but may creep to only 10 inches or so. Propagate by stem cuttings to keep the best colors.

Alternanthera reineckii

Alternanthera reineckii at the feet of Impatiens walleriana in front of Eupatorium rugosum 'Chocolate'

Alternanthera philoxeroides

### Alternanthera philoxeroides
**alligator weed**

Stems of this tropic-loving aquatic root at the edge of the pond and then float out onto the water surface. The leaves are small, rounded, and fleshy. Stems can grow rather large in size and trail for several feet on the water, sometimes up to 20 feet. Flowers are small white powder-puffs held on stalks near the base of the leaves. This species can become a nuisance in warmer climates and should be used with caution in areas where winters do not provide a killing frost. It grows in water up to 3 inches deep, or floating, and can also grow in dryer soil. Crayfish farms often use this plant as a food source, and in the ornamental pond it is a great food for koi, which like to feed on plants.

### Alternanthera reineckii
**copperleaf, ruby runner**

Foliage of this species is a distinctive purple-red, accented by white flowers that resemble blooms of clover. It has an open, trailing habit that makes it suitable for any size pond. Copperleaf is best grown as a marginal, rather than a submerged water plant. It will tolerate deeper water for very short periods of time, but it has a tendency to let go of the soil if the water is deeper than 3 inches. It will float to the surface and find a place to root at the water's edge. Situate it in sun to only part shade.

*Alternanthera sessilis*

### Alternanthera rosaefolia (syn. A. reineckii 'Rosaefolia')
**rose-colored alternanthera**

Leaves of this species are similar to *Alternanthera cardinalis* but are more rose colored, rather than pure red. It will grow to 6–8 inches high. Situate it in sun to only part shade. Though it can grow in soil from moist to submerged, it does best in just wet soil. It will set itself free just like *A. reineckii*. This species propagates easily—stem cuttings will root at the nodes in three or four days at 70°F.

### Alternanthera sessilis
**purple-leafed alternanthera**

This species is yet another aquarium plant that easily adapts to the edge of the pond, or even to an annual planter alongside impatiens and petunias. The foliage color resembles the purple-red of copperleaf (*Alternanthera reineckii*), but its habit is more upright, rather than trailing along the water sur-face. It also differs from the other species by having narrower leaves and a bushier habit. It will grow to a height of 12–18 inches. It tends to flower only when days are short. This species can be grown from seed with results pretty true to type. Start seed on moist soil at about 70°F. Cover lightly with soil and wait up to a month for them to sprout. Starting seed each spring makes for a good alternative to overwintering.

### Anemopsis californica
**yerba-yerba**
**Saururaceae**

White summertime flowers that look just like *Houttuynia*—five petals or more with a big hat or cone in the center. The center is often a white-gray color and the petals are a white that becomes red as the flowers age, like flowers of *Trillium grandiflora*. Red dots first appear and slowly bleed into the rest of the petal. Leathery, oval leaves are dull green with red petioles. It grows to 6 inches high and spreads like a strawberry plant, hopping along making new plants on the ends of runners. It is not invasive, however. It needs sun to part shade and moist soil or up to 3 inches of water. It seems prone to getting mealybugs when not grown in water or when moisture stressed.

This species is native to the southwestern U.S., specifically California, and is listed as hardy in Zone 7, but it has overwintered in our Zone 5 for eight years. To be safe, bring it in over the winter in harsher climates and be sure to give it at least eastern light. Propagate by taking offsets, which root readily. I have never tried starting it from seed.

### Apios
**Fabaceae**

### Apios americana
**water wisteria, Indian potato, ground nut, wild bean, potato bean**

Brick-red to pinkish brown clusters of wisteria-like flowers emerge on vertical stems from summer to fall. Plants left to crawl along the ground rarely flower. Flower clusters are about 3–4 inches long and showiness varies greatly. Hairy, dull green, compound leaves having about five to nine leaflets also look just like those of wisteria. This plant comes in a great variety of colors and flower-cluster lengths, but no selections have been named.

*Apios americana* grows best in part shade but can tolerate sun. It generally climbs as high as 6 feet or so, spreading only 1–3 feet. After a few years, however, a wider colony will have developed. It grows in wet soil and survives seasonal flooding, but it needs water below the crown during the

*Apios americana*

*Arundo donax*

summer to do well. Native to eastern North America. Zone 4 and up. Often late in the year it is infected by spider mites, much like soybeans are. The plants require no special care to overwinter but need to go dormant. They get weak if kept growing year-round.

Propagation by seed is a very easy way to start this plant. Seed do not need much preparation. Simply sow in moist soil and cover. They generally sprout in four to ten days. Another option is to propagate by the tubers produced along the roots like knots on a rope. Divide them off and plant individually. Using the tubers is the only way to keep a selected clone.

### *Apios priceana*
### Price's ground nut

This rare species, growing natively at the convergence of Kentucky, Tennessee, and Illinois, is very similar to *Apios americana*. The difference is in its green-white flowers with a hint of purple at the tips. Otherwise all things are the same.

### *Arundo*
### giant reed
### Poaceae

*Arundo* is a genus of giant grasses that like their feet wet, although they will also grow in a perennial border. They are tall, stately, and highly ornamental—perfect in a natural pond or at the side of a stream. They tolerate wide-ranging environments, including sandy soils to heavy clay, in alkaline or saline conditions. Plants resemble large corn stalks or sugar canes, with wide leaves that can be several inches long, tapering to a point. Flowers are large panicles, silver plumes

Raft made from giant reed (*Arundo*)

that bloom in late summer or fall and quickly turn beige, remaining long into the winter. They are excellent cut flowers and dry well for long-lasting enjoyment indoors.

*Arundo* species are sought after in colder climates for their tropical-looking foliage but are maligned in warmer areas where they may be considered little more than a common weed. *Arundo formosana* is native to Taiwan and China. *Arundo donax* and *A. plinii* are native to southern Europe. They came to North America with settlers from Europe who found the plant extremely useful to create windbreaks in the landscape. *Arundo donax* was especially used to make mats, screens, fences, and even musical instruments. In warmer zones, they grow to massive proportions and can seed themselves in natural habitats. In colder climates, they may not be so hardy and can be a challenge to grow from one year to the next. We find they do best with more fertilizer in the spring than in the summer, allowing them to harden off by fall. It is also extremely important to keep the crown of the plant cool during the winter. A freak warm spell can bring them out of dormancy, causing them to die once the colder weather inevitably returns.

They grow best in full sun but can tolerate some shade. The soil can be dry or take a seasonal inundation of 1–3 inches. We have found that arundos grow best in a site with seasonal moisture that allows the plants to dry out somewhat during the growing season. Giant reed grows as high as 20 feet and spreads 4–8 feet. No pests have been noted.

Hardy in Zones 5–11, arundos will grow throughout the year in warmer climates and need no period of winter dormancy. In colder areas where frost occurs, they will turn brown and die back to the ground. The plants make an interesting winter accent in the pond and can be cut back once they become too tattered from wind and snow.

*Arundo donax*

Although they may be propagated from division or from seed, arundos are best propagated from soaking the stems, or canes, in water. Take a mature cane in late summer to fall, strip it of its foliage, and lay it in a shallow tub of water. Sprouts will appear at the leaf nodes, which may be divided and potted up. These develop into nice bushy plants.

### Arundo donax

Distinctively tropical-looking, this species often grows to 12 feet in the pond and carries 2-foot plumes. Although it is particularly suited to large ponds, where it could be planted in 5 inches of water, this reed performs equally well in the perennial border and can tolerate drought.

## *Arundo donax* 'Variegata'
**variegated giant reed**

This variegated version has bold white and green leaves that create a striking bamboo effect. Shorter than the green form, it is more suitable for a smaller pond. Height 3–8 feet, width 3–5 feet. Moist soil or up to 3 inches of water.

## *Arundo plinii* (syn. *A. pliniana*)
**arrow reed**

Smaller than *Arundo donax*, arrow reed grows 4–6 feet high. This plant has narrower leaves that are often sharply pointed at their tips, consequently it does not have the same elegant appearance as its larger cousins. Attractive as a specimen planting in a medium pond, it grows aggressively in warmer climates and should be containerized for best effect. This species is slightly less hardy, classified for Zones 6–11. It also tolerates less water, taking a depth of only 1 inch.

## *Asclepias*
**milkweed, butterfly plant**
**Asclepiadaceae**

*Asclepias* plants are upright, cheerfully-colored aquatics excellent for the edge of the pond. They are called butterfly plants because they attract so many of these fluttering garden dwellers, especially monarch and viceroy butterflies. Of course, the caterpillars are also attracted to the plants, but do not succumb to the temptation to remove them all. Leave a few to replenish the butterfly population for the coming year. Yellow aphids may also show up. Control with diatomaceous earth or crush individually. All members of the milkweed family contain a toxin that is digested by the insects that chew on the plants, causing the insects to be unpalatable to their predators. The plants have some medicinal value, although care should be taken in view of their toxic propensities.

*Asclepias curassavica*

*Asclepias incarnata*

Native to the Americas, *Asclepias* plants grow in sun to part shade in moist soil or wet meadows. They can stand some seasonal flooding as well. Their pink, orange, yellow, or white flowers bloom in summer. Leaves are willow-like. Height 12–36 inches and spread generally 12 inches. Hardy in Zones 3–11, depending on species. No special overwintering care is required where the species are hardy, but a dormant period is necessary. If bringing the plants indoors for the winter, deep in a cool place. Propagate by seed or take cuttings of select forms. Division is also possible with very mature clumps.

## Asclepias curassavica
### blood flower

Tall plants for the wet edge, these grow 36 inches high and spread just 6 inches. Soil can be up to 1 inch under water. Blood flower blooms all summer with orange-and-yellow or all-gold flowers borne in the leaf axils, not terminally like other forms of *Asclepias*. Native to Mexico and South America, this species carries a hardiness rating just to Zone 10.

Save seeds over the winter to start new plants in spring, or bring plants indoors before frost.

## Asclepias incarnata
### butterfly weed, swamp milkweed

In the water garden landscape these are prized for their late-summer color. Use them in conjunction with other milkweeds in the perennial border (*Asclepias tuberosa*) to link the pond visually with the rest of the landscape. This species will reach a height of 24–36 inches and can tolerate up to 5 inches of water. Foliage is narrow, willow-shaped, and often turns color in the fall. Flowers are small, held in umbels at the top of each stem. They range in color from clear white to light pink to darker rose. There is much variability in the colors, and even bitones are possible. Seed heads have the characteristic half-moon shape and are filled with black seeds attached to strands of silk that float away on the air when the seed heads burst in early fall.

Native to North America, ranging from Quebec to the Gulf of Mexico and westward to North Dakota, Wyoming,

Asclepias incarnata 'Ice Ballet'

Asclepias lanceolata

and New Mexico. Butterfly plant is cold-hardy to Zone 3. Grows best if left in the pond during the winter. Besides the monarch caterpillars, milkweed beetles sometimes eat the seed heads, and aphids in late summer attack young growth and flower buds.

The selection *Asclepias incarnata* 'Ice Ballet', known as white butterfly plant, is also a welcome water plant. The pure white flowers attract butterflies and hummingbirds, and as an added bonus, they make great cut flowers. This is a seed strain, so it can be propagated from seed. Hardiness is the same as for the species, requiring no special care for overwintering. Do not submerge at the bottom of the pond.

### Asclepias lanceolata
**coastal milkweed**

This pale pink milkweed is native to the coastal plains of New Jersey, Florida, and Texas, hardy in Zone 6 and up. This species reaches a height of 24–36 inches. It needs moist soil or water up to 2 inches deep. It will also tolerate seasonal flooding. Propagate by seed or cuttings. Sow seed in spring in 70°F soil. Seed will sprout more reliably if first given a 30-day cold treatment. For cuttings, take in spring from firm growth, before the flowers have set.

### Asclepias longifolia
**long-leafed milkweed**

Native from Virginia to Texas, *Asclepias longifolia* is a tall slender plant with very fine, amsonia-like leaves and white flowers. Give sun to shade exposure and just moist soil. It too will tolerate seasonal flooding. Grows to 24 inches high. Hardy in Zone 6 and up. Best propagated by seed.

Asclepias perennis

### Asclepias perennis
**aquatic milkweed**

A small, compact, bushy plant with fine willowy leaves and gleaming white to pale rose flowers. I was thrilled to first see it at the U.S. Botanic Garden. It was just what I had been looking for—a compact plant covered in white flowers with a pale pink cast. I later encountered this species at the Mercer Botanic Garden in Houston, growing and flowering away in the total shade of large bald cypress trees (*Taxodium distichum*). Native from the Carolinas to Texas.

Give sun to shade exposure and moist soil or up to 6 inches of water. This species takes a lot of moisture. Grows 12–24 inches high. Propagate by cuttings or seed—little cold stratification is needed for this seed. Hardy in Zones 6–11.

*Asclepias rubra*

Taking stem cuttings of *Bacopa*

### Asclepias rubra

Rose to red flowers on bushy plants with small willow-like leaves. I first saw this species at the U.S. Botanic Garden and was taken by its potential in the landscape. Grows just like *Asclepias incarnata* but with smaller leaves. Possibly slightly shorter growing, to 24 inches high. Best in just moist soil but can take seasonal flooding. Propagate by cuttings or seed. Native to coastal plains of New Jersey, Florida, and Texas. Hardy to Zone 6, possibly even Zone 5.

### Bacopa
**water hyssop**
**Scrophulariaceae**

The low-growing tropical marginals in this genus are excellent as ground covers in the bog garden or near the edge of the pond, or as trailing plants in the waterfall or table-top pond. Native to the tropical regions of the Americas, *Bacopa* plants are dainty additions to any water feature, large or small. In water that is neutral to acidic, they will even grow submerged under several inches of water. Foliage is usually small, rounded, and fleshy and often fragrant when crushed. Flowers bloom in summer and range in color from white to pink to blue, depending upon the species. It creeps through sun or shade, generally reaching 2–4 inches high and spreading 24 inches in a season. It needs moist soil or water up to 1 inch deep. Most species will also grow well fully submerged, though they will not flower. The only pest we have noticed is

Planting stem cuttings of *Bacopa*

cucumber beetles on emerged plants. Simply submerge for two to four days to eliminate.

*Bacopa* grows year-round in warmer climates where frost is not an issue. In colder areas, cut about 3 inches from several tips of the plant and bring these tip cuttings indoors for the winter. Simply place them in a cup of water and keep them in a warm, sunny room of the house. They will root and grow during the winter and can be replanted to a pot and placed outdoors when the last chance of freezing has passed. Cuttings are the best method for propagating all species of *Bacopa*, but seed, which is a little smaller than petunia seed, sprouts readily on the surface of moist soil.

*Bacopa caroliniana*

*Bacopa caroliniana*

*Bacopa monnieri*

## *Bacopa caroliniana*
**lemon bacopa, lemon water hyssop**

An easy-to-grow ground cover for the water garden, this *Bacopa* species is a good addition to the container water garden on the patio, where one can enjoy its heavily lemon-scented foliage and bright blue flowers all summer long. There are reports of a white form as well, but I have never seen it. Lemon bacopa is also a good choice for a flooded meadow or storm water detention area, since it will grow fully submerged. Streams and bogs are great environments, too. Native to the coastal plain from Virginia to Florida to Texas. Zones 9–11.

## *Bacopa lenagera* 'Variegata'
**variegated lemon bacopa**

Distinctive gold veining on fleshy, green leaves is a very useful accent even when this plant is not displaying its pale blue blooms. Despite the common name, this plant has no scent—it just looks similar in form to *Bacopa caroliniana*. The species is an all-green form. Native to tropical South America. Zones 9–11.

## *Bacopa monnieri*
**water purslane**

Water purslane is a perfect, creeping ground cover with small light green leaves and nearly ever-blooming white flowers striped pink, lavender, or blue. It can take light foot traffic and would be useful in water detention basins where it can be mowed. It is very adaptable and more tolerant of seasonal water fluctuations than other bacopas. It can grow submerged in clear water, and typically grows in meadows

*Baldellia ranunculoides* f. *repens*

*Baldellia ranunculoides* f. *repens*

## *Baldellia ranunculoides* f. *repens*
### Siberian pink cups
### Alismataceae

Siberian pink cups have dense clouds of ½-inch pink flowers with yellow centers that resemble poppies. The delicate blossoms adorn tufts of foliage 2–10 inches high and 10–12 inches wide all summer long, lending an airy look to the water garden. Excellent for a tub garden, along the pool edge, or in a stream under sun to part shade. Give it moist soil or water up to ½ inch deep. It will also grow submerged in clear water but will not flower.

This species, native to Europe and northern Africa, is rated hardy in Zones 6–11, but it needs some shade to survive south of Zone 8 or the heat will kill it. It needs no special care to overwinter in Zones 6–9, where it will go dormant naturally, but in harsher climates it can be brought in and overwintered in a sunny window or under lights. If not given additional light in the winter, short days of less than 10 hours of sunlight will send it into senescence and you may lose it.

Siberian pink cups naturally form new plantlets on the branches, which are very easy to propagate. Aphids may appear on the plants, but they are generally not bothered by pests.

flooded with water 4–12 inches deep. It reaches up and out of the water, hiding the surface. Native to coastal Virginia, south to Florida, and west to Texas and throughout tropical South America. Zones 6–11.

## *Bacopa myriophylloides*
### thin-leafed bacopa

The most distinguishing feature of this species is its leaves, which are thin and pointed, reminiscent of parrot feather (*Myriophyllum aquaticum*). When growing underwater, it changes from creeping to upright form, and the leaves become wispy and look like strands of hair. This species is more commonly found as an aquarium plant but grows equally well above the water. China-blue flowers appear on the emergent form, which reaches a height of 4–6 inches. Native to tropical South America. Zones 9–11.

*Butomus umbellatus*

*Baumea rubiginosa* 'Variegata'

*Butomus umbellatus*

## *Baumea rubiginosa* 'Variegata' (syn. *Machaerina rubiginosa* 'Variegata')
**golden spears, variegated water chestnut**
**Cyperaceae**

This fine plant has tubular green leaves that are flat like a fencing foil. Leaves are dark green marked with a yellow vertical line that remains stable throughout the growing season. It prefers moist soil or water up to 2 inches over the crown. It does tolerate seasonal flooding of 10 inches or more, however. Flowers are small brown tassels that appear in the fall. It has a running habit and reaches a height of 12–24 inches. Situate in sun to part shade.

Golden spears will overwinter in Zones 6b–11 as long as the roots remain below the freezing line. In very cold areas that can reach down to -20°F, store the plant in a cooler where it will remain damp but will be protected from freezing. Native to Madagascar, Indonesia, Australia, Tasmania.

Propagate by division in the spring. A black spot problem can develop, but it tends to disappear with fertilizing. Also, grasshoppers have been known to chew up the plant.

## *Butomus umbellatus*
**flowering rush**
**Butomaceae**

A delicate beauty, flowering rush displays large umbels of white to pink flowers all summer and onion-like foliage. It is an excellent accompaniment to plantings of tall rushes (*Scirpus*, *Schoenoplectus*, *Phragmites*) and cattails (*Typha*). Two selections are currently available, both from Eberhard Schuster. 'Rosenrot' is pink and 'Schneeweisschen' is white. I have grown these in my garden and find them hard to distinguish. The leaves of the white form are without the characteristic blue blush on stems and leaves.

*Butomus umbellatus* f. *junceus*

*Calla palustris*

Wetland planting of *Butomus umbellatus* f. *junceus*

*Butomus umbellatus* f. *junceus*, from Asia and eastern Russia, is taller and more upright with larger flower heads. It looks far more rushy, with twisted leaves growing in fans. The leaves often get brown as the plant ages.

Flowering rush needs sun to part shade and moist soil or water to 1 inch deep. It tolerates seasonal flooding and can take sustained deeper water, up to 4 inches, in the summer, but it flowers more in shallower water. Generally 12–36 inches high—though *Butomus umbellatus* f. *junceus* can reach 5 feet—and 14 inches wide. Grasshoppers and wooly caterpillars are the only pests I have seen.

With a native range from Europe and across Russia to the Pacific Ocean, it is very hardy, rated for Zones 3–11. It needs no special care over the winter but must have a period

of dormancy. In warmer climates place it in the fridge for about 60 days. Propagation by division of the rootstock is easiest, but seed does sprout after cold stratification for 30–60 days in moist soil.

## *Calla palustris*
**northern calla lily**
**Araceae**

Glossy, heart-shaped leaves on floating stems accented in spring by 2-inch white flowers. A cold-loving aquatic rated hardy in Zones 2–6, *Calla palustris* requires highly acidic water and soil. It overwinters easily in these cold climates as long as it is left with its rhizomes in the water. In its native habitat in Europe, Asia, and North America, it floats out into part or full shade on mats of dead oak and pine foliage. In the fall, it decorates the pond with its seed heads of bright red berries. It reaches only about 4 inches high but has a running spread.

Propagates best by division of its creeping rhizome. It may also be grown from seed, but the seed must not be allowed to dry out. Seed sprouts best if sown fresh and moist and given a cold stratification of 30–60 days. It should sprout then in just over a month. Grow northern calla lily in moist soil or give it free rein to float. It may be bothered by a caterpillar that bores into the stems, but it is occasional and rarely fatal.

*Caltha palustris* in the landscape, northwestern Indiana

## Caltha
### marsh marigold, elkslip
### Ranunculaceae

*Caltha* is much favored by water gardeners for its early spring flowers that open bright yellow or white long before the rest of the pond has come back to life. All the species are characterized by round, usually kidney-shaped leaves that are dark green, glossy, and toothed around the edges. Blooms have five to nine sepals (no petals) and are usually single, although double forms are available. They have a round, mounded habit and grow in clumps, similar to hostas. Plants generally grow in moist to wet, boggy conditions along the edges of creeks, streams, and ponds. They can often be found growing naturally in wet swales, especially under the canopy of tall deciduous trees. In cooler climates they grow from spring through fall, while in warmer areas they may die back to the ground during the strong heat and humidity of summer.

Species of *Caltha* can be found in many areas of the northern hemisphere—Siberia, Japan, North America, the United Kingdom. *Caltha palustris* has the widest range, but several distinct species grow wild in the western part of North America, including *C. asarifolia*, *C. biflora*, *C. leptosepala*, and the dwarf white *C. chelidonii*. Named cultivars are grown in the United Kingdom and are gradually making their way into the North American markets.

Most calthas are best cultivated in moist soil or water up to 1 inch deep under sun or part shade. All like cool weather and do poorly in areas of high summmer heat and humidity. They do best in areas with cool nights. Because of their native habitat, calthas prefer to overwinter in cooler conditions and do require a period of cold dormancy in order to bloom well the following season. Aphids are the only pest I have experienced with calthas.

Propagate by division of offsets in the early spring. Seed propagation is possible, although the offspring may not be true to form. Plus, seed tends to have a short shelf life so sow as soon as ripe. Give seed a period of cold moist stratification before sowing them atop moist soil in early spring. They sprout best in cool soil, before it has reached 70°F.

### Caltha biflora
### twin-flowered marsh marigold

This species, found from Alaska and southward to California and Colorado, is a twin-flowered form, meaning it usually has only two flowers growing on a single stem. It is listed as having white flowers in the flora of the Pacific Northwest, yet all those we have received from collectors have yellow flowers (possibly those are in fact *Caltha asarifolia*.) Height 12 inches, spread 12–18 inches. Rated hardy in Zones 3–7, they survive winters best with good snow cover, because the crowns are very close to the surface or even exposed.

### Caltha howellii (syn. *C. leptosepala* subsp. *howellii*)
### western marsh marigold

Flowers of this species are white with prominent yellow stamens. It is native to the mountain streams of southern Oregon and California, rated hardy in Zones 4–7. Height 24 inches, spread 18–24 inches.

### Caltha leptosepala
### western marsh marigold

One of several species growing wild in western North America, from Alaska to Alberta and southward into Oregon and New Mexico. *Caltha leptosepala* is distinguished by its more oblong foliage and white flowers, though a yellow form is

*Caltha natans*

*Caltha palustris*

listed in the flora of the Pacific Northwest. It sprouts up along the edges of the snow, liking the especially cool environment. Height 12 inches, spread 12–18 inches. Hardy in Zones 4–7, where the summers do not get too hot, like the Pacific Northwest. In the Zone 7 of Tennessee, for example, it does not survive.

### *Caltha natans*
**floating marsh marigold**

This species grows underwater much like a waterlily with floating leaves and submerged stems. It has a small white flower in early spring that floats on the water surface. It is particularly sensitive to warmer temperatures and fades, and then dies, if not kept in the cool, running water that it prefers. It is native to Alaska and southward into northern Minnesota. Zones 3–5. Grow this in part shade at a water depth of 4–6 inches, giving it slightly acidic soil. Height 2 inches above the water—enough for just the flower really—spread 12 inches. In addition to the aphids attracted to most calthas, China mark moth may appear on this species. Propagate by division in autumn or early spring or by seed. Seed are best sown as soon as ripe in late summer. Stand pots in ¾–1¼ inches of water to keep the soil evenly wet. Seed should germinate in one to three months at 59°F.

### *Caltha palustris*
**cowslip**

This harbinger of spring is one of the first marginals to bloom, awakening the pond with bright and cheerful yellow flowers. Leaves are dark green and glossy, resembling those of violets, and usually toothed at the edges. Flowers are yellow, usually single, and shiny. Although it blooms very early in the spring, it may put on a repeat performance in areas

*Caltha palustris* 'Honeydew'

with cool summers. Where summers are hot, however, the leaves sometimes die back. Its native range is circumboreal as far south as Tennessee. Hardy in Zones 3–7. Height 12 inches, spread 12–18 inches. It tolerates seasonal flooding, and some selections grow in up to 6 inches of water.

Propagate by seed or division. Divide root clumps before flowers appear in early spring or when plants are dormant in summer. Sow seed in early summer as soon as it is ripe. Seed-grown plants tend not to bloom until their second year, and double forms do not breed true from seed.

The plant has had some medicinal use, but extreme care should be taken since it is poisonous if eaten raw. When the foliage is boiled at least twice the poisonous elements are removed. Thus prepared the leaves reputedly taste like spinach. Flower buds may also be eaten after pickling.

*Caltha palustris* 'Stagnalis'

*Caltha palustris*, the most widely grown of the species and recipient of the Royal Horticultural Society Award of Garden Merit, has spawned a great number of popular cultivars. Here is a list with basic descriptions:

'Alba'—white flowers smaller than the species
'Auenwald'—large yellow-gold flowers
'Flore Pleno'—double yellow with full-sized petals
'Goldshale'—green-gold flowers
var. *himalensis*—red to orange flowers with red to
    yellow stamens
'Honeydew'—green-yellow with very large petals
'Marilyn'—masses of canary-yellow flowers
'Multiplex'—double orange-yellow with smaller
    petals, like a little mum
'Plena'—double yellow with full-sized petals
var. *radicans*—produces new plants on flower stems
'Semiplena'—lemon-yellow with double row of
    full-sized petals
'Stagnalis'—very upright foliage, gray-green-yellow
    flowers
'Susan'—large lemon-yellow with lots of flowers
    per stem
'Tyermannii'—dark purple stems, yellow flowers

## *Caltha palustris* var. *palustris* (syn. *C. polypetala*)

Native to Iran, the Caucasus, and the East Balkans. More sturdy and vigorous than the North American marsh marigold, though it is rated similarly for Zones 4–7. The yellow flowers may be twice the size of the species, and the plant grows to 24 inches high and 18–24 inches wide.

*Caltha palustris* 'Semiplena'

*Caltha palustris* 'Susan'

## Canna
### Cannaceae

These are the plants your grandma used to grow, only much improved. Tall and impressive, they are topped by extremely colorful flowers that start in midsummer and keep going right until frost. Two kinds of cannas are suitable for the water garden. The true water cannas grow well in saturated soil or with water over their crowns. Generally, *Canna flaccida* and *C. glauca*, as well as the Longwood hybrids 'Ra', 'Endeavor', 'Taney', and 'Erebus', are true water cannas. They grow to varying heights and 2–3 feet wide. All the water cannas bloom throughout the summer.

The second kind is the water-tolerant cannas. These are terrestrial forms that adapt to growing in water-logged soil but that can also grow in the perennial border. Water-tolerant cannas include selections such as 'Florence Vaughn', 'Pretoria', 'Striped Beauty', and 'Durban', but this is not an exclusive list. Try some of your favorites—some usually terrestrial cannas that flower just in late summer will bloom all season when grown in water.

*Canna* foliage is large, long and tapered—very tropical looking. Hues range from bright green to blue-green, dark purple, or crimson. Some are striped in yellow, white, or red. Plants commonly grow to several feet in height in a single season, forming a large mass of tubers at the base. They are suitable as an accent plant in the water garden and make excellent specimens when planted in a container. Lower growing, more creeping water plants, such as *Bacopa* or pennywort (*Hydrocotyle*), are good understory complements to the large, bold effect of a canna.

Leaves and flowers of cannas

Flowers also come in a wide variety of colors, from delicate creams and yellows to brassy oranges and reds. They are either gladiola-type, with large overlapping petals, or plumeria-type, with a more delicate, narrow form. The blooms of *Canna flaccida* are singularly distinctive, reminiscent of bright yellow daffodils with pronounced trumpets.

Full sun is best for bringing out the strongest color and most flowers, but cannas will grow in pretty deep shade. Heights range from 2 to 9 feet and widths from 2 to 6 feet. All take moist soil or water over their crowns to varying depths, up to 12 inches depending on species or cultivar.

Propagate from seed or by division of the tubers. Seed is a useful method only for the species, since seed-grown varieties may not be true to the parent. Stick to division for the named cultivars. If propagating by seed, nick the seed and soak overnight. Sow in moist, not wet, soil at 70°F. They will usually sprout in 7–14 days.

Cannas are rated hardy in Zones 8b–11. The generally accepted view is that cannas are tropical plants that cannot withstand a winter freeze. For this reason it is usually recommended that they be brought indoors for the winter. They can also be left to dry out, so the tubers can be cleaned and stored for the winter. Robert Armstrong, who hybridized the famed Longwood water cannas, reports that he successfully overwinters his hybrids in his Pennsylvania garden by cutting them back and placing them at the bottom of the pond. As long as the rhizomes are not reached by ice during the winter, the plants return the following spring.

Not prone to severe attacks by pests, cannas may be affected by aphids or Japanese beetles during the summer. *Canna glauca* and the Longwood hybrids, though, seem to be rarely bothered by pests. If brought indoors to grow during the winter, they may develop spider mites. Canna rust may also occur among plants that are not kept very wet or are not cleaned well in the fall before being put away for the winter. Rust looks like orange pustules, or iron rust, on the leaves. It usually begins on the lower leaves and progresses up the plant as the infection spreads. Just cut back affected foliage and destroy. Clean tools and wash hands between plants. Sanitation is the best cure for canna rust.

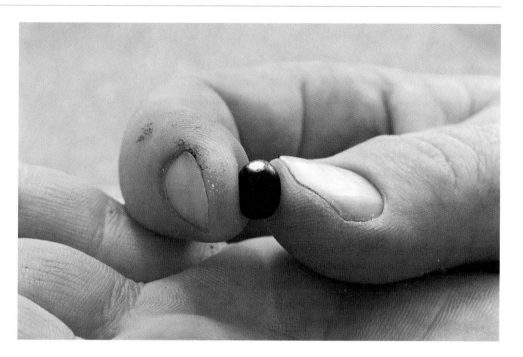

Starting *Canna*

*Canna* 'Black Knight' and 'Intrigue'

*Canna* 'Durban'

## *Canna* 'Black Knight'

This water-tolerant canna, often sold in the trade as a water canna though it does best in just damp soil, is very striking. Flowers open red and fade through orange and into white. Foliage is purple with green stripes. Height 5–6 feet, spread 3–4 feet. Grow in moist soil or water to just 1 inch deep. Japanese beetles tend to be especially attracted to the dark foliage.

## *Canna* 'Durban'

Bright tomato-red flowers sit well above foliage that is flushed in red and streaked with gold. This is a water-tolerant variety sold as a water canna, needing moist to just wet soil. Height 5–8 feet, spread 3–4 feet.

## *Canna* 'Endeavor'
**red water canna**

'Endeavor' is distinguished by its bold, red, butterfly-like flowers. It has blue-green foliage, and the stems have a red blush at the base and the leaves a thin red edge. Height 4–5 feet, spread 2–3 feet. 'Endeavor' grows best in moist soil or up to 6 inches of water. It will tolerate deeper but will not thrive and flowering is poor. 'Endeavor' is a hybrid between a red garden canna and *Canna glauca*. Aside from the color and slightly larger seeds, it can pass for *C. glauca* and is often sold as such.

*Canna 'Endeavor'*

*Canna 'Erebus'*

## *Canna 'Erebus'*
**peach water canna**

These soft, delicate, pinky-peach blooms are a rare color for the water garden. Height 2–6 feet, spread 2–3 feet. Thrives in moist soil or water up to 10 inches deep.

## *Canna flaccida*
**yellow water canna**

This water canna, native to Florida and other states bordering the Gulf of Mexico, has yellow daffodil-like flowers on medium green foliage. These flowers start blooming in early summer, a bit earlier than other cannas. Grow in sun to part shade in moist soil or water up to 10 inches deep. Height 2–4 feet, spread 2–3 feet.

*Canna flaccida*

*Canna* 'Florence Vaughn'

*Canna* 'Intrigue'

### *Canna* 'Florence Vaughn'
**orange-yellow water canna**

Probably the most water tolerant of the non-aquatic cannas, taking as much as 10 inches of water over its crown. The stunning flowers resemble giant pansies of orange edged in yellow. A real showstopper. Flat green foliage. Height 4–6 feet and spread 2–3 feet.

### *Canna glauca*
**yellow water canna**

Native to Brazil and the tropics and subtropics of the Americas, *Canna glauca* is easily identified by its blue-green lance-shaped foliage. It has very narrow leaves. Its pale yellow flowers are recurved, plumeria-type, and appear throughout the summer. Grow in sun to part shade in moist soil or water up to 10 inches deep. It also can grow on a "raft" of its own massed roots. Height 2–6 feet, spread 2–3 feet.

### *Canna* 'Intrigue'
**purple water canna**

A water-tolerant variety often sold as a water canna. 'Intrigue' fills a special niche among cannas with dark purple foliage and pink-orange flowers. It prefers moist soil, but will grow in as much as 10 inches of water. Height 6–10 feet, spread 3–4 feet.

### *Canna* 'Little Lady'

A hybrid from Grass Roots Nursery, it is the same color as 'Erebus' but with five times the flowers. More compact at 2–4 feet high and 1–3 feet wide. Grows in moist soil to water 4 inches deep. It is a great addition and worth seeking out.

*Canna 'Panache'*

*Canna 'Phasion'*

### *Canna* 'Panache'

A much sought after water-tolerant canna, 'Panache' has creamy plumeria-type flowers with raspberry-red throats. Grows 5–6 feet high and 3–4 feet wide. Needs just moist soil. Seems not to be bothered by the usual pests.

### *Canna* 'Phasion'
### Tropicanna™

A water-tolerant canna that many people try to use as a water canna. It works under only moist to wet conditions with no depth of water. Also sold under the trademarked name Tropicanna, this selection has orange flowers. Leaves are heavily flushed in red and streaked with gold. Grows 5–8 feet high and 3–4 feet wide. This patented selection can be propagated by division for personal use only.

### *Canna* 'Pink Sunburst'

A water-tolerant canna often sold as a water canna. The soft pink flowers of 'Pink Sunburst' are accented by large pink-flushed leaves with yellow stripes. Grow in moist soil or water up to 1 inch deep. Height 3–4 feet, spread 2–3 feet.

*Canna 'Pretoria'*

*Canna 'Ra'*

### Canna 'Pretoria'
**variegated water canna**

A water-tolerant canna long sold as a water canna. It has boldly striped banana-like foliage that is topped with large orange flowers streaked red. The effect is very exotic. 'Pretoria' prefers moist soil but will grow well in up to 4 inches of water and will tolerate as much as 10 inches. Height 4–6 feet, spread 2–3 feet.

### Canna 'Ra'
**yellow water canna**

'Ra' is larger than *Canna flaccida* and has strong canary-yellow color. It also has blue-green foliage. It is the tallest of the water cannas, growing 4–6 feet, usually 6 feet, high and 2–3 feet wide. Give it moist soil or water up to 10 inches deep.

### Canna 'Striped Beauty' (syn. 'Bengal Tiger')

A water-tolerant canna that can grow in water up to 1 inch deep. Flowers are gladiola-type with white and yellow petals and red stems. Leaves are bright green striped in white. Reaches 3–5 feet high and 3–4 feet wide.

### Canna 'Stuttgart'

Especially prized among canna collectors, this selection has flowers that open pale yellow and mature to a passion-fruit orange. Leaves are heavily streaked in white. It can be difficult in the landscape, however, because the leaves burn easily, making the plant look damaged. Grow in moist soil or water up to 1 inch deep. Reaches 7–8 feet high and 3–4 feet wide. When dividing, take care to remove the reverted plants—many green shoots are produced without the variegation. Tends not to be bothered by pests.

*Canna* 'Striped Beauty'

*Canna* 'Stuttgart'

## *Canna* 'Taney'
**orange water canna**

A bright, orange flower makes this water canna a particularly welcome addition to the pond. You might also want to try it with some parrot feather (*Myriophyllum aquaticum*) in a tub garden—it makes a perfect accent planting on the porch or patio. Give it moist soil or water up to 6 inches deep. With a slightly smaller spread, 12–24 inches, it grows to a height of 3–4 feet.

*Canna* 'Taney'

## Cardamine pratensis
### lady's smock
### Brassicaceae

*Cardamine pratensis* exhibits patches of cut leaves giving rise to 6-inch stems that in spring bear clubs, or flowers, like giant sweet alyssum or small stock (*Matthiola*). Many varieties are available: single, semidouble, double, deep pink to pale pink, and white. 'Edith', 'William', and 'Flore Pleno' are doubles. They like moist, calcerous soils in sun to part shade and will take water up to 2 inches deep, but they do best in moving water. I have found them in still water of 88°F just sitting in the pond dead. Height 4–10 inches, spread 6–12 inches in a season. Propagate by seed or by division of the offshoots to maintain selected varieties. Divide after flowering. Sow seed in moist soil and give them 30 days of cold stratification. No special care is needed to overwinter where hardy, Zones 4–7. Flea beetles and aphids may be a problem. Native from Minnesota to Indiana and east to New Jersey.

## Carex
### sedge
### Cyperaceae

*Carex* is a genus of grass-like plants forming mounded tufts of foliage that are highly ornamental in the pond and water garden, along a stream or waterfall, or even in a container planting. Being part of the sedge family, several species are truly aquatic. Many others are water-tolerant or at least prefer evenly moist soil in order to grow well. Leaves are commonly triangular, V-, or M- shaped, with a distinctive midrib. They rise from a clump and often arch upward and outward. Flowers are not remarkable, being brown or green spikes that on certain species can only be found with some investigation.

Sedge colonies are common in bogs and fens, in wetland forests, and along the edges of lakes and ponds. They are an important part of the wetland ecology, serving as a kind of buffer zone. They fill in gradually as the shoreline recedes, replacing plants such as pickerel plant (*Pontederia*) and cattail (*Typha*) that grew there when the waters were deeper. Sedges can be difficult to distinguish from grasses, and even more difficult to distinguish from each other. The most remarkable identifying characteristic of a sedge is the presence of a sheath that covers the nutlet, or seed. This sac-like structure is called a perigynium. Its shape, form and texture all help to identify the particular species of *Carex*.

Sedges are found in many parts of the world, ranging from the tropics to more temperate climates. More than 500

*Carex aquatilis*

*Carex comosa*

species of *Carex* are native to North America alone. These are hiding spots for many insects and animals, especially frogs and other small water-loving amphibians. Those growing in shallow water provide spawning ground for fish. Sandhill cranes may be seen making their nests in the hills of a sedge meadow. Sedges did not play much of a role in the medicine chest of old but did have their functions. Farmers once commonly used tussock sedge (*C. stricta*) as supplemental food and bedding for their cows. It was even said to be useful to "keep Milwaukee beer cold until it reached Chicago" (John Eastman, *The Book of Swamp and Bog*, Stackpole Books: Mechanicsburg, Penn.).

Most sedges may be propagated from seed or from division of the clumps in early spring. To propagate by seed, sow and lightly cover, keeping the soil moist. Seed will sprout in about one month or less when soil is at 65–70°F. They grow in sun to part shade in a wide range of pH levels and require no special care to overwinter in their hardiness zones. Mice, grasshoppers, and voles can be a problem. Especially in winter, mice and voles can destroy a stand of sedge by feasting on the shoots and roots.

## Carex aquatilis
### pond sedge

Native throughout the U.S. and Canada, this upright, running plant with blue-green foliage is very similar to Europe's *Carex riparia*. *Carex aquatilis* is very useful in the aquatic landscape for providing drifts of color. The cultivar 'Gold Find' has gold-striped foliage. Also good in wildlife gardens and detention basins. Grows in a wide range of moisture levels. Just moist soil is ideal, but it can take some drought or water up to 6 inches deep. Seasonal flooding is tolerated as well.

*Carex elata* 'Knightshayes' at the Royal Horticultural Society Garden at Wisley

*Carex elata* 'Aurea'

Flowers are green and bloom in spring. It reaches a height of 24–30 inches, and its running spread covers a space 24 inches square in a season. Zone 4, possibly even 3 with snow cover, to 11.

## Carex citrina
### fringed sedge

Native to eastern North America, fringed sedge is similar to the native European *Carex pendula* in shape and size but hardier, reliable to Zone 5. Makes a great accent in the water garden. A large clump forms up to 4 feet tall and 4 feet or more wide in part shade. Grows in full sun but foliage takes on a yellow cast. Tall, pendulous wands of green flowers bloom in spring. Soil is best just moist or up to 4 inches under water. Tolerates seasonal flooding.

## Carex comosa
### bottlebrush sedge

Common in marshes, bogs, and the shorelines of lakes and streams, bottlebrush sedge is distinguished by its dense perigynia, which have long, double-toothed spikes. The effect is rather striking, reminiscent of a long fluffy panicle of grass or wheat. Leaves are M-shaped and rough along the margins. Flowers are brown spikes in summer. Grow in moist soil or water up to 4 inches deep. Height 2–3 feet with flower heads reaching up to 5 feet, spread 2 feet. Zones 4–11. Propagate by seed or division. Native from Maine west to Washington and south to Texas.

## Carex elata 'Aurea' (syn. *C. elata* 'Bowles' Golden')
### golden variegated sedge

This is the European version of the American tussock sedge (*Carex stricta*), similar in form and habitat. The golden cultivar is striking in the pond. It has bright yellow leaves accented by thin green lines. Color is better if grown in full sun, but it can tolerate shade. Flowers are brown spikes in summer. All-yellow foliage can be found on the brassy 'Knightshayes' and the soft 'Sue Ward'. Grow 'Aurea' in moist soil or water to 2 inches deep. It does best if the water is high in spring, then gradually receding in summer to keep the soil just wet. Height 24–36 inches, spread 18 inches. Zones 5–11.

*Carex flacca*

*Carex flacca* 'Bias'

*Carex flacca*

## *Carex flacca* (syn. *C. glauca*)
blue sedge

The glowing, baby-blue foliage of this European native is a worthy addition to the shade garden, although it also grows well in full sun. A perfect companion to hostas in the damp, shaded bog garden. It needs moist soil or water to 1 inch deep. Height 6–12 inches, spread 6–12 inches. Zones 5–11, with evergreen foliage. Brown flowers appear in spring. The selection 'Bias', variegated blue sedge, offers all the virtues of blue sedge with a white margin along one edge, sometimes both edges. The cool blue and white look lights up the darkest corner of the bog garden or pond.

## *Carex hystericina*
porcupine sedge

Native to marshes, ditches and fens of the eastern U.S., this sedge is distinctive for its large puffy seed heads, which resemble spiny cucumbers. The resemblance is created by the perigynia, which are densely clustered and have long spiked tips. They make a great accent for dried arrangements when picked before they turn brown. Flowers are summer-blooming brown spikes. Grow in moist soil or water to 1 inch deep. Height 24–36 inches and spread 18 inches. Zones 4–11.

## *Carex lacustris*
lake sedge, sawgrass

Very similar to *Carex aquatilis*. A taller sedge, this species has blue-green leaves that can reach more than 3 feet in length. Its perigynium has distinctive ribbing and tapers to a point. Native to the eastern U.S. and Great Lakes region, lake sedge is often found growing along the shorelines of streams and lakes. Another similar species, *C. atherodes*, or slough sedge, has fuzzy, hairy leaves and perigynia and is more apt to be found in meadows and prairie potholes. *Carex lacustris* reaches 2–4 feet high and 18 inches wide. It does well in moist soil or water to 1 inch deep. Zones 4–11. It flowers with brown spikes in summer.

## *Carex lasiocarpa*
hairy fruited sedge

Grows in bogs and fens in northeastern U.S. and has fuzzy perigynia. It is a great little clumper that adds variety to a

Carex elata 'Knightshayes'

Carex muskingumensis
'Oehme'

Carex muskingumensis 'Little
Midge' and 'Oehme'

Carex muskingumensis
'Wachtposten'

wet meadow planting, and small birds love the seeds. This has spring flowers that start green and turn brown. Grow in moist soil or water to 4 inches deep. It will tolerate seasonal flooding as well. Height 18–24 inches, spread 24 inches. Grasshoppers and, especially, wooly caterpillars like this plant. Zones 3–11.

## Carex lupulina
**inflated tassel sedge**

Large puffy seed heads resemble spiny cucumbers and are great in dried arrangements. Native to the eastern U.S., this species tolerates considerable shade. It is a fitting choice for a wildlife garden. Flowers are green spikes sent up in spring. Foliage always has a yellow cast. Height 24 inches, spread 18 inches. Zones 6–11. Needs moist soil or water to 1 inch deep.

## Carex muskingumensis
**palm sedge**

A native of the eastern U.S., palm sedge looks like a bushy umbrella grass (*Cyperus*), or perhaps a dwarf water bamboo on steroids (*Dulichium arundinaceum*). It is often used in wetland reclamations. It is easy to grow and forms a clump much like a hosta. It tolerates full shade, yet also grows in full sun, where it will take on a gold-green cast. The green to tan flowers bloom in early summer and are borne on the ends of the stalks. Reaches 12–18 inches high and 12 inches wide. Does well in moist soil or water to 2 inches deep. Zones 4–9. Do not place this at the bottom of the pond to over-winter—it will not survive.

This species has prompted several distinctive selections. 'Ice Fountains' has white-streaked foliage in the spring or in areas of cool nights. It is similar to, and may be the same

Carex muskingumensis 'Little Midge'

plant as, 'Silberstreif' (silver stripe), which has white margins on its leaves and grows slightly smaller than the species. The wonderful 'Little Midge' comes from Limerock Nursery. Just 3–4 inches tall, this cute little sedge looks almost like pine moss or little pine trees. Great as a ground cover or in a small dish garden. 'Oehme' was a sport found in the garden of famed landscape designer Wolfgang Oehme. He gave a piece to Tony Avent of Plant Delights Nursery, who named it in honor of its discoverer. In spring, leaves are evenly green, but in summer the foliage becomes yellow margined and looks almost gilded. And 'Wachtposten' (sentry tower) is a large, more upright form with evenly dark green foliage.

*Carex pendula*

*Cephalanthus occidentalis*

## Carex pendula
### drooping sedge

As its common name suggests, this sedge has long brown flower spikes that dangle like earrings from tall, arching stems that reach 3–6 feet in height. It forms neat clumps 4–5 feet wide and self-sows freely in the moderately warm climate it prefers. Drooping sedge is native to Eurasia and northern Africa, rated hardy in Zone 6, possibly 5, to 11. Where it is not hardy, bring indoors to a sunny window in winter. It does well in moist soil or water to 4 inches deep. It is a favorite of grasshoppers.

'Moonraker' is a selection with heavily variegated foliage. Leaves are mostly cream-yellow with a green streak, especially in the spring. In some climates the variegation tends to fade in the summer and becomes a limey green. Friends in the northwestern U.S. report that it is a great hit, not fading in summer. 'Moonraker' grows somewhat true from seed, but varies a good deal—careful selections should be made from seed crops to ensure reliable variegation.

'Cool Jazz' is another selection, offering cool green leaves with a cream stripe down the center that lasts all summer.

## Carex spissa
### San Diego sedge

A large blue sedge much like a large blue form of *Carex pendula*. Native to southern California. Brown flowers bloom in spring. Grow in sun for the best color, but it will tolerate some shade. Reaches 5 feet tall and 4 feet wide. Does well in moist soil or water to 4 inches deep. Also tolerates seasonal flooding. It needs no special care to overwinter where hardy, Zones 7–11, but elsewhere bring indoors. It tends to self-sow, which can be avoided by cutting the seed heads.

## Carex stricta
### tussock sedge, marsh sedge, marsh hay

As the leaves of this sedge die off, they form a mounded clump, or "tussock," above the waterline. Native to eastern North America, tussock sedge is well suited to a natural garden or a shoreline and provides good cover for birds and frogs. It adds a great shape in the waterscape, too, like little fountains. Green flowers bloom in spring. Height 24–36 inches, spread 12–24 inches. Grow in moist soil or water to 2 inches deep. It tolerates seasonal flooding. Zones 4–9.

## Cephalanthus occidentalis
### button bush
### Rubiaceae

This aquatic woody ornamental is an unusual specimen, truly a shrub rather than a perennial. Each summer it bursts into flower with white globes that look like fluffy, round cotton balls. In the fall, the whole bush turns crimson. No cul-

Cicuta maculata

Combination planting including *Colocasia esculenta* 'Black Magic'

tivars have been formally named, but some very nice red-tipped forms are available, with red petioles and glossy foliage. Native to eastern North America, hardy in Zones 3–10. Grow in sun to part shade in moist soil or water to 18 inches deep. Reaches 3–6 feet high and 6–8 feet wide. No pests have been a problem in our gardens. Propagate by seed or hard or soft wood cuttings.

## Cicuta maculata
### water hemlock
### Apiaceae

*Cicuta maculata* is included here primarily for identification to prevent readers from planting it. It should never be added to a waterscape that is accessible to people. Water hemlock is highly poisonous, as its common name implies, and it has been called the "moist poisonous wild plant in the United States" (*Through the Looking Glass* by S. Borman, R. Korth, and J. Temte, 1997, University of Wisconsin Press: Stevens Point). The roots especially contain the toxin cicutoxin, as do other parts of the plant, which can cause death very quickly.

This North American native grows wild from Nova Scotia and Ontario south to Florida and inland to Missouri. Foliage is formed of three leaflets that are lance-shaped and sharply veined and toothed. Each leaflet is about ⅕–½ inches wide. The summer-blooming flowers are white, formed in umbels, and branch freely from the hollow main stem. It is very similar in appearance to *Sium suave* (water parsnip), for which it is sometimes mistaken, but the foliage of water hemlock gets finer as the plant grows, whereas that of water parsnip grows more coarse. A similar species, *Cicuta bulbifera* (bulb-bearing water hemlock), has narrower leaves no more than ⅕ inch wide and produces small bulbs at the leaf axils.

*Cicuta maculata* does best in part shade, reaching 3–6 feet high and wide. It grows in just moist soil or water up to 12 inches deep and tolerates seasonal flooding. Zones 4–11.

## Colocasia
### elephant ears, taro
### Aracaea

Bold and large-leafed, *Colocasia* is a genus of tender water plants that love lots of fertilizer and hot, humid weather. Commonly named taro or elephant ears because of the size and shape of their lobed leaves, they make dramatic accent plants in the pond. They are ideal for container gardens as well as full-sized ponds because of their eye-catching foliage and graceful habit. Full sun is not their preferred exposure outdoors, and they will produce larger leaves if protected from the afternoon sun.

To grow larger plants, use big pots and make sure to fertilize generously. Transplant every year to keep plants healthy and able to grow their best. Older plants and tubers tend to grow smaller and smaller tops and are more prone to rot.

Native to the tropics of Asia, *Colocasia* species have naturalized throughout most tropical regions of the world. More than 300 varieties are grown in the U.S., especially in Hawaii. Many are grown as a food crop, since all the plant parts can be eaten. Flowers, stems, and leaves are cooked while young and eaten as a vegetable. Leaves are also used to wrap other food and then steamed or baked. Tubers are made into poi, or are fried and sold as taro chips.

For the water garden, interest is more in the colorful leaf and petiole, the leaf stalk, of the cultivars. More often than not it is the petiole that comes in so many beautiful colors, and not the leaf. Concentrate on siting the plant to see "into" it to view the petioles. We tested 38 varieties of taros for their ornamental potential and found five with colored foliage,

Variety in leaves of *Colocasia*

Great range among petioles of *Colocasia*

and smokey colors in between. This plant gives the garden designer a whole palette of colors.

Propagate from corms that are divided away from the main plant, or from "huli" (top or side sprout). Take a ½-inch piece off the top of the main tuber along with the petiole. Let this dry at least overnight, longer if possible. I store mine for up to a month in a paper bag out of direct sun in temperatures between 50°F and 70°F.

Taros may be overwintered in colder climates by bringing them indoors and keeping the pot in a saucer of water in a warm, sunny room. They may also be dried down to a tuber, which can be stored in coarse vermiculite in a sealed container. The plants will also overwinter if they are simply dried down in their pots and left in a cool but frost-free, dark spot where they will remain dormant until brought out again in the spring.

Taros are attractive to quite a number of pests: spider mites, mealybugs, Japanese beetles, and occasionally aphids. In Hawaii, they may also be affected by pink root aphids. They seem susceptible to the incurable Dasheen mosaic virus as well.

one with interesting cup-shaped leaves, and 11 with colored petioles. The petiole colors ranged from purple-black to creamy honeydew-white, with pink, red, striped, streaked,

Planting the huli of *Colocasia*

*Colocasia esculenta*

*Colocasia esculenta* 'Metallica'

*Colocasia esculenta* 'Black Magic'

*Colocasia esculenta* 'Ualtia Pele'

## Colocasia esculenta
### green taro

Green taro makes a good backdrop for more delicate plants, whether in a container garden or a full-sized water feature. Green to pale yellow flowers bloom in summer. It reaches a height of 2–6 feet and spreads 2–4 feet. Grow it in sun to part shade in moist soil or water to 6 inches deep. Zones 9–11.

This species offers many selections in a wide variety of colors and forms. 'Akado' grows to more than 3 feet and displays coffee-colored stems. 'Black Magic' (sometimes sold as 'Jet Black Wonder') has leaves and petioles that are very dark, almost black purple. 'Bun Long' grows to 3 feet and has distinct crinkly, cupped, green foliage that faces upward. It gives a great, unusual texture to the water garden. 'Eleele Naioea' grows to only 2 feet and shows black petioles. 'Elepaio' has the striking look of leaves splattered with white paint. At times leaves are completely white, at other times they are barely touched. Leaves are large given the plant's shorter, 2-foot stature. The remarkable 'Matale' sports bright strawberry-red petioles against large green leaves edged in red. 'Metallica', commonly called violet-stemmed taro, is a particulary elegant cultivar with deep purple petioles and large, velvety, blue-green leaves. 'Nancy's Revenge' is known for a prominant white blotch in the center of the leaf. 'Purple Manalud' offers giant cranberry-colored petioles and big blue-green leaves with a red edge. Even the backs of the leaves have cranberry veins. It grows to 4½ feet tall. 'Ualtia Pele' (sometimes sold as 'Kanapaha' or 'Black Marble') is blue-green overlayed with purple smoke and flecks. Light purple petioles are streaked in dark purple. A perfect accent next to yellows and whites, it makes them shine. It grows to more than 3 feet.

*Colocasia jensii*

## Colocasia jensii
### black princess taro

Slightly shorter than some other taros, this species has bright green leaves with blue-purple blushing between the veining. Petioles are green. The effect is subtle and very pleasing. Plant has a clumping habit and blooms in summer with green flowers blushed with blue-purple. Height 2–4 feet, spread 2–4 feet. Grow in sun to part shade in moist soil or water to 6 inches deep. Zones 9–11.

## Cotula coronopifolia
### golden buttons
Asteraceae

*Cotula coronopifolia*

Accenting the fleshy foliage on this marginal are bright yellow buttons of flowers, reminiscent of daisies, that bloom in summer. It is delightful in the waterfall, at the pond's edge, or in a container water garden. A little shade, especially in the afternoon, helps to keep its bright green color and prevents it from wilting due to high heat and humidity. Height 10 inches, spread 12 inches. Zones 6–8. Native to South Africa. Grow in moist soil or water to 1 inch deep.

Seed propagation is possible—simply sow in moist soil and keep warm and wet—but golden buttons are most easily propagated from stem cuttings, since they root easily from the leaf nodes. Bringing stem cuttings indoors is the easiest way to overwinter in areas colder than Zone 6.

Golden buttons are generally easy to grow and are sometimes listed as invasive. We have found that our ornamental fish nibble on their stems and prevent them from taking over the pond. They also are attractive to mealybugs if not well fed and growing like mad.

## Crinum
**bog lily**
**Amaryllidaceae**

More than 130 species of *Crinum* live in tropical regions around the world. The genus name derives from the Greek word "crinos," meaning comet or hanging hair. The plants are noted for their large flowers composed of six long petals that droop or hang from the center of the blossom. Appearing in summer or early fall, they are very fragrant and look like starbursts. The flowers come in a range of colors from white to deep rose. Foliage is strap-like and leathery, similar to *Amaryllis*, which is a distant relative.

Depending on the species, *Crinum* grows in sun to shade and will range in height from 12 inches to 5 feet. The spread ranges from 12 inches to 4 feet. It tolerates seasonal flooding, but does best in moist soil or water to 2 inches deep. Hardy in Zones 7–11, *Crinum* will grow through the fall and winter in warm, tropical climates. In colder areas, it should be brought indoors and overwintered much like a houseplant. Watch for spider mites and mealybugs at this time.

*Crinum* is usually propagated by removing small offsets of new bulbs that grow from the main bulb. Seed of hybrids are often sterile. Species usually set some seed, which resemble little bulbs. Sow them immediately once they have ripened, by burying half the seed head in damp soil. Keep the seed warm and in bright light. A few years may pass before a new plant reaches sufficient maturity to flower.

Besides the following highlighted species, three others are often sold at pet shops but are not really showy for the pond: *Crinum calamistratum, C. natans, C. thaianum.*

*Crinum americanum*

## Crinum americanum
**water spider lily, swamp lily**

This is the most commonly available species of *Crinum* in North America. It grows wild from Florida southward into Mexico and through Central America into tropical South American regions. Flowers are usually white, although they may take on a pink blush. Blossoms may be as much as 4 inches in diameter and bloom in summer or fall. Grows in sun to only part shade, reaching 12–36 inches high and 12–48 inches wide. Does best in very wet soil or slightly under the water level.

Crinum erubescens 'West Indies'

## *Crinum erubescens* 'West Indies'
### Rastafari crinum

These *Crinum* species native to the West Indies have small white flowers that bloom in summer and little strap-like foliage like large *Liriope*. They make great ground cover, growing to just 10 inches high and spreading 12 inches. Grow in sun to part shade in moist soil or water to 4 inches deep. Zones 9–11. These species do not seem to be bothered by pests.

## *Cypella aquatica*
### water tulip, water orchid
### Iridaceae

An elegant plant for the water garden, *Cypella aquatica* has intense yellow flowers that resemble open tulips, or Chinese lanterns. They bloom in late spring to early summer. Leaves are cordate and resemble palm foliage. Height 12–36 inches, spread 12–36 inches. Grows from bulbs in moist soil or water to 2 inches deep in sun to part shade. Sometimes they are bothered by spider mites. Native to southern Brazil and northern Argentina. Hardy in Zones 9–11. Bring indoors for the winter, or dry down bulbs to be stored like cannas or tropical waterlilies.

Cypella aquatica

Cyperus on display in a container

Seed heads of different Cyperus species

## Cyperus
### Cyperaceae

Members of the sedge family, *Cyperus* species are mostly tropical water plants grown for their ornamental sprays of leaf fronds that resemble thin, papery palms. Overall, the effect is reminiscent of the paper parasols that come with children's "kiddie cocktail" drinks. The large heads are held high atop triangular stems that sprout from a central clump. The "flowers" are really the seed heads, generally small and green, turning tawny brown as the seed develop, usually on display in the summer. The overall appearance of the seed heads is unique to each species.

In ancient days, *Cyperus* foliage, especially from *C. papyrus*, was used to make paper products and to weave mats. Nowadays the plants are useful and attractive accents in the water landscape. One can select a different species of *Cyperus* to suit almost any type of pond. On some the grassy heads are open, with thin and wiry leaves, but others are dense, bushy, and full. Species range in size from very large to very small. Larger specimens are stunning as a central focal point in the waterlily pond. Mixed with other large, tropical water plants, they make the bold statement of tropicalismo possible even in the water garden. *Cyperus* plants provide shade at the edge of the pond and give some relief to shorter plants that benefit from being protected from the sun. All are heavy feeders and should be fertilized at least once a month. Besides their ornamental value, they are also excellent for pond filtration. Only a few species are hardy in colder regions. Most are tender tropic-lovers that will not withstand exposure to freezing temperatures. They overwinter easily in the sunny house or a greenhouse and are suitable as houseplants. They are occasionally bothered by mealybugs, however, when brought indoors in winter.

Although *Cyperus* species may be propagated from division, some are often grown by cutting off the leaf heads just

*Cyperus* foliage

*Cyperus alternifolius*

below the joint with the stem. Trim the fronds to 1 inch, and float the heads in water. They will soon sprout new stems and roots, and can be planted into a pot with soil. This method works for *C. alternifolius*, *C. isocladus*, and *C. textilis*. *Cyperus* species also grow easily from seed—sow on moist soil and keep warm until they sprout.

### Cyperus albostriatus
**broadleaf umbrella grass**

A most striking plant for the container water garden, growing 18 inches high and wide. Highly variegated, individual leaves are broad, almost 1 inch wide, and several inches long, making the head of this species very full and showy. Stems are also striped in white. Seed heads are displayed all year. It resents too much water and will falter if grown with moisture over its crown. For this reason it is best situated in sun to part shade at the very edge of the pond margin, where the

soil stays just evenly moist. Native to southern Africa, it is hardy in Zones 9–11. Where not hardy, bring it indoors and treat as a houseplant for the winter. Propagate by division— seed head will not sprout, for this species is not viviparous.

A popular cultivar is 'Variegatus'. I have noticed two forms of this plant. One, a light green and white, seems to be more available. The other is a deep green with white stripes.

### Cyperus alternifolius (syn. C. involucratus)
**umbrella grass**

This species name and its synonym are so mixed up in the water garden trade that controversy still surrounds them. *Cyperus alternifolius* is the standard umbrella grass most commonly sold to hobby pondkeepers. It is popular for its easy nature and relaxed habit. At 4–6 feet high, it sports a top sprout of leaves that can grow up to 2 feet across in mature specimens, forming the characteristic umbrella

*Cyperus alternifolius* 'Denver Giant'

*Cyperus alternifolius* 'Nanus'

*Cyperus alternifolius* 'Gracilis'

shape for which the plant is named. Individual leaves are generally narrow, about ½ inch wide, but grow to 12 inches or more in length. The plant retains its clean, green color all year long in the warm climate it prefers.

It needs little care other than regular feeding during the spring and summer, and the occasional trimming of brown tips of the leaves. Situate in sun to part shade in moist soil or water to 6 inches deep or more. A quick grower, spreading 24 inches wide, umbrella grass usually requires division every few years. If not divided, the center tends to become woody and empty of foliage. New stems grow from the outer edge of the base, creating a ring around the corky middle of the plant. This species is viviparous and can be propagated by preparing the mature tops to root and produce new plants. Seed can also be sown and will sprout readily. Like grass seed, just sow on the surface of moist soil at 70°F and do not cover.

*Cyperus alternifolius* 'Nanus'

Green young seed head of *Cyperus distans*

This native of Madagascar will tolerate light frosts but not prolonged cold weather. The crown must never be allowed to freeze. Rated hardy for Zones 7–11. In colder climates, bring in tops and float in water, or bring plant indoors, placing pot in a cat-litter tray of water in a sunny, frost-free location.

'Gracilis' (syn. 'Strictus'), miniature umbrella grass, is usually listed as a selection of *Cyperus involucratus*. It has very narrow leaves that give the head a very fine-cut appearance. Refined and elegant, it is well suited to smaller water gardens and table-top ponds, or as a companion plant to bonsai. Grows 12 inches tall the first season and 24 inches the next. Its spread is rather narrow at 12 inches. Give moist soil or water to 4 inches deep.

'Nanus', dwarf umbrella grass, is also usually listed as a selection of *Cyperus involucratus*. It is a compact plant with long umbrella fronds. Although it is shorter than the species, it is taller and lankier than 'Gracilis'. Height 2–4 feet, spread 2–4 feet.

'Variegatus', variegated umbrella grass, offers an even more striking accent in the pond. It is a compact plant–24 inches high and wide—that has irregular white stripes on its long umbrella fronds. It reverts regularly and for no known reason; often all-green plants become variegated again. Beautiful at its peak but difficult to keep there.

'Denver Giant' is a variety that I received from the butterfly garden in Denver where I first saw it growing. Frond heads were 24 inches across and stood 8–9 feet tall—truly an enormous plant for really large scale settings. In my own outside garden it has not attained that height, but it is definitely larger than the others.

*Cyperus giganteus*

*Cyperus distans*

## *Cyperus distans*
**crowned umbrella grass**

The seed heads of this umbrella grass, appearing in the summer, are large and puffy and turn a toasty brown color, giving the plant the appearance of being crowned. Tufts of foliage at its feet make the plant look even more full and regal. Because it can seed itself profusely over the pond, cut off the older foliage and seed heads. Save this seed to start new plants the next season, or bring the plant indoors as a houseplant for the winter. Hardy in Zones 8–11 and native to tropical Asia. *Cyperus distans* grows in sun to shade and moist soil or water to 3 inches deep. Height 30 inches and spread 18 inches. Watch for damage from grasshoppers.

## *Cyperus giganteus*
**Mexican papyrus**

A favorite of many water gardeners, Mexican papyrus has 20-inch spheres of wiry foliage on stiff, very erect, non-arching stems. The overall effect resembles balls of stars. The leaves are flat, rather than the round strands of standard *C. papyrus*. Grows in sun to part shade in moist soil or water to 6 inches deep. Height 5–12 feet, spread 4–5 feet. Native to Mexico and south to South America, rated hardy in Zones 8–11.

Propagate by seed or division. The seed seems to need long days to sprout. Lengthening the short days of winter to more than 12 hours will get them to sprout faster. To overwinter, bring indoors to a bright spot and keep well watered or even place the pot in a shallow tray of water. Keep temperatures above 50°F. During the winter mealybugs may be a problem.

## *Cyperus isocladus* (syn. *C. prolifer*)
**dwarf papyrus**

This compact plant has tight tufts of green strands atop its many stems. It looks like standard *Cyperus papyrus*, only about one-tenth the size. Perfect for a tub garden or table-top pond. Give it sun to part shade and moist soil or water to 4 inches deep. Height 12–18 inches, spread 6–12 inches. Sow seed on wet soil, or propagate from the viviparous top fronds. Overwinter indoors in a sunny spot and keep soil moist at all times, but do not submerge the crown. Watch for mealybugs. Keep winter temperatures above 50°F. Native to eastern Africa and Madagascar. Zones 9–11. This species is sometimes confused with *C. haspan*, but true *C. haspan* is native to Florida and is not really ornamental, more weedy than not.

*Cyperus isocladus*

*Cyperus isocladus*

*Cyperus isocladus* on the patio

*Cyperus isocladus*

*Cyperus longus*

*Cyperus longus*

## Cyperus longus
**hardy umbrella grass, sweet galingale**

Although it is known as the hardy form of umbrella grass, it has also been called sweet galingale because of its pleasing fragrance. This plant is not as showy as its tropical relatives, either. The frond heads have only five leaves or so, instead of the dozen or more that are common on other forms of *Cyperus*. Also, the leaves stand more upright, rather than hanging outward at a right angle from the main stem. Unlike other *Cyperus* species, this one has a running habit.

It is striking in large patches, growing 2–4 feet high. It likes a slightly more acidic soil than the 8.5 pH I have. Closer to neutral produces better plants. It takes sun to part shade and moist soil or water to 6 inches deep, tolerating seasonal flooding. Minor damage from grasshoppers may occur. It is most easily propagated by division in spring, but can also be raised from seed. Over the winter it must go dormant to maintain strong growth but needs no special care where hardy. Zones 4–8. Native to Europe, Asia, and northern Africa.

## Cyperus radiatus
**cosmic cyperus**

The fronds of this species are irregular, giving it a rather spiky appearance. Seed heads appear in the frond and are a deep, rich, chestnut brown. The effect is very striking. Foliage also grows at the base of the plant, making it lush and full. Native to tropical Asia, this plant takes sun to part shade and moist soil or water to 3 inches deep. Height 4 feet, spread 24 inches. Propagate by seed or division, and over-winter by bringing indoors and treating as a houseplant. Zones 8–11.

*Cyperus longus*

## *Cyperus papyrus*
### papyrus

Papyrus is stunning in any garden pond. It has 10-inch balls of long green threads atop a plant 5–12 feet high and 4–5 feet wide. It is understandable why papyrus always looks impressive. This is the plant the Egyptians used to make their paper, or papyrus, where the plant gets its name. Grows in sun to part shade in moist soil or water to 6 inches deep. Native to northern Africa. Zones 8–11.

Seed gives the nicest plants. Like Mexican papyrus (*Cyperus giganteus*), these need extra daylight, at least 12 hours, to sprout. Surface sow on moist or wet soil at 70–75°F. Division is possible, but you will need a chainsaw.

Keep the plants above 60°F through the winter for best results. I find that temps below that cause blinding of the buds on the rootstocks—they may look healthy but do not get any new growth. Mealybugs may be a wintertime problem.

Two selections are worth seeking out. 'Zebra' from San Marcos Growers in Santa Barbara, California, has yellow banding on the stems, and 'Miniature' is about 3 feet tall and small in all ways. It is not the strongest grower but looks great in small ponds.

*Decodon verticillatus*

## *Cyperus fluviatilis* (syn. *Bolboschoenus fluviatilis, Scirpus fluviatilis*)
**giant nut grass**

This plant is noted for its tall, emerald-green, spiky foliage, almost bamboo-like. It is a runner, covering 2–4 feet in a season. It looks great in stands along a lake or in large ponds or detention basins. Grows in full sun or full shade and moist soil or water to 6 inches deep. Reaches a height of 4 feet. Its flower-like seed heads wait to shine until late summer. Native to eastern North America. Zones 4–8. Propagating by division is easiest.

## *Decodon verticillatus*
**swamp loosestrife, water willow**
Lythraceae

Leaves of this very showy plant are lance-shaped and grouped around each squarish stem in sets of twos or threes.

Blooms are a purplish pink and sit close to the leaf axils, borne in summer along the stems as they arch over the water. Seeds form soon after. Stems become woody as they mature—they root and form new plants where they arch into the water. Not invasive. The fall color is blazing red-orange and yellow. It looks like a cross between *Buddleja* and purple loosestrife (*Lythrum salicaria*).

Excellent in large ponds and lakes where it can be used as a hedge, much like burning bush (*Euonymus elatus*). It also makes a good single specimen. Height 4 feet, spread 4–6 feet. Grow in sun to part shade in wet soil or water to 24 inches deep. Zones 3–9. Native to North America, from Florida and Louisiana to Maine and Ontario, westward into Illinois. No special care or protection is needed for overwintering—it fares well in colder climates. It roots freely from stem cuttings, and may also be grown from seed. Japanese beetles and various other beetles may be a problem, but none will kill it outright.

*Dichromena colorata*

*Dichromena latifolia*

## *Dichromena colorata* (syn. *Rhynchospora colorata*)
**white top sedge**
Cyperaceae

White top sedge has seed bracts that resemble 3-inch white stars floating above grassy foliage. The flowers themselves are very small, fuzzy things clustered at the center of the bract. After a time, both the flowers and the surrounding spikes turn a light brown, retaining their star-like appearance. They make excellent cut arrangements and also dry well.

White top sedge is a tender aquatic native to North America, with a natural range that extends from Virginia into Florida and westward into Texas. It has a running habit and is best confined to a pot. It will reach a height of 12–24 inches. Situate in sun to part shade in moist soil or water to 1 inch deep. Divide after a few years, since the plant will spread in a circle around the outer edge and in a few years' time the center of the pot will have few sprouts of new foliage, if any at all. Division of the running rhizomes is the best way to propagate, but it may also be started from seed.

It requires no special care or maintenance and appreciates monthly doses of fertilizer. Hardy in Zones 8–11, it overwinters well in a greenhouse or sunny room in the house.

*Dichromena colorata* is closely related to *D. latifolia*, and the two are often sold interchangeably at nurseries and garden centers. The white seed heads of *D. latifolia* are about one-third larger than those of *D. colorata*. A third species, *D. floridensis*, is smaller and much wispier than *D. colorata* and is good for a small pond or wet meadow.

The species in the genus *Dichromena* have recently been reclassified into the genus *Rhynchospora* but are generally still sold as *Dichromena*. The dichromenas look completely different from any of the original rhynchosporas. Dichromenas grow in loose sods and have orange roots. They are free-flowering and tolerate a wide range of moisture regimes, from fully submerged in spring floods to hot and dry in the summer. They are a great addition to detention ponds and wet grassy areas.

*Dulichium arundinaceum* 'Tigress'

*Dulichium arundinaceum* 'Tigress'

## *Dulichium arundinaceum*
**dwarf water bamboo, three-way sedge**
**Cyperaceae**

True to its common name, the upright, bright green foliage of this 3-foot-tall water plant resembles bamboo, with thin, tapered leaves that stand away from the stems at sharp angles. It is also called three-way sedge for the leaves' tendency to grow in three distinct directions around the stem, a habit apparent by looking straight down on the stem from above. Looking closer will reveal that the leaves spiral in a clockwise direction on some stems, but counterclockwise on others. It is not a true sedge since its stems are round and hollow, not triangular as the sedges are.

Dwarf water bamboo does not have showy flowers, but instead has small brown tassels along the top third of each stem. These bloom in summer. It grows well in full sun or full shade, an added bonus for water gardeners searching for distinctive plants for a shaded pond. It reaches 12–14 inches tall in sun, taking on a yellow cast, but stays a deep green and reaches 36 inches tall in shade. It forms an excellent background to shorter, more showy plants, such as bacopas and alternantheras. With its somewhat unusual foliage, it lends an Oriental flair to the pond.

'Tigress', a new cultivar selection discovered at Charleston Aquatic Nurseries in South Carolina, has clean white margins on each leaf. Very attractive and highly ornamental. Seed heads are white, not brown.

Dwarf water bamboo has a running habit but resents being transplanted—it should not be divided too frequently. To propagate, divide the rhizomes early in the spring before substantial growth has begun. Hardy in Zones 5–11, it can survive a solid freeze provided it is kept in the water. Grow it in moist soil or water to 2 inches deep. Native to North America, growing wild from Newfoundland and British Columbia south to Florida and California.

### Echinodorus
### melon sword
### Alismataceae

Melon sword is noted for its foliage, which is usually lance-shaped, sword-shaped, or spoon-shaped. Many species are grown as aquarium plants because of their attractive underwater appearance. Water gardeners find them interesting for their out-of-water look. The flowers are white and bloom in summer, or year-round where active growth can take place. They are easy to grow and require little maintenance, though they quickly outgrow their pots and benefit from repotting every few years.

Melon sword may be propagated by dividing side plants that can be found at the crown of the mother plant. Often it is grown from the plantlets that sprout where flowers have set. The cultivar *Echinodorus cordifolius* 'Marble Queen' is especially viviparous, setting so many new plantlets that it resembles the common spider plant often sold as a houseplant.

The genus *Echinodorus* is native to many of the warmer regions of the Americas. It generally overwinters well in cool regions, but in areas of considerable frost bring the plant indoors to a greenhouse or warm sunny room for the winter. Mealybugs can be a problem in winter.

I have grown 20 or more selections and species of *Echinodorus*. Many I picked up from the aquarium trade or from collectors. Some very good ones are not readily available in the trade but are worth searching out. They all take the same care but are more tropical than *E. cordifolius*, hardy only to Zone 9 and above.

*Echinodorus cordifolius* growing wild in Missouri

### Echinodorus 'Barthii'
### red melon sword

New growth is red-black. Flower stalks are generally unbranched red sepals with white flowers of ¾–1 inch. Grows in a bird-nest style, reaching 8–10 inches tall and wide. It likes half days of shade.

### Echinodorus cordifolius (syn. *E. radicans*)

This elegant aquatic has all the characteristics for which melon sword is known—clusters of large spoon-shaped leaves and sprays of white summertime flowers that resemble cascades of single roses. The plant grows in a clump and keeps to itself, not trying to force its presence upon other parts of the pond. When not in flower, melon sword can be difficult to distinguish from water plantain (*Alisma*). To tell them apart, gently squeeze the leaf stem. Melon sword has stiff, triangular stems, but those of water plantain are soft and more rounded.

*Echinodorus cordifolius*

Melon swords are highly variable based on where the original plants come from. Native to the central and southern U.S. and into Mexico, this species grows naturally as a submerged or marginal plant in the southern regions of the Mississippi River. It takes sun to part shade and moist soil or water to 6 inches deep. Height 24–36 inches, spread 36 inches. Zones 5b–11.

### Echinodorus cordifolius 'Marble Queen'

The showy creamy white patches on the large spoon-shaped foliage of this melon sword add further beauty to an already noteworthy plant. Just as floriferous as its all-green sibling, with white flowers about 1 inch across blooming in summer. Give full to part shade and moist soil or water to 6 inches deep. This selection can grow submerged and will tolerate seasonal flooding. Height 12–24 inches, spread 24 inches. Zones 5b–11.

### Echinodorus grandiflorus 'Greens Giant'

This selection is tall and vase-shaped. It is probably the tallest melon sword, with flower stalks reaching 6 feet high. Flowers are about 1 inch. The leaves reach to about 5 feet tall, but this is mostly petiole, with leaves about 8–10 inches wide and 12–14 inches long. Foliage is yellow-green. It grows best in part shade, preferably afternoon shade. It produces adventitious plants.

### Echinodorus grisebachii

Foliage reaches 12 inches tall and flower spikes 18 inches. The abundant flower spikes are red-black, flowers are white, and leaves are spoon-shaped. Great in containers.

### Echinodorus horizontalis

Very similar in size and performance to *Echinodorus cordifolius*, and sometimes sold as such, but it is not as hardy.

### Echinodorus macrophyllus

The foliage of this species has a very different look—the sinus often overlaps, cupping the leaves. Most other features are similar to *Echinodorus cordifolius*, and it is often sold is such, but this species is also not as hardy, surviving in Zone 8 and up.

*Echinodorus cordifolius* 'Marble Queen'

### Echinodorus opacus

A nice compact plant for small ponds and containers. Reaches 12 inches high and wide. Flowers stand above the foliage and are ½–¾ inch across. Sometimes sold as a compact *Echinodorus cordifolius*.

### Echinodorus 'Oriental'

New foliage is pink-rose and fades to green with maturity. It is a nice contrast. Grows to 12 inches high and wide in part or full shade.

### Echinodorus osiris

Leaves of this species are copper-colored in new growth. Otherwise, it looks like a small *Echinodorus cordifolius*, growing to about 10 inches high and wide. A variegated form exists and is very showy in ponds and containers.

### Echinodorus 'Ozelot'

Green foliage with red flecks in the new growth. Flowers are relatively few. It prefers shade for half the day, reaching 10 inches high and wide.

### Echinodorus 'Ozelot Marble'

The foliage has the look of being covered with a white netting. New growth has a slight red tint. Grows to 10 inches high and wide in part or full shade.

*Echinodorus palaefolius*

## Echinodorus palaefolius
**giant melon sword**

This giant has the largest leaves of the melon swords, about 18 inches across. They are round and cup-shaped. The leaves rise to 36 inches and the flower stalks to 5 feet. Hundreds of 2-inch flowers are borne all summer long. Propagate by seed or division. It does not produce offsets on the flower stalks.

## Echinodorus paniculatus

Tall, narrow, upright plants look much like *Sagittaria rigida*. It produces many flower stalks and many 1-inch flowers. Grows to 36 inches or higher. It makes a good combination with *Pontederia cordata* or in among cattails and reeds (*Typha* and *Scirpus*).

## Echinodorus parvifolius
**black sword**

Black sword produces ¾-inch flowers on stalks no taller than the leaves. The plants are very full, reaching 12–15 inches high and wide.

## Echinodorus 'Red Flame' (syn. 'Ozelot Nova')

Reaching 12 inches high and wide, this cultivar grows in part or full shade. Flowers are relatively few. The leaves have more red than 'Ozelot' and the color lasts longer into their maturity.

## Echinodorus 'Rose'

Leaves are spoon-shaped and have dark petioles. New growth is copper-colored. Plants grow to 10 inches high and wide. Flowers reach above the foliage.

## Echinodorus 'Rubin'

Small plants grow to just 8 inches high and wide. The ½-inch flowers reach above the foliage. Leaves are red in new growth and are twice as long as wide. This cultivar is very similar to 'Rose'.

## Echinodorus schlueter

Leaves are wavy or ruffled, and flowers are abundant. Sometimes sold as *Echinodorus cordifolius*, this species is very compact and full looking, reaching 12–24 inches tall. 'Leopard' is a red-specked form, but this is only on new growth and quickly fades.

## Echinodorus subulatus

This species reaches 24–36 inches tall and wide, with flowers stalks no taller than the leaves. It is very full and bushy. Petioles are dark, sometimes red.

All green and taller by 4–6 inches, but much narrower, is *Echinodorus subulatus* subsp. *andrieuxii*. Both individual leaves and the plant as a whole are half as wide as the species. This is probably what is often sold as *E.* 'Rigidifolius'.

## Echinodorus tenellus

This very small species reaches just 2 inches tall and has a spreading habit. It is great in streams or floating islands. It was sent to me as frogbit (*Limbonium spongeanum*).

## *Echinodorus uruguayensis*

This species is generally a thin, narrow plant. Narrow foliage is highly variable, depending on the parent stock. It generally reaches 24 inches tall with 3-inch-wide leaves, spreading to 12 inches. Sometimes it has red new growth.

## *Eleocharis*
## hair grass
## Cyperaceae

The genus *Eleocharis* comprises 150 species, including varieties that can be found virtually everywhere in the world. Many of these species are aquatic, growing emerged in the shallow waters of marshes, ponds, and streams. They grow from rhizomes or stolons and bear brown spikelets that look something like heads on a matchstick. Many species are native to North America. They are distinguished by the shape of their leaves and, most especially, by the size and shape of their mature fruit (spikelets and nutlets). Several species have long been used as food crops for their rhizomes that are high in carbohydrates, such as water chestnut (*E. dulcis*). In the U.S., many forms of wildlife eat the fruit on the spiked heads of the foliage, as well as the leaves and rhizomes. Other species are sought for their foliage, which is woven into mats. Large stands of *Eleocharis* help to prevent soil erosion and provide cover to amphibians at the shoreline.

*Eleocharis* species most commonly available to water gardeners are emergent forms with the characteristic straight stems topped with brown heads. Submerged selections are also cultivated for aquariums and may be grown as oxygenating plants in the pond. In the water landscape, *Eleocharis* makes an unusual accent plant. It provides an upright, architectural backdrop for shorter, creeping plants. It is easy to grow and requires little care. Propagate by division or seed, which can be hard to find for those unfamiliar with the plant. Hardiness varies among the different species. Those that are cold tolerant will usually withstand being frozen in the pond and need not be put to the lowest depths of the water garden. More tender selections should be submerged to avoid freezing temperatures. Voles and mice love to overwinter in thick blankets of these plants.

## *Eleocharis acicularis*
## needle rush hair grass

Thin blades of grass-like foliage resemble red fescue (*Festuca rubra*), the main component of seed sold for shady lawns. Summertime flowers are green. This species is great along the shore or in detention ponds needing a grasslike plant to hold the soil, yet that is mowable and can take light

*Eleocharis dulcis*

traffic. This species forms excellent sod. Grow in sun to part shade in moist soil, or grow submerged. It reaches 12 inches high and has a running spread that will cover about 12 inches square in a season in the Chicago area. Geese are really hard on this plant, feeding on it in spring. Native to all of North America. Zones 3–11.

## *Eleocharis dulcis* (syn. *E. tuberosa*)
## Chinese water chestnut

This is the plant that yields the water chestnuts we eat in stir fries. It grows like green drinking straws. Bright green plants form a stand of green tufts 24–36 inches tall. Each tuft will spread no more than 12 inches, but each plant will produce lots of tufts depending on heat and fertilizer. Brown flowers in summer. Situate in sun to part shade in moist soil or water to 6 inches deep. Propagate by dividing the rhizomes. Overwinter indoors as a houseplant or dry down the tubers that form on the ends of the rhizomes and store in a moist but

*Eleocharis acicularis*

*Eleocharis parvula* topiary

not wet place. Zones 8–11. Native to tropical Asia. Mice, voles, and muskrats are probable winter pests, but I have never noted them because I harvest the water chestnuts.

### *Eleocharis obtusa* (syn. *E. montevidensis*) spiked rush

With its many spiked stems, this plant looks like a little hedgehog. Stems are fragile and break easily in heavy rain, but recover and resprout quickly. Situate in sun to part shade in moist soil or water to 2 inches deep. Height 12 inches, spread 12 inches. Native to North America. Hardy in Zones 3–11. Geese can be pests when grown in large ponds.

Be careful not to handle or brush the stems too often while the brown clubs appear in summer or the plant will freely seed itself around the pond. But it plays well with others, not taking over and killing other plants. It grows in sites that are open. Propagate by division or seed. Seed is best sown fresh but can be stored. I find the seed is easier to

sprout if sown and left outside for the winter underwater or in flooded trays. In spring then lower the water level until the soil is just wet and they will sprout easily.

### *Eleocharis parvula* miniature rush

Looking more like moss or bent grass, this tiny fine-bladed plant is great for lining streams and ponds or for dripping fountains, aquatic topiary, or miniature water gardens. Displays silver-green flowers in summer. Situate in sun or shade—it does fine in low light. Height 2 inches with a creeping spread. Grow submerged or in moist soil. Native from Minnesota to the tropics. Zones 3–11. Propagate by division—simply cut out little squares of the sod and place on wet soil. Protect this species from both grass carp and geese, which will destroy it.

*Epilobium hirsutum*

*Equisetum*

## *Eleocharis vivipara*
**miniature jumping rush**

This species looks like thin green hair-like strands with little plants formed on the ends. Flowers are silver-green and bloom in summer. It is great in small ponds and container ponds and is also nice in waterfalls and streams. Native to the coastal plain of the southeastern U.S. Zones 9–11. Bring indoors where not hardy and treat as a houseplant, but watch for mealybugs. Grow in sun to part shade in moist soil, or grow it submerged entirely. Height 12 inches, spread 18 inches. Propagate by division or plant up the little plants from the ends of the stems.

## *Epilobium hirsutum*
**pink water jewel**
Onagraceae

This is a moisture-loving perennial in need of moist to wet soil and tolerant of seasonal flooding. Situate in sun to part shade. Height 18 inches, spread 6 inches. With pink flowers blooming in summer, it is a great performer in wet gardens and marginal plantings. Native to Europe. Zones 5–7. Propagation is very easy by surface sowing the seed. White and pale pink forms are also available.

## *Equisetum*
**horsetail, scouring rush**
Equisetaceae

The genus *Equisetum* is the only member of its family, the Equisetaceae. Roughly 30 species are in the genus; only a few are truly aquatic although several will adapt well to wet soils. They grow wild in most temperate areas of the world. They are easily identified by their straight, hollow stems, which are grooved. Each joint is a distinct part of the stem and has a black band at its edge. They reproduce by spores that are borne on cones that grow atop each stem and so are classified as cryptogams, plants that bear no flowers or seeds.

Equisetum fluviatile

Equisetum hyemale

*Equisetum* is commonly called horsetail because the stems resemble the tail of a horse. This is also a direct translation of the Latin name: *equus* for horse and *setrum* for tail. Fossils of horsetail have been found in the U.S. and in Europe. They are said to date from the Carboniferous period, and at that time were truly giant in proportion. Our contemporary species are generally much smaller. Like their ancestors, though, they contain high qualities of minerals, vitamins, salts, and silica. The plants' uptake of silica, which is deposited as silica crystals in their tissue, causes their stems to be hard and gritty. For this characteristic they were much favored for scrubbing pots and pans and earned another common name, scouring rush. They were also once used medicinally to treat illnesses. Modern research has discovered that *Equisetum* extracts have an enzyme that destroys thiamine. Equisetums are grazed by wildfowl, muskrats, and moose, and they are an important food source for breeding trumpeter swans.

Most species are extremely cold tolerant, hardy to Zone 4 at least. They will survive freezing temperatures and last through the winter at the edge of the pond, leaving no need to move them below the frost line. Equisetums are usually propagated by dividing their underground rhizomes in the spring, although they will tolerate division during summer or early fall.

### Equisetum fluviatile
**water horsetail**

A true aquatic, water horsetail requires water to survive— from fully moist soil to floating—and will not invade its terrestrial neighbors. It has green stalks with large black bands accented by thin pink bands. This species will sprout from stem sections that contain a joint when the section is floated in water. Water horsetail branches freely and grows very thin, long side shoots that radiate from each main stem. Stems are not perennial like those of *Equisetum hyemale*. Situate in sun to shade. Height 24 inches with a running spread. Native to Canada and the Great Lakes area, south to Indiana. Zones 4–11. Coots may feed on this in the spring.

### Equisetum hyemale
**common horsetail**

This species of *Equisetum* grows equally well in wet or dry soil, but not with its crown under the waterline. It can be a bit of a thug in the garden because of its running habit, and so is best always kept in a pot. Stems often remain green throughout the winter, even in colder climates. Situate in sun to part shade. Height 24 inches with a running spread. Native from Newfoundland to Guatemala. Zones 4–11. Division is the simplest method of propagation.

For some variety, *Equisetum* 'Bandit' has yellow striping in the stalks. *Equisetum hyemale* 'Robustum' is larger than the species by a third with thicker stems up to ½ inch across.

*Equisetum scirpoides*

## *Equisetum palustre*
### marsh horsetail

This well branched plant looks like little Christmas trees. It grows in loose stands in shaded areas or part shade. It gives a very woodsy effect but take caution: this plant runs and is almost impossible to get rid of once established. It does not do well in hot weather, however, and can look toasty in temperatures over 90°F. It needs moist soil or water to 2 inches deep. It tolerates seasonal flooding and does not like drying out. Height 12–14 inches. Zones 2–6. Native to Canada and the Great Lakes region.

## *Equisetum scirpoides*
### dwarf horsetail

Native to North America and evergreen in most areas. It has diminutive, needle-like foliage that serves as a good cover in a bog garden or near the edge of the pond. Height 8 inches with a running spread. Needs moist soil and tolerates seasonal flooding but will not grow in any depth of water. Situate in sun to part shade. Zones 4–9. 'Contorta' is a twisted form—the plant looks like a wad of steel wool.

## *Equisetum sylvaticum*
### wood horsetail, swamp horsetail

This very pretty, airy plant looks like little Douglas firs or hemlocks. Keep it contained, which also keeps it from spreading itself too thin, and situate in part to full shade. Full sun will cause it to yellow, if not kill it. Height 18 inches with a running spread. Needs wet soil and can take seasonal flooding. Zone 3 and up. Native to North America.

## *Equisetum telmateia*
### giant horsetail

Like *Equisetum sylvaticum* but larger and bushier, like a big fluffy fox's tail. It is very green and well branched. It is one of my favorite plants, but it hates the high pH in my nursery. Best in acidic soils in part shade in seasonally high water or seeps and wet streamsides (moist soil or water to 4 inches deep). It can be very invasive and must be contained. Reaches 30 inches high in my experience, though some sources claim 8 feet. Zone 6 and up. Native to the western U.S.

## *Eriocaulon*
### pipewort, hat pins
### Eriocaulaceae

Small fleshy leaves like irises or grasses form a tuft at the base of the plant. Out of this tuft a stiff stem arises holding a gray-white button on top in summer. It looks very much like an old-fashioned ladies' hat pin. The different species vary in size, from 12 to 30 inches tall. *Eriocaulon decangulare* is the largest and the showiest at over 24 inches tall, and *E. compressum* is just as showy but only 18 inches tall. Otherwise, the species look the same and require the same culture. Give sun to part shade and wet soil or water to 6 inches deep. Spreads to 12 inches. Propagate by division, but when the plants are healthy and strong they will seed freely. Most are native to coastal North America from New Jersey to Texas. One species, *E. aquaticum*, is hardy into Canada and is found in the acidic waters of the Great Lakes region. Hardy in Zones 4–5. Where it is not hardy, bring indoors and treat as a houseplant for the winter, being sure to keep it wet.

## *Eriophorum*
### cotton grass
### Cyperaceae

*Eriophorum* is commonly referred to as cotton grass because of the hair-like white tufts of perianth bristles on the flower heads that continue all summer and the thin, grass-like foliage that grows in dense clumps. It is not truly a grass but instead is a sedge, with triangular leaves that have sharp edges. Cotton grass does best in cooler climates and is not a stout water plant in southern regions with hot, muggy summers. Native to bogs, it grows best in neutral to acidic water, and will not tolerate ponds with alkaline water. It often grows wild in cranberry bogs with other acid-loving plants and shrubs, such as bog rosemary and blueberry (*Andromeda glaucophylla* and *Vaccinium*). It is very useful in large groups, like in a wet meadow or carnivorous plant bog.

*Eriophorum* species can be found throughout the northern hemisphere and many are listed as native to the U.S. and Canada. They all look about the same and grow with basically the same needs. Full sun is best, but just morning sun farther south will help keep them from overheating. Height 10–24 inches with a running spread. They are best containerized if not designed to be a drift, or they will look rather sparse. Keep soil wet or under 2 inches of water. Most species can take seasonal flooding—in spring, because the water is colder, it holds more oxygen. Propagate by dividing the rhizomes in early spring, but they may also be grown from seed. The seed is so wet, though, that it needs three months of cold stratification. Hardiness ranges vary, but they usually overwinter well at the edge of the pond. Voles and mice love these plants and will eat any parts that are not submerged.

### *Eriophorum angustifolium*
**narrow-leafed cotton grass**

In late spring or early summer, narrow-leafed cotton grass is covered with large flower tufts that lift and sway in the slightest breeze. It is distinguished from the standard cotton grass (*Eriophorum latifolium*) by its narrower foliage. Height 8–40 inches. Native to North America from Greenland to Alaska and from New York through Iowa to Washington. It is common in the U.K. and native to Eurasia. Some sources say it ranges the furthest south of all the cotton grasses, reaching into northern New Mexico. Zones 3–7. This species seems to be unappealing to mice and voles.

### *Eriophorum gracile*
**slender cotton grass**

Native to northern North America, growing from Canada down into Indiana and northern California and Colorado. It also grows in Eurasia. The flower heads reach 24 inches high, though the leaves will stop at about two-thirds that height. Zones 3 or 4–5. Pests are not a problem for this species.

### *Eriophorum latifolium*
**broadleaf cotton grass**

This is possibly the prettiest cotton grass, with multiple, very white tufts of seeds on wands extending well above the foliage. Height 24–30 inches. It forms tussocks, then sends out runners to form new tussocks—it is very grassy. Spreads 12 inches or runs. Though less common than *Eriophorum angustifolium*, it is considered the standard for the genus. Native to Eurasia. Zones 3 or 4–5.

*Eriophorum vaginatum*

### *Eriophorum vaginatum*
**hare's tail cotton grass**

Gray-green foliage stops just below the flower heads, setting off their orange or rust color. Like *Eriophorum latifolium*, this species sends out runners to start new tussocks, creating the look of a tussock that is more broad and dense than the open sod of other species. The seed heads are dense, having one, not multiple, tufts. Height 12–20 inches, spread 12 inches. Needs full sun. Pests do not seem to like this species. It is circumboreal in the northern hemisphere and is rated hardy in Zones 3 or 4–5.

### *Eriophorum virginicum*
**tawny cotton grass, Virginia cotton grass**

This species forms clumps to 36 inches tall and 18 inches wide, with tufts that are white or tawny. It tolerates warm, humid summers better than other species, but still needs part shade in the southern part of its range. Native only to North America, from Canada to Tennessee, some say as far south as Florida. Hardy in Zones 3–9.

*Glyceria aquatica* 'Variegata'

## *Glyceria*
Poaceae

*Glyceria* species can be found in the temperate and subarctic regions of both North and South America. Several species are aquatic and grow naturally in North America. Although an important food source for wildlife, they are not usually considered ornamental and for this reason most are not commonly available at nurseries or garden centers. *Glyceria* species are generally cold tolerant and overwinter easily in the pond. They require winter submersion beneath only enough water to cover the crown of the plant, with no need to move them deeper into the pond. Glycerias grow by undergrown rhizomes that are easily divided in the spring, and may also be grown from seed.

### *Glyceria aquatica* 'Variegata' (syn. *G. maxima* 'Variegata')
variegated manna grass

A rambling aquatic with narrow, 2-inch-wide leaves that are usually 12 inches or so in height, variegated manna grass has leaves striped in creamy white and bright green. In the spring and fall, when the weather is cool, the leaves take on a delightful pink tinge. Flowers are negligible tan blooms in summer. A strong grower in the moist to wet soil, or water to 1 inch deep, that it prefers, variegated manna grass runs freely and should be restrained in a pot so that it does not intefere with its neighbors. In larger earthen plantings, it should be kept in check by pulling. Situate in sun to part shade. Zones 4–11. Reversion to its all-green form is not

*Glyceria aquatica* 'Variegata'

uncommon but is easily corrected by removing the rhizomes from which the green leaves have sprouted. Mice and voles are usually a problem in winter, and coots in spring. Native to Europe and Asia, this form can be found from many commercial sources.

### *Glyceria canadensis*
rattlesnake manna grass

This plant looks like aquatic *Briza* and is quite showy in flower. The large flower heads are very effective when planted with *Asclepias* and *Hibiscus*. It is loose growing, as are the other species. Height 24 inches, spread 24–36 inches. Zones 3–7.

*Gymnocoronis spilanthoides* 'Variegata'

Monarch butterfly on *Gymnocoronis*

## *Gymnocoronis spilanthoides*
**water snowball, Senegal tea**
**Asteraceae**

A bushy plant with very glossy green leaves, this tropical South American native has many clusters of ½-inch, white flowers that are made up of tiny white filaments, thus earning the common name water snowball. It branches freely, floating out on the water surface and still growing to 3 feet high and wide. Although it is an excellent plant for the pond margin, taking moist soil or water to 12 inches deep, including seasonal flooding, it also grows submerged and is sometimes sold as an aquarium plant. Situate in sun to full shade. Propagate by cuttings. It is rated hardy for Zones 9–11, but it has come back here in Zone 5 after being placed at the bottom of the pond, below the freeze line for the winter.

Water snowball blooms in summer and smells like baby powder. It is one of the best butterfly-attracting plants in our water gardens. Especially during the fall migration, it is covered with monarch butterflies. It may also attract aphids, though these are rarely a problem. When they are, just submerge for a few days.

*Gymnocoronis spilanthoides* 'Variegata' is a form with white irregular margins on the leaves. Another form has wine-red stems.

*Hibiscus* and *Colocasia esculenta* 'Black Magic'

### *Habenaria repens*
**bog orchid, water spider orchid**
Orchidaceae

Leafy stems sport green flowers in summer. It grows in patches in sun to part shade, reaching 6–12 inches high and 6 inches wide. It grows in wet soil or even no soil, forming floating mats instead. Propagate by division or seed. Native throughout the Caribbean and north to the Carolinas. Hardy in Zones 8–12, otherwise bring indoors for the winter and keep frost-free at temperatures between 60°F and 70°F. Watch for aphids.

### *Hibiscus*
**mallow**
Malvaceae

Large summertime flowers lasting but a day are borne on shrubby plants up to 6 feet high, depending on the species. The flowers are generally in the red to white range, usually with a strong eye zone of color. The tropical forms are more vibrant in color than the other species. After flowering, hibiscus develop papery-covered green fruits that some people find attractive. The plants die to the ground in winter, growing again in the spring and summer. Situate in full sun for best color. Propagating by seed is easiest, but cuttings may be taken from cultivars. Weevils that eat the seed can be a problem.

### *Hibiscus coccineus*
**water hibiscus**

This southern belle has deep crimson flowers 5–8 inches wide. They are among the reddest in the plant kingdom and are always showstoppers. Palmate leaves have three, five, or

*Hibiscus moscheutos*

seven points and are divided into narrow segments, resembling a Japanese maple leaf. The red-flowered 'Lord Baltimore' is probably a selection or hybrid of *Hibiscus coccineus* though it is usually sold as a selection of *H. moscheutos*.

Grows 6–9 feet high and 3–6 feet wide, but it can vary depending on cultivation and when plants are started. The base of the plant will become quite woody. It does best with a tip pruning in early summer to encourage branching, for it can get floppy because it gets so tall. Situate in sun to part shade, but sun is best. It needs moist soil or water to 4 inches deep, and it tolerates seasonal flooding. Native to Georgia and Florida, it will not survive north of Philadelphia. Rated hardy in Zones 7–11. Overwinter where not hardy by applying a heavy mulch, or bring it indoors to a cool location, like a garage.

### *Hibiscus lasiocarpus*
**wooly mallow**

Creamy flowers with a red eye are borne atop stout stems that reach 4–6 feet high. Give full sun exposure and moist soil or

*Hibiscus militaris*

*Hibiscus moscheutos*

*Hibiscus moscheutos*

*Hibiscus moscheutos*

water to 3 inches deep. It does best with seasonal flooding and receding water. Spreads to more than 3 feet. Native to southern Indiana and south to Texas. Zone 6 and up.

## Hibiscus militaris (syn. H. laevis)
### halberd-leafed marsh mallow

Large shrubby plant with an open vase shape. The slightly rounded, large, 4–6 inch flowers are more tubular than flat. They are pink to white, generally with a rose eye. The leaves are distinct in that they have two short lobes on either side of a much longer center lobe. This species is native throughout the eastern U.S. from Illinois to Florida to Texas—hardy in Zone 5 and up. Situate in full sun for best flowering, growth, and shape—it tends to get floppy in shady sites. Height 4–6 feet, spread 4 feet. Grow in moist soil or water to 24 inches deep. It also tolerates seasonal flooding and is great for detention basins. Besides weevils, aphids can also be a problem for this species.

## Hibiscus moscheutos
### water hibiscus, swamp mallow, swamp rose mallow

This medium-sized shrub has stunning 10–12 inch flowers ranging in color from white through deep red, with or without eye zones. It is usually larger-flowering and bushier than *Hibiscus palustris* but not as water-tolerant, preferring moist soil or water to 4 inches deep, though it will tolerate seasonal flooding and even dry soil. I have witnessed this growing in 12 inches of water, though it was not as strong. It also tolerates brackish water up to 15 parts per million and is very adaptable from high pH to acidic conditions. Grows well in sun to part shade, but best in full sun. Height ranges from 24 inches for the dwarf selections to more than 6 feet. Spread 2–4 feet. Highly variable over its North American range—

*Hibiscus moscheutos* 'Kopper King'

*Hibiscus moscheutos* 'Lord Baltimore'

found in the Northeast through to Illinois and south to Florida.

Very easy to grow and performs well in a planting, needing little care. Excellent along lake shores and streams and in seasonally flooded areas—good in detention areas and along retention ponds. Propagate by seed, division, or cuttings taken in early summer. Cut back the stems for the winter and mulch heavily where not hardy. Hardy in Zone 5 and up. It may be slow to reappear in the spring. This species can be propagated by division. Attracts butterflies and even hummingbirds, and does not seem to be bothered by weevils or aphids.

Many hybrids and cultivars are available, with many breeders working on these great plants. Many more cultivars than those listed here are coming onto the market—look for them and try them out.

   'Anne Arundel'—strong, true pink
   'Blue River'—clear white
   'Fantasia'—soft pink
   'Fire Ball'—red with red foliage
   'Flare'—fuchsia-red and sterile
   'Kopper King'—red foliage and white flowers with
     rose radiating from a carmine eye
   'Lady Baltimore'—pink with a wide carmine eye
   'Lord Baltimore'—red
   'Moy Grande'—12-inch rose-pink flowers
   'Old Yella'—cream
   'Sweet Caroline'—ruffled pink
   'Turn of the Century'—pinwheel of rose and white
   Southern Belle Group

### *Hibiscus palustris*
### water hibiscus

A true aquatic that thrives in wet soil to flowing water, even tolerating up to 2 feet of seasonal flooding, *Hibiscus palustris* is native to the Mississippi Valley. Plants listed under this name in the trade, however, are *H. laevis*, *H. moscheutos*, or a hybrid of the two. It branches freely and has pink or white flowers with a rose throat. It grows in sun to part shade, reaching 4–6 feet high and 2–4 feet wide. Zones 5–11.

### *Hippuris vulgaris*
### mare's tail
### Hippuridaceae

The leaves of this aquatic are very similar to those of *Myriophyllum aquaticum* but are generally shorter and more linear and not so finely or delicately cut. The white summer-blooming flowers are inconspicuous and barely visible to the naked eye. It grows as a creeping rhizome under sun to part shade, covering 24 square inches in a season. Height is 6–12 inches. Grow as a marginal in wet soil or grow submerged, and overwinter below water. The species is circumboreal, rated hardy for Zone 4 and up. Propagate by stem cuttings, from which it readily grows. It is grown in the U.K. but is not generally available in the U.S., though I remember seeing this in Estes Park in Colorado. I have sometimes noticed aphids on ours, but they are easy to eradicate by submersion.

*Hippuris vulgaris*

*Hottonia palustris*

*Hippuris vulgaris*

## *Hottonia*
**featherfoil, water violet**
**Primulaceae**

### *Hottonia inflata*

Leaves are very finely cut, like those of *Hottonia palustris*, but the flowers of this North American native are much smaller, only ⅓ inch long and usually white. They bloom earlier, too, in spring to early summer. Much more noticeable are the stems on which the flowers appear—they are thick, inflated, and hollow. Height 8 inches, spread 12 inches. Plants will grow freely for one season and then not reappear for several years. They often grow out into a foot or two of water. Natural stands may be found in ditches and ponds from Maine and New York to Illinois and southward into Texas and Florida. Zone 6 and up. Grow in sun to part shade. Propagate and overwinter as for *H. palustris*. The two species attract the same pests, as well.

### *Hottonia palustris*

A delightful plant native to Europe and Asia that roots at the edge of the pond and then floats out onto the water surface. Leaves of this unusual marginal are thin and deeply cut, arising as a whorl from a central rosette. Flowers look like tiny primula blossoms, usually white or lilac with a yellow throat, and bloom in summer. Grows in sun to shade in water 12–24 inches deep. It grows best in softer water. It reaches a height of 4 inches above the water surface and spreads 4–12 inches. Propagate by turions and cuttings taken in spring, but I find it difficult to establish. It must strike root before the water heats up past 70°F and the plants set bud. Once they set buds they do not want to root and will flower and die. Overwintering takes no special care where hardy—Zone 6 and up—but if it must be brought in keep potted in a cool place, like a refrigerator. China mark moth and aphids can be a problem.

*Houttuynia* to the left of *Typha* and underneath *Caltha* and *Salix*

## *Houttuynia cordata*
## Saururaceae

A very rampant runner in the moist soil it prefers, houttuynia has heart-shaped leaves that grow in a dense mat. In the fall, as the weather cools, they turn a dark maroon-purple that has a very striking impact in the garden. Plus, the foliage is fragrant. Flowers appear in early summer. They are white, single, and look somewhat like single-petaled roses. Height 6 inches. It will tolerate seasonal flooding but does best if water is not constantly over its crown. Grow in sun to shade and keep within bounds, in a pot or other enclosure, for best results. Hardy in Zones 5–11, but do not allow it to freeze in winter. It must be submerged to the depths of the pond or, alternately, mulched into the perennial border. Native to Japan, Taiwan, and India. Attractive to Japanese beetles.

Several worthy cultivars are available. 'Chameleon' is the variegated form of houttuynia, much appreciated by gardeners as long as its running habit can be contained. Foliage is splashed with white and red all year long and never looks tattered or dirty. It reverts easily to the all-green form, which will quickly overtake the variegated patches if not cut out right away. 'Tricolor' is green, pink, and white. 'Flore Pleno' (syn. 'Plena') has double flowers. 'Flame' has more orange in it than 'Chameleon', and 'Boo-Boo' is red and green.

*Houttuynia cordata* 'Chameleon'

*Houttuynia cordata* 'Flore Pleno'

*Houttuynia cordata* 'Flame'

*Houttuynia cordata* 'Boo-Boo'

## *Hydrocotyle*
pennywort
Apiaceae

*Hydrocotyle* species are low-growing, running aquatics with round, umbrella-like, often toothed leaves that stand up straight from running stems. Leaves are fleshy and usually shiny. They may be anywhere from 3 inches to a mere ½ inch in diameter. Many species can be found in various parts of the world—it may almost be considered cosmopolitan. Because of their ability to breed across species, it is sometimes difficult to determine which one is which.

There is something cheerful about a plant that remains green from spring through fall and bears leaves with serrated eges that look like smiles connected at the corners. Hydrocotyles are useful in the water garden for their ability to quickly create shade over the pond, as many species will grow running stems that float out over the water surface. They scramble between plants, covering pots and making a soft edge between water and taller plants such as sweet flags (*Acorus*) or cattails (*Typha*). In a container water garden, they will spill over and trail downward from the edge of the pot. They are usually grown for their foliage; flowers are inconspicuous, white or sometimes green tufts that often remain underneath the leaves. Some species are considered weeds for their rampant growth. If left unchecked, these species can soon overtake the pond, smothering out less exuberant neighbors.

Most species grow well in sun to part shade. Though division is the best means of propagation for several species, hydrocotyles can be grown from seed—just sow on moist soil at 70–75°F for most species—and are easily grown by stem cuttings, roots sprouting from virtually every leaf node. For tender species that are grown in colder climates, bring stem cuttings indoors to root in warm water. Keep in a sunny windowsill. Cold-tolerant species overwinter well in the pond but should not freeze—move them to the bottom with the waterlilies.

*Hydrocotyle bonariensis*

## *Hydrocotyle americana*
hairy pennywort

These fuzzy green leaves are ½–1¾ inches wide and veined in purple with purple stems. This species trails freely and is an excellent plant for waterfalls, the edges of ponds or streams, tub gardens, or table-top ponds. It will grow submerged in clear water, although not in water that is cloudy or green. It is also one of the few pennyworts with noticeable white flowers, which rise above the foliage in white tufts. A native of North America, growing from Nova Scotia and Newfoundland southward into New England and the Carolinas and westward to Tennessee and Minnesota. Zones 7–11. Reaches a height of 2–4 inches in moist soil or water to 4 inches deep. Propagate by division or cuttings, and seed is possible but can be hard to collect. Sow moist and allow 30–60 days cold stratification, then warm to 70°F.

## *Hydrocotyle bonariensis*
giant pennywort

A large species of *Hydrocotyle*, with leaves up to 3 inches in diameter. It has large sprays of white flowers throughout the summer. Best suited to a large pond where it can ramble without taking over other plants. Height 4–6 inches in moist soil or water to 4 inches deep. Native from Virginia to Florida and widespread in tropical South America. Zones 6–11. Best to propagate this species by division. Aphids may be attracted to it but are generally not a problem.

Hydrocotyle sibthorpioides 'Variegata'

Hydrocotyle lemnoides, left, and Eleocharis parvula in topiary with Houttuynia and Myriophyllum aquaticum in the foreground

Hydrocotyle sibthorpioides 'Variegata'

### Hydrocotyle lemnoides
**mini pennywort**

A diminutive form of *Hydrocotyle*, with leaves no more than ½ inch wide and overall height the same. The habit is reminiscent of baby's tears (*Soleirolia soleirolii*). Excellent for a small pond to soften a rock edge, or in moss topiary. It will grow submerged under clear water, but otherwise does best in moist soil. Division is the most practical method of propagation. Native to Australia. Zones 7–11. Where not hardy, bring indoors and treat as a houseplant.

### Hydrocotyle ranunculoides
**bull's-eye pennywort, cut-leafed pennywort**

The fleshy leaves of this pennywort are irregularly cut and highly scalloped, giving the appearance of petticoats. They are dark green and marked with a bright red dot in the cen-

ter. Height 4–6 inches. Grows in moist soil or water to 6 inches deep. Native from Pennsylvania to South America. Zones 5–11. Overwinter indoors as houseplant where not hardy, though spider mites may be a problem. Division is the most practical means of propagation.

'Ruffles', or ruffled pennywort, is a more tender selection (Zones 8–11) that was first found in the bayous outside New Orleans. It has very ruffled edges on its felty, green leaves. At 3 inches it is slightly shorter than other pennyworts we have grown. Grows in moist soil or water to 4 inches deep.

### Hydrocotyle sibthorpioides 'Variegata'
**crystal confetti**

This dainty pennywort forms a full carpet of 1-inch, frilled, heart-shaped, jade-green leaves that are edged in cream. As the plant matures, the foliage develops pink margins and

*Hydrocotyle ranunculoides*

*Hydrocotyle verticillata*

*Hydrocotyle umbellata*

*Hydrocotyle verticillata* 'Little Umbrellas'

burgundy stems. Because it is just 1 inch tall and trails freely, it is excellent for container water gardens, where the soil can stay evenly moist to wet. Also perfect for waterfalls or in bogs or in aquatic topiary. It is more shade-tolerant than other pennyworts, taking sun to full shade. Native to Japan and China. Hardy in Zone 6, with cover, to 10. Treat as a houseplant where not hardy. Propagate by division.

## *Hydrocotyle umbellata*
### giant floating pennywort

This species is the largest of all the pennyworts, with big umbrellas of leaves and floating stems that creep out across the water. In fact, the whole plant will grow floating, or in moist soil. Very attractive when trailing down a waterfall or along a stream. Height 4–10 inches. This species is variable depending on the source. Native from Minnesota to South America. Zones 5–11. Treat as a houseplant where not

hardy. Propagate by division. Aphids may attack in late summer.

## *Hydrocotyle verticillata*

Native from Missouri to South America, including the southeastern United States. Grows in sun to shade in moist soil or water so deep it floats. Height 6 inches or more with the usual running spread. It can cover 24 inches in a season. Propagate by division. Zones 5–11.

We selected 'Little Umbrellas' because the glossy green foliage resembles an armful of little umbrellas. It stays more compact and is shorter than the species and other selections, reaching 2–4 inches high. Grows in sun to part shade in moist soil or water to 4 inches deep.

*Hygrophila corymbosa* 'Stricta'

*Hygrophila corymbosa* 'Stricta'

## *Hygrophila*
**hygro, temple plant**
**Acanthaceae**

A confusing genus of several species all sold interchangeably as the same plant. Many are sold as aquarium plants, some of which are also suitable as marginal plants in the water garden. The ones listed here have purple-blue flowers that look something like tiny snapdragons, blooming anytime the plant is not submerged. Leaves are usually long and thin, wider toward the middle, opposite. Some forms are ruffled. They grow in sun to shade and are easily propagated from stem cuttings. Bring cuttings inside in the winter to root in warm water. Native to southeast Asia.

## *Hygrophila corymbosa* 'Stricta'
**dragon lanterns**

Upright, fast growing plant with foliage that is tinted in purple when the weather is cool, in spring and fall. It is very free-flowering and is often covered with clusters of tiny blue flowers looking like turtles' heads sitting near the central stem. Reaches 12 inches high and wide, though in shade it will grow to 36 inches tall. Grows in moist soil or submerged. Zones 9–11. Bring indoors and treat as a houseplant for the winter where not hardy, keeping it wet. Spider mites may attack in the winter, but simply submerge the plant for a few days to kill them.

Several other cultivars of *Hygrophila corymbosa* are great for the water garden. 'Willow Leaf' has thin willowy leaves and red stems. 'Siamensis Narrow Leaf' has narrow leaves and darker purple stems than 'Willow Leaf'. 'Fine Leaf' has leaves of very fine texture, much like *Alternanthera*. 'Greta' has very large ruffly leaves, and 'Ruffle Leaf' has a very red cast to the whole plant, much like 'Fine Leaf' but with wavy-edged leaves. 'Siamensis' is similar to 'Stricta' but has larger foliage.

*Hygrophila difformis*

*Hymenocallis liriosome*

## *Hygrophila difformis*
**water wisteria**

Water wisteria has mint-like foliage and tiny blue flowers borne at the leaf joints on long, trailing stems. When it is grown submerged, its foliage becomes ferny and very finely cut. Foliage is very sticky when emerged. Great in containers and in the margins of ornamental ponds to hide pots. Grow in sun to just part shade in moist soil or water to 2 inches deep. Height 6–10 inches with a running spread. Aphids may appear in late summer. Overwinter inside as a houseplant or in an aquarium. Native to southeast Asia and India. Zones 9–11. 'Variegata', or variegated water wisteria, has white striping in the foliage of submerged leaves and slight mottling in emerged leaves.

## *Hymenocallis*
Amaryllidaceae

*Hymenocallis* species are grown for their showy white flowers, which resemble both a common white daffodil (*Narcissus*) and bog lily (*Crinum americanum*). The petals are connected by a hymen. Foliage is long and straplike, thick, also like *Crinum*. Easy of culture, they bloom when they want, sometimes in early summer and again in the fall. They grow in sun to part shade in moist soil or water to 6 inches over the crown. Most are tolerant of seasonal flooding. Height can be from 6 inches to 24 inches, depending on the species, and spread is 12–20 inches. Most species are native to tropical regions of the world, and a few grow wild in warmer, temperate regions. Propagate by offsets of bulbs or seed sown fresh (they are like little bulbs). To overwinter in colder climates, dig up bulbs and store in a cool, dry place. Some people recommend leaving the soil on the bulbs and storing them dry in a bag or box in a cool dry place not above 60°F. Or, bring them indoors in a pot and treat as a houseplant.

## *Hymenocallis caribaea* 'Variegata'
**variegated spider lily**

White flowers in midsummer set off the foliage, which is striped in creamy white. An extremely attractive plant for the water garden even when it is not in bloom. Grows into nice clumps like clivias. Can take more shade than others, growing in sun to shade. Reaches 12–18 inches high and 12 inches wide. Hardy in Zones 7–11. Propagate by division only. Bulbs may be kept in the pond over the winter as long as they are below the freeze line.

## *Hymenocallis crassifolia*
**bog lily**

Thin, very green foliage looks like a big daylily (*Hemerocallis*). It grows well in streams and wet-seeps. A large block of these plants looks very impressive when in bloom—large white flowers are 2–3 inches across with five connected petals. Native to the southern U.S., it needs a sunny exposure and moist soil or water to 6 inches deep. I have observed this growing in deeper water in streams, but never in ponds. Height 24 inches and spread 18 inches. Hardy in Zone 8 and up.

## *Hymenocallis liriosome*
**spider lily**

The name of this species means "fragrant lily." Flowers are up to 7 inches wide, having a long tube and then six lobes and a cup, or crown, of white from which stamens rise. They look like spiders because of their long petals and sepals. Leaves are narrow, less than 1 inch wide, and 12 inches or more in length. Like *Amaryllis*, the leaves are long, strap-like, and deeply grooved. Plant reaches a height of 18 inches and spreads to 24 inches, making nice clumps. Grows in moist soil or water to 2 inches, but tolerates seasonal flooding very well. Native to Louisiana and Texas. Zones 7–11.

### *Hymenocallis occidentalis* (syn. *H. caroliniana*)
**swamp lily**

This species bears three to nine flowers on each scape. The fragrant flowers have tubes to ½ inch long, perianth lobes to 4 inches long, coronas to more than 1½ inches long. Looks great in large groups and is excellent in detention ponds. Overwinter by digging up a clump and storing in a paper bag where it will stay cool and dry. Zone 7 and up. Native to Georgia and Alabama, north to Missouri and southern Illinois and Indiana. Height 24 inches or more, spread 12 inches. Grows in moist soil or water to 6 inches deep.

### *Hymenocallis palmeri*
**Palmer's swamp lily**

A smaller hymenocallis with small strap-like leaves that are very dark green. Produces one to three flowers at a time. Height only 6 inches or more and spread 6–12 inches. Grows in moist soil and tolerates seasonal flooding. Zone 9 and up. Native to Florida and Georgia.

### *Impatiens*
**touch-me-not**
**Balsaminaceae**

Widely used as annuals in American gardens, *Impatiens walleriana* and the New Guinea Hybrids make up the bulk of garden plants. The genus *Impatiens* is a large group, however, extending from the Americas into Asia and the islands of the Pacific. All impatiens need some shade and constant moisture. The species listed here are wet-seep or stream-edge plants. They are very colorful, with flowers that hang under the layers of foliage without being hidden.

Impatiens propel their seed from recoiling seed pods. Those species listed here are difficult to transplant and prefer to be sown directly into place. I sow seed on the soil surface in the fall and let it come up in spring. No covering is needed for the seed, although they will come up through a soil or mulch covering of up to ½ inch.

*Impatiens capensis*

### *Impatiens capensis*
**spotted touch-me-not**

*Impatiens capensis* displays pale to bright orange flowers with red dots in mid to late summer. Sometimes they have only a few spots, and sometimes the flowers appear almost red. The tall, 2–5-foot, umbrella-like plant is full and branched, with flowers hanging just under the foliage. Spreading to 24 inches it grows nicely in a stand or alone as a specimen. A form with golden new growth is available from Glasshouse Works in Stewart, Ohio. This North American native is truly annual, but once planted it self sows and keeps going and going. Grows in sun to part shade, but is really best in part shade. Soil may be wet to dry. Spider mites may appear in late summer but do not seem to be a problem. The juice of this species is said to cure poison ivy. I have tried it myself and it seems to work.

*Ipomoea aquatica*

*Impatiens pallida*

## Impatiens glandulifera
**mountain impatiens**

Purple to white flowers, and all shades in between, adorn what looks like a small shrub. Willowy leaves and very large showy flowers are borne in abundance. Height 4–6 feet, spread 24–36 inches. Grows in sun to shade in wet to dry soil. Great for seasonally flooded areas. This annual can become a pest, however, because of the exploding seed dispersal. Propagate by seed, which is best, or cuttings. Native to China.

## Impatiens pallida
**pale touch-me-not**

These pale to bright yellow flowers are displayed in summer on this annual from eastern North America. Reaching 2–4 feet high and spreading 24 inches, it grows in sun to shade in wet to sometimes dry soil. It is great for wet woods or shady pond edges for naturalistic ponds. Propagate by seed. Watch for spider mites.

## Ipomoea aquatica
**water spinach, water morning glory**
**Convolvulaceae**

Water spinach—known by a number of names, including *kong xin cai*, in Asian groceries—is an Oriental vegetable. The young shoots of this aquatic are often used in stir-fry dishes. It has 3-inch white flowers in late spring or early summer and again in early fall when the weather cools and days become shorter. This native of tropical regions of Asia is considered a noxious weed in warmer climates for its ability to grow very rapidly out on the water surface. Do not plant it in sites that are connected to natural bodies of water—it must not be allowed to spread. It grows fast to help shade a pond and can tolerate koi predation.

It grows 8–10 inches high in sun to part shade and has a running, floating spread. When rooted to the bottom it grows in water 4–18 inches deep; in deeper water it forms floating mats. Hardy in Zones 9–11. In colder climates, bring in new shoots and grow the plant in a bowl of warm water in a sunny room. Or plant the new shoots in pots—I like hanging baskets in a sunny window. It almost stops growing in winter when the days are short, then resumes when the days get longer in March. It can be easily propagated from stem cuttings, which root quickly from the leaf nodes. Mealybugs and spider mites may attack in winter, but simply submerge for a few days to control.

## Isolepis
Cyperaceae

### Isolepis prolifer
New Zealand jumping rush

This novel rush native to New Zealand has blades up to a foot long that end in little plants. These little plants have long blades that also end in little plants, and so on. A perfect accent plant, its stems are chestnut colored at the base, bright green at the tips. Easy to grow. May be invasive, but not destructive, in warmer climates. Grows in full sun to full shade and does not flower. Height 6 inches with a running spread. Grows in moist soil or water to 2 inches deep. Propagate by offsets—just cut off the little plants from the ends of the leaves and plant them. Hardy in Zones 6–11. In colder regions bring in the small plantlets before the first frost and treat as houseplants.

### Isolepis cernua
mini jumping rush

Tufts of thin green hair forms tufts of new hair at the ends, forming a spreading mat or trailing wave of green—it looks like hair that wants to spread. It is very fine and does not flower—looks great in mixed planters. Grows in sun in moist soil to submerged. Height 3–6 inches, spread 12 inches. Zone 6 and up. Propagate by offsets from the ends of the blades, and bring these indoors in winter to treat as houseplants. Mealybugs may be a problem indoors in winter, but just submerge for a few days to control.

## Juncus
Juncaceae

Many species of *Juncus* have strongly upright foliage that is important in the water garden landscape because it provides a useful background for other pondside plants with a bolder or more delicate nature. Foliage is stiff and hollow. Flowers appear as brown tassels that droop from near or at the tip of the leaves. The look is interesting, but not highly ornamental. Most *Juncus* species have little or few leaves, and are noted for their long, spiked stems. These are usually dark green, but light blue selections are also available. Foliage dries well and the plants are much favored in floral arrangements. In many climates the foliage will be evergreen throughout the winter—cut these back to the ground every few years to remove older growth that may be more tattered. Annual foliage should be cut back in late winter. They may be grown in the perennial border as long as they are given adequate moisture. *Juncus* grows from underground rhi-

zomes that are linked by stolons. It is easily divided at these rootstocks, but may also be grown from seed.

Species of *Juncus* may be found in most parts of the world. Several North American species are cultivated for sale to water gardeners. Because they are usually cold-tolerant, *Juncus* may be overwintered in the pond with no need to be placed at the bottom with waterlilies or lotus. Tender species may be brought indoors and kept as houseplants.

Some species have selections with tightly curled foliage and are commonly called corkscrew rush. In the U.S., corkscrew rush is sold as *Juncus effusus* 'Spiralis'. However, it is just as likely that the plant being sold is really *J. balticus* 'Spiralis'. This distinction is not insignificant. *Juncus balticus* has a running habit and open, lax growth. *Juncus effusus* grows in a clump and has sturdier foliage with more upright growth habit. Also, the genus *Scirpus* is often confused with *Juncus*. Although they resemble each other, the two genera are not related. The easiest way to distinguish them is to examine their brown flowers. *Juncus* flowers and seed divide into three; *Scirpus* do not. Also, *Scirpus* seed heads are scaly and are shaped somewhat like small cones.

Stands of *Juncus* are useful in earthen ponds as spawning ground for bluegills and sunnies. Dragonfly larvae often use the upright leaves to rise from the water, clinging to the foliage while they metamorphose into adult dragonflies. They provide important shelter to fish, fowl, and insects.

### Juncus balticus 'Spiralis'
Baltic corkscrew rush

Often sold as corkscrew rush, this selection has a somewhat lax habit as well as a tendency to flop and run. It is best sited near a staunchly vertical marginal, such as *Iris*, to help hold up its foliage. It resembles a bed of springs, very twisty but not as easily kinked up as *Juncus effusus* 'Spiralis'. It does not keep its foliage in winter—just cut back in fall for a fresh start in spring. Hardy in Zones 4–9. Native to Europe. Grows in sun to part shade in moist soil or water to 4 inches deep. Reaches 24 inches high with a running spread. Division is the best method of propagation, but a fair amount of the seed comes true as curly.

### Juncus 'China Blue'

Very slender blue leaves form nice, upright clumps. Seed heads are a chestnut color. It is very graceful and ornamental and, like the other blue juncus, it keeps its foliage year-round and can tolerate some drying. Moist soil or water to 4 inches is ideal, but it tolerates seasonal flooding and generally deeper water than the other blue rushes. Grows in sun to shade. Height 18–24 inches, spread 12 inches. Native to China. Zone 5 and up.

### Juncus conglomeratus
**compact rush**

This European native is not compact, but the seed heads are. Slender stems are very upright and shorter than those of *Juncus effusus*. Grows in sun to part shade in moist soil or water to 4 inches deep. Tolerates seasonal flooding and brackish water, but avoid limy soils. Height 15–24 inches, spread 12 inches. Zone 5 and up. It requires a dormant period to stay healthy. 'Spiralis', the twisted version of this plant, is often confused with and sold as *J. effusus* 'Spiralis'.

### Juncus decipiens 'Curly-wurly'
**miniature corkscrew rush**

This is the Shirley Temple of the *Juncus* cultivars, with tightly curled miniature stems. The stems are about as thick as pencil lead. Although it prefers moist soil, it will grow in up to 1 inch of water. It tolerates seasonal flooding as long as the summers are just damp. Height 6 inches and spread 6–8 inches in sun to part shade. Zones 6–11. To propagate by seed, surface sow and keep moist. A delightful, carefree plant for the container water garden or for a small, intimate pond.

### Juncus effusus
**common rush, soft rush, hard rush**

A good vertical accent plant, the circumboreal common rush has stiff spines of green foliage. It often retains its color all year long, even in colder climates. Hardy in Zones 3–11. Grows in sun to part shade in moist soil or water to 4 inches deep. It does best if the water level drops in the summer to just wet soil. Height 24–36 inches, spread 12 inches. Propagate by division, especially for the selected cultivars, or by seed surface sown.

It has a long history of use in Asia for weaving mats and baskets. It was used for many years as "rushlights," candles made by peeling away the outer skin and dipping the inner gauze-like, even-burning pith in tallow. During World War II in England, common rush was gathered from wetlands to make rushlights because candles were in short supply.

'Cuckoo', or variegated common rush, has straight stems accented with yellow stripes that run the length of the leaf. A strong grower, it is not as heavily variegated as 'Gold Strike' and variegation is irregular and prone to reversion. Though stunning when at its best—often full stems are yellow—I consider it to need too much maintenance for the garden. Best really only for collectors.

'Gold Strike' is similar to 'Cuckoo' but has more consistent gold striping along the length of its dark green foliage.

*Juncus effusus*

*Juncus effusus* 'Gold Strike', left, with *Baumea rubiginosa* 'Variegata'

*Juncus effusus* 'Unicorn'

*Juncus ensifolius*

'Lemon Twist' is a twisted version of 'Gold Strike'. A bright gold stripe covering about a quarter of the diameter of the blade runs up every curl.

*Juncus* 'Silver Spears' is a white variegated form growing to 24 inches tall and 12 inches wide.

'Spiralis', or the true corkscrew rush, has tightly coiled foliage that is excellent in fresh or dry floral arrangements. Grows to 12–18 inches high and wide. Almost evergreen even in colder climates. Good as an accent for more bold foliage like *Iris pseudacorus* or *Pontederia*.

'Unicorn', or giant corkscrew rush, has dark green, twisted foliage that is much larger and taller, at 24 inches high and wide, than the standard *Juncus effusus* 'Spiralis'. It retains its bold shape and texture throughout the summer and even into the fall and winter.

'Vittatus' is a variegated form similar to 'Cuckoo'. It is very unstable and is prone to reversion. I recommend it only for collectors.

## *Juncus ensifolius*
### flat sedge, dagger leaf

Broad leaves look like small *Iris* seedlings. Slightly blue-green in color with dark black-brown seed heads all summer. Great when used with irises and other finer-foliaged plants. Grows in sun to shade in moist soil or water to 2 inches deep. Tolerates seasonal flooding. Reaches 10–20 inches high and 12 inches wide. Hardy to Zone 4 and up. It is more northern in distribution, found mostly across Canada and the upper Midwest, to Alaska and south to California. Grasshoppers may attack this species.

## *Juncus filiformis*
### thread rush

Often sold as *Juncus effusus* 'Spiralis' in the nursery trade, thread rush is a nice alternative to that coarser plant. Native to the northern U.S., it is hardy in Zone 3 and up, needing to

*Juncus filiformis* 'Blonde Ambition'

*Juncus filiformis* 'Blonde Ambition'

*Juncus glaucus*

go dormant to stay healthy. Grows in sun to shade and moist soil or water to 4 inches deep. Height 12–18 inches, spread 12 inches. Propagate by division or seed—even *J. filiformis* 'Spiralis' comes true from seed.

'Blonde Ambition' is an almost completely yellow selection, with about a quarter of the blade still green. It has semi-lax leaves and really brightens up an area. A real treat for the pond. Originated at Collector's Nursery in Battle Ground, Washington. It is usually listed as a selection of *Juncus effusus*.

## *Juncus glaucus* (syn. *J. inflexus* var. *glaucus*) blue rush

The upright, baby-blue leaves of this rush resemble fescue (*Festuca*) at the edge of the pond. Foliage stays all winter for great off-season interest. Blue rush is very nice in any pond. Grows in full sun in moist soil or water to 2 inches deep. Reaches 12–24 inches high and 24 inches wide. Zones 4–11. Native to Europe.

*Juncus inflexus* 'Afro'

*Juncus* spp.

## *Juncus inflexus*
### hard rush, European hard rush

Native to Europe as well as other temperate regions of the world, *Juncus inflexus* appears more narrowly upright and gray-green—though some forms are quite blue—than the common rush (*J. effusus*). It reaches 24–36 inches tall and 18 inches wide. Grows in sun to part shade in moist soil or water to 4 inches deep. Its blue or green tubular foliage resembles that of *J. glaucus* but is larger and more dramatic. In the fall, cold weather causes some of the green forms to turn dark purple. Zones 5–11. This, like *J. effusus*, is quite variable so know your source.

'Afro', or blue medusa corkscrew rush, has billowy curls of powdery blue foliage that make the perfect accent for ponds, streams, waterfalls, and even the moist perennial or bog garden. Ever-blue even in colder climates, blue medusa is a marked improvement over standard corkscrew rush, *J. effusus* 'Spiralis'. The foliage has better substance, holding its curled form longer. Height 12–18 inches and spread 24 inches. Propagate by division. It also grows from seed but is then variable.

## *Juncus marginatus*
### fireworks sedge

Clumps or small patches of thin foliage form red seed heads that give the appearance of fireworks all summer. Very nice as a specimen or mixed with other plants like *Asclepias*, *Butomus*, *Cyperus*, and *Ruellia*. Great in containers. Height 12–18 inches and spread 12 inches. Grows in sun to shade in wet soil or water to 4 inches deep. Tolerates seasonal flooding. Zone 4 and up. Native to the U.S. Often confused in the trade with *Juncus accuminatus*, a very similar but taller plant.

## *Juncus nodatus*
### baby's breath rush, bird nest rush

Extensive, branched, golden red seed heads form clouds of color on this plant in the summer, giving it a creeping baby's breath appearance. The plants are short at 6 inches but full, spreading to 12 inches, which makes them great for combining with other plants like arrowhead (*Sagittaria*) and blue rushes (*Butomus*). Easy to grow, and may seed about a little in a pond with open soil. Grows in sun to shade, but color is best in full sun. Takes moist soil or water to 2 inches deep, and tolerates seasonal flooding. Native to the Mississippi Valley, it is hardy in Zone 5 and up. In colder areas remove from the pond and mulch heavily—it needs to go dormant to maintain health.

## *Juncus patens*
### California gray rush

A tender, clump-forming rush with slender foliage just ⅛ to ³⁄₁₆ inch in diameter that is stiff and dark gray. Excellent in pots. Grows in sun to shade, but has a tendency to flop in too much shade. Will grow in the perennial border if given enough moisture. Prefers moist soil or water to 6 inches deep. Height 18–30 inches and spread 24 inches. Zones 6–11. Native to California and, some experts say, along the Pacific Rim, including Japan, China, Korea, Russia, and Alaska.

*Juncus patens*

African thatching rush in a container garden with *Ranunculus ficaria*, *Hydrocotyle sibthorpioides* 'Variegata', *Samolus*, *Lemna major*, and *Juncus decipiens* 'Curly-wurly'

'Carmen's Grey' is a fantastic rush that was selected and brought back from Japan by Ed Carmen. This rush is widely popular and often grown from seed—some are not as nice as the original.

'Elk Blue' is a worthy cultivar discovered by Randy Baldwin in the hills southeast of Elk, California.

'Quartz Creek' is a selection from southern Oregon made by David Fross of Native Sons Nursery in Arroyo Grande, California. It reaches a height of 24–36 inches and spreads slowly to 24–36 inches wide.

### Juncus polyanthemus
**Australian silver rush**

Silvery-blue foliage gracefully arches and sways in the breeze. Very sculptural. Native to Australia. Forms large clumps. Excellent in containers. Generally 3–4 feet high, but sometimes even 5 feet. Spreads to 2–6 feet. Grows in sun to part shade, and it may lose its blue color if the shade is too dense. Takes moist soil or water to 1 inch. Zones 8–10. Bring in and treat as a houseplant where not hardy. It is great for indoor ponds because it does not go dormant.

### Juncus repens
**creeping rush**

Trailing runners clamber over sides of pots in containers, over waterfalls, down streams, and over rocks and edges. This species is great to soften the pond edge and weave between stones. Stems have a red cast, and chestnut-red seed heads add color all season, making it look like a flowering sedge. Roots form all along the stem. Grows in sun to shade in wet soil or water to 2 inches deep. It will also grow float-ing and submerged in flowing water. Height 6 inches, spreading 24 inches or more. Native to the U.S. Zone 5 and up. Bring in and treat as a houseplant in colder areas.

### Juncus spp.
**African thatching rush**

Very sturdy, dark hunter-green foliage that grows tall and thin, this rush is used for thatching in Africa. Upright habit when young, arching out as it matures. Looks and feels like plastic. This tolerates a lot of traffic without much harm. Can be used to overflow a container or the edge of a pond. Grows in sun to part shade in moist soil or, preferably, 1 inch of water, though it tolerates up to 6 inches. Height 36 inches and spread 2–6 feet. Hardy in Zone 8, otherwise bring indoors and treat as a houseplant. I originally received this plant from John Greenlee and have loved it ever since—a great plant.

### Juncus torreyi
**Torrey's sedge**

Reddish to deep brown seed heads form thick pom-poms about the size of a nickel. Stiff leaves that form colonies, not clumps, are very dark green with reddish bases. With its running spread it can get out of hand in a small pond if not potted, but can do nicely in a larger pond around taller plants that need socks. Grows in sun to shade in moist soil or water to 4 inches deep. Tolerates seasonal flooding. Height 12–18 inches, depending on exposure—more shade brings more height. Native to most of Canada and the very northern U.S. Zone 3 and up.

Justicia americana

### Justicia americana
### water willow
### Acanthaceae

A hardy relative to the shrimp plant (*Justicia brandegeeana*), *J. americana* produces masses of 1-inch clusters of white to pink-purple flowers in summer. Foliage is narrow, like willow leaves, and grows on shrubby plants 12–18 inches high and 12 inches wide. It grows in full sun or part shade and reaches about the same height whether grown in moist soil or up to 10 inches of water, and so creates a "fishable edge" in the earth-bottom pond. Grows from underground stoloniferous rhizomes and forms colonies, similar to the habit of lizard tail (*Saururus cernuus*). It is easily propagated by dividing the rhizomes in early spring before it gains significant new growth. Seed is easy to start but difficult to collect because it is spring loaded, much like *Ruellia* seed. Overwinter it in the pond—no need to submerge. Hardy in Zones 4–11. It grows wild in eastern North America, from Ontario and Quebec south to Georgia and Texas, and westward to Oklahoma and Wisconsin. Other species or subspecies in the genus may be localized. *Justicia ovata*, from Virginia to Florida, is said to have "more loosely flowered spikes." Much underused in the water garden and in wetland reclamation projects, *J. americana* is very attractive, easy to care for, and free-flowering. Water willow is an excellent plant to control soil erosion and is great in streams and other areas that have wave action or moving water.

### Laurentia palustris
### azure carpet
### Lobeliaceae

Narrow, short leaves form a dense tuft of bright green. Dainty flowers that resemble small blue lobelias appear in late spring to early summer. Height ⅛ inch with a creeping spread. Good for moist groundcover among rocks at the edge of the stream or waterfall, or in the moist soil of a bog garden. Grows in sun to part shade. Propagate by dividing the plant into smaller clumps in early spring. Hardy in Zones 6–11. Overwinter in colder climates by bringing inside and keeping as a houseplant. Slugs can occasionally be a problem.

### Lilium michiganense
### Michigan lily
### Liliaceae

This midwestern native has large, recurved, red-orange petals on tall plants. Plants resemble small-flowered tiger lilies. Grows 24–60 inches high and produces as few as one or as many as 25 flowers. Flowers are 4–5 inches across, generally orange with red throats and red spots. Grows in sun to

*Lilium michiganense* in the wild

shade in wet to evenly moist soil. Tolerates seasonal inundation. Great along a shady stream. Divide as a lily or start from seed or scale cuttings. Selections have been made in different colors, but it takes some searching to find them. Yellows, reds, and spot-free forms exist.

## *Limnocharis flava*
### velvet leaf
### Limnocharitaceae

Leaves of this tender marginal are spoon-shaped, pointed at their tips, and are soft and velvety to the touch. The plant has an open, mounded habit, reaching 12–18 inches high and 6 inches wide. Summer flowers are creamy yellow, single, three-petaled, open, rounded, and accented by a brown center. Blooms resemble those of *Hydrocleys nymphoides*, a member of the same family. Grows in sun to shade in moist soil or water to 3 inches deep. Propagate by dividing offshoots, or it is also viviparous. Hardy in Zones 9–11, it does not survive a frost. Bring indoors and keep as a houseplant in colder climates. It is native to the Americas south of Zone 10, including Mexico, Central America, and the Caribbean. It has naturalized in India, where it is considered a pest, and in southeast Asia, where it is eaten and used as fodder.

## *Limnophila aromatica*
### Scrophulariaceae

Generally limnophilas are sold as submerged aquarium plants, where they have finely cut foliage much like *Cabomba*. But emerged, growing in 2–4 inches of water, the foliage is toothed and opposite. Leaves are similar to garden phlox (*Phlox paniculata*). Flowers are ¾ inch and lavender, borne in the leaf axils toward the top of the plant. Height 12–14 inches. I have grown only *Limnophila aromatica* and *L. sessiliflora*. *Limnophila aromatica* is easier as an emerged plant. It flowers easily, sending out blooms anytime it is above water, and is useful for filling in around *Thalia* and tall *Pontederia*. Grows in sun to part shade, but seems to prefer part shade. Native to southeast Asia. Hardy in Zones 9–11. Overwinter indoors in a fish tank or as a houseplant. Stem cuttings are the best form of propagation.

## *Lobelia*
### Lobeliaceae

A favorite of the bog and perennial garden, lobelias are cherished for their brilliant flowers, which appear in late summer through fall. Flower petals are divided in half, with two tips pointing upward and three pointing downward, somewhat like a split-petaled snapdragon. Flower colors vary from bright red or bright blue through crimson and purple. On some selections, the foliage is purple or dark red. Leaves are narrow and grow alternately on a central stem. The plant does not usually branch, each stem growing from a separate crown. *Lobelia* species range from less than 12 inches to 5 feet in height. The dryland form, *L. inflata*, has many medicinal uses and has an effect like nicotine, where it excites nerve cells and then paralyzes them. Although lobelias have been used medicinally, their milky juices contain toxins.

Lobelias attract butterflies and hummingbirds, which help in pollination. The lower petals of *Lobelia siphilitica* form a definite platform for pollinating insects. The cardinal flower, which lacks this petal formation, is pollinated by hummingbirds, which do so "on the wing."

Lobelias are easily propagated by division in spring. *Lobelia siphilitica* and *L. cardinalis* may also be propagated by floating mature stems in water. Plantlets will sprout at the leaf node. Once they have begun to root, they may be divided and planted out in the water garden. They also grow well from seed. As always, seed is good for the species, division for cultivars.

Native to Europe, the British Isles, and North America. Some species are not reliably hardy in cold climates. It is best to place them deep in the pond for the winter or to mulch them well in the perennial bed. Sometimes they will not return in the spring despite a gardener's best efforts.

Lobelia cardinalis

Lobelia cardinalis 'Red Giant'

## Lobelia cardinalis
### cardinal flower

This species is known for its bright crimson flowers, which appear from July through September on single stems that reach up to 3 feet in height. Leaves are ovate, clothing the stems until the terminal flower spikes occur. Grows in sun to part shade in moist soil or water to 3 inches deep. Spreads to 12 inches. Zones 5–11, but Zone 3 with snow cover. Native to North America.

The large-sized selection, 'Red Giant', reaches to more than 5 feet in height when in flower. Cardinal flower is often hybridized with *Lobelia siphilitica* to produce cultivars that are spectacular for their flower color. *Lobelia* 'Tania' has bronze foliage with large, fuchsia-blue flowers, and *L.* 'Russian Princess' has burgundy foliage and bright red flowers. Many more selections and hybrids are introduced every year.

## Lobelia dortmanna
### water lobelia

A native of colder areas of North America, water lobelia grows with submerged foliage along sandy shores or in the shallow waters of soft-water lakes. It has thin leaves ⅛ inch wide and 1 inch or so long that are actually two hollow tubes joined together. Tips are rounded and recurved. Plants are clump-forming, spreading to 6 inches, connected by underground stolons. Flowers are blue or white and less than 1 inch long, held above the water surface. Stems rise 6–12 inches above the leaf clump in water less than 6 inches deep. Grows in sun to part shade in water no deeper than 8 feet, in which it grows fully submerged and does not flower. Zones 4–9. I have grown this, and it is great in a little pool in a stream.

Lobelia 'Russian Princess'

Lobelia siphilitica 'Alba'

## Lobelia fulgens
**red-leafed lobelia**

Native to Mexico and the southern U.S., this red-flowered species is similar to *Lobelia cardinalis* but has dark red stems and, sometimes, leaves. Grows in sun to part shade in moist soil or water to 3 inches deep. Height 12–36 inches, spread 12 inches. Zones 9–11. Overwinter in a cold frame.

'Queen Victoria' is possibly a cultivar of *Lobelia fulgens* or a hybrid between that and *L. cardinalis*. It has dark red leaves and stems and scarlet flowers, growing to 4 feet high.

## Lobelia kalmii
**brook lobelia**

Growing wild in fens of the northern United States and into Canada, this lobelia grows to about 15 inches tall and 3 inches wide. It has linear, basal leaves that are spatula-shaped and that may be deciduous. It keeps a basal rosette but it may

be very compressed. Flowers are small on spikes about 2¾–5¼ inches, and are blue with a pronounced white eye. Flowers from July to October. It is "characteristic of calcareous fens and shores" and "also occurs on calcareous soils of wet to wet-mesic prairies and wet lake dune flats if groundwater seepages are present" (*Plants of the Chicago Region*, 4th ed., by F. Swink and G. Wilhelm, 1994, Indiana Academy of Science: Indianapolis). It grows best in part shade in ephemeral ponds that are just damp by fall. This is great in a pool of a stream. Zones 3–6.

## Lobelia sessilifolia

Native to Japan and southeast Asia, this species grows about 15–24 inches tall and 4–12 inches wide with lance-shaped, toothed leaves. Its violet-colored flowers appear at the leaf axils, blooming in June and July. It likes acid soil and moist conditions in sun to part shade. Tolerates winter flooding. Hardy to Zone 5.

## Lobelia siphilitica
**giant blue lobelia**

Native to fens of eastern North America, giant blue lobelia is very similar to cardinal flower in form and habit. Leaves are slightly more lance-shaped and irregularly toothed. Flowers are bright blue. Flower spikes are densely covered with blooms from July through October. Grows in sun to part shade in moist soil or water to 3 inches deep. Performs best in neutral or alkaline soil. Height 12–36 inches and spread 12 inches. Zones 3–11.

A dwarf selection, 'Nana', is available, as well as white forms. 'Alba', giant white lobelia, is a popular selection.

*Lobelia siphilitica*

*Ludwigia arcuta*

A tetraploid strain called *Lobelia ×speciosa*, created by Wray Bowden of Ontario, Canada, through crossing *L. cardinalis* with *L. siphilitica* and *L. fulgens*, is very winter hardy and flowers in red, pink, and purple shades. Also *L. ×gerardii*, another product of crossing *L. cardinalis* with *L. siphilitica*, has purple-violet flowers and leaves that are broadly lanceolate and dark green, turning reddish. Uses and culture are like *L. fulgens*, but it is hardy to Zone 8, possibly Zone 7. *L. ×gerardii* 'Rosencavalier' is a pink form that comes true from seed and reportedly was originated from *L. ×gerardii* 'Blauzauber'.

## Ludwigia
**water primrose**
Onagraceae

*Ludwigia* species range in size from large—more than 8 feet tall—to very small—less than 6 inches tall. They are almost cosmopolitan, occurring in most parts of the world. Leaves are usually rounded, toothed, and shiny. Flowers are mostly yellow, single, flat, and four-petaled. They often form pneumatophores, spongy white spikes that appear at the base of the stem and help the plant absorb oxygen from the water. They grow in sun to part shade in moist soil or water to varying depths. Ludwigias propagate easily from stem cuttings and may also be grown from seed. Sow moist and keep them at 70°F and they will sprout in about one month. I surface sow, then dust sand on top. Frost-tender species are best overwintered as a houseplant in colder climates, or bring in stem cuttings and keep in a vase of water in a warm, sunny windowsill.

## Ludwigia alternifolia

This form is similar to *Ludwigia decurrens* and *L. leptocarpaare*. It is covered all summer with 1–2-inch yellow flowers. It has wide, deep green leaves that resemble a willow. It complements hibiscus, asclepias, and red rice. Grows to 4 feet tall and 2–4 feet wide in 2–12 inches of water. Zones 5–11.

## Ludwigia arcuta
**primrose creeper**

A great pond cover, primrose creeper creates an unusual visual effect in the water garden. As it floats out over the water, it holds the last 6 inches or so of its foliage straight up from the water surface. Summertime flowers are a cheerful, bright yellow, about 1 inch wide. Spreads 12–24 inches. Water to 2 inches deep. Zones 6–11. 'Grandiflora', or improved primrose creeper, has many more flowers than the standard form.

*Ludwigia arcuta*

*Ludwigia ascendens*

*Ludwigia arcuta 'Grandiflora'*

## Ludwigia ascendens

This species is very similar to other water primroses but has white flowers. Its shiny leaves creep along on stems that float on the water surface. They never stand up out of the water, but rather mound along. It spreads 4 feet or more and reaches 4–6 inches high. Grows in moist soil or water to 6 inches deep, floating in deeper water. *Ludwigia ascendens* makes a wonderful contribution to the all-white garden and shines beautifully at the base of taller pickerel plants (*Pontederia cordata*). Zones 9–11.

## Ludwigia decurrens

This species is similar to both *Ludwigia alternifolia* and *L. leptocarpaare*. It is covered all summer long with 1–2-inch, medium yellow flowers. Wide, deep green leaves, similar to willow leaves, add to the beauty of this plant. Its many branches add the fullness that any pondscape needs. Looks great with hibiscus, asclepias, and red rice. Grows to 4 feet tall and 2–4 feet wide in moist soil or water to 6 inches deep. Zones 7–11.

*Ludwigia leptocarpaare*

*Ludwigia linearis*

## Ludwigia leptocarpaare

*Ludwigia leptocarpaare* is similar to both *L. alternifolia* and *L. decurrens*. It complements hibiscus, asclepias and red rice. The plant is covered all summer long with 1–2-inch, medium yellow flowers. Wide, deep green leaves, similar to willow leaves, on well-branched plants help transition the pond to the rest of the garden. Reaching 4 feet tall it provides needed height to the pondscape. It spreads 2–4 feet wide in moist soil or water to 4 inches deep. Zones 9–11.

## Ludwigia linearis

It has very willowy, shiny leaves on tall, often unbranched, upright stems. You will need a few of these plants to achieve an appearance of fullness. Flowers are very yellow and can exceed 2 inches in diameter. They look great planted with blue ruellias or red hibiscus. This species also looks great along a shoreline or mixed into a bed of arrowhead (*Sagit-*

*taria*) or lizard tail (*Saururus cernuus*). Tolerates sun to part shade, growing in moist soil or water to 6 inches deep. Height 4 feet and spread 2–4 feet. Hardy to Zone 6, but it reseeds itself in colder areas.

## Ludwigia maritima

This species is very similar to *Ludwigia virgata*. It also has two or more upright stems that branch from the base, creating a fuller bush. Reaches 2–4 feet high and wide. It produces yellow flowers that average 1–1½ inches. Grows in moist soil or water to 6 inches deep. Great with taros (*Colocasia*) and other large foliage plants.

## Ludwigia palustris

This form of *Ludwigia* is most often grown submerged, creating a beautiful, underwater ground cover. While submerged, the foliage is green or, in some forms, a deep

*Ludwigia peploides*

*Ludwigia peruviana*

*Ludwigia peruviana*

red-brown color. When grown out of the water, it makes a great ground cover around pots or trailing down a water-fall. It grows very densely in full sunlight and less so in shade, reaching 6 inches high and 24 inches wide. It has small flowers but these do not add to the aesthetic value of the plants. Overwinter by submerging to the bottom of the pond. Hardy to Zone 4.

### *Ludwigia peploides*
**dwarf primrose creeper**

Similar to *Ludwigia repens*, with a creeping habit, this selection has yellow-orange flowers of 1–1½ inches. Grows in moist soil or water to 3 inches deep. Height 4–6 inches, spread 2–4 feet. Zones 8–11.

### *Ludwigia peruviana*
**sunshine bush**

This is a shrubby form that can grow into a small tree 2–8 feet high in a single season. It will reach this size from seed sown in February and planted out as 1-foot-tall seedlings in mid-May here in the Chicago area. It has 1–2-inch flowers all summer long. Grows in full sun to part shade in water to 10 inches deep. Spreads 2–8 feet. Zones 9–11. Great in containers or large ponds.

### *Ludwigia repens*
**red ludwigia**

A creeping form spreading to 24 inches with bright green leaves on red stems. Flowers are very tiny, with extremely small petals or none at all, so that they may look green. A small plant reaching 6–10 inches high, it is ideal for a waterfall or as a groundcover at the edge of a pond or bog. Water to 2 inches deep and tolerates seasonal submersion. Zones 5–11. Some forms are a deep red.

*Lychnis flos-cuculi*

*Lychnis flos-cuculi*

### Ludwigia sedioides

This species is distinctive because its leaves float on the water surface, similar to a waterlily. It looks the least like a ludwigia. The leaves are shaped like a square paddle, with teeth on two edges. They arise from a central core and, as they grow, form a pattern reminiscent of a mosaic. They are red tinted and very shiny when the plant is in flower. Single, bright yellow flowers rise slightly out of the water. The plant prefers acid water of less than 7.5 pH, and will languish and die in water that is neutral to alkaline. It grows best in sun to part shade, reaching 2–4 inches high and branching freely to form large patches with a 12-inch spread. *Ludwigia sedioides* is native to Brazil and grows in moist soil or water to 3–12 inches deep. Zones 9–11.

### Ludwigia uruguayensis

This species has hairy leaves and is more upright, reaching 6 inches tall. It grows in moist soil or water to 2 inches deep, spreading 12–24 inches. Its clear yellow flowers usually rise up out of the water. Zones 6–11.

### Ludwigia virgata

This form is similar to *Ludwigia linearis* but is smaller. It has two or more upright stems that branch from the base, creating a fuller bush. It produces yellow flowers that average 1–1½ inches in diameter. Reaches 4 feet high and 2–4 feet wide in moist soil or water to 6 inches deep. They are very attractive with taros (*Colocasia*) and other large foliage plants.

### Lychnis flos-cuculi
**ragged robin**
Caryophyllaceae

Leaves of this wet-tolerant perennial are narrow, just ½ inch wide and 2–3 inches long. Flowers rise above the base of the plant on tall, 12–24-inch, arching stems. White or pink, finely cut blooms of ½–¾ inch appear at the tip in a cluster. A very delicate plant that is delightful in moist soil at the edge of the pond margin or in the bog garden. It tolerates about a week of high water, as in drainage basins. Grows in sun to 10 inches tall or part shade to 24 inches. Spreads 10 inches. Propagate by division of clumps in early spring, as for a daylily (*Hemerocallis*). Zones 5–8. Not particularly cold-tolerant, it should be heavily mulched. The foliage is evergreen and is damaged below 10°F. European native that has naturalized in eastern North America. 'Nana' is a dwarf form available in both white and pink. It grows to only 4–6 inches tall and wide.

Lycopus americanus

Lycopus europaeus

## Lycopus americanus
### American bugleweed, cut-leafed water horehound
### Lamiaceae

Native to North America, this species has square stems and toothed leaves. Small white to pink flowers bloom at the leaf axils in summer but are not highly ornamental. It is usually grown for its foliage, which has a highly cut texture, like Italian parsley. It is a very common wetland plant, occurring in sedge meadows, marshes, fens, wet mesic prairies, floodplains, and ditches. Grows in sun to shade to 12–24 inches high and 12 inches wide. Best if kept contained, for it can muscle out other plants. Propagate by seed or division. Hardy in Zones 4–11.

Its rambunctious European cousin *Lycopus europaeus* is not recommended for the water garden or the perennial bed. It has often hairy leaves that are opposite, lance-shaped, deeply toothed, and an even green color. In the spring and fall, foliage takes on a bright burgundy color. It quickly crowds out other perennials in the pond margin, and worse yet, it seeds itself into the perennial border, where it grows with equal force and vigor. The two species are virtually the same, but *L. americanus* has more finely cut foliage that is not hairy.

## Lysichiton
### skunk cabbage
### Aracaea

Lysichitons are noted for their large, rippled leaves and unusual "hoods" that cloak spathes of flowers in early spring, April or May, often as the leaves are only just starting to break through the soil. As the flowers pass away, the foliage takes center stage. The common name comes from the musky odor released when the leaves or flowers are crushed. The sap from the leaves and roots can make your hands itch. Very striking in damp shade, often growing among trees along stream beds and creeks. Propagate from seed or by dividing off side-eyes of mature clumps. They

*Lysichiton americanum*

overwinter well in northern climates and need no special care or protection. A hybrid of *Lysichiton americanum* and *L. camtschatcensis* is available with cream flowers.

### Lysichiton americanum
**yellow skunk cabbage**

The "hood" of this species is bright yellow. It grows to 10 inches high and about 3–5 inches wide. Leaves appear later and reach 3–4 feet tall. Grows in part shade in moist soil. Spreads 3–4 feet. Striking at the edge of a stream or pond. Native to western North America, from Alaska southward into California and eastward to Montana. Tolerates seasonal flooding. Best planted under a canopy of deciduous trees to provide shade during the heat of summer. Zones 4–7.

### Lysichiton camtschatcensis
**white skunk cabbage**

Similar to other species, but with a white hood that is shorter, broader, and more rounded than that of *Lysichiton*

*americanum*. Mature foliage is slightly shorter than other species, 3–3½ feet high. Needs acid soil, moist to wet. Tolerates some flooding. Grows in part shade, spreading 3–3½ feet. Not quite as cold-tolerant as yellow skunk cabbage. Native to northern and eastern Russia and Japan. Zones 5–7.

### Lysimachia
**Primulaceae**

*Lysimachia* is a cheerful clan of moisture-loving plants that usually have yellow flowers that bloom in summer at or near the leaf axils, although flower shape varies considerably among the different species. Many adapt well to the perennial border, although they grow equally well in sun to part shade at the margins of the pond or in container water gardens. Besides the species listed here, Leo Jelitto and Wilhelm Schacht in *Hardy Herbaceous Perennials* (3rd ed., 1990, Timber Press: Portland, Ore.) refer to *L. barystachys*, *L. ephemerum*, *L. lanceolata*, *L. nemorum*, and *L. vulgaris*. They say that all prefer wet soil but will grow in the perennial border.

*Lysimachia* species are native to temperate regions of the northern hemisphere. Several grow naturally in North America. Most species are cold tolerant and require no special protection through the winter. They are usually propagated by dividing the fleshy underground stems, which root easily, but can also be grown from seed.

### Lysimachia ciliata
**golden lanterns**

Leaves of this species are similar to those of other lysimachias, ovate and tipped, slightly toothed, about 1 inch wide and 3 inches long. In the summer, yellow flowers that look like pagoda lanterns appear near the leaf axils. They dry well and make interesting additions to floral arrangements. Grows best in moist soil or tolerates water 6 inches deep. Height 36 inches, spread 24 inches. Zones 5–11.

### Lysimachia clethroides
**gooseneck loosestrife**

Foliage is lance-shaped and hairy. Small white blooms appear in spikes at the end of stems in July through September. The spikes lean horizontally and often tilt at the tip, giving them the look of a goose's head. Reaches 36 inches high with a running spread. This species is not a true aquatic but tolerates moist soil, making it very useful at the edge of the pond margin and in the higher reaches of the bog garden. Zones 4–11. Native to Japan, China, and Korea.

*Lysimachia clethroides*

*Lysimachia nummularia 'Aurea'*

*Lysimachia nummularia 'Aurea'*

*Lysimachia nummularia*

## *Lysimachia nummularia*
## creeping Jenny

An excellent ground cover for the edge of the water garden or pond, creeping Jenny also is well suited to scramble down a waterfall or tumble from the edge of a tub garden. Grows to 1 inch high and creeping in moist soil or water to 1 inch deep. It has rounded leaves that clasp on opposite sides of its stem, forming a tight, dense chain of foliage. Yellow flowers appear in the summer, with rounded petals that form open blooms held at the leaf axils. A variegated form, 'Aurea', or golden creeping Jenny, is very popular for its clear yellow foliage. It does not flower as freely as the species. Zones 4–10. Native to Europe and widely naturalized in many parts of the world.

*Lysimachia punctata*

## *Lysimachia punctata*
**golden candles**

Native to Europe and Asia and now naturalized throughout North America, this species has oval to lance-shaped, pointed leaves that are slightly toothed. Its bright yellow flowers are held close to the stem and are slightly cup-shaped. Reaching 24 inches high and 6 inches wide in moist soil, it is almost indestructible. A variegated form, 'Alexander', or variegated golden candles, has creamy white margins on its leaves. In the spring and again in the fall, leaves are tinged in pink. With the same bright yellow flowers, the overall effect is quite stunning. 'Golden Alexander' is a variegated form with gold-margined foliage.

*Lysimachia punctata* 'Alexander'

*Lysimachia punctata* 'Alexander' in spring

*Lysimachia terrestris*

*Lysimachia terrestris*

## *Lysimachia terrestris*
### swamp candles

A tall, showy species native to North America, growing as far south as Georgia. Height 8–18 inches and spread 6 inches. Flowers are borne terminally, comprising the top 4–6 inches of the plant. Some forms have a red eye in the flowers. Grows in sun to full shade, shorter in sun and taller in shade, in moist soil or water to 2–6 inches deep. Lightly branching, it forms loose stands somewhat like lizard tail (*Saururus cernuus*). Bright yellow fall color. Zones 4–9.

## *Lysimachia thyrsiflora*
### tufts of gold

Smaller than other upright species, this wetland plant has thin, ½-inch-wide leaves that are ovate and pointed, about 2 inches long. Flowers look like tufts of yellow, held near the stem and leaf axil. They appear in mid-spring and last for several days. In the fall, withered stems turn a brilliant yellow. Excellent for the front of the bog garden or at the edge of the stream. I like to mix this with *Asclepias incarnata* and *Iris virginica* in detention areas. Grows in moist soil or water to 6 inches deep, reaching 12 inches high and wide. Zones 5–8.

## *Lythrum*
### Lythraceae

*Lythrum* is a cosmopolitan genus, with various species occurring in temperate climates around the world. *Lythrum salicaria* and *L. virgatum*, both commonly called purple loosestrife, brought from Europe and Asia in the 1800s, now overtake wetlands in North America, especially those in the East and Midwest. Although these exotic species are reputedly sterile, they cross freely with each other to create fertile hybrids that are just as invasive as their parents. It is illegal in many states to sell, distribute, plant, or cultivate them. Nevertheless many sources sell them and many gardeners plant them, to the detriment of our disappearing wetlands and the wildlife that depends upon them.

Lysimachia thyrsiflora

Lythrum 'Blush'

*Lythrum* is characterized by lance-shaped leaves that clasp directly to the square stem. The plant grows quickly, usually reaching about 3 feet in height. From late summer through frost, it has terminal flower spikes that are covered with hundreds of small purple flowers. These flowers produce hundreds of seeds, which need only about eight weeks to reach bloom size. The species native to North America, *L. alatum* or winged loosestrife, has flowers with shorter petals that are solitary on most of the leaf axils. It is not invasive like its exotic cousins, and its presence in our native wetlands is threatened by the non-native species. Authorities have released beetles and weevils that prey upon the exotic species in an effort to bring them under control. Initial trials indicated that the insects posed little danger to agricultural crops and most native plants. Unfortunately, it appears that the insects may not be able to distinguish between the non-native forms of *Lythrum* and our own native species. In addition to winged loosestrife, our native swamp loosestrife (*Decodon verticillatus*) also appears to be at risk.

Lythrum 'Morden Pink'

*Marsilea mutica*

*Marsilea mutica* 'Micro Mini'

*Marsilea drummondii*

*Marsilea drummondii*

### Marsilea
### water clover
### Marsileaceae

Delightful additions to the water garden, *Marsilea* species are the lucky charms of the pond. Their clover-shaped foliage belies the fact that they are really ferns, which reproduce by spores. Sporocarps are the spore-bearing bodies of the plants, like modified fronds. The location and shape of the sporocarps are generally the key to proper identification. Marsileas are grown for their attractive foliage and ease of care, not for any floral attributes. Most species have foliage that emerges above the water surface. Only one species, *M. mutica*, has leaves that float on the water. The emerged leaves open in the morning and close at night, giving the appearance of many small butterflies at rest. All species have four lobes to each leaf. Some have leaves that are hairy, others smooth. Marsileas are easily propagated by stem cuttings. They grow natively in many parts of the world, mostly tropical to warm regions. In very cold climates, overwinter by bringing indoors and keeping as houseplants.

### Marsilea drummondii
### hairy water clover

Leaves are silvery, accented by brown stems. Grows in sun to shade in moist soil or water to 4 inches deep. Reaches 3–6 inches high with a running spread. Zones 5–11.

### Marsilea mutica 'Micro Mini'

Probably three different plants are sold under this name. All are very similar, but insufficient work has been done on their

*Marsilea quadrifolia*

*Marsilea schelpiana*

true identity. Leaves about the size of a dime float on the water surface or rise slightly above it. Ideal for container water gardens. Dense growth can reach 3 inches high, but usually is no more than 1 inch above the soil line. It has a running spread. Grows in sun to shade in moist soil or water to 4 inches deep. Zones 5–11.

### Marsilea quadrifolia
**upright water clover**

Growing from Spain to Japan and naturalized in eastern North America, this species has very upright and triangular leaves. Good for waterfalls and for giving small fish a place to hide. A rampant grower in sun to shade in moist soil or water to 4 inches deep. Reaches 6 inches high with a running spread. Zones 5–11.

### Marsilea rotundifolia
**butterfly water clover**

Two or more plants are sold under this name, their exact identities remaining unclear. Foliage is more rounded than in other species. This species is not cold-tolerant, rated hardy in Zones 8–11. Grows in sun to shade in moist soil or water to 6 inches or more deep. Reaches 6 inches high with a running spread.

*Marsilea rotundifolia*

### Marsilea schelpiana
**cut-leafed water clover**

Leaves are finely and irregularly cut, giving the plant a lacy and delicate air. Grows in sun to shade in moist soil or water to 3 inches deep. Reaches 6 inches high with a running spread. Zones 6–11.

Planting stem cuttings of *Mentha*

## *Mentha*
## mint
## Lamiaceae

*Mentha* species are highly fragrant and have long been used for their aromatic qualities. Garden mints are European and have been introduced into many other parts of the world, including North America. Many other mints are native across the northern hemisphere. Several species are tolerant of wet soils, even those that are usually grown in the perennial border (spearmint, *M. spicata*, for example). The ones listed here require wet conditions in order to grow and prosper. Mint leaves are lance-shaped, lobed, toothed, and often hairy, especially on the bottom. Color is an attractive, even green. Flowers are clustered balls of tiny blue or pink flowers surrounding the stem like little pom-poms. Blossoms appear in midsummer and continue until fall. When cool weather arrives, foliage turns purple. Because of their running habit, *Mentha* species should be kept containerized for best effect. They are easy to propagate, especially from stem cuttings, or by division. And they will tolerate freezing temperatures and conditions, so no special care is required in colder climates.

## *Mentha aquatica*
### aquatic mint

This species is always a favorite with water gardeners. It is highly fragrant, flowers well with lavender-pink blooms, and attracts plenty of butterflies. Foliage can be used in teas and jellies. Grows in sun to part shade in moist soil or water to 2 inches deep. It reaches 3–12 inches high with a running habit. Zones 5-11.

## *Mentha arvensis*
### wild mint

This native mint has leaves that are lance-shaped and sharply toothed. Pink flowers appear at the leaf axils, surrounding the stem like little pom-poms, and bloom from July through frost. It can be found growing in northern areas in sedge meadows, fens, alder thickets, and shallow marshes, along streams and shores. Grows in sun to part shade in wet soil or water to 1 inch deep. Reaches 12–24 inches tall with a running spread. Zone 4 and up.

## *Mentha pulegium*
### brook mint

A much more diminutive version, this species has airy, dainty flowers of sky blue. It is just as fragrant as other mints and attracts just as many butterflies—it is probably the "mintiest" of the mints. Perfect for growing among rocks at the edge of the pond or in the nooks and crannies of a bog garden. Grows in sun to part shade in moist soil or water to ½-inch deep. Reaches just ½ inch tall with a running habit. Zones 5–11.

*Mentha aquatica*

*Menyanthes trifoliata*

*Menyanthes trifoliata*

## *Menyanthes trifoliata*
**bog bean, buck bean**
**Menyanthaceae**

Growing wild in bogs and shallow lakes, bog bean has large, three-lobed leaves that are lance-shaped and markedly veined. The foliage grows from a creeping rhizome that frequently floats out onto the water surface. It does best in 1–3 inches of water but can grow out from the margin, floating on the pond. I have also observed this growing floating over 6 feet of water. Flower buds are pink clusters that open to white, fringed, star-shaped blooms that are highly fragrant, not unlike the scent of vanilla. The flower stalks generally stand 2–6 inches taller than the leaves, giving the plant an overall height of 6–9 inches. Blossoms appear anywhere from late May through July but are rather short-lived. For the rest of the growing season, the foliage forms a quite dense mat on the water surface. Situate in full sun to part shade. Zones 2–7, given its circumboreal origins. It may freeze solid in the winter as long as it is kept in water. Best propagated by dividing the rootstock in summer after flowering.

## *Mimulus*
**monkey flower**
**Scrophulariaceae**

Mimulus species are best known for their flowers, which are tubular and resemble snapdragons. They range in color from blue to purple and occasionally white, yellow, or red. Leaves are lance-shaped or ovoid and either toothed or lobed. Although they grow adequately in full sun, they prefer part shade, where they grow taller and stay greener. Deadheading encourages more blooms and stretches the growing season. Much underused and overlooked. Useful for margins and along streams. Found in many parts of the temperate climates of the world, especially North America. It overwinters well in colder climates, and may be propagated by division, seed, or stem cuttings. Cuttings can be taken anytime until they set seed. Root in moist soil or sand.

*Mimulus alatus*

*Mimulus cardinalis*

## *Mimulus alatus*
### sharp-winged monkey flower

Use this species to add height to shady pond plantings—it is great with *Carex* or American skunk cabbage (*Symplocarpus foetidus*). *Mimulus alatus* is native to North America, more common in southern climates. It has stalked leaves and a winged stem. Flowers are usually lavender. Grows in part to full shade in moist soil or water to 6 inches deep. Height 12–36 inches, spread 12 inches. Zones 5–11. A rare white-flowering form, 'Snow Crystal', is commercially available. Easily crosses with other *Mimulus* species, especially *M. ringens.*

## *Mimulus cardinalis*
### red, cardinal, or scarlet monkey flower

This great native has large, 1–2-inch flowers of tomato-red to cherry-red. Leaves are hairy and sticky, with prominent joints that look like knuckles. Hardy in Zones 5–8, possibly 9 with shade. It does poorly in humid weather. Grows 24 inches tall and 12 inches wide in just wet soil. It is easy to grow from seed, but divide or take cuttings of good selections. Aphids can sometimes be a problem, as well as a root rot fungus like fusarium when stressed. When conditions are right it is easy to grow. Grows in part shade and thrives in mountain sites that are sunny but cool in summer. I have observed many examples of this plant in Yosemite National Park growing in dripping seeps on the mountainside. A yellow form is also available.

*Mimulus guttatus*

*Mimulus guttatus*

### *Mimulus guttatus*
**yellow monkey flower, seep spring monkey flower**

Highly variable, this species may grow from 6 inches to 3 feet in height. Grows throughout North America, but is not as cold tolerant as other species. Has yellow flowers with characteristic shape but up to 1½ inches in size. Grows in part to full shade in moist soil or water to 1 inch deep. Spread 8–10 inches. Zones 6–9. A variegated cultivar, 'Variegatus' (syn. 'Richard Bish') has gold splashes on its foliage and is very striking even when not in bloom. There is also a double form called hose in hose.

*Mimulus* 'Lothian Fire'

*Mimulus* 'Lothian Fire'

*Mimulus ringens*

## *Mimulus* 'Lothian Fire'
**red monkey flower**

Although this plant may not be very tall, its bold flowers make a lasting impression. The blooms are bright red trumpets with yellow throats. They are well accented by shiny green leaves that have red stems. Stunning when cascading down a stream or waterfall. Give sun to part shade and moist soil or water to 1 inch deep. It does best in moving water. Height 12 inches, spread 12 inches. Zones 7–9.

## *Mimulus ringens*
**lavender monkey flower**

This species grows freely through much of North America, from Nova Scotia to Georgia and into Texas. It has unstalked leaves that are oblong and somewhat toothed. Flowers are a lovely lavender color, varying from almost grape to almost white, peeking out from between the shiny jade-green leaves. It blooms profusely. Grows in sun to part shade in water up to 6 inches deep. Reaches 20–30 inches high and 12–20 inches wide. Zones 5–11. Great with sedges, *Scirpus*, *Juncus*, or *Asclepias*.

## Myosotis
### Boraginaceae

The genus *Myosotis* includes both wetland and dryland species. The wetland species are delightful front-of-the-pond margin plants that bring in the early summer with sprays of flowers that resemble small, delicate, single roses. Color ranges from white to pink to light blue and bright blue, depending upon the cultivar. Most grow to about 6 inches or so in height, spreading to about 12 inches, with small, oblong leaves that are usually clear green and somewhat hairy. They form a dense mat that grows well not only at the edge of the water garden, but also in a stream or waterfall. Grows easily from seed, stem cuttings, or division. Colors come true from seed if different colors are not growing right next to each other. After its first flowering, myosotis will often flower intermittently throughout the summer as long as the weather stays cool. In warm, humid climates, the plants will wither some and may turn dark, black, and crispy. Trim these unhappy leaves and wait until cooler days return. The plants will resprout and begin to rebloom. In very southern climates of the United States, they are best grown as winter annuals, much like pansies. Generally hardy in Zones 4–9, they overwinter well in colder climates, being native to Europe and Siberia. *Myosotis* species are widely naturalized in temperate regions, including North America.

Although it resembles the myosotis that grows in the perennial border, wetland myosotis will not survive the drier conditions that exist outside the pond. There is no way to look at the foliage or flowers in order to distinguish a dryland from a wetland species, unless you are a botanist. If it grows in the pond, it is an aquatic form; if it withers and starts to die in the pond, then it belongs in the perennial bed. *Myosotis* grows well in moving water, benefiting from the additional oxygen that comes with the flow of water through its roots. It is good for filtration and helps reduce the occurrence of green algae in the pond.

*Myosotis laxa*, or small-flowered forget-me-not, has much smaller flowers than *M. scorpioides*. This wetland species is native to North America, but is not commonly available for sale. It grows about 12 inches tall and is almost grassy-looking.

*Myosotis laxa*

### *Myosotis scorpioides* 'Mayfair'
### variegated water forget-me-not

Leaves of this selection are margined in creamy white, making the plant attractive even when it is not in flower. In spring, it has characteristic blue blossoms. Grows in sun to part shade in moist soil or water to 1 inch deep. It is difficult to grow but can be stunning.

### *Myosotis scorpioides* 'Mermaid'
### blue water forget-me-not

An improved selection, 'Mermaid' has larger blue flowers that are dotted with white eyes. Blooms in spring. Leaves are also slightly larger than on other cultivars. Grows in sun to part shade in moist soil or water to 1 inch deep. It is more compact with short internodes, forming a nice mound. Slightly more tender with hardiness rated at Zones 5–9.

*Myosotis scorpioides* 'Mermaid'

*Myosotis scorpioides* 'Pinkie'

*Myosotis scorpioides* 'Snowflakes'

### *Myosotis scorpioides* 'Pinkie'
**pink water forget-me-not**

Growing just like its blue siblings, 'Pinkie' forms a creeping cushion of cotton-candy-pink flowers with white eyes in spring. Excellent for underplanting around larger marginals in the pond, or tucked into a pocket along a stream or waterfall. Also performs well in a table-top pond. Grows in sun to bright shade in moist soil or water to 1 inch deep. Spread is smaller at 6–10 inches.

### *Myosotis scorpioides* 'Snowflakes'
**white water forget-me-not**

'Snowflakes' is a unique cultivar with crystal white flowers starting in spring and continuing through summer. Blooms are large and long lasting, covering a vigorous plant that is easy to grow. Situate in sun to part shade in moist soil or water to 1 inch deep. This selection originated from Pineknot Gardens in North Carolina.

### *Myosotis scorpioides* 'Wisconsin'
**blue water forget-me-not**

Starting in spring, this selection has blue flowers that fade to pink. It continues to flower off and on throughout the summer, and blooms heavier again in the fall. Situate in sun to part shade in moist soil or water to 1 inch deep. Zones 4–9.

*Myriophyllum aquaticum*

*Myriophyllum aquaticum*

*Myriophyllum papillosum*

## *Myriophyllum aquaticum*
**parrot feather**
**Haloragaceae**

An old standby in the water garden, parrot feather has feathery foliage that floats out effortlessly over the water surface. Grows well at the edge of the pond as well as the side of a stream or waterfall. Whorls of leaves may be 3 inches or more in diameter, growing on long trailing stems. If the plant starts to look scraggly, simply cut off the last 6 or 8 inches of new growth and discard the more mature foliage. Or cut the long stringy stems back into 6–8-inch pieces, bundle them together with a rubber band, and pot them up. They will root readily and form more full plants, much like pinching back petunias.

Although it is sometimes listed as an oxygenating plant, *Myriophyllum aquaticum* is not a species that is commonly grown underwater. There are many, many submerged forms of *Myriophyllum*. They bear some resemblance to *M. aquaticum* but grow more readily beneath the water surface. One underwater species introduced from Europe—*M. spicatum*, or Eurasian water milfoil—is considered an invasive weed for its ability to form dense underwater mats. It should not be grown in the pond or water garden. Other species, native to North America, are valued for their contributions to the aquatic community. *Myriophyllum farwellii* is listed as a "special concern" because of its scarceness. For more about underwater species, see Chapter 11.

The ease of growth that parrot feather displays has earned it a place on the prohibited noxious weed list in some states. Care should be taken to check with authorities before growing the plant in warmer climates. It grows in sun to part shade. Height 6 inches when rooted in soil, with a running spread. Does best in moist soil or up to 6 inches of water, but will grow floating over any depth. *Myriophyllum aquaticum* is native to South America. Hardy in Zones 6–11. In colder climates where frost may occur, bring stem cuttings into the house for the winter. The plant may survive a winter freeze if submerged beneath the water, but it is not reliably hardy in cold regions.

The same in all respects but smaller is *Myriophyllum papillosum* var. *pulcherrima*, dwarf parrot feather or red stem parrot feather. It is one-third to half the size of *M. aquaticum* and is a great selection for small ponds and containers. It grows more full with more branching.

## Oenanthe
### Apiaceae

Oenanthes have finely cut foliage that resembles the leaves of celery or parsley. They are aromatic and even edible, having a peppery, celery-like flavor that is suitable for salads and stuffings. Leaves grow from running stems that root quickly at the leaf nodes, making stem cuttings the easiest form of propagation, though division works too. Flowers are umbels of small, white, star-like blossoms that appear in summer and continue through to fall. The plants are excellent for filtration, taking up nutrients that would otherwise contribute to green algae in the pond. *Oenanthe* overwinters easily in colder climates and will withstand being frozen in the pond with no special care or attention. It is so hardy that the plants start to grow in the ice in the spring, the dark foliage melting the ice with the sun's rays. It will also grow in the house during the winter.

*Oenanthe javanica* 'Flamingo'

*Oenanthe javanica* 'Flamingo'

### *Oenanthe javanica* 'Flamingo'
**rainbow water parsley**

A Korean native, this lovely plant has pink, white, and green frilly foliage that resembles compact carrot tops. I use it to make flavored vinegars, where it imparts its pink color. Grows well along the edge of the pond, stream, or waterfall. Also suitable in a larger container water garden. The pink fades in the heat of summer but returns in the fall. It makes a great ground cover in wet areas. The variegated form does not flower as profusely as its green parent, *Oenanthe javanica*, nor does it grow as rampantly at the edge of the pond. Situate in sun to part shade in moist soil or water to 2 inches deep. Height 6 inches. Zones 5–11.

*Oenanthe sarmentosa*

*Oenanthe sarmentosa*

*Onoclea sensibilis*

## *Oenanthe sarmentosa*
**water parsley**

The lush, green foliage of this plant provides an excellent foil to larger, more full-leafed plants, such as cannas, cyperus, and colocasias. It grows very quickly, sometimes too quickly, and can cover a small pond in a single summer as its stems grow out across the water surface. It is best contained to the upper pond or biofilter or its own corner of the water garden. It can be a bit of a thug in the moist conditions it prefers—rooted in moist soil or floating. Grows in sun to full shade, reaching 6–12 inches high. Zones 5–11. Native to both sides of the Pacific.

## *Onoclea sensibilis*
**sensitive fern**
**Woodsiaceae**

I have photographed this plant across much of its native range from Canada to Florida. It varies some in its appearance but mostly in its adaptability to water. Make sure the plants you buy come from wet-tolerant parents. Grows in moist to wet soil and tolerates seasonal flooding. Reaches 12–18 inches high as it slowly creeps at a rate of about 18 inches a year. Division is easiest method of propagation, but plants can be started from the spores, which take about 18 months to reach transplant size. A modified frond that resembles a rattle carries the spores. The spore case remains all winter and provides interest. Overwintering takes no special care. Hardy in Zones 3–9. No pests other than the occasional deer in spring.

*Orontium aquaticum*

*Osmunda regalis* 'Purpurascens'

*Orontium aquaticum*

*Orontium aquaticum*

### *Orontium aquaticum*
**golden club**
**Araceae**

*Orontium aquaticum* is noted for its velvety, lance-shaped leaves that are dark olive-green and can reach 5 to 12 inches in length. In late spring or early summer, the plant has unusual white flower spadices with terminal spikes of many very small yellow flowers. The overall effect is very striking. An easy-to-grow plant, it forms tight clumps, like hostas. Grows in part sun to full shade in moist soil or water to 6 inches or more deep. Height 6–10 inches, spread 12–18 inches. I have observed this growing in 5 feet of water in a tannin-darkened stream with 12-inch-long leaves and seed heads above the water. Native to North America. Zones 5–11. It varies a little over its range. The large plants in the South are less hardy. Overwinters well in colder climates and withstands being frozen in the pond. Best propagated by division of the rootstock. May also be grown from seed sown fresh in damp to wet soil. Allow cold stratification for 30 days, then they will sprout in two to three weeks at 60°F. Red-stemmed and variegated forms are also coming onto the market.

### *Osmunda*
**Osmundaceae**

#### *Osmunda regalis*

This tropical-looking fern can reach up to 6 feet tall and wide when growing in water up to the crown in part shade. It is a truly impressive plant. Generally it grows to 3–4 feet tall and wide in sun to part shade. Foliage is a dull, army-green color. Great for pond edges or seasonally wet woods under bald cypress (*Taxodium*). Found circumboreally in the temperate northern hemisphere, it grows from Canada to Central America. Hardy in Zone 3 and up. Fronds can be fertile or produce a terminal spore structure. Propagate by spores or tissue culture of select cultivars. Division is possible but difficult because of the fibrous roots.

Several selections are available. 'Crispa' (syn. 'Undulata') has wavy margins on the leaflets and grows to 2 feet tall and wide. 'Cristata' is a crested form that is very showy in the right place. Instead of coming to a terminal tip, many tips develop. It grows to 3 feet tall and wide. 'Gracilis' (syn. 'Grandiceps') has coppery new growth and reaches 3 feet tall and wide. 'Purpurascens' has purplish stems and a purple cast to new growth that remains on some of the fronds through maturity. Grows to just over 3 feet tall and wide.

## Osmunda cinnamomea
### cinnamon fern

Very feathery fronds are covered in copper-colored hairs. Grows to 3–5 feet tall and 12–36 inches wide in wet soil with water 1–2 inches below the crown. Grows along shady streams and wet woodlands or shady ponds. Grows from Canada to Central America. Hardy in Zone 3 and up.

## Pedicularis groenlandica
### elephant head, lousewort

Having yarrow-like foliage (*Achillea*) with a slender spike, this species grows up to 24 inches tall and about 6 inches wide in wet soil. Tolerates spring floods up to 6 inches deep. Grows in full sun to part shade. The flowers comprise 6-inch spikes that are rosy purple to shiny black-purple, and each flower looks like the front view of an elephant's head with trunk. The common name lousewort comes from the belief that when cows ate this plant they became infected with lice. Native to Canada and northern parts of the U.S. Hardy in Zones 3–9. Likes cool water and is great along streams. Propagate by division. Needs winter protection for the leaves, either snow cover or mulch. Many other pedicularis like wet, springy sites and come in a wide range of colors: yellows, pinks, blues, whites.

*Peltandra virginica*

## Peltandra virginica
### bog arum, arrow arum
### Araceae

The foliage of this plant forms a dense clump that resembles arrowhead (*Sagittaria*) but that will not spread in an earthen pond, as arrowhead are wont to do. The green flowers resemble jack-in-the-pulpit (*Arisaema triphyllum*), appearing below the foliage in summer. A strong grower, bog arum is suitable for the edge of the pond and makes an excellent accent plant. Grows in moist soil or water to 6 inches or more deep in sun to part shade. Height 24 inches, spread 24 inches. Native to North America. Zones 5–9. Can be frozen in the pond. Propagate by division of rootstock. May also be grown from seed. Sow fresh, or keep in moist sphagnum until sown, in moist soil. Germinates in two to three weeks in temperatures above 60°F.

*Peltandra virginica*

*Peltandra 'Snow Splash'*

Peltrandras do best in 6 inches of water or less, but I have observed them in 4 feet of water and still growing, though not at their best. Like many plants with a wide geographic range, the appearance and form can vary greatly from one population to the next—at one time 40 species were listed. I have seen plants that grew to 5 feet with 18-inch-wide leaves; plants with red petioles; plants with long, pointed, triangular leaves like a jester's hat; plants 12 inches tall with spoon-shaped foliage; plants with orange, large flowers; plants with small, green, spotted flowers. *Peltandra sagittifolia* has white flowers and red seeds instead of green. Currently only one hybrid selection exists, *P.* 'Snow Splash'. It has white variegation that starts minimally in spring and grows to cover half the foliage by summer.

## *Peltiphyllum peltatum* (syn. *Darmera peltata*) umbrella plant, Indian rhubarb
### Saxifragaceae

Small pink to almost white flowers on stalks borne before the foliage. Slowly creeping rhizomes like astilbe grow in very wet soil. Grows to 36 inches high and 24–36 inches wide with leaves of 12–14 inches across and round, like inverted umbrellas. I observed this at Yosemite National Park where it grew along streams and in wet depressions, even growing on rock outcroppings in the middle of the river. It does best in wet and cool conditions and suffers in the heat. It also does not adapt to a pH above 7.5. Great for carnivorous plant bogs. Native to the Sierra Nevada. Hardy in Zones 6–9. Propagate by division or seed sown on damp soil and left uncovered.

'Nana' is about half the size of the species, growing 12–15 inches tall with 6–8-inch leaves. This is a cutie. I have grown it in my stream garden but our hot summers and cold winters did it in. While alive it was 6 inches tall with 4-inch leaves with a red cast to the edges.

*Penthorum sedoides* in flower

Flower of *Penthorum sedoides*

*Penthorum sedoides* in fruit

### Penthorum sedoides
### star fruit
### Crassulaceae

Much underused in the water garden, star fruit has three to five flowering wands that radiate from the center of the plant, forming a star. Each stem supports a star-shaped green flower composed of five sections. But the flowers are secondary to the fruit, which turns pink and looks like flowers. In the fall, stems and seed capsules turn pink while the foliage turns a bright, golden yellow. Grows in sun to part shade in moist soil or water to 4 inches deep. Height 10–18 inches, spread 10 inches. Native to North America. Zones 4–11. Withstands being frozen in the pond. Propagate by dividing the rootstock, or it is easy to grow from seed. Surface sow in wet soil at 70°F. Seed sprouts in two weeks at

50 percent and above. Winter buds can be very small, so be patient. In spring it can seed a lot on barren soil, but it bows to other plants and is never invasive.

### Petasites
### Compositae

Grown especially for their large, rounded foliage that looks like rhubarb (*Rheum*)—their leaves are also eaten—petasites are vigorous growers that do best in large sites where they may run freely, reaching 3–4 feet high. Excellent for naturalizing along the edge of earthen ponds and streams. In smaller water gardens, they should be kept in containers so they do not overtake their neighbors. Petasites have unusual flowers that appear early in spring before foliage has even sprouted. The flower spikes may be from 6 inches to 12 inches or so in height, adorned with small tufted flowers that may be white, green, or even dark red. The stalk is purpled-red. The blooms last only a week or so, quickly followed by the appearance of the foliage. Petasites prefer cooler tem-

*Petasites hybridus*

*Petasites hybridus*

*Petasites japonicus* 'Giganteus'

peratures and part to full shade. They can wilt in the heat and humidity of summer if they are not given at least afternoon shade. Species may be found in Europe, Asia, and North America. They are generally hardy in Zones 5–9, overwintering in moist soil or in the perennial border in colder climates. Fall mulch is beneficial. Propagate by division of the rootstock in spring before it has flowered, or later, after blooming but before substantial leaf development. You may propagate even after foliage is well developed by simply digging up a clump and cutting the leaves back to 6 inches or so from the ground, and replanting. If foliage gets tattered, clear cut to the ground for a fresh flush.

## *Petasites hybridus*
### butter burr

Flower stalks of this species are dark red. The triangular, cupped leaves are large at 18–24 inches across and reach up to 4 feet tall. They lend a bold, architectural element to the pond and are best suited for large water gardens or bogs.

## *Petasites japonicus*
### Japanese butter burr

This species native to Japan and eastern Asia has yellow-green flowers that appear on low umbels that look like little tufted mounds of blossoms. Grows to about 24–36 inches tall with leaves 12–18 inches around. Leaves of 'Giganteus' are very rounded and can be up to 3 feet or more in diameter, and 'Variegatus' (syn. 'Nishiki-buki') is the same as the species but for its very striking yellow-splashed foliage. A very nice, smaller form reaching 18 inches tall with 12-inch leaves is *Petasites japonicus* f. *purpureus*. It has deep red-purple petioles and a red cast to its green foliage.

Roots of *Phragmites*

*Phalaris arundinacea*

## *Phalaris arundinacea*
**reed canary grass, ribbon grass**
**Poaceae**

A running grass of cosmopolitan origin that has been used to stabilize shorelines and lake banks, phalaris is considered an invasive weed in some parts of North America. Only the variegated forms are cultivated for the garden and pond, where they make excellent accent plants and are easily kept in pots. Leaf blades are roughly 14 inches long and ¾ inch wide. Those of the species are a bright, even green. Thin, silvery plumes appear in late summer and reach up to roughly 7 feet tall on the green form and about 4 feet on the variegated forms. They grow in sun to part shade in moist soil, prefering cooler climates. In areas with hot, humid summers, they are prone to slow their growth and may even go semi- or completely dormant. Once the weather cools again in the fall, they resume growth and remain attractive until winter. Hardy in Zones 4–11, overwintering well in the pond. Propagate by division of the running rhizome. If foliage gets tattered, just clear cut to bring on fresh new growth.

*Phalaris arundinacea* var. *picta* 'Luteopicta' (syn. 'Aureovariegata') is a cultivar variegated in long stripes of yellow and cream over much of the foliage, though it often turns green in the heat of summer. 'Strawberries and Cream' (syn. 'Feesey'), about 12–14 inches tall, is mostly creamy white with thin green stripes. In the spring and again in the fall, it is tinged in pink. It is an improvement over the old standby, 'Picta', which has the same stripes but does not turn pink in cooler weather. 'Picta' grows to 24–36 inches tall. Another cultivar, 'Tricolor', reaches 12–14 inches tall and turns pink in spring and fall, but does not have as much white as 'Strawberries and Cream.' Yet another selection, 'Woods Dwarf', is shorter and more compact than 'Picta', reaching 10–12 inches tall, but otherwise has the same features. About the same size as 'Picta' is 'Blonde', a very creamy white selection with green stripes.

## *Phragmites*
**Poaceae**

Taller than *Phalaris arundinacea*, *Phragmites* also has wider and longer leaves, roughly ¾–1¼ inches by 24 inches. Foliage is blue-green and grows quickly in spring once the weather warms. Plants can grow up to 18 feet, depending on selection. Plumes are larger too, about 12–24 inches. They emerge dark red or purple and then change to silver as they mature. Depending on the selection, seed heads can be green, silver, tan, black, brown, yellow, purple, or reddish silver. Seeds are rarely fertile and plants grow mostly by underground, spreading rhizomes. Because it also has a tendency

*Phragmites australis*

*Phragmites australis* subsp. *australis* 'Variegatus'

to run, *Phragmites* should be kept in a pot in most water garden landscapes. It is a great choice for filtration to remove pollutants from the water. Propagate by division of the rhizome or by seed. Leave it in the pond to overwinter in colder climates. Cosmopolitan in origin, it was used in England for centuries to make reed thatch roofs. Much lore surrounds it in Europe and Russia, but it was never used to much benefit in North America, where it has naturalized. Seeds make porridge for Native American Indians.

### *Phragmites australis* (syn. *P. communis*)
**pampas reed**

Best suited for very large ponds. Makes an imposing, bamboo-like appearance. The closest thing to pampas grass (*Cortaderia*) the North will ever see. The silver-white plumes may be harvested in early fall. Left to dry, they make wonderful accents in dried floral arrangements. Grows in sun to part shade in moist soil or water to 24 inches deep. Height 7 feet.

Zones 4–11. A very, very tall subspecies, *Phragmites australis* subsp. *altissimus*, grows up to 18 feet high. Also *P. australis* subsp. *pseudodonax* is a real monster. It has blue-green, large leaves 1–1½ inches wide and 12 inches or more long. Canes are 12–18 feet tall and ¾ inch thick. It is great for screening.

### *Phragmites australis* subsp. *australis* 'Variegatus'
**gold rush reed**

This selection has bright green stripes on dark green leaves. It is smaller than other species and cultivars, reaching 3–6 feet tall, and is easy to grow. Situate in sun to full shade in moist soil or water to 4 inches deep. Late summer plumes are gold rather than silver. Zones 4–11.

### *Phragmites australis* 'Towada'

A shorter form, with yellow and green foliage that is marked in red. The seed heads also have a red cast. Grows 24–30 inches tall. Widely available in Japan, it has not yet made its presence felt in other commercial markets.

*Phragmites karka* 'Candy Stripe'

*Phyla lanceolata*

### *Phragmites karka* 'Candy Stripe'
candy stripe reed

Brought into cultivation from its native Japan and China by James Waddick. Leaves are narrower, at most 1½ inches wide. 'Candy Stripe' may be the same as 'Variegatus' which has clear white stripes and is tinted pink in spring and fall. Grows in sun to part shade in moist soil or water to 4 inches deep and can tolerate water to 24 inches. Reaches 4–8 feet high. Zones 5–11.

### *Phyla lanceolata*
frog fruit
Verbenaceae

An ideal ground cover for the wet spot in the yard, or for a rocky margin at the edge of the pond, *Phyla lanceolata* tolerates some foot traffic and may even be mowed. It has small, lance-shaped leaves that are toothed and an even green. In the fall, foliage turns a wonderful crimson-purple color. Starting in early summer and continuing throughout until fall, it is covered in tiny white flowers that resemble verbena. As they mature, they change to yellow and then pink. Great for containers or for use as a walkable shoreline for fishing or boat access. Grows in sun to part shade in moist soil or water to 4 inches deep. Reaches 2 inches high with a trailing spread. Propagates very easily from stem cuttings. Overwinters well in northern climates without any special care or attention. Simply leave it in the pond or at the margins of the water garden. Zones 5–11. Can be found growing wild in North America.

*Phyla lanceolata*

## Physostegia leptophylla
**water obedient plant**
**Labiatae**

This is the water-loving cousin to the perennial form of *Physostegia* commonly found in many backyard gardens. Like its land-loving relatives, the aquatic form has tubular lavender-pink flowers that appear throughout the summer. Leaves are lance-shaped and toothed. Height 3–4 feet and spread 24 inches. Grows in sun to part shade, and tolerates deep shade, in moist soil or water to 1 inch deep. Propagates easily from stem cuttings or by division, and may also be grown from seed. Native to the southeastern U.S. Zones 5–11. Overwinters well in the pond as long as the pot is submerged in the water below the freeze line. Other species that take seasonally wet soil are *P. angustifolia, P. intermedia,* and *P. virginiana.* Try these above the waterline in wet to moist soil.

*Physostegia leptophylla*

*Pontederia*
pickerel plant
**Pontederiaceae**

Pontederias are much-favored pondside plants for their shiny, heart-shaped leaves and striking spikes of summer flowers ranging in color from blue to white into lavender and pink, all with a prominent yellow spot on the middle lobe called a "bee." The plant itself has a compact habit, growing from a rhizome that sits, like an iris, near the surface of the soil. Its native range includes North America, from Florida and Oklahoma northward to Minnesota, Nova Scotia, and Ontario, extending into South America.

*Pontederia* earned the common name pickerel plant or pickerel weed because it was thought that pickerel fish would be found wherever the plant was growing. Not only young pickerel appreciate the foliage when grown in deeper water, so, too, do other fish, frogs, and other amphibians. Pickerel plant attracts butterflies, skippers, and hummingbirds, and dragonflies and damselflies use the upright stems as perches to shed their final larval stage and become adults. Wildfowl eat the seed. Young leaves can be used in salads or cooked as a vegetable, and the seed may be eaten like nuts or ground to make a flour. Pickerel plant is also appreciated for its excellent filtration abilities. The cultivar *P. cordata* 'Crown Point' has been rated as one of the best overall filtration plants in studies performed by Michael Kane at the University of Florida, Gainesville.

Pickerel plant propagates most readily from division of its rootstock in spring. It may also be grown from seed, but requires a period of cold, wet dormancy. The winter tolerance of pickerel plant depends heavily upon its local heritage. Those grown in more southern climates with mild winters, or with none at all, do not generally survive a winter freeze if they are moved to more northern areas. Make sure to select one that has been raised for the particular climate in which it will be grown. Overwinters best in cold climates if the rootstock is protected from freezing. Place the rootstock well below the frost line of the pond, or remove the plant to cold, damp quarters until spring returns.

Flowering habit varies from one plant to another. The flower spike consists of a collection of five budded spikes. On some, flowers open at the bottom of the spike and then progress upward. Others open haphazardly over the spike. Some open top to bottom like rows of corn or like a hyacinth blossom. When the flowers have finished, the spikes often lean into the water so that the seed may disperse. Look closely at the flowers and it is apparent that pontederias are related to water hyacinth (*Eichhornia crassipes*). Flowers are funnel-shaped. The upper lip has three lobes, with a bee on the middle lobe. The lower lip is separated into three parts. The flowers close at night and open in the morning as it warms. Pickerel plant is tristyly, meaning it produces three types of flowers with style and stamens of different lengths for each type, and each plant produces flowers of one type. Each type can only be fertilized by pollen of another flower with the opposite combination of style and stamen lengths. Not many water plants are like this—another is *Lythrum*.

Dividing *Pontederia*

*Pontederia cordata*

*Pontederia cordata*

## *Pontederia cordata*
### blue pickerel plant

Considered one of the mainstays of the water garden pond, *Pontederia cordata* has shiny, jade green, heart-shaped foliage and large spikes of blue flowers. Grows in sun to part shade in moist soil or water to 10 inches deep. Height 24–30 inches, spread 12–24 inches. Zones 5–11. I have observed wild populations as far north as Duluth, Minnesota, but have not found plants sold that are that cold hardy.

It is unclear whether there are two species of *Pontederia* in the U.S., or whether all are the same species, forming instead separate subspecies. Listed as separate species are *P. cordata* and *P. lancifolia*, which has more narrow, lance-shaped leaves. Also listed erroneously is *P. angustifolia*, which is in truth a selection of *P. cordata*. I hold the opinion that all are forms of one species.

*Pontederia cordata*

Pontederia cordata 'Alba'

### Pontederia cordata 'Alba'
### white pickerel plant

Flowers of this selection are white rather than blue. Blossoms are often tinged in pink, especially at the base of the flower. Leaves are shiny, green, and spoon-shaped. Grows in sun to part shade in moist soil or water to 10 inches deep. Height 24–30 inches, spread 12–24 inches. Zones 5–11. This refers to a color subset that is collected in the wild and grown from seed, and more recently from division and tissue culture. You may receive different plants from different suppliers.

### Pontederia cordata 'Angustifolia' (syn. 'Lanceolata')

This is a very upright, 3–5-foot plant with icy, sky-blue flowers. Foliage is dark green. Zones 5–11.

### Pontederia cordata 'Crown Point'

More compact and bushy than the species, 'Crown Point' is extremely hardy. Its leaves and its flower spikes are more rounded than those of other pickerel plants. Flowers are bright, deep blue. Reaches 12–18 inches high and wide. Grows in sun to part shade in moist soil or water to 18 inches deep. A versatile plant that is well suited for reclamation and wetland sites due to its hardiness in cold weather and its ability to filter pollutants from the water. Zones 4–11.

Pontederia cordata 'Alba'

*Pontederia cordata* 'Dilatata'

*Pontederia cordata* 'Pink Pons'

## *Pontederia cordata* 'Dilatata'

Often sold as a species, *Pontederia dilatata*, it is in truth a form of *P. cordata*. Also, this is sold in Europe as *P. cordata* 'Angustifolia'. It is a very nice 3–5-foot plant that spreads to 24 inches. Flower spikes of more than 6 inches display dark blue-purple blooms. Zones 5–11.

## *Pontederia cordata* 'Pink Pons'
**pink pickerel plant**

Blooms of 'Pink Pons' are pink-lavender, noticeably pink when placed next to their standard blue brethren. Grows in sun to part shade in moist soil or water to 6 inches deep. Height 24–30 inches, spread 12–18 inches. Zones 5–11.

## *Pontederia cordata* 'Spoon River'

Leaves are very narrow, spoon- or lance-shaped, only ¾ inch wide and up to 7 inches long. Flowers are intensely blue and stay erect after blooming. Grows in sun to part shade in moist soil or water to 6 inches deep. Height 24–30 inches, spread only 6–12 inches. Zones 5–11.

## *Pontederia sagittata* 'Singapore Pink'

A pink-flowering pontederia from tropical South America, this is often sold as a form of *Pontederia cordata*. It will flower in winter in an indoor pond given enough light. It never needs to go dormant. Hardy in Zone 9 and up. A frost can kill it.

*Potentilla palustris*

*Pontederia sagittata* 'Singapore Pink'

*Potentilla palustris*

## *Potentilla palustris*
**marsh cinquefoil**
**Rosaceae**

One of the few members of the rose family that is truly aquatic, *Potentilla palustris* has leaves that are formed of three to five leaflets, each lance-shaped and heavily toothed. A low, creeping plant up to 12 inches tall and wide, it roots at the edge of the pond, stream, or waterfall and then floats out across the water surface. It is rather open, not a bushy, full plant like the popular landscape shrub *P. fruticosa*. In midsummer it produces dark red flowers that resemble dainty, single roses. It is native to North America where it grows along the edges of lakes, streams, swamps, and bogs. Often listed as circumboreal. Zones 3–9. It grows in sun to part shade rooted in wet soil or just floating on the water surface. It does best in moving water 1–3 inches deep, such as along a stream. Propagate by division.

*Preslia cervina*

*Ranunculus acris*

## *Pratia angulata*
### heavenly stars
### Lobeliaceae

Very similar to azure carpet (*Laurentia palustris*), heavenly stars grows as creeping, dense, green clumps with narrow leaves just ⅛ inch long. The plant can be ¼ inch to 5 inches tall. In the summer this pond-edge plant has white flowers that closely resemble *Lobelia*. Grows in sun to part shade in moist soil. Does best just wet but tolerates seasonal flooding in spring for seven to ten days at a time. Zones 6–11. Native to New Zealand. Overwinter in colder climates by bringing inside and keeping as a houseplant. Propagate by dividing plant into smaller clumps in early spring, or take stem cuttings anytime. Just press the cuttings into the soil to root.

## *Preslia cervina*
### Labiatae

This hardy mint relative is a real treasure. Very fragrant, it reaches 12–20 inches tall. Leaves are very fine, like thyme or rosemary. Grows in moist soil to water 4 inches deep. Tolerates shade but prefers full sun. Great along the edge of the pond or in a stream. Butterflies love it. Flowers bloom in midsummer for about three weeks in blue-purple or white. Cut back after flowering to keep it looking nice. Zones 5–9.

## *Ranunculus*
### Ranunculaceae

*Ranunculus* species are found in many parts of the world, from the tropics to the arctic. They propagate well from stem offsets or by division of the rootstock. Many overwinter well in water gardens in colder climates with no special care or attention and may also be overwintered in the perennial bed with mulch for protection. Leaves can be spoon-shaped to seven-lobed and highly cut. Roots can be hair-like or tuberous. Flowers are tepals of five or more and generally yellow-orange to white.

*Ranunculus acris* 'Citrinus'

*Ranunculus acris*

## *Ranunculus acris*
### tall buttercup

A native of Europe that has naturalized throughout the world, this buttercup grows to almost 36 inches in height. The rounded and finely cut leaves form a mound about 24 inches high and 12 inches or so wide, with the flowers appearing higher on long, arching stems. It is covered with waxy yellow flowers in spring, and with deadheading will continue to bloom intermittently throughout the summer. Grows in sun to part shade in moist soil. Tolerates seasonal flooding for a couple days at a time. Zones 4–9. Needs no special care to overwinter where hardy. Propagate by seed for colors—they come mostly true. Propagate by division for varieties. Popular cultivars include 'Citrinus', a pale lemon-yellow; 'Sulphureus' in golden yellow; and 'Flore Pleno' in double chrome-yellow.

*Ranunculus acris* 'Flore Pleno'

*Ranunculus lingua*

*Ranunculus flammula*

## Ranunculus lingua
### tongue buttercup, greater spearwort

This lightly branched, tall plant of 24–36 inches high and 12 inches wide is great for mixing with *Scirpus*, *Cyperus longus*, or *Asclepias*. Flowers of ½–¾ inch are a bright, brassy yellow all summer. Plants spread by underground rhizomes or from stems that fall over and produce new plants. Leaves are spear-shaped. Grows in wet soil to water 6 inches deep. Tolerates seasonal spring flooding. Native to Europe. Hardy in Zones 5–9. Where not hardy, sink to the bottom of the pond and bring back up as soon as the ice is off the pond. Propagate by division, cuttings, or offsets from the stems. Or sow seed on moist soil and cover lightly with sand. 'Grandiflora' is the same but for its 1-inch flowers.

## Ranunculus flammula
### creeping spearwort, tongue buttercup

A native of Europe, this diminutive ranunculus grows both above and below the water surface. It has narrow leaves less than ⅙ inch wide and 2½ inches long that grow in a star-like fashion from the plant's crown. Running stolons also emerge from the crown, landing a few inches away and forming a new plant. Flowers are small, bright yellow, and buttercup-like. Each stem has at least one flower. They bloom in shallow water of 1–3 inches or when growing along the margin of the pond. Grows in sun to part shade, reaching 12–24 inches high and 12 inches wide. Zones 5–9.

## Ranunculus flammula 'Thor'

Similar to the species, but with much larger flowers. In the summer, the plant is literally covered with 1-inch, waxy, single-petaled, yellow flowers. The foliage and flowers have a very thick substance, almost like plastic. Extremely robust, well branched, and compact, reaching 10 inches high and 6–10 inches wide, 'Thor' is superior to the species and easier to grow. It is well suited to the container water garden or the edge of the pond. Grows slowly in sun to part shade in moist soil or submerged, losing its ability to bloom in water deeper than 3 inches. Zones 5–9.

## Ranunculus repens
### creeping buttercup

A common plant for the perennial border, this creeping buttercup also grows well at the edge of the pond and makes a great ground cover for wet soil. It has rounded leaves that are deeply cut and single flowers with waxy yellow petals that bloom in spring. Height 4 inches. Because of its rampant habit, it must be containerized or grown in a location where it can be easily cut back and controlled. Grows in sun to shade in moist soil or water to 1 inch deep. Zones 4–9.

'Pleniflorus' has double yellow flowers and shiny green foliage. 'Buttered Popcorn' is a beautiful gold overlaid with metallic silver. It is especially well suited to wet areas in full shade, and even tolerates some foot traffic. Also, it is not as aggressive a runner as its all-green parent.

*Ranunculus repens* 'Pleniflorus'

*Ranunculus repens* 'Buttered Popcorn'

*Ranunculus repens* 'Buttered Popcorn'

*Regnellidium diphyllum* (upper left) and planting stem cuttings of *Regnellidium diphyllum*

## *Regnellidium diphyllum*
### twin-leafed water clover
### Marsileaceae

Foliage of this marginal water plant is fleshy, and leaves are two-lobed, resembling water clover (*Marsilea mutica*) but without the markings. The color is lighter, more khaki-green than other water clovers. Height 3 inches with a running spread. Grows in sun to part shade in moist soil or water to 4 inches deep. This is a great choice for a shady pond. It will float out on the water surface or scramble among the rocks at the edge of the pond or in a bog. This is a fern with spores, but it propagates easily from stem cuttings. Reportedly hardy to Zone 7, but mine have never lived past a frost. Zones 9–11. It does not tolerate freezing conditions and must be brought indoors for the winter in colder climates. Keep as a houseplant until spring returns. Native to southern Brazil and northern Argentina.

## *Rorippa nasturtium-aquaticum* (syn. *Nasturtium officinale*)
### watercress
### Brassicaceae

Flowers of this water-loving plant bloom in spring and are white with four petals, the customary amount for members of the mustard family (Brassicaceae). It has toothy, mustard leaves. The plant has a trailing habit and stems often float out over the water surface. It grows in sun to shade in wet soil or water to 4 inches deep and will grow floating in deeper water. Height 6–12 inches and spread 12 inches. In many areas, even those with cold winters, the foliage will stay evergreen through the winter, even when frozen in the ice. Hardy in Zones 4–9. Watercress is well known for its medicinal uses and is valued as an herb in cooking because of its pungent, peppery flavor. When selecting watercress that will be eaten, though, it is advisable to choose those offered in grocery stores and not those growing in your own backyard stream, pond, or waterfall. Watercress is excellent for removing pollutants from the water, pollutants which end up in the plant's foliage. It has also been discovered that a microscopic form of snail often lives in the plant's foliage. The snail has been linked to liver flukes, which can damage your liver if ingested. It can also be susceptible to flea beetles, aphids, snails, cabbage loopers, and leaf miners. Propagate from division, cuttings, or seed sown wet and given cold stratification for 30 days. When I want to start some, I go to the grocery store and buy a bunch, bring it home, stick the end of it under a rock in the stream, and away it grows. Watercress is native to Europe, and it has become so naturalized in North America that it is also said to be native here.

*Rorippa nasturtium-aquaticum*

*Rorippa nasturtium-aquaticum*

## *Rosa palustris*
### swamp rose, marsh rose
### Rosaceae

One of the few roses that grows in soil that is always moist to wet—but not in any depth of water, though it tolerates some seasonal flooding—swamp rose has characteristic rose-like foliage that is gray-green. Stems are very thorny. Flowers are single, pink, and usually appear in June. After flowering, the plant produces noticeable, ornamental bright-red rose hips. These are a favorite food for several wildfowl as well as deer. Grows in sun to part shade, reaching 4–8 feet high and 6–8 feet wide. Propagates by seed, division of rootstock, or from hardwood cuttings taken in fall or winter. Hardy in Zones 4–9, it overwinters well in northern climates, withstanding freezing temperatures. Swamp rose is native to North America, grow-

*Rotala rotundifolia*

*Ruellia brittoniana* 'Katie'

ing from Ontario to Nova Scotia, into Wisconsin, Michigan, and Minnesota, southward into Arkansas and Florida. Not commonly offered by commercial sources, but a double form exists that is sold by many specialty rose growers.

### *Rotala rotundifolia*
**pink sprite**
Lythraceae

*Rotala* species are located in many tropical and warm regions of the world. A charming aquatic from India into Japan and southeast Asia, *Rotala rotundifolia* has lovely red, pink, and green leaves with red stems. Leaves are small, fleshy, very rounded, holding closely to the stem. In spring and fall, when days are short, giving less than 10 hours of sunlight, the 2-inch-tall, creeping plant is covered with pink flowers that look like miniature astilbes. Excellent for table-top ponds. Also good for indoor ponds, where it will flower all winter. Grows in sun to shade in moist soil or submerged. Propagates freely from stem cuttings. Hardy in Zones 9–11, it must be overwintered indoors as a houseplant.

### *Ruellia*
Acanthaceae

Though other perennial forms of *Ruellia* are often considered weeds of little ornamental significance, *Ruellia* species that grow in wet soil are sought out by water gardeners. The water-loving species are noted for their large, petunia-like flowers that appear all year long in the tropical climates they prefer. Foliage is usually narrow and lance-shaped, not unlike willow leaves. In colder climates, the foliage often turns dark purple once night temperatures begin to

cool into the 40s and low 50s. Propagates equally well from stem cuttings and seed. Does not withstand cold temperatures—hardy in Zones 9–11—and must be overwintered indoors as a houseplant.

### *Ruellia brittoniana*
**water bluebell**

Much favored by water gardeners, this species is constantly covered with 1–2-inch lavender-blue flowers. Very easy to grow, it takes sun to part shade and moist soil or water to 6 inches deep. It reaches 2–4 feet high, sometimes more in the Deep South, and 24 inches wide.

A delightful pink variation, 'Chi Chi', or pink water bluebell, is just as free-flowering as other water bluebells. Foliage turns burgundy in autumn when the temperatures fall. Makes a nice, bushy statement that is great with hibiscus or ludwigias.

### *Ruellia brittoniana* 'Katie'
**dwarf water bluebell**

The purple-blue, geranium-blue flowers of this selection nestle against the leaf stems. Due to its near lack of internodes, the plant has a dwarf, compact habit, not usually reaching more than 10 inches or so high and 12 inches wide. Instead of the usual 1–3 inches between nodes, the leaves are stacked one atop the other. Flower stems are also reduced by half, but leaves and blooms are the same size as those of the species. Grows in sun to part shade in moist soil or water to 1 inch deep.

Four cultivars are in this dwarf group. Two are commonly sold as 'Pink Katie' and 'White Katie', the only differ-

Ruellia squarrosa 'Alba'

ence being their flower colors, pink and white, respectively. 'Strawberries and Cream', or variegated dwarf water bluebell, is a newer variegated cultivar with the same compact habit as 'Katie.' Its leaves are speckled in cream, pink, white, and green, becoming more green with age. Flowers are a soft, purplish-blue.

### *Ruellia squarrosa* 'Alba'
**white water bluebell**

This form has crepe-paper-white flowers. The leaf shape is a little different—rounded rather than pointed and willowy. Grows in sun to part shade in moist soil or water to 6 inches deep. Height 2–4 feet, spread 24 inches. It is often sold as *Ruellia brittoniana* 'Alba', because the species look so similar except for the leaves—white forms of *R. brittoniana* do exist but they are weak growers.

### *Rumex orbiculatus* (syn. *R. brittanica*)
**water dock, great water dock**
**Polygonaceae**

A much-underused and unnoticed marginal plant, *Rumex orbiculatus* has shiny, dark green, lance-shaped leaves that are about 2 inches wide and 4 inches long. In the summer, green flower heads appear as a drooping plume, turning to brown and taking on a graceful, almost feathery appearance. Grows in sun to part shade in moist soil or water to 6 inches deep. Reaches 36 inches high and 24 inches wide. Propagate by dividing the rootstock or from seed. Cold and frost tolerant, this water plant requires no special care or maintenance to survive the winter in cold climates. Zones 5–11. Native to temperate regions, including North America.

*Rumex orbiculatus*

Range of *Sagittaria* leaves

*Sagittaria australis* 'Benni' Silk Stockings™

## *Sagittaria*
## arrowhead
## Alismataceae

Named for its arrow-shaped leaves that are held atop long stems that rise from a central base, *Sagittaria* is highly ornamental at the edge of the pond and is very easy to grow. Many species are extremely variable in their height, leaf shape, and flowering, depending on the parent population. Leaves may be broad or narrow, depending upon the particular species, and some are lobed. Flowers are usually single and white, resembling small single-petaled roses; of course, a double form is available as well. Blossoms are held on a long stalk that rises from the central base of the plant, appearing first in June and recurring throughout the summer. In the fall, arrowhead develops underground tubers, and the mother plant dies off completely. These small tubers, called turions, will sprout and grow the coming spring. Water gardeners

often believe that their arrowhead plant has died, only to find that it has set turions at the bottom of the pot. Finding the turions early each spring and repotting them will continue the arrowhead heritage in the pond for years to come. They may also be divided in summer by digging up actively growing plants or offsets. *Sagittaria* can be grown from seed—surface sow on wet soil and provide long days. For the cold-hardy ones, sow and refrigerate for 30 days then provide lots of light and warmth of 70°F. Arrowhead contributes to the water garden landscape with both its clean, geometric foliage and delicate white flowers. They are attractive when mixed with pontederias or planted near hibiscus and grasses like *Phragmites* and *Scirpus*.

Cold-tolerant species are native to much of North America, with numerous species growing in localized areas or parts of the continent. Tropical species are native to tropical regions of Central and South America, and the odd plant occurs here or there in the rest of the world. Many species were valued for their food content. Tubers were harvested and cooked like potatoes. The tubers and seeds are also favored by wildlife, foraged by muskrats and beavers as well as several species of wildfowl.

### Sagittaria australis

In every respect, this species looks like a form of *Sagittaria latifolia* or *S. sagittifolia*, and it grows in the same conditions. Tubers are smaller than for those species, however, and it is hardy in Zones 5–11. A selection called 'Benni' Silk Stockings™, developed by Aquascapes Unlimited in Pipersville, Pennsylvania, has red new growth, but the older foliage looks dirty with the red overlay.

### Sagittaria 'Bloomin' Baby'

A dwarf, extremely free-flowering form of arrowhead that is most likely a form of *Sagittaria cuneata*. It emerges earlier than other arrowheads and often starts to bloom when it is only 3 inches tall. Grows in sun to part shade in moist soil or water to 2 inches deep. Will grow in water 24 inches deep but will send up floating foliage; however, mine never flower when this deep. Reaches 3–10 inches tall with a running spread. Found growing wild in the Midwest. Zones 5–11.

### Sagittaria brevirostra

This species looks and grows just like *Sagittaria latifolia*, but the white flowers are generally held above the foliage. Grows in sun to part shade in moist soil or water to 6 inches or more deep. Height 12–20 inches with a running spread. Zones 3–11.

### Sagittaria engelmanniana

Coastal in distribution, from Massachusetts to Mississippi, it looks like a small form of *Sagittaria latifolia* f. *gracilis*. It reaches about 12 inches tall with flowers held above the foliage. Great for small ponds and containers. Zones 8–10.

### Sagittaria graminea
**narrow-leafed, lance-leafed, grass-leafed, or slender arrowhead**

Foliage of this species is narrower than that of other arrowheads. In just 1 inch or so of water, it will often have submerged leaves. This underwater foliage is narrow and tape-like, similar in appearance to *Vallisneria* and submerged melon sword (*Echinodorus*). Emerged leaves are shaped like tongue depressors. Narrow-leafed arrowhead is

*Sagittaria* 'Bloomin' Baby'

usually shorter in stature than the standard *Sagittaria latifolia*, reaching only 12 inches or so in height. It has the same running spread and white flowers that are common to many in the species. It is a good choice for a small pond or a container water garden. Grows in sun to part shade in moist soil or water to 4 inches deep. Zones 3–11.

### Sagittaria graminea 'Crushed Ice'
**variegated lance-leafed arrowhead**

'Crushed Ice' is distinctly variegated, with blotches of white appearing on each leaf and slightly twisted foliage. The look is not unlike *Echinodorus cordifolius* 'Marble Queen'. Like its green counterpart, 'Crushed Ice' is a more diminutive arrowhead ideally suited for smaller ponds and water gardens. Grows in sun to part shade, but because of its variegation, it may melt in very hot, humid summers and would benefit from some afternoon shade. Height 12 inches, spread 12 inches. Grows in moist soil to submerged in up to 5 feet of water as long as the water is clear. This variegated form comes true from seed somewhat. Zones 5–11.

*Sagittaria lancifolia*

*Sagittaria latifolia*

*Sagittaria lancifolia* f. *ruminoides*

### *Sagittaria lancifolia*
### white swan

A tender species of *Sagittaria*, white swan has tall lance-shaped leaves that arch outward from their iris-like rhizome. The overall effect creates the impression of the wings of a swan. Its single white flowers appear throughout the summer on a long stem that also arches up and outward, complementing the sway of the foliage. Grows in sun to part shade in moist soil or water to 10 inches deep. Height 1–4 feet, spread 12–24 inches. Zones 8–11.

 *Sagittaria lancifolia* f. *ruminoides*, or red swan, is similar in all respects to the species, except that the base of each leaf stem is brushed in bright red. This can vary from supplier, from lightly blushed to almost black to a spotted or striped pattern.

Sagittaria latifolia

Sagittaria latifolia 'Brevifolia'

## Sagittaria latifolia

The standard arrowhead, *Sagittaria latifolia* is widely distributed across North America and through Central and South America. It sports the characteristic arrow-shaped leaves and clear white flowers. Leaves may grow submerged, becoming long and tapered, closely resembling *Vallisneria*. Often selected as a wetland reclamation plant, it self-seeds readily and takes up water quickly. Grows in sun to part shade in moist soil or water to 6 inches or more deep. Height 12–20 inches with a running spread. Zones 3–11. This is a favorite food of muskrats. It can form large colonies that shade out other aquatics like *Sabatia* and *Myosotis*, so plant wisely.

Because of the large range this species covers it varies greatly, from flowering above the foliage or below, from hav-

Sagittaria latifolia 'Flore Pleno'

Sagittaria montevidensis

Sagittaria rigida

ing narrow bladeless leaves to very narrow sagittate leaves to broad and rounded sagittate leaves. Some have hair on the foliage, others have red or brown spotting on juvenile foliage or others on mature. Some have a red cast to new growth. Some have branched flower stalks. Tuber size varies as does hardiness, based on provenance of original plant material. Some selections that take advantage of these variations have been made and named, but a lot of room remains for interesting selections in this species.

'Brevifolia', needle-leaf arrowhead, has extremely narrow leaves that are sharply pointed at each of their three corners. It has a more delicate and angular appearance than the species, but is just as easy to care for. Its very vertical foliage is perfect for a more grassy or Oriental look. 'Flore Pleno', double arrowhead, displays very double, ruffled, frilly flowers. The earlier flowers on small plants tend to be not as showy but look like wet popcorn. 'Leopard Spot' has prominent brown-purple spots on rounded sagittate foliage and grows to 24 inches high and wide.

### Sagittaria montevidensis
### Aztec arrowhead

This tropical beauty has giant foliage that is deeply veined and of a stronger texture than other arrowheads. Flowers are abundant, with single white petals marked with a red dot and yellow centers. Grows in sun to part shade in moist soil or water to 5 inches deep. Height 2–4 feet, spread 36 inches. Zones 8–11. In Zones 8–9 some plants produce a corm-like overwintering structure. This is truly an annual species, however, producing copious amounts of seed rather than tubers. Native from South America to South Dakota, a few subspecies make up the range. *Sagittaria montevidensis* subsp. *montevidensis* has large, 1–2-inch flowers, each petal with a red blotch at the base, on up to 5-foot branched stalks. Less showy are *S. montevidensis* subsp. *calycina* and *S. montevidensis* subsp. *spongiosa*.

### Sagittaria rigida

This species is gaining favor with aquatic landscapers because of its upright, spoon-shaped foliage that does not hide the flowers. Also, it does not shade out other plants as badly as *Sagittaria latifolia* does. Grows to 24 inches high with a spread of 12 inches. Spreads by seed and tuber. I find it too coarse and plain en masse in ponds. The foliage is a dull green. Good in 12–20 inches of water where the foliage just peeks out of the water and the flowers lie on the surface. Zones 3–10.

## Sagittaria sinensis
### Chinese arrowhead

The Oriental form of arrowhead, grown extensively for its value as a food crop, this species has leaves that are not as glossy as other forms. The leaves are pointed and shaped almost exactly like triangles, and even the petioles are strongly triangular in cross section. It has greater value in the water garden landscape for its leaf texture, since it does not often produce flowers. The double form produces small, double, white, rose-like blooms, but alas they are mostly hidden by the foliage. I also observed some forms growing in Nanjing, China, in 1997, with red anther and pistil disks. Grows in sun to part shade in moist soil or water to 6 inches or more deep. Height 12–20 inches with a running spread. Zones 3–11. I buy tubers at the Chinese grocery, and if they are missing a terminal bud I simply float them in well-aerated water in half-days of sun. They sprout in a couple weeks' time.

## Samolus parviflorus
### water alyssum
### Primulaceae

Leaves of this dainty water plant grow in basal rosettes that form a neat clump. Flowers rise a few inches above the foliage in summer—white sprays of blooms that are small and fine-textured. It is good for a ground cover or as an accent plant near the edge of the pond. Also good for containers. Grows in sun to part shade in moist soil to submerged. Height 6–12 inches, spread 6 inches. Propagates easily from stem cuttings, rootstock division, or from seed. *Samolus* species are found in many parts of the world, mainly in the southern hemisphere. This species has proven cold-tolerant in the pond in Zone 5.

## Sarracenia
### pitcher plant
### Sarraceniaceae

This large group of species and cultivars are becoming widely available because of tissue culture. Once only for collectors, select varieties are now available in large numbers. Sarracenias make a great addition to the neutral to acid water garden, conditions they need for survival. They are like no other water plant, with alien-looking, pitcher-shaped leaves and flowers like Japanese processional lanterns. They are very effective at trapping and killing insects—I have found them so full of mosquitoes that I had to scoop them out to keep the pitchers from being damaged.

*Samolus parviflorus*

*Sarracenia flava*

*Sarracenia* mixed

*Sarracenia flava*

*Sarracenia purpurea*

They grow in sun to part shade, producing white, yellow, red, or pink pitchers in summer. *Sarracenia flava* has yellow pitchers to 24 inches, *S. leucophylla* has white pitchers to 18 inches, and *S. leucophylla* 'Turnock' has double, red-yellow flowers on standard pitchers. *Sarracenia purpurea* 'Blood Vessel' is a 12-inch selection with deep red veins from Itsaul Plants in Atlanta, Georgia. *Sarracenia ×catesbyi* is copper-colored, growing to 12 inches high and wide. The following hybrids from the work of Rob Gardener and Larry Mellichamp are good to try. *Sarracenia* 'Ladies in Waiting' has many red pitchers up to 24 inches tall with white dots. 'Flies Demise' has dusty orange and red pitchers to 10 inches tall. 'Dixie Lace' has new pitchers emerging all season and reaching 18 inches in a coppery butterscotch color with red veins. 'Mardi Gras' has many large cobra hoods of white, green, and red on 12-inch plants.

Depending on species or selection, height is 6–24 inches, spread 6 inches. Grows in moist soil or water to 1 inch deep. Plant in live sphagnum for best results. Some growers have success with a mix of sand and peat moss. Most are hardy to Zone 7, but *Sarracenia purpurea* is the hardiest at Zone 3. I have often seen it growing on moss and willow islands in the lakes of northern Minnesota. See *Carnivorous Plants of the World* by James Pietropaolo and Patricia Pietropaolo (1986, Timber Press: Portland, Ore.) for much more about sarracenias.

## *Saururus*
## Saururaceae

*Saururus* species, found in North America and in southeast Asia, are known for their heart-shaped leaves that appear alternately on tall stems that grow from creeping rhizomes. The plant forms dense colonies of upright stems topped with drooping spikes of white flowers. Both the flowers and the stems are aromatic, having a pleasant fragrance similar to vanilla or ginger. It grows well from stem cuttings or division of rootstock, and although it will withstand a frost, it cannot tolerate being frozen in the pond. Rated hardy in Zones 4–11. Move the underground rhizomes so that they will not freeze during the winter.

*Sarracenia* hybrids

*Sarracenia ×catesbyi*

*Saururus cernuus*

*Saururus cernuus*

*Saururus cernuus* var. *ruminoides*

## *Saururus cernuus*
### lizard tail

Lizard tail is well suited to the water garden landscape, providing a taller backdrop for smaller plants. It is useful because its white flowers bloom for a long period, usually for about a month in early summer, and it returns year after year. Plants are somewhat variable. Grows in sun to part shade in moist soil or water to 6 inches deep. Height 12–36 inches with a running spread. It tolerates seasonal flooding and grows well along streams or in shady wetlands. Good for detention ponds with a wet corner. *Saururus cernuus* var. *ruminoides*, or red-stemmed lizard tail, is the same as the species, but with red stems that make the plant even more attractive in the pond landscape.

*Saururus chinensis*

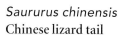

*Scirpus albescens*

## *Saururus chinensis*
**Chinese lizard tail**

An extremely attractive pondside plant, Chinese lizard tail has a white splotch on the topmost leaves, like bracts on a poinsettia, that make the plant ornamental even when it is not in flower. Grows in sun to part shade in moist soil or water to 6 inches deep. Height 18–36 inches with a running spread. Height is greatly affected by exposure, however. I have seen plants 40 inches tall in shade and 12 inches in full sun. Very showy but slow to grow is 'Oregon Gold', an all-gold selection from Hughes Water Gardens in Tualatin, Oregon.

## *Scirpus*
**rush**
**Cyperaceae**

*Scirpus* species can be found in many parts of the world, including North America. Certain species have been reclas- sified from *Scirpus* to *Schoenoplectus*. They are grouped together here because they are still more commonly known as *Scirpus*. *Scirpus* (and *Schoenoplectus*) species usually have foliage that is thin, narrow, and tall. Flowers are brown clubs or plumes that appear in mid to late summer. Rushes are most commonly propagated by division, but may also be grown from seed. Many species are cold tolerant and will survive a winter freeze as long as they remain in the pond. Rushes are excellent for shoreline stabilization in a natural pond or stream. They provide important cover for wildlife, including birds and amphibians, as well as nesting grounds for wildlife and fishes.

## *Scirpus albescens* (syn. *Schoenoplectus lacustris* subsp. *tabernaemontani* 'Albescens')
**white rush**

Foliage of this rush is cylindrical. In spring, it has strong white vertical stripes, but these markings are not so pro-

*Scirpus cyperinus*

*Scirpus cyperinus*

nounced in summer when the weather turns warm and muggy. The excellent, upright habit of this marginal makes a good accent in the pond. Grows in sun to part shade in moist soil or water to 3 inches deep. It will grow in water 24 inches deep but will be a much less dense, more open stand. Reaches 4–6 feet high with a running spread. Zones 5–9.

### Scirpus americanus (syn. *S. pungens*)
**three-square rush**

Foliage is blue-green and triangular, forming long, arching wands. It tolerates deep water up to 24 inches, but does best in moist soil or water up to 6 inches deep. It is an excellent source of food for wildlife, forming a loose, open stand that is great for shorelines and fish. Grows in full sun, reaching 3–6 feet high with a running spread.

### Scirpus californicus
**giant bulrush**

A tropical species of rush with very tall, rounded green stems. The plant sways and bends in the breeze, providing excellent height, form, and texture to the water garden. Grows in sun to part shade in moist soil or water to 10 inches deep. It will also grow floating in deeper water creating matted floating islands. Reaches 3–7½ feet high with a running spread. Zones 7–11.

### Scirpus cyperinus
**wooly rush**

Distinguished by its fluffy, silken tassels of tawny brown that appear at the ends of stiff, dark green foliage. The plant forms a dense clump 4 feet high and 24 inches wide and does not run, unlike other *Scirpus* species. It looks more like a cyperus than a scirpus. Grows in sun to part shade, taking moist soil or water to 4 inches deep. Zones 3–9.

### Scirpus fluviatilis
**giant nut grass**

Another *Scirpus* species that does not look like one, giant nut grass is noteworthy for its tall parasols of emerald-green foliage. The effect is similar to giant palm sedge (*Carex muskingumensis*). Grows in full sun. Reaches 4 feet high and 2–4 feet wide with a running spread in moist soil or water to 6 inches deep. Zones 4–8. This poor plant has been through the ringer on names, but *S. fluviatilis* seems to be currently accepted as correct. A very similar species is *S. robustus*.

*Scirpus validus*

*Scirpus validus* with *Pontederia*

## *Scirpus validus*
**soft rush**

Graceful, green cylinders of foliage have large, brown pen-dulous flowers. Combined with pickerel plant (*Pontederia*) or *Peltandra*, it is a knockout. Height 2–6 feet. Grows with a running spread in sun to part shade. Takes moist soil or water to 10 inches deep. Zones 3–11. It has a huge native range and now either has many subspecies or is due for a name change. A form from Rumsey Gardens in the U.K. is very showy with shocking yellow stems in spring that turn green in summer.

## *Scirpus zebrinus* (syn. *Schoenoplectus lacustris* subsp. *tabernaemontani* 'Zebrinus')
**zebra rush**

Highly ornamental from spring through fall, zebra rush has white bands or markings that appear every few inches along its tall, green foliage. The marks do not fade or burn as the plant ages, but as a general rule, the white patches are more pronounced when weather is cool or the plant is well fed and actively growing. Grows in sun to part shade in moist soil or water to 3 inches deep, though it tolerates deeper water. Height 4–6 feet with a running spread. Zones 5–9.

## *Scutellaria galericulata*
**common skullcap**
**Lamiaceae**

This undemanding perennial grows in wet shade to full sun with up to ½ inch of water over its crown. It can also toler-ate seasonal flooding. In full sun it grows to about 10–12 inches tall and wide, in shade to almost 24 inches. Half-inch blue-violet flowers bloom for 4–6 weeks in summer and will rebloom if deadheaded. Pink and white forms are also avail-able. The leaves have almost no petiole, giving the well branched plant a bushy, full look. It looks much like an aquatic form of *Nepeta*. Propagate by division, seed, or stem cuttings taken before flowering. Seed comes true for the color type as long as it is isolated from the others. Excellent in containers and along streams, it is not invasive and in fact easily gets crowded out. Native from Canada to the Ohio River and from the Pacific to the Atlantic. Hardy in Zones 3–6, possibly warmer.

A related species, *Scutellaria laterifolia* differs in just three respects. Flowers are half the size of the other species but twice as abundant. The leaves have petioles half as long as the foliage, giving this plant an airy look. Also, it grows from Canada to as far south as central Florida, hardy in Zones 3–10.

## Sesbania punicea
**lobster claw, scarlet rain tree**
**Fabaceae**

Introduced from the Caribbean and naturalized from North Carolina to Texas, this species is hardy in Zones 8–11. Blooming in summer on new wood are trusses of vibrant orangey red flowers like sweet peas. Plants can be shrubby or trained into a tree. Spreads by seed or runners, forming small colonies. Grows to 3–10 feet tall with a 5-foot spread. It is a great annual for the North or can be treated like cannas and cut to 4–6 inches from the ground and brought in from freezing temperatures. Grows in wet soil to water 6 inches deep and tolerates seasonal flooding. Propagate from seed, cuttings, or division. Nick seed to help them germinate, then sow in moist soil at 70–80°F or warmer. They will sprout in one to four weeks. Great in containers for hot patios. It likes it hot and is not for areas where summer nights routinely drop below 70°F.

## Sium suave
**water parsnip**
**Apiaceae**

The submerged leaves of water parsnip are very finely cut, more so even than the leaves of carrots. As they emerge above the water they become coarser until they look like parsnip foliage, or Italian parsley if crowded. One stalk, if planted alone, forms almost a shrub. The plant grows from a central stalk that shoots forth umbels of starry white flowers in summer through fall. Native to temperate regions of North America, it grows in moist soil or water to 6 inches deep, overwintering well in the pond with no special care or protection. Zones 4–11. Grows in sun to part shade, reaching 3–5 feet high with a spread of 2–3 feet. Propagates from division of rootstock in early spring, or very easily by seed. It

*Sium suave*

looks great with *Pontederia* or *Thalia*, giving a baby's breath effect. Should be used more.

## Sparganium
**burr reed**
**Sparganiaceae**

Daylily-like foliage grows submerged in deep water or emerged in shallow. Most emerged foliage is just over 24 inches tall. Each plant spreads to only 4–6 inches, but they form colonies like cattails (*Typha*). Flowers are little white balls on zigzag stems, some branched, some not. They are sweetly scented and are attractive to skipper butterflies. They bloom all summer, followed by spiny-looking balls of fruit. Leaves are a bright, translucent celery-green, and fall color is banana-yellow with a hint of pumpkin. Very showy. Fairly open growing, so it does not crowd out other plants.

Fourteen species are native throughout the northern hemisphere and into Australasia. Most of the North American

*Sium suave*

*Sparganium*

species look very similar when emerged. All are useful in the water garden, either in containers or in drifts. Look for *Sparganium eurycarpum*, *S. glomeratum*, *S. natans*, *S. emersum*, *S. americanum*, *S. fluctuans*, and *S. androcladum*. The mature seed of these species is about the only way to tell them apart. All are hardy in Zones 2–10 and are very adaptable. Easy to grow from seed sown fresh, given 30 days of cold treatment, then warmed up. Will sprout in four to 30 days. Also easy to divide offsets in summer, or they produce corms for overwintering, which can be lifted and planted separately.

## Stachys palustris
**marsh betony**
**Labiatae**

A hardy and reliable water plant native to North America, marsh betony has thick spikes of pink or purple flowers in summer. Leaves resemble those of *Monarda* and are hairy. In the fall, foliage takes on a maroon or yellow color. Its running spread may be invasive in the very moist soil that it prefers. Can grow in water as deep as 5 inches, reaching a height of 6–24 inches. Grows readily from stem cuttings, rootstock division, or from seed. Overwinters in cold climates with no special care or protection, as long as its pot remains submerged in the water. Zones 4–8.

Another species, *Stachys cooleyae*, or great hedge nettle, grows naturally in southern British Columbia and Oregon. It has deep red-lavender flowers. A few other species are also useful. They are very similar in size, color, and hardiness, but foliage and flower size varies. I have tried *S. tenuifolia*, with larger branched flower heads, and *S. aspera*, with smaller and bushier foliage.

*Stachys palustris*

*Thalia dealbata*

*Stachys palustris*

*Symplocarpus foetidus*

## *Symplocarpus foetidus*
### American skunk cabbage
### Araceae

Very similar in appearance to yellow and white skunk cabbage (*Lysichiton* spp.), this species has large, leathery, and lance- to spade-shaped leaves. Springtime flowers are smaller than other skunk cabbage, with a pointed, shell-like spathe of dark red, brown, green, or speckled, which encloses a small spadix. Native to North America, it grows in the eastern and midwestern parts of the continent, as well as temperate east Asia and Japan. Zones 3–9. Overwinters in colder climates without special protection—the heat of its growth in spring actually melts the snow around it. Grows in part shade in moist soil or water to 3 inches deep, reaching 36 inches high and wide. The Asian forms are shorter, reaching 12–18 inches, with very red, shiny flowers. A variegated form also exists. Best propagated from seed, but also may be divided at the rootstock.

## *Thalia*
### Marantaceae

*Thalia* species are grown primarily for their striking, lush foliage. Leaves are ovate to lance-shaped and can become rather large, up to 24 inches across at their widest, and often more than 36 inches in length. Flowers are unusual silvery-purple beads that droop from long, arching stems. *Thalia* species are native to tropical regions of the Americas, and most can be readily propagated by division of the rootstock.

*Thalia dealbata*

*Symplocarpus foetidus*

## *Thalia dealbata*
**purple thalia**

*Thalia dealbata* is a hardy species, overwintering in colder climates, to Zone 5, with no special protection. It grows in sun to part shade in moist soil or water to 6 inches deep, reaching a height of 2–6 feet with a spread of 24 inches. Its purple flowers bloom in late summer. 'Blue Cup Leaf Form' is a selection with blue leaves that are more cup-shaped than those of the species. And 'Broad Leafed Form' has leaves that are flat and more triangular in shape. The foliage looks very tropical and has a slight powdery blue color.

## *Thalia geniculata*
**alligator flag**

The common name of this thalia derives from its usefulness in "flagging" the presence of an alligator—as the gator swims through the glade, it rustles the plant, causing the leaves to

*Thalia geniculata*

*Thalia geniculata*

*Thalia*

*Tillaea americana*

swing back and forth. Foliage is more yellow-green than that of *Thalia dealbata*, and the late-summer flowers are silvery blue. Grows in sun to part shade in moist soil or water to 10 inches deep. Height 2–9 feet, spread 2–6 feet. This is a more tender species that will not survive a winter frost. Zones 9–11. Bring it indoors to spend the winter.

 *Thalia geniculata* f. *ruminoides*, or red-stemmed alligator flag, has stems streaked in red and sometimes solid red, giving it an even greater accent value in the pond. This form grows slightly larger, as well, reaching 2–10 feet high and 2–6 feet wide.

### *Tillaea recurva*
### water sedum
### Crassulaceae

A miniature aquatic that looks just like garden *Sedum*, only much, much smaller. Diminutive white flowers appear through the summer. Leaves flush a rosy red in cooler weather. Adapts well to the moist to wet perennial bed, the bog garden, or the pond, growing in moist soil to submerged. It will not tolerate drying. Situate in sun to part shade where it will reach 1–3 inches high with its running spread. Zones 5–9. Overwinters well in cooler water and withstands freezing temperatures. Propagates easily from stem cuttings. A popular aquatic plant in British water gardens, it has become a pest because it spreads so readily. *Tillaea americana* is similar, but native to the U.S. It is less of a weed and often annual.

*Typha laxmannii*

*Typha angustifolia*

*Typha latifolia* 'Variegata'

## Typha
cattail
Typhaceae

Foliage of cattails is narrow, anywhere from ½ inch to 2 inches wide, depending upon the species. Height can range from 6 inches to more than 12 feet tall. Leaves are generally flat on one side and more rounded on the other. Flowers are long catkins that turn brown as they mature, releasing downy seeds that float away on the breeze. Cattails grow in freshwater marshes and colonize wide areas with their stiff, running rhizomes. They tolerate water over their crown and provide important habitat for fish and amphibians. Their foliage serves as a nesting source for many species of wild birds, and their roots are often eaten by muskrats. Leaves and roots have also had their place as a source of food for humans—the rootstock can be ground into flour, and the new shoots may be boiled and eaten as a vegetable. Cattails can be grown from seed, but they propagate quickly from division of the rhizomes. They overwinter well in cooler water and withstand freezing temperatures. Native to many parts of the world, *Typha* grows wild in North America, from Newfoundland to Alaska and southward into Mexico.

### Typha angustifolia
graceful cattail

More narrow-leafed than the standard *Typha latifolia*, foliage arches and sways gracefully in the breeze. Very elegant. Suitable for most ponds and large container water gardens. Height 4–6 feet. Catkins are very thin and make attractive additions to floral arrangements. Grows in sun to part shade in moist soil or water to 12 inches deep. Zones 3–11.

### Typha domingensis
giant cattail

A towering species of *Typha*, it grows 8–11 feet tall and has catkins up to 24 inches long. Foliage is thin and narrow, similar to *T. angustifolia*, only 1 inch or so wide. Grows in sun to part shade in moist soil or water to 24 inches deep. Zones 7–11.

### Typha latifolia

A bold vertical accent in any pond, this is the standard cattail commonly seen growing in ditches and in wetlands. It is excellent for water filtration and should not be dismissed for its value in the water garden landscape. Grows in sun to part shade in moist soil or water to 12 inches deep. Reaches 7 feet tall. Zones 3–11.

### Typha latifolia 'Variegata'
variegated cattail

The variegation in this cattail is bold, forming clean, bright green and white, longitudinal stripes. An elegant addition

*Typha minima*

*Typha minima*

to any pond, it does not grow as readily as other cattails and does not appreciate being transplanted. Grows in sun to part shade in moist soil or water to 12 inches deep. Height 5–6 feet. Zones 4–11.

### *Typha laxmannii*
**dwarf cattail**

Ideal for small ponds and container water gardens, dwarf cattail has very narrow foliage and small catkins. Growing to only about 36 inches in height, it is not as heat tolerant as other cattails. Zones 3–10. Grows in sun to part shade in moist soil or water to just 4 inches deep.

### *Typha minima*
**miniature cattail**

Perfect for the very small pond or container garden, this miniature species has petite, round catkins on petite, vertical plants. Height is just 12–18 inches. Foliage is often an attractive blue-green color. Grows in sun to part shade in moist soil or water to 3 inches deep. Zones 3–9.

*Veronica americana*

*Veronica anagallis-aquatica*

## *Veronica*
### Scrophulariaceae

*Veronica* species are native to northern temperate regions, including North America, Zones 5–9. Of the 250 species in the genus, about 10 are aquatic. The low creeping or bushy plants are covered in blue flowers, and some exhibit burgundy fall color. The foliage varies dramatically among the species, from round to stringy, but the flowers are generally the same deep to pale blue. They propagate easily from stem cuttings or from seed surface sown anytime, and overwinter well in colder climates with no special protection. They can simply remain in the pond throughout the winter.

## *Veronica americana*
### American brooklime

This North American native has lance-shaped leaves that are slightly toothed. Flowers are tubular and light blue, appearing on spikes that grow from the leaf axils. Very free-flowering in spring and early summer. It has an upright, bushy habit and does not run into or interfere with its neighbors. Height 4–12 inches, spread 10–12 inches. Suitable for the edge of the pond or bog garden, or in a table-top pond. Situate in sun to part shade in moist soil or water to 3 inches deep. Zones 5–9. Reproduces readily from seed but is never a pest. May be annual in some ponds, but new seedlings are up and ready by fall for overwintering in the pond.

Two other species are virtually the same as *Veronica americana*. *Veronica anagallis-aquatica* is more likely to be perennial. It has leaves that clasp the stem and deep blue to almost white flowers in abundance all summer. *Veronica scutellata*, also more perennial, has very narrow, heavily toothed foliage and is great in containers or streams.

*Veronica beccabunga*

*Veronica beccabunga*

## *Veronica beccabunga*
### European brooklime

Native to Europe, this species has a shorter, more creeping habit. Foliage is rounded and slightly toothed, shiny, and fleshy. It displays great fall color of intense crimson. Flowers are bright blue, appearing at the leaf axils in spring to summer. A delightful addition to the pond, it has a tendency to run and needs some pruning to restrain its presence. Particularly well suited for a small tub garden or table-top pond. Grows in sun to part shade in moist soil or water to 3 inches deep. Height 4 inches and spread 12 inches. Zones 5–9.

## *Viola*
### violet
### Violaceae

The violets include a group of species adapted to seasonally wet soils. With their familiar blue-to-white-faced flowers they lend spring color to even the shadiest pond. Many are tolerant of very wet soil year-round. Generally considered northern plants, hardy in Zones 4–7, they may be dormant by midsummer or foliage may endure all summer. Hot summers in wet soil seem to spell death. All are easy to propagate by division or from seed sown fresh and cold stratified. All those species for the water garden landscape take wet shade to full sun. None tolerate water over the crown for any length of time. Foliage is the major difference between the species, and flower color, though most come in a range of darker or lighter selections. They grow to 4–6 inches tall and wide. All are excellent when used with *Carex* or *Glyceria*. They are free of pests and diseases save for deer, which grazed my planting down to the ground two years in a row.

*Viola palustris*

### Viola cucullata

Looks like a common blue violet. Very nice in a wet shady shore or seasonally flooded woods. It can tolerate water over the crown for three to five days.

### Viola labradorica
**Labrador violet**

This species has a mounding habit and heart-shaped foliage. A deep-purple-leafed form is sold in the perennial market and is worth a try in a wet spot.

### Viola lanceolata

This is often sold as *Viola palustris*—four times I have ordered *V. palustris* and received *V. lanceolata*. Far more heat tolerant than *V. palustris*, *V. lanceolata* is the best violet for water. Flowers are white with pale blue faces and darker whiskers.

### Viola macloskeyi

Very adaptable and heat tolerant. Blooms a long time—three weeks—here in the Chicago area. Flowers are a very pale blue.

### Viola nephrophylla

Similar to *Viola lanceolata*, but two-thirds the size and a darker color. Very tolerant of high pH in the water and soil.

*Viola palustris*

### Viola palustris

The least heat tolerant of the species listed here. It does not do well south of Zone 6. The summers are just too hot. It is very similar to *Viola lanceolata*, but the foliage is wider and the flowers a little bluer.

*Wedelia trilobata*

## *Wedelia trilobata*
**golden water zinnia**
Asteraceae

A trailing plant with yellow, zinnia-like flowers in summer, this tropical is excellent in waterfalls or on the pond edge, in moist soil or water to 1 inch deep. It also tolerates drought. Grows in sun to shade, reaching 6 inches high. It propagates readily from stem cuttings, and requires protection during winter. Bring inside and treat as a houseplant. Hardy in Zones 9–11. A variegated form is available with yellow-splashed foliage. It is a nice addition, especially in shade, but be vigilant to remove all-green shoots.

## *Xyris*
**yellow-eyed grass**
Xyridaceae

The acid-requiring plants in the genus *Xyris* have grassy or iris-like foliage at the base and club-like flower heads that rise above the foliage. Bright yellow, three-petaled flowers are borne on these clubs all summer long. Foliage is often tinged with red or purple. Seed look like little hemlock cones. The 250 species are found throughout the world. Ten to 15 species are native to the U.S. The major difference between the species listed here are size and hardiness. They grow 4–24 inches tall and wide, depending on species, in full sun to shade in moist soil or water to 4 inches deep. They are great in combination with *Sarracenia*. More should be done in adding them to the waterscape. Easy to propagate by seed or division of clumps. They need no special care to overwinter where hardy. Otherwise, bring indoors and treat as a houseplant.

*Xyris*

## *Xyris difformis*

Flowers are ⅔ inch and continue all summer. Grows 12–18 inches tall. Hardy in Zone 5 and up. Very grassy foliage.

## *Xyris fimbriata*

Hardy in Zone 8 and up. Large ½-inch flowers on plants that grow up to 24 inches tall. Leaves are narrower at ½ inch wide, forming clumps 24 inches across. I have observed specimens in the wild with 20 stems and almost red foliage and deep red stems. Very showy with *Sarracenia flava* or any of the new red-leafed cultivars.

## *Xyris montana*

Flowers are ⅓–½ inch. Reaches 12 inches tall. Hardy in Zone 4 and up.

*Zantedeschia aethiopica*

## Xyris torta

This species has wider foliage, like *Xyris fimbriata*, but it is twisted. Flowers are up to ½ inch. Hardy in Zone 4 and up.

## Zantedeschia
calla lily
Araceae

The six species in the genus *Zantedeschia* are native to South Africa. Hardy to Zone 6 or 7, depending on selection and protection. I generally regard them as tender and bring them indoors for the winter, letting them dry in the pot until one month before setting them out, then I water them and place them in a sunny window. They vary in height from 6 inches to 4 feet, with similar spreads. Much breeding has been done to create brilliant hybrids that need to be explored for the water garden. Foliage is arrow-shaped to lanceolate, depending on selection. Foliage can be green or dotted with white. A selection occurs that has yellow streaking in the foliage— it is interesting as a specimen but too much en masse. Flower color ranges from white to almost black-red, including yellows, pinks, and reds. There are no blues. All like very moist to wet soils but no water over the crown. Propagate by division for selections or seed for species. Seed must be defleshed before sowing, but sow fresh on moist soil at 70°F.

*Zantedeschia aethiopica*

*Zantedeschia aethiopica* 'Crowborough Variegated'

*Zephyranthes candida*

### Zantedeschia aethiopica

The classic large, white calla lily. Great as a specimen or in a stand. Grows to 4 feet high and wide. A great number of outstanding cultivars have been selected from this species:

'Apple Court Babe'—dwarf at 12 inches tall with lots of 2–4-inch flowers; hardier than others

'Crowborough'—white flowers; grows 18–24 inches tall; a British selection said to be hardy, but not as hardy as 'Apple Court Babe'

'Crowborough Variegated'—yellow-splashed foliage; grows 18 inches tall and 12 inches wide; very unstable and easily reverts

'Green Goddess'—white flowers with green tips; grows to 4 feet tall

'Little Gem'—creamy white; grows to 12 inches tall

'Whipped Cream'—white flowers and heavily spotted foliage; 36 inches tall

'White Giant'—white flowers and white-spotted foliage; a 6½-foot-tall monster

### Zephyranthes
### rain lily
### Amaryllidaceae

Native to the U.S. and Mexico, the rain lilies go dormant in the dry season and grow and flower in the wet season. They can grow year-round in wet sites but tend to flower better if they get a dry period. All are between 3 and 10 inches tall with grassy foliage. The six-petaled flowers are 1–3 inches across in white, yellow, or pink. They grow in full sun to part shade in moist soil or water to 3 inches deep. They are tender perennial bulbs, so are hardy in Zone 8 and up. *Zephyranthes candida*, however, has survived in my Zone 5 or 6 garden for years. Where not hardy, they can be overwintered indoors. Just do not water them until returning them to the pond in the spring. Following are some species and varieties of note:

*Z. atamasco*—pure white, open-faced flowers

*Z. candida*—white flowers with a crocus-like shape, betraying their common name of water crocus

*Z. flavissima*—flat, yellow flowers

*Z. grandiflora*—hot pink, open flowers

*Z.* 'Grandjax'—A pale pink hybrid from Ray Flagg

*Z. jonesii*—small yellow flowers

*Z.* 'Labuffarosa'—very showy large, flat, pink to white flowers from Yucca Do Nursery in Hempstead, Texas

*Z. reginae*—small yellow, crocus-like flowers with a hint of orange on the backs

*Z.* Sunset Strain—pinky yellow and very showy

*Zephyranthes candida*

*Zizania aquatica*

## *Zizania*
### wild rice
### Poaceae

Leaves of *Zizania* are usually about ½–1 inch wide and 3–4 feet long, forming long, arching shapes that have an elegant appeal in the pond. Plants can reach 6 feet or more high and 4 feet or more wide. Flower heads are 3–4 feet tall, standing above the arching leaves. They are large panicles of roughly pyramidal shape, with very showy male flowers appearing on the lower stems and less showy female flowers on the upper stems. The rice, which forms on the upper, female flowers, is dark red and usually ripens starting in late August and continuing through September. As the rice ripens, it falls off the stalk and tumbles into the water. It floats downstream and waits until spring to sprout and grow. *Zizania* species are generally annual, but can be perennial the farther south they grow, and depend upon annual seed production to maintain the rice paddies in successive years. All are hardy as

perennials at least to Zone 5. They can also be propagated by division, however. They grow best where there is some moving water, and in the wild generally will not grow in areas where water is stagnant.

Wild rice has long been a food staple for Native American Indians. It was an important food source for Indians in the Great Lakes region. In fact, the name Menominee means "wild rice people." Wild rice is still grown and harvested in some areas, including Manitoba, Ontario, Minnesota, and California. Wildfowl of many species also favor wild rice, as do muskrats, deer, and moose.

### *Zizania aquatica*

A tall, stately water plant that is much underused in the water garden landscape. Plumes appear in midsummer and continue throughout the fall, giving a very exotic appearance to the pond. Very easy to grow, it has a tendency to run by its underground rhizomes. Best suited to a large pot, even

*Zizania aquatica*

in the earth-bottom pond. Grows in full sun, producing floating foliage with 24–36-inch flower stalks above the water in water deeper than 36 inches. In shallower water of 12 inches deep or less, plants can grow to 7 feet or more. Flower panicles are large, generally between 12 and 24 inches in length and 12 inches wide. Native to North America, growing wild from Nova Scotia to Manitoba, into Minnesota, Nebraska, and Texas.

## *Zizania latifolia*

The Asian form of wild rice, native to Japan, China, Korea and Siberia. It is often infected with smut to form a culinary delicacy. It looks very similar to *Zizania aquatica* but it grows in shallow water of 12 inches deep or less, never much deeper.

## *Zizania palustris*
### northern wild rice

The debate continues over whether *Zizania palustris* is a separate species or just a form of *Z. aquatica*. It is usually shorter than *Z. aquatica* and the female flowers are flatter. The rice is larger on *Z. palustris*, making it more important commercially, and it is the more common species in northern Wisconsin (*Through the Looking Glass* by S. Borman, R. Korth, and J. Temte, 1997, University of Wisconsin Press, Stevens Point). *Wetland Plants and Plant Communities of Minnesota and Wisconsin* (S. Eggers and D. Reed, 1997, U.S. Army Corps of Engineers, St. Paul District) also refers to this separate species, saying that "Ownbey and Morley (1991) apply the name *Z. palustris* with two varieties for the wild rice found in Minnesota." It grows in colder water, rarely in water warmer than 65°F. Panicles are generally half the size of those of *Z. aquatica* and tend to be 12–24 inches above the water. Grows in clear water to 6 feet deep.

# CHAPTER 8

# IRISES

I have been fascinated with irises for the water garden ever since I was a young boy exploring the Mississippi River in northern Minnesota. The first water-inhabiting iris I ever found was a muddy blue color, a wild-growing cultivar of *Iris versicolor* whose beauty and appeal only I seemed to appreciate. Giving it ample water, I grew it in my father's prized patch of German bearded iris cultivars, much to the family's chagrin. Everyone but me was surprised when it sprouted new foliage and flourished for many seasons.

Over the years I have found more irises that tolerate or require either wet or water-saturated soil. Growers and hybridizers are developing many new, exciting cultivars with larger flowers, greater color, and enhanced hardiness. There is no need nowadays to look along the shores of a local pond, stream, or river to find excellent, sturdy, free-flowering irises for the water garden. Resilient and remarkably pest-free, water-side irises reward the gardener with years of early summer flowers.

Two broad categories of irises grow in and near the pond. The first group comprises the true water irises, which grow best with water over their crown throughout the year, even in fall and winter. These include *Iris pseudacorus* (yellow flag), *I. virginica* (southern blue flag), *I. versicolor* (blue flag), *I. laevigata* (rabbit ear iris), the Louisiana irises, *I. fulva* (red flag or copper iris), and *I. prismatica* (cube-seed iris). The other general grouping of irises contains those that grow best with wet soils for some of the growing season, but in most climates prefer drier conditions for the remainder of the year. These are *I. ensata* (Japanese iris), the Siberian irises, *I. missouriensis* (Rocky Mountain iris), and *I. setosa* (Alaskan blue flag). Many irises are commonly called a type of "flag" because they marked the shallow area in a stream where travelers could safely cross over.

*Iris pseudacorus*

Back to front, *Carex elata* 'Knightshayes', *Houttuynia cordata* 'Flore Pleno' to the left of *Iris laevigata* 'Variegata', then *Acorus gramineus*, and *Menyanthes*

*Iris pseudacorus* 'Variegata' stands at the front of the pond margin with, counterclockwise, *Juniperus*, *Viburnum lantana* 'Holden Gold', *Euphorbia palustris*, *Symphytum*, *Sium suave*, and *Rudbeckia*

## LANDSCAPE USES

Although important distinctions exist among the *Iris* species discussed in this chapter, they share one common trait: all are central landscape plants for the water garden. Each iris blooms in the spring, sometime between May and July depending upon cultivar and climate. Colors range from the whitest whites to the deepest blues, with purple and lavender hues, and reds, yellows, browns and greens—essentially every color in the rainbow. Some are deeply veined or heavily marked with a yellow glow toward the center of the petals. Certain cultivars even rebloom in the fall, if they are grown in the climates they prefer. The flowers of water garden irises generally rise above the leaves of the plant, and often they appear to be floating on air. From a distance, one could easily mistake them for brightly colored butterflies.

The substantial root systems of many water garden *Iris* species often make them excellent for holding back soil erosion along the banks of natural ponds and streams. Some iris species tolerate seasonal drought as well as seasonal flooding, thus earning them a place in detention or retention areas in the larger, corporate landscape. Even a ditch or a wet spot in the homeowner's backyard is perfectly suited to many moisture-loving *Iris* species.

Water garden irises are amiable sorts that blend well with many other pondside plants, especially those that grow closer to the water surface and have delicate foliage. Parrot feather (*Myriophyllum aquaticum*) is an excellent accent plant when grown at the base of a water iris. Its finely-cut, emerald green, fluffy foliage softens the water line and contrasts well with the iris's larger, sword-shaped, architectural foliage. Iris leaves also serve to shade smaller inhabitants, like marsh marigold (*Caltha palustris*) or candelabra primula (*Primula japonica*), which shun the heat of the summer sun.

## BLOOM SEASON

Predicting the dates on which irises will bloom is an inexact science. When the flowers appear depends heavily upon climate and cultivar. In our midwestern garden, the earliest to blossom are usually *Iris versicolor*, *I. setosa*, and *I. prismatica*. Generally, they open toward the end of May and last through to the end of June. Within a few days after the appearance of the early bloomers, *I. pseudacorus* bursts into flower, starting at the very end of May and continuing through to the third week of June. *Iris virginica* awakens about a week after *I. pseudacorus*, in early June, followed by *I. laevigata* in mid-June. Both flower for two to three weeks. By the middle or end of June, *I. missouriensis* and *I. fulva* have started to blossom, as well as the Siberian irises. The Siberians last for several weeks, while *I. fulva* only flowers for a week or so. The last but by no means the least are the *I. ensata* cultivars, which begin their show at the end of June and continue through to the middle of July. Louisiana iris cultivars vary greatly in their bloom dates and range over several weeks, some starting as early as late May or early June, and others not beginning to flower until the end of June through and into July.

Based upon our discussions with other iris activists, we have found that, as a very general rule, these guidelines can be adjusted based upon relative climate. Thus, for every hundred miles or so north of Chicago, bloom season will start about a week later than what we experience. Similarly, for every hundred miles or so south of Chicago, water garden irises will begin to bloom about a week earlier. Of course these are only rough estimates, and particular cultivars may bloom much earlier or later than the species, depending upon its individual predilections.

A few *Iris* species or cultivars will put forth a repeat bloom later in the season. For the most part this reappearance of flowers occurs after the plant has had a few weeks' rest. Some cultivars will put forth a new set of flowers in the fall, but they are rare. A few cultivars bloom even better on their second flush of flowers than they did on their first.

## SUNLIGHT, WIND, AND WATER DEPTH

All the irises discussed in this chapter perform well if they receive a full day of sunlight. They also grow well and bloom reliably if given at least six hours of sun. Cultivars whose flowers are white or light-colored often prefer some shade to protect their blossoms from drying out too quickly. Gener-ally, water garden iris will not flower if sunlight drops to an average of less than four hours per day. At reduced exposures, most iris species will wither and eventually die out completely.

If an iris plant is to be placed in a partially shaded spot, morning sun is usually preferable to afternoon sun. The warming rays in the morning will help to evaporate dew from the plant's leaves, reducing the risks of attack from fungus or bacteria. Cutworms, too, will retreat to a subterranean slumber once exposed to sunlight. Morning light is less harsh to iris flowers, but afternoon sun can easily burn up the paper-thin petals of lighter-hued blossoms.

Gentle breezes can be an aesthetic benefit to a water garden with irises, sending ripples across the water and gently nudging the iris blossoms so that they dance lightheartedly above the pond. Too much wind, however, can cause substantial damage to iris flowers and can even reduce the height of the foliage. It is best to create a sort of windscreen to protect irises from excessive blowing winds, whether these may occur all year long or only seasonally. Grasses planted around the pond, outside the liner, make a great windscreen.

Proper water depth for pondside plants is determined by measuring the distance between the crown of the plant and the surface of the water. An iris whose proper water depth is 3 inches should be placed with its crown 3 inches below the water surface. Moist soil is that which retains water, but does not have any water standing over it. Most *Iris* species will tolerate a range of water depths, say from moist soil to water a few inches over the crown. These irises do not require that the plant be set or planted at precisely a certain water depth. Submersion within the range given will provide them with proper growing conditions. For some species, the degree of water tolerance changes at different times in the year—these requirements are discussed with respect to seasonal care and maintenance.

## SEASONAL CARE AND MAINTENANCE

Water irises are dependent upon seasonal changes in day length and water or soil temperature to induce them to go dormant in the winter and to prompt them to start growing again in the spring. This being so, it is critical that potted water irises be brought up near the surface of the pond in the early spring where the water is warmer. This warming temperature awakens the irises from their winter slumber and causes them to begin bud formation. Irises that are planted in soil near the edge of the pond should be cleaned of mulch and debris in early spring to allow the sun's rays to warm the plant and its soil environment.

Water garden irises are heavy feeders and benefit from early spring fertilizer to supplement the soil's nutrients. The more fertilizer they receive, the more they will grow and flower—reduced fertilizer will not shock the plants into setting bud or flowering, as can happen with many other plants. As a general rule, begin fertilizing irises when the pond temperature reaches 65°F and continue to fertilize at one-month intervals through the season, well after they have started to sprout. Stop fertilizing about a month before the last frost-free date in the area, to allow the irises to harden off for the winter. In climates without frost, withhold fertilizer once the plants show signs of going dormant, for example, when they begin to stop growing new foliage and older leaves begin to wither and turn brown.

Irises are carefree plants and need minimal attention through the summer. Deadheading spent flowers will curtail the impulse of those especially energetic strains to seed themselves throughout the pond. Other more restrained varieties benefit from deadheading simply for the sake of appearance. For the same reason, trim back older leaves as they develop a tan or brown color. Trimming off old or unsightly foliage reduces the threat of pests and diseases, another excellent reason to keep the plants well tended. Fall cleaning of irises also prevents diseases or insects from overwintering on the plant, waiting for spring to come to life and attack the new plants.

Proper winter care depends upon the particular species of *Iris*. Generally, irises that like to grow in water year-round (*I. pseudacorus*, *I. virginica*, *I. versicolor*, *I. laevigata*, and *I. prismatica*) are easily prepared for winter's cold winds. As the foliage dies down in the fall when water temperature cools, trim the leaves back to just an inch or so above the crown of the plant. Leave the plants in the pond, making sure that they will stay wet throughout the winter. Some gardeners prefer to mulch them into the perennial border, while others move them to the bottom of the pond. We have found that these irises do well if they are simply left on the shelf or margin of the pond. They should not be exposed to winter's cold winds by being taken out of the pond and simply left to freeze dry in their pots.

Other water garden irises cannot tolerate water over their crown during the cold winter months of northern climates. These include *Iris ensata*, *I. missouriensis*, and the Siberian irises. As a general rule, none of these species will survive a period of dormancy with their crowns submerged below water. They do perform well, however, if they are grown in a boggy area where the soil stays moist but the

*Scirpus albescens*, left, and irises, center, line a stream

crown of the plant is not covered with water. Growing these species at the edge of a natural pond or stream, where they will not be subjected to a winter drowning, is the ideal solution. If they are in pots in a pond, remove them from the water garden in the fall, dig a temporary hole for them in an open spot of the perennial border, and mulch them heavily for the winter. Make sure to trim off most of the foliage to prevent dormant insects or their eggs from spending their winter in cozy hibernation with the iris plants.

In warmer climates where the temperature does not drop below 25°F, mulching is unnecessary if pots are removed from the pond. Just do not let them dry out. Place them in a pan filled with water 1–4 inches deep, keeping the crowns of the plants above the water level.

# PLANTING

Water garden irises prefer a soil that is high in clay, to provide structural support and to allow the plants' roots to move freely for adequate strength and nutrition. Although organic matter, such as decomposed cow manure, may be added to the soil, be very careful. Organic matter is fine in a perennial border, but in the water garden it breaks down quickly once the water temperature warms, creating salts that can burn the roots of water plants. Too much organic matter can also cause an algae bloom in the pond. I recommend keeping the soil somewhat "lean" in organic matter and supplementing it with regular feedings of fertilizer.

There is no one specific recipe for the proper acidity or alkalinity of soil for irises that grow in or near the pond. Water-tolerant irises have widely divergent ranges of tolerance to acid or alkaline soil conditions (see the table "Recommended Soil pH for Water Irises"). Soil that is too high in dissolved salts can burn the roots of the plant, weakening the iris and eventually killing it altogether. Likewise, soil that is too alkaline or too acid will starve the iris by preventing it from taking up needed nutrients from the soil and water.

## Recommended Soil pH for Water Irises

| *Iris* Species | Soil pH |
| --- | --- |
| I. ensata | Acid (6) to neutral (7) |
| I. fulva | Any soil type, but prefers neutral to alkaline (7+) |
| I. laevigata | Acid (6) to neutral (7) |
| I. missouriensis | Prefers neutral (7), but will tolerate acid (6) to alkaline (8) |
| I. prismatica | Acid (6) to neutral (7), but will grow in alkaline (8.5) |
| I. pseudacorus | Wide range, from acid (5.5) to alkaline (9) |
| I. setosa | Prefers somewhat acid (6.5–7.2), but will tolerate alkaline (to 8.5) |
| I. versicolor | Slightly acid (6.5) to alkaline (8.5) |
| I. virginica | Neutral (7) to alkaline (9) |
| Louisiana irises | Wide range, from acid (5.5) to alkaline (9) |
| Siberian irises | Acid (6) to alkaline (8) |

Irises grow best in pots that are wide and shallow. The rhizomes grow close to the surface of the soil, much like German bearded irises, in more or less a straight line. Plant the rhizome toward the edge of the pot with the growing tip pointing toward the center, to maximize the pot's space. Spread the roots out on a mound of soil, so that they are not all tangled together underneath the rhizome. Then add soil over the rhizome and growing tip. The rhizome should be underneath the soil, with the growing tip just barely below the soil surface.

The exception to this general rule is *Iris prismatica*, which grows by sending out what appear to be underground "runners," which sprout and form new fans of iris. *Iris prismatica* will fill the entire pot with its running fans, looking much like a lawn. It, too, may be planted with its growing tip slightly below the soil surface.

When water-tolerant irises outgrow their living quarters, they have a tendency to push against the edge of the pot and then "jump" out of the pot entirely. Finding a pot that is at least a foot in diameter will help keep this from happening too frequently. Louisiana iris cultivars are such exuberant growers that they are especially prone to running and easily jump from their pots in a single season. Make sure to use a pot that is wide enough to accommodate at least a year's growth. Better yet, grow them in a large, shallow tray to avoid the necessity of replanting them in midseason.

In my experience, planting or transplanting an iris when it is in bud or bloom is not best, as this will cause the plant to forfeit the flowers in favor of acclimating to its new environment. I recommend planting and transplanting irises immediately after they have finished flowering, when they are actively growing new roots, which they started to do just as they began flowering. Although other sources recommend planting irises in late summer or early fall, we in our midwestern (Zone 5) climate have suffered severe losses through the winter with irises planted out in August or September. The plants are not able to grow sufficient retractal roots before the onset of fall dormancy, and they heave from the ground through the successive freezes and thaws of our winters. In such colder climates, if transplanting must wait until later in the summer, it is imperative that the plants be mulched heavily to withstand the winter cold.

Fall transplanting is appropriate in warmer climates where the irises will not be exposed to a winter of freezing temperatures and blowing winds. In southern climates, water irises that are planted or transplanted just after flowering will have to endure not only transplant shock, but also the long, hot, muggy weather of southern summers. Many irises cannot survive such a double-punch, and succumb before the new season has begun.

Perhaps the best advice is to experiment with a few fans of iris to test the viability of planting or transplanting at different times of the year, before committing the entire stock of iris plants. Look for guidance and information from other water garden enthusiasts who also grow irises and knowledgeable nursery personnel.

# PROPAGATION

## Starting from Seed

To start irises from seed, the seed must have an average of a six-week period of cold, moist dormancy. Remove the seed from the seed pod, and then remove the outer corky seed covering to find the thin seed inside. Lay out several seed on a few layers of paper towel and roll it up loosely. Wet the paper towel roll until it is just damp and put it in a plastic bag. Seal the bag and store it in the refrigerator—we put them in the vegetable crisper drawer—at about 45°F, for six weeks.

Once the seed have passed their cold, moist dormancy, remove them from the plastic bag and the paper towel roll. Place them on dampened potting mix—any seed-starting mix will do—and cover them lightly with more dampened potting mix. Keep the soil evenly and continuously moist. Peat pots work well, as do small plastic pots with bottom and side holes. Keep them at about 75°F and give them at least eight hours of sunlight per day, either naturally or with artificial grow lights. Then do not be impatient—iris seed can take up to three years to germinate after cold stratification. But generally, plants should have sprouted in about two weeks. Sprouting is evident when small grass-like blades start to peak out from under the potting mix.

After the seedlings have sprouted, feed them with a light solution of fertilizer (10-10-10). Transplant them to larger pots when they begin to look crowded and have grown at least a few roots. Seedlings that are well cared for and well fed generally will flower a year after they have sprouted.

## Dividing

Propagating irises from division is an uncomplicated task. Dig up the plant or remove it from its pot, and wash all the soil off the roots. If the clump is especially large, use two garden forks, back to back, to split the clump apart into smaller, more manageable sections of rhizome. Rinse off as much of the soil as possible, using the strong jets of a garden hose. Then, using a sharp knife, divide the iris rhizome into smaller clumps, or into sections with one, two, or three fans. Make sure that each rhizome section retains some growing roots and is at least 3–4 inches long. Wash the rhizomes clean of soil and inspect the plants for dead or damaged roots. Trim the roots back so that they are about 4 inches or so in length. Foliage can be trimmed back to about 6 inches or so, reducing stress to the plant and allowing new foliage to grow more quickly.

In colder climates irises are best divided just after they have finished flowering, in midsummer. This is the time of year when they are best able to recover from the shock of division, grow new roots, send up new foliage, and yet still be able to harden off for the fall. In warmer climates where winters are not cold and frozen, divide and transplant irises later in the fall, after the baking heat of summer has passed. During the fall and into the mild winter, the irises grow new roots and go through a period of dormancy, preparing for the new spring season ahead.

*Iris laevigata* stands to the left of *Scirpus albescens*; *Menyanthes* is at the feet of the scirpus, with *Houttuynia* on the bank to the right

*Iris ensata* 'Southern Son'

*Iris ensata* 'Flying Tiger'

## *Iris ensata*
### Japanese iris

*Iris ensata*, also formerly known as *I. kaempferi*, is the renowned Japanese iris. Growing naturally in Japan and on the Asian continent, it has been widely cultivated in the Orient and in the United States, as well as in the United Kingdom. Although characteristics vary from one selection to another, Japanese irises generally grow to about 24–36 inches in height, sometimes taller, with thin, upright foliage. Flowers are usually held well above the foliage, and may be single, double, or multipetaled. Colors range from deep, velvety purple through to the cleanest white. The blossoms are generally flat, with most of the petals hanging downward. In the water garden, they are exquisite, with midsummer flowers usually 6 inches or more in diameter.

Japanese irises prefer wet soils in the spring and summer, and will tolerate up to 2–3 inches of water over the crown during these times of year. It has been our experience that in the spring or summer Japanese irises do not survive seasonal flooding of a few feet of water over the crown.

*Iris ensata* is generally regarded as a plant that should not be left in the water over the winter, especially in colder climates. Ice formation around the crown of the plant often leads to its demise, and it will not reappear the following spring. In our own experience, however, certain cultivars have, for a year or two, survived a cold, midwestern winter in the pond. These instances were extremely rare, and I cannot say that the results were typical. The safest practice is to follow the time-honored rule that *I. ensata* should be removed from the pond and placed in a cool, dark place for the winter. Mulching them over in the perennial border is an ideal solution. In warmer climates with more temperate winters, our friends and customers have found that *I. ensata* is more likely to flourish even if it remains in the pond for the winter.

Many, many cultivars of Japanese irises have been registered with the American Iris Society. Much literature has

*Iris ensata* 'Lasting Pleasure'

*Iris ensata* 'Hue and Cry'

been devoted to these wonderful, edge-of-the-pond plants. For a thorough discussion of all aspects of their care, as well as the hundreds of cultivars that are available, consult *The Japanese Iris* by Currier McEwen (1990, Brandeis Univerisity Press: Hanover, Mass.). Following is a list of some of the most recent introductions of *I. ensata*.

'Crown Imperial' (Bauer and Coble) is a white double formed from rolling, ruffled petals. Numerous blue veins radiate out from a small blue halo surrounding the yellow signal. The crowning glory of the flower is the centerpiece of erect, multiple, imperial blue styles with large matching blue crests. Blooms in midseason. Forms one to two branches and reaches 36–40 inches tall.

'Dark Lightning' (Bauer and Coble) is a very dark blue-violet with a lightning-white halo surrounding the yellow signal and sparkling white rays that strike only halfway down the falls.

'Dragon Mane' (Bauer and Coble) is a large, dramatic, multipetaled white with red-violet veins and purple styles.

'Edged Delight' is white with a delightful blue rim around the standards.

'Epimethius' is wine-red with splashes, speckles, and streaks of white, lavender, and lilac. Grows to 40 inches tall and blooms in mid to late season.

'Espata' (Copeland) is a lightly ruffled dark plum-violet with lighter shoulders and edges of rose-violet. A dark blue-violet halo surrounds the yellow signal. White to light violet sanded styles hold large and flared violet crests. Very vigorous and has performed well in a wide range of soils.

'Fond Kiss' (Schafer-Sack) has large warm white flowers with a pink flush on the falls. Grows to 33 inches tall and blooms in midseason.

'Frosted Plum' (Bauer and Coble) is white with purple halo and veins, plum-purple styles, and white wire rims.

'Muffington' (Bauer and Coble) is pearl-white with plum halo and veining out to white rims. Styles are purple.

'Peak of Pink' (Bauer and Coble) is a near white pink with sharp, true pink styles and style crests.

'Pinkerton' (Bauer and Coble) is the truest pink. It has darker pink veins and cream-pink styles with pink crests. It forms two to three branches.

'Pooh Bah' is bright red-violet with white rays. Styles are white with red-violet crests.

'Rafferty' (Bauer and Coble) is lavender-pink with stamens that produce petaloids to full extra petals.

'Rosewater' (Copeland) is rose-violet with a blue halo and violet styles. Its flaring form blooms in late season.

'Ruby Star' is bright red with a white star halo. Styles are white with red crests.

*Iris fulva*

*Iris fulva* 'Marvell Gold'

'Sapphire Crown' (Bauer and Coble) is white with blue-violet halo and veins and purple style arms.

'Shinto Rings' has bright white flowers with ½-inch ring edges of rose to red-violet. Arching cream-white styles have white crests with just a fringe edge of rose-violet. The large, horizontal blooms are displayed right on top of the foliage. Grows to 32–36 inches tall with one branch and blooms in midseason.

'Silver Band' has red-wine species blooms on cream variegated foliage.

## *Iris fulva*
### copper iris, red flag

*Iris fulva* is native to the central and southern U.S. east of the Mississippi River, ranging from Illinois and Missouri southward to Georgia and Louisiana. It is a smaller iris in both plant and flower, growing to 12 inches or so in height. Its slender leaves droop slightly at the tips, giving the plant a graceful air. The falls and standards of the 3-inch flower also hang downward, causing the blooms to resemble miniature, copper-colored *I. laevigata* or *I. ensata*.

*Iris fulva* grows well in full sun or part shade. It usually flowers in mid-June, about the same time as other Louisiana irises, for which it is one of the parents. Preferred water depth is generally from evenly moist soil to water about 3 inches over the crown of the plant. It is the most water-tolerant of the irises for the water garden. It performs well in sites that dry out during the summer, and also tolerates seasonal flooding. It has large, corky seed coats that permit the seeds to float downstream once flowering is completed.

Copper irises are perfectly hardy in colder climates, Zones 5–11, and easily survive a winter freeze, provided they remain in the pond water. In very warm climates, the plant should be permitted to spend some time in dormancy—

*Iris laevigata* 'Variegata'

*Iris laevigata* 'Variegata'

cease fertilizing and allow it to dry out to just damp. No hard-and-fast rules determine the required degree of dormancy—it depends largely upon the cultivar.

Selections of *Iris fulva* were registered from the 1930s through the 1940s, but many of these are no longer commonly available. One cultivar that was found in 1932 near Marvell, Arizona, and has been recently reintroduced, is 'Marvell Gold' (Waddick, 1991). It has golden yellow flowers that glow in the water garden.

## Iris laevigata
### rabbit ear iris

The common name of *Iris laevigata* is quite appropriate, given its rounded, short, upright petals. Originating in eastern Asia, *I. laevigata* is especially grown, cultivated, and appreciated in Japan. A few cultivars are available in the U.S., and the list grows longer every year.

*Iris laevigata* requires moist soils throughout the entire year; it does not tolerate seasonal drought. Hardy in Zones 4–9, it grows to about 36 inches in height and has a spread of approximately 12 inches. Because it prefers cooler summers, it usually reaches only 12–18 inches tall in our midwestern gardens. This preference for milder climates has made *I. laevigata* a much favored plant in English water gardens and in the ponds of those living in the Pacific Northwest. It can be more difficult to establish in the South and Midwest. Preferred water depth is from moist soil to 6 inches of water over the crown.

The blossoms of *Iris laevigata*, usually 3–4 inches wide, are stunning additions to the pond garden. They appear in midsummer, sparkling white, elegant blue, or royal reddish-purple blooms that dance over arching green foliage that sways in the breeze. The coloring is more like water colors, not veined like the blooms of *I. versicolor*.

Only a handful of cultivars of *Iris laevigata* have been registered by the American Iris Society. Following are those that are more readily available in the United States and the United Kingdom.

*Iris laevigata* var. *alba* (unregistered) is a marvelous iris with snow-white flowers having three drooping falls. Often confused with 'Snowdrift', which has six falls. Generally grown from seed.

'Albopurpurea' is a taller cultivar with light blue flowers marked with a broad white border.

'Colchesterensis' (Wallace and Co., 1910) is an older selection with six drooping falls. Its petals are pure white and heavily mottled in rich blue.

'Midnight Wine' (Reid, 1992) is a cultivar selected for its very deep maroon color. A slash of white marks the center of the falls.

'Monstrosa' (unregistered) has at least six falls, all medium blue edged in white, with a white signal spear washed with yellow.

'Mottled Beauty' (Perry's Farm, 1960) is full-flowering selection with creamy white blooms that are mottled with violet spots and streaks.

'Regal' (Perry's Farm, 1960) is a lovely cultivar with rose-magenta flowers that have flaring, slender falls.

'Royal Cartwheel' (Reid, 1981) has blossoms of deep navy-blue-purple, each petal carrying a slash of white down the center.

'Semperflorens' (Perry, 1919) is another older cultivar, with deep blue-violet flowers. It frequently reblooms in the fall in the environment and climate it prefers.

'Snowdrift' (unregistered) has very clear, white blossoms marked with a yellow signal. It has six drooping falls and is often confused with *Iris laevigata* var. *alba*.

'Variegata' (Tubergen, 1916) is cherished by water gardeners for its clean white stripes that run the length of each leaf. Blooms are a medium blue.

'Violet Parasol' (Hager, 1977) is a clear violet-blue, marked by a yellow spear in the center of each petal.

## Iris missouriensis
### Rocky Mountain iris

The common name reveals the natural habitat of this wetland plant, native to the western portion of North America from Nova Scotia and Alberta southward into South Dakota and Arizona. Growing to about 36 inches in height, it bears 3-inch flowers in late spring or early summer. Colors range from light blue to lilac to deep blue, with an occasional lavender or white. The blossoms are usually veined and sport a bright yellow signal. Plants are hardy in Zones 3–9.

*Iris missouriensis* prefers soil that is wet in the spring and early summer, but that dries out once the plant has finished blooming, mimicking its natural habitat of spring snow-melt floods followed by dry summers. Generally, it blooms between May and July, the precise date often depending upon the altitude at which it is grown. It performs particularly well along streams or in a stream garden, or planted in a high mound in the bog garden.

The current state of cultivars available for *I. missouriensis* is similar to that of *I. prismatica*. Several selections were registered with the American Iris Society in the 1960s, but only one has been registered recently near the start of the twenty-first century. Selections are made and offered on the basis of color and form rather than cultivar name.

## Iris prismatica
### cube-seed iris

Native to the eastern seaboard of North America, *Iris prismatica* is a sod-forming plant adorned with early summer flowers of white, light blue, dark blue, purple, or even pink. Unlike other irises, it has rhizomes that are small and more rounded. It grows by sending out thin extension rhizomes that sprout and form a new clump of fans. Because of this growth habit, *I. prismatica* competes well with grasses and forbs in the wet meadows, damp fields, and open marshes that it prefers.

Cube-seed iris grows to about 8–14 inches or so in height, and forms a tight clump about 12 inches wide. Its blooms are diminutive, only 1–2 inches in diameter. It is hardy in Zones 2–9 and will tolerate the salty conditions of the seaside. It prefers soil that is moist or only slightly submerged. It can withstand some summer drought and occasional seasonal flooding. The plant should not be submerged to the bottom of the pond for over-wintering, but will last until spring quite well if simply left in place at the margin of the water garden.

Although *Iris prismatica* has been sold in the United States and in the United Kingdom for many years, only a few cultivars are registered with the American Iris Society. They are more commonly sold by color, rather than by cultivar. The only registered selection recently available is 'Polly Spout' (Duval, 1985), a pale blue-purple that is prominently veined in dark blue-purple. It has a large, yellow signal that is faintly veined in purple. The foliage flushes purple at the base of the fans.

## Iris pseudacorus
### yellow flag

*Iris pseudacorus* is commonly known as yellow flag, owing to its bright yellow flowers that appear in early spring. It originates from Europe, where it was often used as a dye plant and a medicinal herb. These valuable traits earned it a place on the trip westward to America in the eighteenth century. Yellow flag has now naturalized over most of North America from Canada to Florida, growing in full sun or part shade, in shallow or deep waters. It is an exuberant seeder and should never be planted in a natural lake or on the edge of a natural stream.

Generally hardy in Zones 4–9, *Iris pseudacorus* usually grows to about 3–4 feet tall and has a spread of 24–30 inches.

*Iris pseudacorus*

*Iris pseudacorus* × *I. ensata*

*Iris pseudacorus*

Blooms are usually 3 inches wide. It tolerates water over its crown, up to 6 inches, and withstands seasonal flooding. It also survives periods of drought during the summer.

The species boasts more than 60 named cultivars, of which approximately 40 have been registered with the American Iris Society. Following are some of the more noteworthy cultivars currently available from nurseries and growers.

'Alba' is the ivory-white form, a delicate blossom that performs better in part shade. Similar flower colors can be found in 'Ecru' and 'Ivory', both of which are cream colored. All these lighter yellow flags grow to about 4 feet high with a 24-inch spread. Prolific bloomers, they should be deadheaded once flowering is past so that they do not self-seed throughout the pond.

'Bastardii' has pale, primrose-yellow flowers with very faint brown markings on the falls of the blossom. Often

*Iris pseudacorus* 'Bastardii'

'Variegata' sports yellow-striped foliage in early spring, fading to clear green as the heat of summer sets in. Adorned with yellow flowers in early summer, it should be dead-headed once blooms are spent. Because of its bold, architectural foliage, variegated yellow flag is highly prized for its ornamental value in the water garden, even when not in flower.

A dwarf form is available that has not yet been registered with the American Iris Society. A strong springtime bloomer, it lacks a brown signal on its falls. The plant remains about 12 inches or so tall until it is finished blooming, with its flowers generally rising up to 4 inches over the tops of the leaves. Once bloom season is passed, it resumes foliage growth and eventually reaches the standard yellow flag height of 3–4 feet.

## *Iris setosa*
### Alaskan blue flag

This water iris is native to the eastern seaboard of Russia, China, and Korea and has extended its range through Japan and eastward to Alaska, southward to Labrador, Newfoundland, and through Quebec, Ontario, and Maine. It is hardy in Zones 4–7.

A sturdy and attractive iris, this extremely cold-hardy species grows approximately 10–30 inches tall, with an equal spread, depending on day length. It gets taller the farther north it grows. Its glaucous blue leaves are slender and often tinged in red at the base. Flowers are 2–3 inches wide and are rather flat, giving the blossom the appearance of having only three petals. The blooms of *Iris setosa* growing wild in Asia and in the western portions of North America are usually a purple-blue. Those growing in the eastern part of North America are generally a clear blue color. Petals are marked with a yellow or white signal.

A number of cultivars have been registered with the American Iris Society, several in the recent years near the start of the twenty-first century, but they are difficult to obtain. Nevertheless many are grown from seed strains and are sold by color rather than selection name. These two cultivars are choice. 'Arctic Rebloomer' (Lankow, 1992) has blue-violet flowers. In the Pacific Northwest, it blooms first in spring and again in the fall. 'Moorsee' (Berlin, 1979) is a cultivar of strong blue resulting from colchicine-treated seed. The flowers have more texture and substance and longer durability than those of the species.

grown from seed, the selections available show some variability. The cultivar grows to 3 feet tall with a 24-inch spread.

'Beuron' is a tetraploid—it has twice as many chromosomes as the standard *Iris pseudacorus*. This causes the flowers to be of greater substance and durability than those of the species. The cultivar generally grows to almost 4 feet in height, with flowers appearing on the outside of the clump, slightly below the top edge of the foliage. Blossoms are a bright yellow, almost the color of a school bus in fact, with a strong brown signal.

'Lime Sorbet' (Brown) has all yellow foliage in spring, fading to a bright lemon-lime-green in summer.

'Sun Cascade' (Huber) is a stunning double yellow flag with characteristic brown signals on the falls. Almost sterile, it will not spread itself about the water garden as readily as some other cultivars. It, too, grows to 4 feet or so, and enjoys having several inches of water over the crown.

*Iris versicolor*

Knees of *Iris virginica* 'Purple Fan'

### Iris versicolor, I. virginica
**blue flag, beet root iris**

*Iris versicolor* and *I. virginica* are best known as the blue flags, because of their light blue flowers that bloom in midspring. Their other common name derives from the beet-colored "knees" they display in early spring, when their blue-green, sword-shaped leaves take on a dark red stain that flares from the base toward the tips of the foliage. Native to North America, both blue flags are naturalized throughout the eastern United States, from Canada southward to Texas and westward to the Mississippi Valley. *Iris versicolor* is hardy in Zones 3–9, but *I. virginica* requires a slightly warmer climate, being hardy in Zones 4–9.

*Iris versicolor* is slightly shorter than *I. virginica*, but not by much. *Iris versicolor* grows to 24–30 inches tall, and *I. virginica* reaches up to 36 inches or more. Both have a spread of approximately 12 inches. *Iris versicolor* prefers water that is up to 3 inches or so over its crown. *Iris virginica* enjoys

deeper water, up to 6 inches over its crown. On the other hand, *I. virginica* tolerates drought better than *I. versicolor*, making it a perfect plant for retention areas or wet spots in the lawn. The flowers of *I. virginica* are usually 2–4 inches wide, slightly larger than the 2-inch blooms of *I. versicolor*, but *I. virginica* has only about half as many as *I. versicolor*.

More than four dozen cultivars of blue flags have been registered with the American Iris Society, and they are enjoying somewhat of a rediscovery in recent years. Here are some of the more noteworthy cultivars.

*Iris versicolor* 'Between the Lines' (Schafer-Sack, 1991) is a free-flowering selection that reaches almost 24 inches in height. Its flowers are white but are heavily veined in violet, giving the blossoms a light blue appearance. A yellow signal on the falls adds a touch of a halo to the bloom.

*Iris versicolor* 'Candystriper' (Warburton, 1991) also grows to no more than 24 inches. Its abundant white flowers are deeply veined in rose. Although no water irises come in

*Iris versicolor* 'Mysterious Monique'

*Iris versicolor* 'Springbrook'

red or pink, the effect of the veining gives this blossom a pink glow.

*Iris versicolor* 'Little Rhyme' (Schafer-Sack, 1990) is a clear white-flowering cultivar with a bright yellow signal. It grows to about 12 inches in height, and blooms profusely. To date, this is by far the best white selection of *I. versicolor*.

*Iris versicolor* 'Mint Fresh' (Warburton, 1991) is a slightly larger cultivar with bright white flowers that are heavily striped with red veining. The plentiful blossoms always remind me of peppermint candy.

*Iris versicolor* 'Mysterious Monique' (Knoepnadel, 1986) is a most extraordinary cultivar for the pool-side garden. It flowers liberally with very dark violet flowers—the petals are like black velvet—accented by a distinct white signal. At almost 36 inches tall, it catches your eye almost immediately and rivets your attention.

*Iris versicolor* 'Party Line' (Warburton, 1988) sports red-purple flowers veined in darker red-purple. It has a pale yellow signal that changes to white with red-purple veining. Style arms are pure white with a red-purple midrib. A most attractive and free-flowering cultivar, it grows to about 18 inches.

*Iris versicolor* 'Pink Peaks' (Schafer-Sack, 1988) is certainly the most diminutive cultivar available, growing to about 9 inches in height. A steady bloomer, it has dark pink flowers with red-purple veining. Its white signal is also veined in red-purple. Styles are dark pink with pure white curls on the tips.

*Iris versicolor* 'Shape Up' (Warburton, 1986) is distinctive for its orange-red signals veined in black and edged in white. Flowers are dark red-violet and are borne in profusion. The cultivar grows to about 18 inches tall.

*Iris virginica* 'Dottie's Double'

*Iris virginica* 'Contraband Girl' (unregistered) is bright blue with a hint of lavender. Sturdy and vigorous, it grows to about 36 inches tall.

*Iris virginica* 'Dottie's Double' (Warrell, 1983) has unusual, double-petaled flowers veined in orchid-lavender. The flowers have six signals and six falls and look like spinning pinwheels.

*Iris virginica* 'Pond Crown Point'

*Iris virginica* 'Pond Crown Point' (Speichert, 1996) is a Cub-Scout-blue flower with a strong yellow signal. It has large flowers and good bud count on strong, erect stems.

*Iris virginica* 'Pond Lilac Dream' (Speichert, 1996) has white flowers that unfurl to dainty lavender-pink, accented by a creamy yellow signal. It grows to about 4 feet tall.

## Louisiana Irises

Louisiana irises are hybrids of the five to eight *Iris* species in the series *Hexagonae*. Louisianas will grow from drought conditions to water as deep as 4–6 inches, and they tolerate seasonal flooding. They do well in the garden with supplemental watering. Most are not hardy north of Zone 5 and many only to Zone 6, but they need no special care to overwinter where hardy. They produce more running rhizomes than the other irises discussed in this chapter, with some growing 24 inches or more in a season. Plant height varies from 18 to 36 inches. The only pests seem to be borers, like the rest of the irises, and grasshoppers. The seed tend to be very large, corky things and much less abundant than those produced by the other species. For more information, see *The Louisiana Iris: The Taming of a Native American Wildflower* (2nd ed., The Society for the Louisiana Iris, 2000, Timber Press: Portland, Ore.).

'Acacia Rhumba' is an early, ruffled, soft lemon-yellow bitone with falls of a heavily veined green. Grows to 28 inches.

'Bayou Bandit' is a rare variant of *Iris fulva*. The color is soft chocolate-brown with underlying pink and a sheen of lavender. Blooms early to midseason, reaching 32 inches high.

'Bushfire Moon' is a nicely ruffled, rich orange-yellow that blooms early to midseason. It grows to 30 inches.

'Cajun Sunrise' is a magnificent, flat, strong brick-red with a broad, golden yellow edging and a sunburst-yellow ray pattern on the falls. Blooms in midseason and reaches 33 inches high.

'Cyclamint' is a purple self with minty, yellow-green signals on all petals. Blooms in midseason and grows to 30 inches tall.

'Elaine's Wedding' blooms in midseason with lightly ruffled lavender blooms that have a deep yellow-green line signal with a deep spot at the end. Styles are lacy and green. Reaches 34 inches high.

'Jazz Hot' is smoky red with a white rim. Ruffled and with a lemon-yellow reverse, it reaches 35 inches tall and blooms in mid to late season.

'Joie de Vivre' is cerise purple with a red flush, fading to an old rose coloring with deeper purple flush. Reaches 35 inches high and blooms in mid to late season.

'Lake Quachita' blooms in midseason in light blue with a small yellow steeple signal. Grows to 26 inches high.

'Professor Neil' is a tetraploid in deep wine-red with large, brilliant yellow signals. Grows to 36 inches and blooms in midseason.

'Swamp Pioneers' is a light creamy peach. Standards are upright and light peach with a yellow line signal, and falls carry a light yellow crest that radiates over a white background. Style arms are solid yellow. It blooms early and grows to 36 inches tall.

## Siberian Irises

Eleven species make up the series *Sibiricae* as classified by the American Iris Society. The first to come to mind is *Iris sibirica*. It shares many characteristics with the other ten species that form the Siberian group, most importantly their preference for seasonal moisture in the garden. Although each of the species is currently available, their common offspring are much more widespread in the trade. Since 1970 or so, hybridizers have been cross-pollinating the various species in the Siberian group with *I. sibirica*, creating hybrids whose parentage is now so complicated that the cultivars are no longer listed with a species name. Several hundred Siberian iris cultivars are registered with the American Iris Society. *The Siberian Iris* by Currier McEwen (1996, Timber Press: Portland, Ore.) is an excellent source of information, written by the foremost hybridizer of Siberian irises in the United States.

Siberian iris cultivars are excellent for the bog garden, for the edge of the stream, or for a seasonal wet spot in the backyard. In colder climates, they prefer wet soils in the spring and summer, but generally require drier conditions in the fall and winter. If they are placed in the pond in the spring, they should be removed before winter frost arrives, and mulched in the perennial border. In warmer climes, where the temperatures do not drop below 20°F, they do not need mulch.

When first offered, Siberian irises were limited in color to blue and white. Now, the range has been greatly expanded to include deep purple-reds to light lavender-pinks. The true red color still eludes hybriziders for the moment, but it is only a matter of time before this color, too, will be included in the palette of Siberian iris flowers. There are new cottage colors, and yellows, as well as repeat bloomers. Flowers are anywhere from 2 to 4 inches wide, depending upon the selection.

'Banish Misfortune' (Schafer-Sack) has small species-like flowers with more full form. Medium lavender flowers have a large yellow to cream signal and are veined in deep purple. Grows to 45 inches tall and blooms in early to late season.

'Blueberry Fair' (Hollingworth) has light blue-violet standards. Styles are multishaded blue-violet to blue. Ruffled, flared falls are medium blue-violet with a veined white signal.

'Careless Sally' (Schafer-Sack) is a blend of rose, blue, and yellow. It is a large flower with very full, round, and ruffled falls, pale ruffled standards, and wide styles with large curls. Signals are sunrise-yellow. This is a rebloomer.

'Countess Cathleen' (Schafer-Sack) has light blue-violet falls, white signals with blue-violet veining, and ruffled standards and styles. Reaches 30 inches high and blooms in midseason.

'Dandy's Hornpipe' (Schafer-Sack) has unique coloring of pale lavender standards lightly flushed with red-violet and pearly styles with blue-green midribs. Falls are lavender and yellow, heavily dappled and veined with red-violet. Signal is sunset colored. Grows to 29 inches tall and blooms in midseason. This is a rebloomer.

'Drops of Brandy' (Schafer-Sack) is an unusual blue-violet bitone. Light blue standards are wide, full, and ruffled. The blue-violet falls are dappled and have a lighter ½-inch, washed rim and are so wide and ruffled they overlap. Grows to 27 inches and blooms in mid to late season.

'Helicopter' (Shidara) is a six-fall double with open, flat form. It has dark blue-violet falls and no standards.

'Jewelled Crown' (Hollingworth) is a large, deep wine-red. Standards are waved at the edge. Falls are ruffled with a large circular blaze. Reaches 24 inches tall and blooms in midseason.

'Kita-no-Seiza' (Shidara) is a six-fall double in dark violet with large white signals and violet styles.

'Mesa Pearl' (Bauer and Coble) is pale lavender with near white edges. Falls have a few darker veins in center and an overall pearl sheen. Blooms are flat.

'Nagareboshi' (Shidara) has six falls in dark blue-violet with white signals.

'Over in Gloryland' (Hollingworth) is tetraploid. It opens very dark velvety blue-purple with a prominent light gold blaze. Round ruffled form.

'Parasol' (Shidara) is a new registered name for 'Hare-sugata'. It has six falls of lavender pink and six yellow signals.

'Pleasures of May' (Schafer-Sack) has pale lavender standards and white style arms. Falls are light violet and the small white signal is veined in light violet. Grows to 30 inches tall and blooms in early to late season.

'Ranman' (Shidara) is multipetaled with six to nine falls, its stamens and styles often transformed into petals forming a pink rosebud above the lavender falls. Full form with very wide petals.

'Riverdance' (Schafer-Sack) has rich blue, well ruffled flowers. The falls and style arms have white wire edges. Grows to 43 inches tall and blooms in midseason.

'Roaring Jelly' (Schafer-Sack) has falls dappled bright raspberry with pale lavender standards also lightly dappled. Full, round, slightly recurved flowers bloom in midseason on 36-inch-tall plants.

'Shall We Dance' (Hollingworth) is a blue-violet bitone tetraploid. Ruffled falls are light with prominent darker veining. Standards are very pale blue. Reaches 31 inches tall and blooms in late season.

'Shebang' (Bauer and Coble) has rose-violet petals. The six falls are darker and the six to nine standards and petaloids are lighter.

'Somebody Loves Me' (Hollingworth) is a ruffled tetraploid of medium blue-violet. Falls have a very large white blaze. Style arms are light blue. Grows to 32 inches tall and blooms in early to midseason.

'Sprinkles' (Bauer and Coble) has a lavender ground evenly sprinkled with violet-lavender, except at the pale rims. Blooms in late season.

'Trim the Velvet' (Schafer-Sack) is a rich blue-purple self. Velvety falls have white edges. Standards and falls are gently ruffled. Signals are small and white and veined in blue-purple. Grows to 30 inches tall and blooms in mid-season.

## Wide Species Crosses

Taking the pollen from one iris species and using it to fertilize the flower of another iris species is the general process commonly called "wide species crosses." The objective is to create a new iris hybrid that will have all the best characteristics of the two parent irises. In the perfect example, crossing *Iris ensata* with *I. versicolor* would result in a new iris hybrid—*I. ×versata* perhaps—that will have the superior bloom color and shape of *I. ensata*, and yet have the greater water tolerance and increased bud count of *I. versicolor*.

Of course, not all attempted crosses develop hybrids with exactly all the best characteristics of the parent plants. Sometimes the hybrid will look exactly like just one of the parents, because that parent's genetic make-up is dominant over that of the other parent. In my experience, *Iris pseudacorus* is especially prone to overwhelm the traits of other parents. Yet one or two plants from any cross usually will show some promise. By further crossing these hybrids, improvements in bloom color, size, or plant sturdiness can be fortified.

Simply placing the pollen of one parent on the stigma of another flower does not guarantee that the cross will be successful. Attempted crosses commonly fail to yield a single viable seed pod. Many factors, such as climate, humidity, sunlight, and soil chemistry, may affect the success of a cross-pollination. The primary impediment to successful wide species crosses is in the plants themselves, specifically the difference in chromosome counts between the many *Iris* species that are water tolerant. If the chromosome counts of the two parents are not the same, or at least capable of being combined and reproduced, then the cross is unlikely to ever be successful.

Efforts by many hybridizers from many parts of the world are yielding some remarkable and highly garden-worthy wide species crosses. Water gardeners will be able to reap the rewards of these efforts, as the new cultivars become available. The following paragraphs describe some wide species crosses that are more readily sold.

### Iris versicolor × I. ensata

Almost a dozen selections of this wide species cross are registered with the American Iris Society. The aim is to produce

*Iris versicolor* × *I. laevigata*

a cross that has the flower quality of *Iris ensata* and the increased water depth preference and greater flower count of *I. versicolor*. One of the most available offspring of this cross is 'Oriental Touch' (Huber, 1992), which grows to almost 4 feet in height. It has dark violet falls with a light creamy yellow signal.

### Iris pseudacorus × I. ensata

Only a few cultivars of this cross have been registered with the American Iris Society. The objective is to join the sturdiness and glowing yellow flower color of *Iris pseudacorus* with the beauty and enhanced flower size of *I. ensata*. A good recent selection is 'Chance Beauty' (Ellis, 1988), which earned the Royal Horticultural Society Award of Garden Merit in 1998. It has yellow falls that are veined in chocolate brown, with a deep yellow signal patch.

Iris ×robusta

## Iris versicolor × I. laevigata

Although just a few cultivars are registered, much work is being done on this cross by hybridizers and propagators. Their goal is find a hybrid that will have the high bloom count of *Iris versicolor* with the greater flower size and richer bloom color of *I. laevigata*. Readers should know of the following stunning selections.

'Aquatic Alliance' (Reid, 1994) has light violet flowers that are veined in dark purple and that have large gold signals edged in white.

'Asian Alliance' (Witt, 1988) has medium red-violet falls marked by a yellow signal.

'Berlin Versilaev' (Tamberg, 1988) is a dark yellow heavily veined in reddish brown. Falls are marked with a yellowish white signal.

## Iris pseudacorus × I. versicolor

This is another wide species cross receiving considerable attention from current hybridizers and propagators. The cross is hoped to have the sturdiness of *Iris pseudacorus* and the increased bud count of *I. versicolor*. 'Limbo' (Ellis, 1988) received a Preliminary Commendation from the British Iris Society in 1987. It has clear white falls veined in deep blue-purple. The yellow signal is veined in purple. A strong grower, it reaches more than 36 inches in height.

'Holden Clough' (Patton, 1971) is another excellent cultivar, with yellow flowers that are lined in purple, giving the flower a brown appearance. Although registered as a cross between *Iris pseudacorus* and *I. chrysographes*, that parentage is questioned. Some hybridizers believe that it is more likely a cross between *I. pseudacorus* and *I. foetidissima* or its reciprocal. Others contend that it is probably a cross between *I. pseudacorus* and *I. versicolor*. Chromosome mapping may shed some light on this mystery, but whatever its parentage, it deserves a prominent place in the water garden.

Two seedlings of 'Holden Clough' have been registered in their own right. 'Berlin Tiger' (Tamberg, 1988), raised from colchicine-treated seed, is a striking selection with yellow blooms that are heavily veined in intense brown. The signal patch on the falls is also brown. 'Roy Davidson' (Hager, 1987) has light yellow falls that are lightly veined in chocolate brown. The signal is a deep brown crescent outlined by deep yellow.

## (Iris virginica × I. versicolor) and (I. versicolor × I. virginica)

These crosses are naturally occurring, resulting in an iris usually named *Iris ×robusta*. They generally have greater water depth tolerance and higher bud count. We have found many variations of *I. ×robusta* in our midwestern climate, growing in ditches and low spots in open meadows or marshes. A few selections have been registered with the American Iris Society. The following three are most commonly available.

'Gem Dandy' (Kennedy, 1984) is a true gem in the water garden, with free-flowering blue blooms that cover the plant in midsummer, plus low seed production.

'Gerald Darby' (Darby, 1968) is similar but has larger flowers that are deep violet-blue. It is not prone to seed itself in the pond.

'Mountain Brook' (Kennedy, 1984) is a delightful selection with purple-blue flowers that have a strong white signal. It has a narrow, upright shape, owing to its very erect stems and equally erect foliage. It should be deadheaded after flowering to prevent its appearance elsewhere in the pond.

# CHAPTER 9

# WATERLILY-LIKE PLANTS

Several very attractive water plants grow like waterlilies but are not properly members of the genus *Nymphaea*. These "waterlily-like" plants produce rhizomes, tubers, and roots that grow in soil that is several inches, sometimes even several feet, below the water surface. With long stems or petioles, the plants bear foliage that floats on the water far above the soil surface. Their flowers also appear on, or above, the waterline.

Besides this common growth habit, waterlily-like plants are widely divergent in their plant shape and habit, flower color and size, and even their hardiness. They give water gardeners a wide range of selections when waterlilies will not work in the landscape design. Waterlily-like plants such as the water snowflakes (*Nymphoides*) grow well in small container and table-top ponds, both of which are too small for most waterlilies. Often waterlily-like plants are less expensive than waterlilies, as well. Most waterlily-like plants also grow and flower better in shade than do hardy or tropical waterlilies.

## LANDSCAPE USES

Waterlily-like plants are a great substitute for lilies in containers or small ponds. Those that have a smaller spread, such as water poppy (*Hydrocleys nymphoides*) and painted white water snowflake (*Nymphoides cristata*), are ideal additions to tub water gardens. *Nymphoides peltata*, *Aponogeton*, *Brasenia*, and *Hydrocleys peruviana* are good in larger ponds. Waterlily-like plants can be used in regular ponds to force a perspective—plant larger lilies in the front, dwarf lilies in the middle, then waterlily-like plants in the back to make the pond look wider and bigger. They are also good in shady ponds to replace lilies. They add color and dimension along the edge of marginals or in between rushes (*Scirpus*). Waterlily-like plants can add more color to a lotus planting. Use water hawthorne (*Aponogeton distachyus*) with waterlilies to provide early and late season interest—since they grow in cooler water than waterlilies they can add a month of interest before and after the waterlily season.

Waterlilies and *Stratiotes aloides* in a formal pond

*Nymphoides peltata*

*Nymphoides peltata* floats on the water and *Colocasia esculenta* displays its large leaves in front of the bridge

Waterlily-like plants spread by seeds and runners more readily than waterlilies. Some can take over an area in a short period of time. The most invasive are *Nymphoides peltata*, by far the most persistent, followed by *Brasenia*, and then *Trapa*. All three plants can be controlled with pulling and spraying. All seem to succumb to koi and goldfish in a pond so that they never get out of hand, but never plant these in a natural body of water.

## SUNLIGHT, WIND, AND WATER DEPTH

Most waterlily-like plants grow and flower best in full sun. All can handle shade, however, and will still grow. In fact, though they may not color as well or flower as much, they still will perform better in shade than most waterlilies would.

Like waterlilies, the plants covered in this chapter "breathe" through the upper portions of their floating leaves. They need quiet, calm waters away from splashing. If they are splashed from a fountain or waterfall, they begin to suffer from lack of oxygen. The leaves will often turn yellow, then brown, and become mushy and die. They are also susceptible to foliar disease brought on by water getting into the stomata on the surface of the leaves. Wave action can also be detrimental, pulling the leaves away from the plant or uprooting them. *Aponogeton* and *Potamogeton* species handle moving water the best.

Most waterlily-like plants prefer shallower waters than do waterlilies. Water no deeper than 24 inches is advisable. *Aponogeton, Brasenia*, and some of the *Nymphoides* species can grow in deeper water, but still perform best in 24 inches or less.

## SEASONAL CARE

Waterlily-like plants that are cold hardy will revive from their winter dormancy as the ice thaws from the pond and the water warms. They should be fertilized once they show active growth, according to the fertilizer manufacturer's directions. In warmer climates where the pond has not frozen, the plants should be cleaned and fertilized in the spring as they begin to put on new growth. Tender plants may be safely returned to the pond once the water temperature consistently reaches 70°F. Make sure they have been potted in fresh soil and fertilized so they are prepared to start new growth and flowering.

In the summer, remove spent leaves and flowers, and fertilize regularly. When water temperature reaches 80°F in the height of summer, plants appreciate a feeding every two weeks.

For fall maintenance, running plants like *Brasenia* and *Nymphoides peltata* may need the runner wound back into the pot or simply cut back to 12 inches or so from the base of the plant.

To survive the winter, then, hardy waterlily-like plants may remain in the cold pond, with no special attention other than placing them deep enough that their rhizomes or crowns will not be subjected to a freeze. Tender plants should be brought indoors and kept in an aquarium. Use a heater to maintain a water temperature of at least 70°F and lights to supply 12 hours of at least 1000 foot-candles.

## PLANTING

Waterlily-like plants are easy to pot up. Use wide, shallow pots, since most grow across the surface rather than down into the soil. Use good aquatic soil, such as a clay and sand mix, or an equivalent. Soilless media are acceptable but may be buoyant, needing a topping of small stones in order to hold the pot under the water.

After selecting the pot and soil, fill the pot with the soil, top with sand or pea gravel, and thoroughly water. Then make a hole in the soil, place the crown of the plant about 1 inch below the soil surface, and firm the soil over the roots. Submerge the pot in the pond, roughly 6 inches or so below the water surface.

Because these plants have such brittle stems and dehydrate so easily, it is extremely important to keep them as moist as possible before they are transplanted, and to return them to the pond as soon as planting is done.

## PROPAGATION

Most waterlily-like plants propagate readily from runners that develop freely during the summer. This includes the water poppies (*Hydrocleys*) and the water snowflakes (*Nymphoides*), which often start new plantlets along their long growing stems. Water hawthorne (*Aponogeton distachyus*), however, is best propagated from seed, since it produces few, if any eyes or offshoots, and is not easily propagated by other means.

## PESTS

The most common problems with waterlily-like plants are aphids and China mark moth, problems that also confront waterlilies. If detected early, they may be washed from the plants with a stiff spray of water. For further information see Chapter 12.

*Oenanthe javanica* 'Flamingo', on the rocks in back center, and *Cyperus alternifolius* 'Nanus', in the pond at the right

*Aponogeton distachyus*

## *Aponogeton distachyus* (syn. *A. distachyos*)
### water hawthorne
### Aponogetonaceae

*Aponogeton distachyus* is one of more than 40 species in the genus, most of which have completely submerged foliage and flowers. Commonly called water hawthorne, it holds its blooms and leaves on the water surface and makes an extremely attractive plant for cooler water. It flowers in spring and again in fall, accompanied by the blooms of such marginals as marsh marigold (*Caltha*). In southern climates, the plant will often bloom all winter long. In colder areas, it can be grown indoors in the winter in a cool greenhouse or sun porch. Water hawthorne extends the season of flowers in the pond, blooming before waterlilies have begun to show color in the spring, and flowering again in the fall after waterlilies have ended their display.

Flowers are a crisp white accented by black stamens, although variants can be found with blooms that are laven-der or even pink. This is an area ripe for further selection and refinement. Blossoms have a clean, vanilla fragrance that is carried on the wind for several feet. The foliage of water hawthorne is elliptical, shiny and dark green, some-times with a tinge of purple. It grows in sun to part shade in water from 6 inches to 4 feet deep, spreading 24–30 inches. The plant prefers cool water and may go completely dor-mant in ponds where the summer water temperature con-sistently exceeds 70°F. It is hardy in cold water and can withstand a freeze, needing no particular winter care or attention. Zones 5–11. It is also generally unaffected by pests or diseases.

Water hawthorne does not set many side-eyes on its tubers and cannot be propagated by division or stem cut-tings. It is best propagated by starting its small, bulb-like seed. Simply plant the seed in a shallow pan that has been topped with a dusting of sand, and place the pan in about 12 inches of water. I have also had great luck just floating the

Tubers of *Aponogeton distachyus*

*Callitriche palustris*

seed in the pond in a plastic bag of water or in a mesh bag so the seed can photosynthesize.

In South Africa, where it is native, water hawthorne's buds are canned and pickled like olives. The tubers are also edible. Water hawthorne has naturalized throughout Australia, New Zealand, and South America. It is often sold commercially in North America. Other species of *Aponogeton* can be found in many tropical and temperate regions of Europe and Asia.

### Brasenia schreberi
**watershield**
Cabombaceae

Watershield has elliptical, rounded, shiny leaves, 4½ inches by 2½ inches, that float on the surface much like waterlily foliage. Stems join the floating leaves at their centers, rather than at one edge. The underside of watershield foliage is dark red or maroon, as are the submerged stems. The underwater parts of the plant are covered with a mucilaginous jelly.

Flowers are small, less than ½ inch tall and wide, and unusual, lacking any obvious petals and having purplish red stamens tipped in white. The plant is more often grown for its foliage than its flowers. It grows in sun to part shade in water 6–24 inches deep, preferably. It will survive in as much as 5 feet of water.

Watershield is best propagated by division. Seed are small and difficult to collect. The plant is very hardy in colder climates, given its ability to pull its creeping rootstock deep into the mud where the ice cannot reach it. Zones 4–10. It is rarely bothered by pests or diseases.

*Brasenia* is native to Africa, Asia, Australia, and North and Central America. The species *B. schreberi* is naturalized throughout the southern United States. Seeds are often eaten by waterfowl, and in Japanese cuisine, young leaves are considered a delicacy.

### Callitriche
**starwort**
Callitrichaceae

Being the only genus in its family, *Callitriche* is virtually cosmopolitan in its distribution and circumboreal in origin. It has sparse, opposite underwater foliage and more rounded and dense floating leaves. On the surface, the leaves often form rosettes of bright green that soon make a thick mat that shades out sunlight. When crowded, the leaves look like tiny stars, giving it the common name of starwort. The whitish flowers are minuscule and often go completely undetected.

*Callitriche palustris* (common water starwort or water chickweed) grows in shallow streams in the United States and Canada. Other species, such as *C. hermaphroditica* (autumnal water starwort), *C. heterophylla* (large water starwort), and *C. marginata*, are common in North and Central America. A European species, *C. stagnalis*, has been found growing in streams in Connecticut. The distinguishing features among the species are the differences in size and shape of the leaves, but the distinctions are more recognizable to botanists than water gardeners. Most species are rarely found for sale in the United States, Canada, or even the U.K. The most widely available is *C. palustris*, often sold in the U.K., but less so in North America.

*Callitriche palustris*

The diminutive *C. palustris* prefers cool, oxygen-infused water, growing in sun to part shade in depths of 6–24 inches. Its leaves crowd together to form a dense mat about 12 inches wide on the water surface. Individual leaves are very small, less than ½ inch wide, and elongated with a pointed tip. The tiny, white, and not very showy flowers bloom from April to September.

*Callitriche* also grows submerged, doing best in cool streams and clear ponds about 36 inches deep. It grows in sun or part shade in warmer areas. Submerged *Callitriche* looks very similar to *Elodea*, but it can be distinguished by its leaves—those of *Callitriche* are in pairs, those of *Elodea* form sets of threes. Also, *Callitriche* foliage is a deeper jade-green, as opposed to the cellophane-green of *Elodea*.

Because its seeds are difficult to collect, *Callitriche* is best propagated by division or stem cuttings made in summer—just cut off the top 4–6 inches and plant the cuttings in soil. Hardy in Zones 4–10, it overwinters well in cooler climates without special care or attention. In the winter, the plant dies back to its crown at the soil surface. This crown can freeze solid in the pond's icy waters and still resprout in spring. It also forms dormant buds in late fall that settle in the mud at the bottom of the pond. These buds, and self-sown seed, start to grow early in the spring. It is rarely bothered by pests, with aphids being the only culprit likely to appear, especially in hot, muggy summers.

I have observed starwort in slow-moving streams in both Estes Park, Colorado, and in England. It is good green food for fish and safe haven for aquatic insects, but uses are limited because of its need for cool water temperatures.

## *Hydrocleys*
### Limnocharitaceae

Native to Central and South America, species of *Hydrocleys* have shiny, rounded leaves with a prominent midrib and a spongy internal layer that keeps the foliage afloat. They are cordate (or nearly so) at the base where the leaf joins the submerged petiole. Flowers are single, usually three-petaled, and creamy yellow, with numerous black or brown stamens. Stems of flowers and foliage are usually marked with veining that gives the appearance of being jointed. Blooms last only a day but are borne in profusion once the weather warms.

Although plants grow from a crown that is nestled in the soil beneath the water surface, they produce many floating runners that sprout new foliage and roots. It is these sprouted, floating runners that usually flower, not the original plant rooted in soil. The many floating runners, with leaves and blossoms, quickly cover the water surface in the warm weather the plants prefer. The plants are beneficial for their ability to provide this surface cover, but for this reason they may also be considered a nuisance in some areas and may be prohibited as a noxious weed in states with warmer temperatures all year long. In cooler weather and under short days, the stems and runners tend to die back to the plantlets formed along the stem. Hydrocleys are easily propagated by dividing off floating stems that have rooted and produced foliage. They may also be grown from seed; however, finding seed may be difficult.

Because they are frost-tender, hydrocleys must be brought indoors for the winter. Keep them in an aquarium with a grow light and a water heater. They need water in the range of 75°F or more in order to thrive. They may also be overwintered by keeping them moist in a hanging basket like a houseplant, although care must be taken lest they die due to the variation from their normal wet growing conditions. We have found them hardy to Zone 9, although other sources report them hardy into Zone 8.

*Hydrocleys nymphoides*

*Ludwigia sedioides*

### Hydrocleys martii
**golden water poppy**

This species has large foliage about the size of *Hydrocleys peruviana* and flowers with all-gold petals and yellow to green stamens. Very showy. The petals are separate and do not overlap to form a cup like the other species. It has more flowers that *H. peruviana*, but not as many as *H. nymphoides*. Grows in sun to part shade in water 4–36 inches deep.

### Hydrocleys nymphoides
**water poppy**

Water poppy has rounded leaves and creamy yellow flowers that are about 2 inches in diameter. An easy plant to grow, it starts blooming once the water temperature reaches 70–75°F and continues unabated unless killed by frost. An excellent addition to ponds in cooler climates, where its running habit that spreads over 1–6 feet can be restrained. If the gardener is willing to prune it back, it grows well in container ponds and small water gardens. Water poppy is also a favorite water plant because it tolerates a lot of shade, though it prefers sun, and grows in water as much as 3 feet deep, though it prefers 4–12 inches.

### Hydrocleys peruviana
**giant water poppy**

With a habit and form similar to water poppy, the giant form has flowers and foliage approximately 50 percent larger. It is more suitable for a larger pond, given its tendency to run across the water surface. It provides good coverage to shade fish during the heat of summer. Giant water poppy does not flower as profusely as its smaller cousin and has blooms that are more green-yellow. Grows in sun to part shade in water 4–18 inches deep but will tolerate as much as 36 inches of water.

### Ludwigia sedioides
**mosaic plant**
**Onagraceae**

While most species of *Ludwigia* are marginals that grow along the edge of the pond, this species grows as a mostly submerged plant. Its small, single yellow flowers blooming in summer resemble those of the other species, though, giving away its genus affiliation.

The plant's common name harkens to its leaves' overall diamond to squarish shape. They grow from a central radius so that the foliage forms a mosaic-like circle. The floating leaves are green with red edges, stems, and petioles. Mosaic plant is an unusual and attractive plant that quickly provides water coverage in the warm and sunny to partly shady conditions it prefers. Intolerant of water that is not acidic or at least neutral, it will wither and die in pond water above a pH of 8. Although it grows best in 12–18 inches of warm water, it survives depths of up to 36 inches, as well as cooler water temperatures. Its running spread usually covers 24 inches in a single season, each rosette spreading to 4 inches.

Native to Brazil, mosaic plant is easily propagated from cuttings and from division of the rosettes. Hardy in Zones 8–11. To overwinter in cooler climates, bring it indoors and keep it in a warm aquarium of at least 65°F with supplemental light to stretch the daylight the plant receives. In cool water or short days, it will produce dormant eyes or buds

Luronium natans

Nymphoides indica

that fall to the bottom of the pond. Many gardeners have difficulty getting the buds to resprout in the spring. Other than the occasional aphid or China mark moth, the plant is not bothered by insects or diseases.

## Luronium natans
### floating water plantain
### Alismataceae

An endangered plant in the United Kingdom, *Luronium natans* has submerged leaves that are long, thin, and ribbon-like. Leaves that reach the water surface are floating, oval, and often tipped. The flowers, which also float on the water surface through spring and summer, are single and white-petaled with yellow stamens. It grows in sun to part shade in still waters and does not care for the phosphate or nitrate that can be left in the water from pollution run-off in the wild or liquid fertilizer in the pond. Native to central and western Europe, where it is apparently more vigorous, this is the only species in the genus.

As its flowers reveal, floating water plantain is related to Siberian pink cups (*Baldellia ranunculoides* f. *repens*), water plantain (*Alisma*), and arrowhead (*Sagittaria*), all of which have single, three-petaled blooms resembling roses. The leaves of floating water plantain resemble small leaves of water poppy (*Hydrocleys nymphoides*).

Floating water plantain will grow in as little as 4 inches and as much as 30 inches of water, but optimally 12–18 inches. Its floating mass usually spreads to about 10 inches wide. It is ideal for colder climates that do not produce enough heat to grow water poppies. It hates hot weather, and is hardy only in Zones 2–5. It does not appear to grow from

Nymphoides geminata

division. Fortunately it self-sows readily and under ideal conditions comes up in profusion, although not so much that it becomes a nuisance. It is bothered only by China mark moth, and then only rarely.

## Nymphoides
### water snowflake
### Menyanthaceae

In many ways *Nymphoides* is similar to *Hydrocleys*. Both have rooted crowns but floating stems that sprout, producing leaves, flowers, and still more rooted crowns. Both have blooms that last only a day. But they have important differences. *Nymphoides* leaves are rounded but have a sinus, and they are flatter and thinner than those of *Hydrocleys*. The leaves of *Nymphoides* are often dark red or brown underneath and sometimes veined in burgundy on top, and the edges are toothed or crinkled. *Hydrocleys* has leaves that are always green, top and bottom, and always smooth-edged. The summer-blooming flowers of *Nymphoides* are smaller and distinctly star-shaped, with five petals, and sometimes with fringed edges. Those of *Hydrocleys* are larger, with three rounded, overlapping petals. Besides its similarity to *Hydrocleys*, the taxonomy within the genus *Nymphoides* is confusing and the various species are often labeled differently by different authorities.

Species of *Nymphoides* are native to and grow in most temperate and tropical climates; the genus is cosmopolitan. Hardy forms may be overwintered like hardy waterlilies, placed in the bottom of the pond where they will not freeze. Tender species must be brought indoors to be protected from cold temperatures. Keep them in an aquarium with a grow light and a small water heater.

Nymphoides are easily grown from offsets of viviparous leaves that have rooted and sprouted their own foliage. Some may also be grown from the runners that form roots all along themselves. Simply cut off a section of runner with roots and plant it. A new shoot will arise where the roots are. If the section is long, simply coil it up, lay it in the pot on soil, and cover with pea gravel. The wreath of stems will sprout a colony of plants.

Propagation from seed is also possible. Some, like *Nymphoides geminata*, produce large seed and pods, large enough to find anyway. The seed is about the size of pepper seed. I sow mine in a clear storage container with about 1–2 inches of heavy soil on the bottom covered in ¼ inch of sand. Sow the seed on the surface, then lightly add more sand, just to cover. I use this method with all species except *N. geminata*. It needs vernalization, the normal up-and-down temperatures of the pond in spring. For the tropical or tender species just bring the water up to 70°F.

I sow in a clear storage box that I place in the pond or a large fish tank—the seedlings seem to rot if not part of a larger body of water. If the fish are a problem, I put the clear lid on the box with holes drilled in it, or use ¼-inch hardware cloth.

Although no hybrids of *Nymphoides* species are currently available on the market in the United States or overseas, some hybridization has been noted in the wild. This area needs to be explored in order to increase the range of colors and forms in this wonderful genus.

## Nymphoides aquatica
**banana plant, floating heart**

Sometimes also sold as a submerged or aquarium plant, *Nymphoides aquatica* can be grown for its round leaves and star-shaped white flowers that sit on the water surface. Its leaves are green with reddish purple undersides. Flowers rise from the leaf petiole union rather than from the crown of the plant. Grows in sun to part shade in moist soil or water to 36 inches deep, spreading 12–24 inches or more wide. Hardy in Zones 7–11. It is commonly named banana plant for its tubers, which look like little bunches of green bananas, not unlike those produced by the semihardy waterlily *Nymphaea mexicana*. *Nymphoides aquatica* has also earned the name floating heart for its added ability to grow as a floating water plant. Large leaves can develop with roots and flowers, and the petiole can rot away or snap off in deep water or crowded conditions.

## Nymphoides cordata

Hardy in Zones 5–10 and native to eastern North America, this species is a small form with 2-inch, ovate leaves and flowers creamy to white, formed in umbels. Books on the flora of South Carolina say it has purple leaves with white flowers arising from the leaf axils. It grows in sun to shade and spreads 12–24 inches. It grows in up to 24 inches of water but also tolerates seasonal flooding and will grow submerged foliage for a time.

## Nymphoides crenata
**painted yellow water snowflake**

Foliage of this species is heavily mottled in dark red or brown, prompting it to be called "painted." Often the leaves are noticeably toothed. I have seen some variations with liver-colored leaves accented by green veins. Flowers are yellow, star-shaped, and fringed. Grows with a running spread in 4–24 inches of water. Zones 7–11.

## Nymphoides cristata
**painted white water snowflake**

Like its yellow counterpart, leaves of this painted species are heavily variegated in dark burgundy. Flowers are small, dainty, white, star-shaped, and lightly crinkled—they really do look like snowflakes floating on the water surface. This white-flowering form produces more blooms than any other

*Nymphoides geminata*

species. Excellent for container and tub gardens, and for small water gardens it provides beneficial cover for small fish. It is easy to grow, thriving in water 4–24 inches deep. It reproduces from viviparous leaves and is not a running form of *Nymphoides*, spreading to 12–24 inches. Zones 7–11.

### *Nymphoides geminata* (syn. *N. peltata*)
### yellow water snowflake

This hardier form of water snowflake is grown for its cheerful yellow, star-shaped flowers that have very frilly, fringed edges. Blooms are borne on running stems rather than from the leaf axils. Leaves are slightly toothed and an even green, although sometimes shadowed with a hint of brown. It is very free-flowering and fast growing, with a running spread. Though ideally it grows in 4–24 inches of water, I have even seen yellow water snowflake growing in damp soil. Hardy in Zones 5–11.

### *Nymphoides hydrocharioides*
### orange water snowflake

This species, native to Australia, has orange, star-shaped flowers that rise from the leaf axils. Its leaves are green with dark red or brown variegation. Grows in 4–24 inches of water with a running spread. Zones 7–11.

*Nymphoides geminata*

### *Nymphoides indica*
### white water snowflake

With frilly flowers similar to those of yellow water snowflake (*Nymphoides geminata*), this white-flowering form is not as hardy. Also, it sets blooms directly from the leaf axils rather than from running stems. It spreads by viviparous leaves and does not have the overpowering coverage of other forms of *Nymphoides*. Grows to 12–24 inches or more wide in water 4–24 inches deep. Zones 8–11. 'Gigantea' is a cultivar with flowers 1 inch or so wide and leaves up to 6 inches across. Its spread can be more than 36 inches.

*Polygonum amphibium*

*Stratiotes aloides*

## Polygonum amphibium
**willow grass, amphibious bistort**
**Polygonaceae**

This lovely pond plant has long, narrow, floating leaves often tinged in red, accented by a red or black chevron and with a prominent midrib. In the summer, it produces hot pink flowers that resemble little bottle brushes. In China I have seen white variations of this highly variable species, as well as pale pink forms elsewhere. A versatile creeping plant, it adapts well to moist soil or as much as 4 feet of water over its crown. When growing in the margin of the pond it reaches up to 40 inches in height. For optimal growth, place the plant in about 12–18 inches of water in sun to part shade. It propagates readily by cuttings but can also grow from seed sown on moist soil. Zones 5–9.

## Stratiotes aloides
**water soldier, water aloe**
**Hydrocharitaceae**

Until the late 1990s prohibited in the United States as a noxious weed, *Stratiotes aloides* looks like an underwater pineapple. The plant produces a 6-inch, pineapple-like bud for overwintering. These dormant buds fall to the bottom of the pond in the autumn and so remain until spring. In summer, when the plant is ready to flower, the buds float to the surface, sending up long, pointed, stiff, and heavily toothed leaves from around a central crown that also produces white, single, three-petaled flowers. Growing in sun to part shade in any depth of water, though it does best in water 2–4 feet deep, the floating plant reaches 10–12 inches tall above the waterline. Spread of each plant is 4–10 inches.

*Stratiotes aloides*

*Stratiotes aloides*

Water soldier is a popular plant in the United Kingdom, but is far less common in the United States because of its former federal status. It is native to Europe and central Asia and is related to *Egeria densa*, as well as species of *Hydrilla*, *Elodea*, and *Lagarosiphon*, which its flowers resemble. It produces buds like those of *Hydrilla*, but is slow to spread, covering just 24 inches in a season. Does best in waters low in alkalinity. It spreads by stolons and is usually propagated by offsets. Plants may be either male or female, which is evident by the either staminate or pistilate flowers. Hardy in Zones 3–11. To overwinter, simply allow the buds to drop below the freeze line in the pond. Propagate by division of the offshoots. I have noticed no pests—koi only pick at it.

## Trapa
### Trapaceae

*Trapa* species are noted for their clusters of triangular leaves that float on the water surface. Leaves are green, sometimes with red chevrons, and may be toothed. Flowers are small, usually white and three-petaled, held close to the water surface above the foliage. They grow well as pond coverage but should never be released in natural bodies of water. Some plants are tropical, needing indoor protection with warm water and supplemental light in order to survive a cold, dark winter.

*Trapa* is native primarily to Europe and Asia. It is often grown in Asia for its seed, which is shelled and boiled—to remove its toxin—to produce, reportedly, a crunchy texture albeit bland flavor. Some species have naturalized in North America, much to the chagrin of those who must navigate its waterways. Trapas propagate by seed or offset of their floating crown. They are sometimes bothered by aphids or China mark moth. In a backyard pond, they are likely to be nibbled by the resident koi and goldfish.

### *Trapa bicornis*
**giant mosaic plant**

This species has seed with only two horns, which it only rarely produces, and is not currently prohibited from production or sale in the United States. It has larger white flowers than *Trapa natans* and is a showier plant. Leaves are dark green with a maroon chevron and have red undersides. Giant mosaic plant is often sold as an aquarium plant and grows readily as a floating plant with no potted crown in the pond. It spreads to 8 inches wide in sun to part shade, preferring water at 4–12 inches deep, if not allowed to float. Hardy in Zones 8–11.

### *Trapa natans*

Now considered an invasive species and prohibited under federal law in the United States, *Trapa natans* has spread along the waterways of the eastern seaboard. For a homeowner the more immediate concern is the seed that it produces, which have four extraordinarily sharp spines. A better selection is *T. bicornis*, which has only two spines on its seed.

# CHAPTER 10

# FLOATING WATER PLANTS

Floating water plants are the ultimate in easy care water gardening—no potting is necessary. Like little boats, the plants simply drift effortlessly in the pond. Their roots dangle down into the water, drawing nutrients for the plant's growth. Some of the best plants for filtering pond water are members of this group. They act as the pond's feather dusters, removing suspended particles from the water. Floating plants are important for shading the pond to protect fish and other wildlife from baking under the hot summer sun. The plants also provide a way for wildlife to hide from predators, such as herons and raccoons. Floating plants are fertile spawning grounds in the spring and hideaways for the young fry that hatch and grow in the summer.

Plants that grow on the water's surface have developed special means to keep themselves afloat. Some, such as water hyacinth (*Eichhornia*), have enlarged air sacs in their leaves that act much like buoys. Others, such as frogbit (*Hydrocharis morsus-ranae*), use repellent waxes to keep the water from being absorbed into their foliage. Still others, such as water lettuce (*Pistia stratiotes*), have water repellent hairs that use surface tension to allow the leaves literally to stand on the water. All floating water plants use their ability to float to exploit an environmental niche—growing in water that is too deep for other plants or that appears only seasonally, such as floodwater—in order to grow in water that is rich in nutrients.

The ease of care for which floating plants are so well known has also earned them considerable notoriety in warmer climates. In states with warmer winters, from Florida through to California, water hyacinth and water lettuce are not only discouraged, but literally banned from possession. Never, never add a single floating plant to a natural body of water. Even in tiny portions, they can quickly grow and spread, causing enormous trouble with their floating mats of vegetation over the water. When in doubt, compost them into your vegetable bed.

*Pistia stratiotes*

*Neptunia aquatica*

## LANDSCAPE USES

Larger floating water plants, such as the sensitive plants, water lettuce, and water hyacinth (*Neptunia aquatica*, *Pistia stratiotes*, and *Eichhornia*, respectively), grow well in ponds of all sizes. Keep them in the top, "header" pond of a stream or waterfall to aid in biological filtration. Smaller plants are more appropriate for container and tub gardens. In large, earthen ponds, it takes quite a few to make an impression.

Floating plants are best not permitted to completely cover a pond's surface. Too many plants can reduce oxygen in the water to levels that are dangerous to fish and other underwater animals. Complete cover is not a problem, however, in container water gardens that do not have any fish inhabitants. As a very general rule, about one-third of the pond's water surface should be covered with vegetation. As floating plants take over more of the pond in the late summer, they should be thinned and removed. Use them as mulch or compost, since they return nitrogen to the soil.

In ponds designed to house fish and other underwater wildlife, good choices are plants with long, flowing root systems, such as water hyacinth and water lettuce. These are favored by fish as ideal places to lay eggs during the spring spawning season. Aquatic insects and similar underwater inhabitants often use the long roots to hide and forage for still smaller aquatic wildlife that is a source of food.

For small container ponds on the deck or patio, or even in a window box, many of the floating plants make wonderful and easy-care accents. Smaller forms of water hyacinth and water lettuce, as well as the water ferns (*Ceratopteris thalictroides*), all fit well into a mixed water planting of a container water feature.

## SUNLIGHT, WIND, AND WATER DEPTH

Most floating water plants grow well in full sun, even in harsh summer climates where the temperature exceeds 100°F and the humidity is high. Many also grow well in part shade, and water lettuce (*Pistia stratiotes*) as well as water ferns (*Ceratopteris thalictroides*) often prefer at least part shade in order to grow well.

Since they can bounce and move along with the rippled movements of wind and waves, floating water plants are often able to withstand and adapt to such conditions. Water hyacinth (*Eichhornia*) and water lettuce can even grow into a large mat that will absorb some of the motion associated with waves or wind. Very small water plants, such as azollas or duckweed (*Lemna*), can withstand the movements even when they are completely upturned. The wax on their leaf surface causes the plants to flip over in a wave, and even if the plants are submerged the wax will cause them to rise to the water surface.

Since they simply sit on the water surface, floating water plants are unaffected by water depth, except that they do generally prefer some depth of water and do not adapt to being stranded on moist soil. They grow well in water from just a few inches deep to waters that are several feet or more.

## WATER CHEMISTRY AND FILTRATION

Water plants that float in the pond are usually tolerant of a wide range of pH in the water, as well as variations in alkalinity. Some such as water hyacinth are even used in the water filtration industry and have been found effective in absorbing pollutants such as heavy metals from the water. Water ferns (*Ceratopteris thalictroides*) and sensitive plants (*Neptunia aquatica*) do not grow well in alkaline waters, where the pH is above 8.

Floating water plants are among the most sensitive to the addition of salt to the pond. Salt quickly dries out the plants, causing them to shrivel, wither, and die. In some the salt acts to change the plant's osmotic potential, drawing water from the leaf surface. In others the salt appears to breach the leaf membrane's ability to repel water, allowing salted water to enter the plant's cells. Whenever salt will be added to the pond, make sure to remove floating water plants to a holding tank until the need for the salt has passed and the water may be desalinated with fresh water.

Floating water plants absorb nitrates and phosphates from the water. Water hyacinth (*Eichhornia*) and water lettuce (*Pistia stratiotes*), in fact, are so efficient that they are often recommended to aid filtration. Their dangling roots quickly take in nutrients that would otherwise promote algae growth and turn the water green. Duckweed (*Lemna*) is also an able filtration plant, often used in sewage lagoons. Other floating plants, such as frogbit (*Hydrocharis morsus-ranae*) or sensitive plant, have only an average ability to filter nutrients from the water and are not recommended to combat green water in the pond.

## SEASONAL CARE

Floaters that require warm summer temperatures should not be placed in the pond until the water temperature has reached a consistent 65°F. Floating water plants that are from tropical regions tolerate elevated air and water temperatures and will thrive in the heat and humidity of summer. For these plants, cooler water that falls below 65°F can cause their foliage to yellow and form black streaks. Floating plants from cooler regions, such as frogbit (*Hydrocharis morsus-ranae*), suffer from the heat and will start to yellow when the water rises past 80°F. They should be moved to a shady spot in the pond when summer heat is at its greatest.

Once out in the pond, floating plants need regular fertilizing and an occasional cleaning to remove dead or tattered foliage and spent flowers. The long, flowing roots can be trimmed back to 6–10 inches if they become too matted or dirty.

Fertilize floating water plants by placing them in a separate bucket of pond water in which fertilizer has been dissolved at half the strength recommended by the manufacturer. Take care not to add too much fertilizer for it can quicky cause the plant's roots to burn off and rot, seriously harming its growth. Leave the plant in the bucket overnight and then return it to the pond, rinsing its roots thoroughly so that the remnant fertilizer will not leach into the pond water and cause an algae bloom. Doing this every week or so will keep floating plants happy and healthy even in ponds that are crystal clear.

Another way to fertilize long-rooted floating plants is to grow them in the center of a tomato cage that has been secured in a pot of soil at the bottom of the pond. The floaters will stay in the center of the tomato cage ring, and as their roots grow, they will reach the pot filled with soil and root into the soil. The pot of soil can be fertilized with tablets every few weeks, feeding the roots that have anchored there.

Tropical floating water plants can be difficult to over-winter in colder climates. They cannot remain outdoors but must be brought in for the winter. They can be kept in an aquarium or just floated in anything that can hold water, even a brandy snifter. Often they will winter well in a warm sunny windowsill for several weeks, so that the pondkeeper will be convinced the plants will survive until spring. Suddenly, in February or so, the plants will simply turn to mush and melt away, with no apparent reason for their demise. The problem is the lack of adequate light intensity.

When the days begin to lengthen in February, the plants start growing, but the natural light is not bright enough to permit proper growth. The tender new growth starts to falter for lack of adequate light and then falls prey to mold or other bacterial infections. Soon the entire plant becomes feeble and dies. Tropical floating water plants, such as water hyacinth (*Eichhornia*) and water lettuce (*Pistia stratiotes*), need water temperatures of at least 70°F and at least 14 hours of sunlight of at least 1000 foot-candles. This is equivalent to four fluorescent bulbs held about 12 inches over the water.

Considering the amount of energy and electricity required to keep tropical water plants alive for an entire winter, it is often cheaper to simply mulch them into the vegetable garden in the fall, and buy new ones the following spring.

## PLANTING

Floating water plants are not usually grown in soil, but a few can be potted. This is often done in the winter in order to keep the plants growing indoors. Water hyacinth (*Eichhornia*) and water lettuce (*Pistia stratiotes*) may be grown in this fashion, as well as the sensitive plants (*Neptunia aquatica*). Even azollas will grow on moist soil, or a similar growing medium. Some gardeners prefer to grow water hyacinth and water lettuce in pots so they stay contained and are easier to feed, leading to improved growth and better blooming. Once they are potted, though, they are unable to filter nutrients from the water and their value as filtration plants is essentially negated.

## PROPAGATION

Most floating plants are propagated by dividing off new growth that is produced on side-shoots. Once the new growth has developed enough roots to support itself, it can be detached from the main plant. Water hyacinth (*Eichhornia*) and water lettuce (*Pistia stratiotes*) are commonly propagated in this fashion, as are the sensitive plants (*Neptunia aquatica*). Smaller floating plants, such as duckweed (*Lemna*), salvinias, and azollas, quickly produce new self-sustaining plants. The water ferns (*Ceratopteris thalictroides*) have an unusual method of reproduction where the odd leaf, having fallen into the water, sprouts new plantlets which may be separated once they have grown their own roots.

The sensitive plants also reproduce well from seed sown on evenly moist soil. Other floating plants, since they reproduce so quickly from vegetative growth, are not generally propagated from seed. Some are so small, in fact, that it would be very difficult to collect any seed to grow.

I am not aware of any current efforts to hybridize floating plants grown by water gardeners. Certain plants, such as azollas, duckweed, and salvinias, are too small to make hybridization practical. There is little perceived reason to produce improved selections of water hyacinth or water lettuce, since their sale and transport is restricted or in some states completely prohibited. We must await the chance sport found in someone's backyard pond, or new species collected from the wild.

## PESTS AND DISEASES

Floaters with soft, spongy foliage are prime targets for sucking insects, especially aphids, which are often found on water lettuce (*Pistia stratiotes*), and to a lesser extent water hyacinth (*Eichhornia*), in our hot, humid summers. China mark moth can affect water hyacinth and water lettuce, and weevils may infest some water hyacinth.

Molds can also take hold when the plants are subjected to cooler waters or are grown indoors with poor air circulation. Water lettuce is especially prone to mold.

Fish can be a problem because they tug on the plant's roots and tear at their leaves. Koi are probably the most prevalent pest of water hyacinth and water lettuce. Deer, raccoons, and muskrats also like to munch on these leaves.

*Primula japonica* is tucked to the left of *Gunnera* in the margin while a hardy waterlily floats on the water

*Aeschynomene fluitans*

*Aeschynomene fluitan*s

## *Aeschynomene fluitans*
**giant water sensitive plant**
**Fabaceae**

Giant water sensitive plant has long, 1–3-inch leaves that grow alternately on a single stem. This stem floats on the water, becoming swollen, white, and somewhat furry as it ages. The plant's summer-blooming, large, 1-inch flowers are yellow and resemble blossoms of the common sweet pea, although they have no fragrance. Leaves are sensitive and close when touched (though not as readily as those of *Neptunia aquatica*). A quick grower, it is native to warm regions of the world and may be grown free-floating or rooted to the edge of the pond with its stems trailing out on the water surface. It grows in sun to part shade and reaches 2 inches high with a running spread.

Giant water sensitive plant propagates by division or cuttings. It may also be grown from seed sown on moist soil, which usually sprouts in a few weeks. To overwinter the plant, make sure to keep it in water that is frost-free, preferably above 60°F. Mealybugs and spider mites may affect the plants, mostly in winter. Hardy in Zones 9–11.

## *Azolla*
**Azollaceae**

A true fern, this aquatic has leaves that are fuzzy and finely toothed. A bright green in summer, leaves turn red in spring and fall when the water is cool. Excellent pond cover for fish and other wildlife. *Azolla* species hold a blue-green algae that fixes nitrogen, fertilizing the plants, so be sure to put any that are skimmed from the pond into the compost or use as a mulch in the perennial garden. *Azolla* species are very sen-

sitive to the number of daylight hours they receive, giving them a tendency to die out during the shorter days of winter. They grow in sun to shade, reaching ½ inch high with a running spread. Hardy in Zones 9–11.

## *Azolla caroliniana*
**fairy moss, mosquito fern**

Fairy moss is native to North America. It can be found growing wild as far north as Michigan and Wisconsin and into the New England states. Plants are rounded, not triangular, like branches of arborvitae (*Thuja*). They overwinter by freezing in the ice and thawing in spring.

## *Azolla pinnata*
**Christmas tree fern**

A species native to South America, *Azolla pinnata* has triangular-shaped foliage that looks something like a flat Christ-

*Azolla caroliniana*

*Ceratopteris thalictroides*

*Azolla caroliniana* in cool water

mas tree. It is considered invasive and is prohibited under U.S. federal law. Ours always died during the short days of winter because of its dependency on long hours of daylight.

### *Ceratopteris thalictroides*
### water fern
### Parkeriaceae

Leaves of this unusual floating plant look like big, puffy leaves of Italian parsley. The plant is said to resemble a fern because of its highly cut and serrated leaves. It usually reaches 12 inches high and wide. The species *Ceratopteris pteridoides* has slightly coarser foliage and is slightly larger. Any part of the foliage that lies on the water surface sprouts

a plantlet and will root to become a new plant. Water fern also grows in soil in a few inches of water; when so planted, its foliage looks like curly parsley, still more finely cut. It grows best in full shade, and needs at least part shade to survive. To overwinter water fern, which is hardy in Zones 9–11, keep it in water of at least 65°F. Bring it indoors into a warm fish tank. It is not bothered by pests or diseases.

### *Eichhornia*
### water hyacinth
### Pontederiaceae

Well known for lavender-blue flowers and shiny green foliage, the tender floating aquatic species of *Eichhornia* are known as water hyacinths. Leaves are spongy and inflated at the base, making them buoyant in water. Plants reach about 12 inches high with a running spread. Water hyacinths make great container plants—just drop them in any pot that will hold water, throw in some fertilizer, and be rewarded with tons of flowers for the entire summer. Excellent for filtration, their roots draw nutrients out of the water that would otherwise promote an algae bloom. The species *E. crassipes* is so highly regarded for its filtration abilities that it is routinely grown for sewage treatment.

In very clean, well-tended ponds, water hyacinths can suffer for lack of adequate nutrition. Fertilize them weekly in a bucket of pond water as for other floating plants. Or, water hyacinths can be fertilized like other marginal water plants. Although usually grown as floating water plants, water hyacinths also grow when planted in a container with soil. Provided there is a bit of water over the crown, the plants will thrive in these conditions.

Roots of *Eichhornia azurea*

*Eichhornia azurea*

The thick, long roots of water hyacinths are black and feathered and can grow to 12 inches or more in length. Trim them back or thin periodically so that older roots do not start to decompose in the pond or clog filtering systems.

*Eichhornia* species grow best in sun to part shade in warm water and will not survive a winter freeze. They are hardy in Zones 9–11. Because cool spring temperatures can cause severe setback, wait until the pond temperature is consistently at 65°F before putting plants out in the spring. In colder climates, treating them like annuals is easiest and often cheapest. Use them as winter mulch in the vegetable or perennial garden, and buy new plants in the spring. Overwintering them requires water temperatures of at least 60°F and sunlight for at least 10 hours every day.

In southern states, the plants are considered noxious weeds because of their ability to clog waterways. Federal law in the U.S. prohibits their sale in some states. Studies are being undertaken to determine whether a natural predator, a species of weevil, can be used in warmer climates to eradicate its spread in natural waterways.

### *Eichhornia azurea*
**creeping water hyacinth, peacock water hyacinth**

The lavender-blue flowers of creeping water hyacinth are more lavender than those of *Eichhornia crassipes* and have a noticeable yellow dot like a peacock's feather. For this yellow dot the plant is also sometimes known as peacock water hyacinth. Flowers are slightly smaller and more rounded. Leaves are spoon-shaped and clasp the central growing stem, which floats and creeps out on the water much like bog bean (*Menyanthes trifoliata*).

Creeping water hyacinth is useful to soften the edges of ponds. I have also found it very attractive when planted in container water gardens under larger marginals, such as *Cyperus*, *Thalia*, or *Colocasia*.

Just as beneficial for filtration, it has roots that are not as feathered and prominent as those of *Eichhornia crassipes*. It is easily propagated by breaking its running stem once the new stem has developed a few roots. *Eichhornia azurea* is believed to be native to Central and South America, but it is so widespread that many people argue this point. The stems have been used to make furniture and baskets that resemble rattan.

Although some sources report a yellow-flowering form of water hyacinth, I have never seen one and know of no one who ever has. I suspect that the yellow water hyacinth is a water garden myth that has developed through a misunderstanding about its flower color. Many books and catalogs describe the water hyacinth as having "blue and yellow flow-

*Eichhornia crassipes*

*Eichhornia crassipes*

ers." Inexperienced readers have understood this to mean that there are two flower colors—one blue, one yellow—when in fact it is describing only one flower type, that of *Eichhornia azurea*'s blue flowers with yellow markings.

### Eichhornia crassipes

Noted for its prominent lavender-blue flowers and fleshy, rounded, floating leaves, water hyacinth grows quickly in warm water. A few plants bought in the spring can easily turn into a few hundred by fall (they are excellent for compost in the perennial border or the vegetable garden). Plants propagate readily from leaf shoots which develop into new plants, like strawberry plants. It is prohibited from sale or possession in southern states. Where it can be grown legally it is a welcome addition to the water garden for its ability to filter out unwanted nutrients and for its attractive flowers. Although each flower lasts only a day or two, they are borne

in abundance. *Eichhornia crassipes* is believed to be native to the African Congo basin, but it too is so extensive that many people disagree on its origin.

### Hydrocharis morsus-ranae
### (see also *Limbonium spongeanum*)
### frogbit
### Hydrocharitaceae

The common name frogbit is applied to several different plants—*Hydrocharis morsus-ranae* and *Limbonium spongeanum* the two most common—and is unfortunately the object of some confusion. *Hydrocharis morsus-ranae* is the prettier plant, with small, white, three-petaled flowers that look like miniature water poppies (*Hydrocleys*). Leaves are shiny and heart-shaped and have a "floating sac" on the undersides. It is a great plant for the small pond and for containers because it is pretty and easy to grow. Grows in sun to

*Lemna*

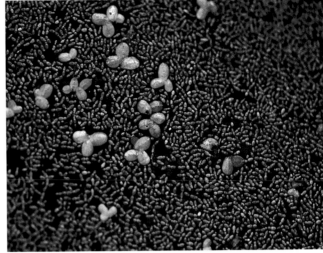

*Lemna*

part shade with a running spread, reaching up to ½ inch tall. It forms buds that sink to the bottom of the pond to overwinter until spring. Hardy in Zones 4–10.

### *Hygroyza aristata*
### floating purple spike
### Poaceae

A small floating, creeping grass of warm waters, this plant is ideal for containers and small water gardens. It also works well at the edge of the pond or as a floating cover beneath taller plants. As the plant matures, it develops a burgundy chevron in the center of each leaf, providing additional foliar interest. It is able to float because its leaf sheath becomes spongy. As it does, it takes on a reddish tan color. Its flowers are uneventful, about 2 inches tall, appearing as black or brown spikes in late summer. Grows in part shade to part sun. Although the plant will grow in soil that is only moist or even dry, it is best planted where the stems may float on the water surface. A native of southeast Asia, it is often sold as a fish tank or aquarium plant. As with any other water plants, especially those for warmer climates, it should never be introduced to natural bodies of water. Hardy in Zones 9–11. Bring indoors into a well lit fish tank for the winter.

### *Lemna*
### duckweed
### Lemnaceae

Known as the smallest flowering plant in the world, many species make up the genus *Lemna*, commonly called duckweed. Most duckweeds have leaves that are round or almost round. They are light green and less than ⅛ inch in diame-

ter, with a single root growing from the underside of the leaf. Although they do flower, the blooms are so minute they defy detection by the naked eye. Duckweeds grow in sun to part shade with a running spread, quickly covering the water surface. They have "budding pouches" on the edge of the leaf, from which grow new single-leafed plants. Hardy in Zones 3–11, they overwinter by producing buds that sink to the bottom of the pond.

Duckweed is often seen covering large areas of earthen ponds. Fish love to eat duckweed, and it may have a hard time staying alive in a pond shared with koi or goldfish. I do not use duckweed as an ornamental plant, but instead as a food source for koi and goldfish to eat in early spring when it is still too early to feed them regular fish food. Adding goldfish to a pond is an excellent way to rid the water of duckweed in a short period of time, without having to resort to the use of harmful pesticides.

### *Limbonium spongeanum* (see also *Hydrocharis morsus-ranae*)
### frogbit
### Hydrocharitaceae

*Limbonium spongeanum*, another frogbit, looks very much like *Hydrocharis morsus-ranae*, but its shiny leaves are oval, not heart-shaped. It, too, has a "floating sac" on the underside of each leaf. Blossoms are not very showy, just ¼-inch, scrizzly mops of pale cream. The plant produces shorter runners, and more of them, than the hydrocharis. Grows in sun to part shade with a running spread, reaching ½ inch tall. Hardy in Zones 4–10. Overwinters through similar buds. *Limbonium spongeanum* is often sold in garden centers

Limbonium spongeanum

as floating heart, which is more appropriately the common name for *Nymphoides aquatica*, a waterlily-like plant that can also be grown floating on the water surface.

### *Neptunia aquatica*
### sensitive plant
### Fabaceae

Sensitive plant, so named for its foliage that contracts at the slightest touch, has leaflets that are opposite, growing on either side of the petiole, arranged to resemble dragonfly wings. Its flowers are yellow tufts about 1 inch wide, appearing freely throughout the summer on the running stems. The plant's main floating stem becomes stout, white, and matted as the plant matures. Growing naturally in warm regions, sensitive plant is native to South America. Although it is often sold as a floating water plant, it also grows well rooted in soil at the edge of the pond, where it reaches about 6 inches tall. Situate in sun to part shade. Hardy in Zones 9–11.

*Neptunia aquatica*

*Pistia stratiotes*

*Pistia stratiotes* 'Angyo Splash'

## *Pistia stratiotes*
### water lettuce
### Araceae

Foliage of this plant grows like a rosette from a single crown—it really does resemble a floating head of lettuce or cabbage. Leaves are spongy and crinkled and velvety in texture. Color is usually light green or lime-green. When mature each leaf may reach up to 12 inches in height and several inches wide. An individual plant overall may reach more than 24 inches in diameter, though water lettuce has a running spread. It grows best in part shade, especially in very hot climates, and can tolerate full shade. Flowers are tiny, white circles that appear just at the base of the leaves. Something akin to microscopic peace lilies, they are only visible by searching for them. Water lettuce reproduces by offsets that grow from the base of the mature plant, like strawberry plants. Hardy in Zones 9–11. Difficult to overwinter.

*Pistia stratiotes* 'Angyo Splash'

Several selected cultivars of *Pistia stratiotes* offer some variety. These all grow smaller than the species, individual plants reaching about 6 inches high and 6 inches wide, though they have the same running spread. 'Aqua Velvet', or blue water lettuce, is light blue and, with its smaller form, more suitable for smaller, backyard ponds. On 'Ruffles', or ruffled water lettuce, the top edges of each leaf are more crinkled and ruffled than the species. The plant forms a tight rosette and is the smallest form of water lettuce that I have seen, generally reaching just 2–4 inches tall and wide. The Japanese selection 'Angyo Splash', or variegated water lettuce, has leaves streaked and blotched in creamy yellow. The effect is unusual and somewhat ornamental, but the plant may be more valuable to the collector of variegated plants

than it would be to most water gardeners. Like many variegated plants, this selection has a tendency to revert; the offenders must be culled and removed. Leaves are sometimes more twisted and bent, a probable result of the variegation.

## *Salvinia*
### water velvet, cat's tongue
### Salviniaceae

Like *Azolla*, *Salvinia* is a genus of true ferns. The leaves grow on a long, central stem that resembles a chain. Leaves are velvety and spongy, having surface hairs that are water repellent and underwater hairs that are water attracting to help them stick to the water. They are most useful in small ponds

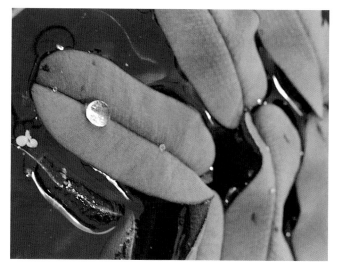

Salvinia longifolia

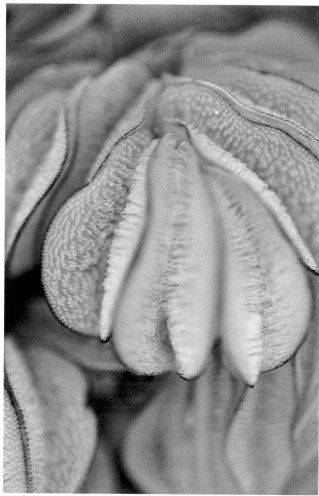

Salvinia molesta

Salvinia molesta

and containers, although they may not last long in koi ponds, since they are a favorite food of koi. Their best color is achieved in part shade, where they turn an attractive khaki or "fatigues"-green. Though they grow in full sun, the plants take on an unappealing brown tint. Native to Mexico and into South America, they are hardy in Zones 10–11.

### Salvinia longifolia
**giant velvet leaf**

Each leaf of this unusual *Salvinia* species reaches 2–3 inches in length and 1 inch in width. The hairy, furry leaves grow alternately from their central, running stem, all floating directly on the water surface.

### Salvinia molesta (syn. *S. rotundifolia, S. minima*)

Listed as a prohibited aquatic plant under U.S. federal law, *Salvinia molesta* has fuzzy, round, ½-inch leaves that are connected in long, running chains. In fall, as the water cools, the leaves become more "bent," with their edges folded up out of the water. In northern climates it is very cold sensitive, requiring a minimum water temperature of approximately 45°F.

# CHAPTER 11

# SUBMERGED WATER PLANTS

Submerged water plants are the unsung heroes in the war against green water, the one battle all pondkeepers are sure to face sooner or later. Important to water quality as well as water clarity, underwater plants help filter unwanted nutrients and add important oxygen to the water during the day. Besides their usefulness, many are highly decorative as well. Some have finely cut foliage while others are long strap-like creatures that undulate in the current. Certain submerged plants were once popular in aquariums, but having become troublesome weeds in natural lakes and streams, may be unlawful to sell or keep under applicable laws. Fortunately, alternatives to those prohibited plants are available that are helpful to the pond ecology.

Underwater plants are sometimes referred to as "oxygenators" because they add oxygen to the water in the pond. This label is a bit of a misnomer, since they produce oxygen only during the day. At night, submerged plants reverse the process and remove oxygen from the water. Many marginal pond plants have submerged forms often sold as oxygenators, but they often do not perform in the pond as they do in the fish tank.

Underwater plants vary greatly in their foliage and flower habits. They generally fall into three groups. Some, such as mermaid's fan (*Proserpinaca palustris*) and *Ranunculus*, have both submerged and emerged foliage, each very different. Others, such as *Cabomba*, have only submerged leaves but float their flowers on or above the water surface. Still others, such as *Najas* and hornwort (*Ceratophyllum*), have both submerged leaves and flowers.

Submerged plants with floating flowers often bloom in late spring or early summer, sometimes continuing intermittently throughout the summer. Although each blossom may be very small, a large grouping can make an attractive addition to the early summer pond, when waterlilies have only just begun to flower, or to accompany water hawthorne (*Aponogeton distachyus*).

Foliage of submerged water plants is very distinct from that of emerged plants. Some leaves are thick and strap-like, while others are very thin and finely cut. Often the leaves and stems are easily torn or broken; since they are viviparous, this brittleness permits the plants'

*Menyanthes, Nymphaea 'Sioux', and Azolla float in front; Acorus calamus 'Variegatus' stands before the rocks with Nymphoides peltata on the water surface to the right; and in back, left to right, Onoclea sensibilis, Colocasia esculenta 'Black Magic', and Hibiscus moscheutos*

*Potamogeton illinoensis*

proliferation in a wide area, especially in large earthen ponds. These plants can quickly overrun an earth-bottom pond.

Roots of underwater plants are often long and fibrous, serving both to anchor the plant and to draw nutrients from the soil. The exception is hornwort, which has no roots to speak of but instead floats in the water and absorbs nutrients through its foliage. Many underwater plants that root in the soil produce subsoil runners from which new plantlets quickly sprout. These plants, such as *Vallisneria* and *Sagittaria*, are able to form a carpet on the pond floor that holds soil in place, much like a sod. Potamogetons, myriophyllums, and hydrillas can form thick, branching mats anchored to the pond bottom that smother everything under them.

## LANDSCAPE USES

Thanks to their diversity, submerged plants can be selected to grow well in almost any kind of pond or water garden setting. Very large earthen ponds are ideal for sagittarias and vallisnerias, which will even withstand visits from geese and other foraging animals. Smaller lined backyard ponds can grow almost any kind of submerged plant. Ranunculus and potamogetons grow well in calm or moving water. Myriophyllums will grow in up to 10 feet of water, and dwarf forms of *Sagittaria* and *Utricularia* will thrive in just a few inches of water in a table-top pond. Some, such as hornwort (*Ceratophyllum*), prefer full sun, but others, such as

anacharis (*Egeria densa*), can grow quite well with almost total shade.

In a pond for fish and wildlife, most oxygenators make good spawning beds but they are hard to remove from the pond when the fish are done. Hornwort, though, does not seek to root, making it an excellent spawning ground for fish in the spring, as they swim around and through the hornwort to mate and lay down their eggs. You can then dip out the plant and move it to a new home to raise the fry if you like. Also because of the course texture of the plants the fish tend not to eat it.

## POND FILTRATION

Submerged plants perform a vital role in creating and maintaining an ecosystem suitable for fish and other wildlife. Through photosynthesis, submerged plants draw nutrients directly from the water, absorbing nitrates and phosphates through their leaves as well as their roots. *Sagittaria subulata* is particularly effective at removing phosphates from pond water, using it before it can be converted to energy by algaes that would quickly turn the water green. *Vallisneria* strips calcium carbonate from the water, depositing it on its leaves and forming a white sand at its base as the calcium flakes off. This has the overall long-term effect of lowering the pH of the pond—not so seriously as to make it acidic but moving it to neutral so other plants, like *Utricularia*, can thrive.

Submerged plants also make great dust mops. As they photosynthesize their leaves become charged and attract dust and dirt out of the water column, effectively cleaning the water. Too much dirt in the water can eventually kill the plants by interfering with photosynthesis. *Cabomba*, foxtail (*Myriophyllum heterophyllum*), and hornwort (*Ceratophyllum*) are the best cleaners—they can be removed from the pond in a bucket and rinsed to remove the soil from the leaves and the pond at the same time.

"How many?" is the often-asked question, and for pond stores the answer is "you can never have too many." Too many submerged plants in a small pond, however, can cause violent pH swings from day to night because of their oxygenating properties—the loss of carbonate molecules during the day plunges the pH and the release during the evening brings it back up. I have heard recommendations from two bunches per square foot of surface to two bushels per acre. Now who is right? Both and neither—you have to consider the application. I have found that for most lined ornamental ponds you need about 10–15 bunches of oxgenators for every 10 foot by 10 foot area 2–3 feet deep. But still, this depends on the depth. If a pond is mostly shallow, like 6 inches deep with a small deeper part, start with a few and add.

## SUN, WIND, AND WATER DEPTH

Submerged plants grow in a wide range of conditions, from full sun to full shade, depending on the individual plant species and cultivar. Those that tolerate greater water depth in sunny conditions, such as *Myriophyllum*, will often grow well in more shallow, shadier areas as well. Some experimentation may yield a few surprises. In our ponds *Sagittaria*, *Vallisneria*, *Cabomba*, and *Egeria densa*, which usually require sunny exposures, have all also done well in the shade.

Certain submerged plants grow well in moving water, such as the pockets in streams and under waterfalls. Others require still, placid water to grow well. *Vallisneria*, *Ranunculus*, *Sagittaria*, and *Potamogeton* all do well in slowly to moderately moving water. They look great in pond narrows were the water will flow and give the plants direction, adding to the effect of the moving water. Anacharis (*Egeria densa*) and elodeas both do poorly in moving water—they tend to break up and uproot.

Those that perform well in greater wind and wave movement are also suitable near fountains and the mouths of waterfalls. One of my favorite places to plant *Vallisneria americana* 'Giant' is in a deep stream or near the edge of a waterfall, where its long, strap-like leaves can undulate in the moving water. Dwarf sagittaria (*Sagittaria subulata*) is great in 4–12 inches of wavy water where it forms an aquatic sod.

Turbidity is a problem for submerged plants because it means that soil, dirt, and silt will be deposited on the leaves of the plants. This can harm them and in extreme circumstances can cause their death. In large ponds where soil may be dragged up from the bottom and become suspended in the water, where it will settle onto the plants, plant in sand to avoid this problem. In small ponds, if a pot becomes overturned and coats the submerged plants with dirt, simply remove the plant and rinse the leaves so that the soil will be removed.

Submerged plants grow in a wide range of water depth, some tolerating just 6–8 inches of water. Others take several feet, and a few will take even deeper water. But most will grow in water from 4 inches to 6 feet deep if the water is clear. Dark or dirty water will simply shade the plants to

death, much like the Aqua Shade product, which kills algae by dying the water black to prevent sunlight from entering the pond. Some plants, however, do get sunburned and may need a little protection in the form of shade from emerged plants or from deeper water. A piece of styrofoam also works—float it on the water during the heat of the day and take it off again in the evening. Shade may be especially helpful in acclimating plants new to the pond to the new light levels. Deeper water, since it experiences little wave action, can also be helpful by giving plants a place of calm in which to grow. When calm-loving plants grow into the wave zone they are usually broken up or "shaved."

## WATER CHEMISTRY

Underwater plants tolerate a wide range of soil and pH conditions. They do best in waters that are low in dissolved calcium or total hardness. Simply put, pH is a function of the available hydrogen ions and is related to dissolved calcium and total hardness, which deal with dissolved mineral concentration. Rain water has few, if any, dissolved minerals, but well water can be so concentrated as to interfere with oxygenators' ability to pull carbon dioxide out of the water. Our ponds' pH levels run anywhere from 7 to 8.8 with little interruption in the plants' growth. Rooted plants seem to manage better than bunches without roots. Some ponds may require a pH reducer. Although you need to be careful with it, many people lower the pH with swimming pool acid, or muratic acid, which is a 10 percent solution of hydrochloric acid.

A generally accepted rule is that most submerged plants are highly sensitive to salt (sodium chloride) and will not fare well if salt is added to the pond. The validity of this rule has not been tested by the water gardening community, at least to my knowledge, and it may well be that certain submerged plants are better able to tolerate at least a certain level of salt concentration than may be commonly thought. In our experience salt tolerance and the hardness or softness of the water go hand in hand—if the water has elevated hardness then the salt tolerance of the plants is reduced, and if the water is soft then the salt tolerance is higher.

Sodium chloride levels are an issue because many of the pond fish treatments include salt and many koi clubs recommend it. Some string algae treatments also have salt in them. It is important to monitor your plants when adding these products, or better yet, remove the submerged plants from the pond and keep them in temporary salt-free quarters while adding salt to the pond. Make sure that water changes have removed all salt residue before returning the submerged plants to the pond.

Water temperature is also an important factor affecting the chemistry of the pond. Water, heat, and oxygen have a special relationship. As the water temperature rises the level of dissolved gasses drops, including the oxygen needed by fish and the carbon dioxide needed by plants for photosynthesis. To help keep up the level of dissolved gasses, maintain water circulation in hot weather and even lower the temperature if it begins to approach 90°F. Although the plants would probably be fine, they can lower the oxygen level at night under those conditions to kill off the fish and the biological filter. Although it sounds like the answer would be to eliminate the plants, if they are replaced by algae then the problem still exists.

## SEASONAL CARE

Summer care for submerged plants is minimal. Although underwater plants absorb nutrients through their leaves and roots, they benefit from supplemental fertilizer added to the soil. Fertilize regularly according to manufacturer's directions. Remove old, tattered leaves. Plants that grow long stems, such as *Cabomba* and *Egeria*, sometimes begin to look long and leggy. They can be trimmed by cutting off several inches of stem and pushing these new ends into the soil. They will soon root and grow. Plants that grow from underground stolons, such as *Vallisneria*, often need no additional care except an occasional brushing of their leaves to remove accumulated soil, algae, or similar debris.

In the fall, stop fertilizing submerged plants about three weeks before the average frost date. In warm climates where frost is not a concern, stop fertilizing when the pond temperature falls below 60°F. For the winter, submerged plants that are hardy in the area may be left in the pond. More tender plants should be brought indoors. Submerge them in a bowl of water or fish tank on a warm, sunny windowsill. For plants such as anacharis (*Egeria densa*) that grow from a running stem, we often trim off the newest 5–6 inches of growth and plant this in soil, submerging it in several inches of water and keeping it warm and sunny.

## PLANTING

Submerged plants grow best if they are planted in a pot and fertilized regularly. Use a pot that is wide and shallow. Another alternative is to plant the underwater plant in the same pot with waterlilies or water hawthorne (*Aponogeton distachyus*), reducing the number of separate pots that must be maintained in the pond. Use the same soil suitable for other water plants—clay mixed with sand, or an equivalent. Gravel is also acceptable, although it will not hold fertilizer.

All stem-cut submerged plants, such as foxtail (*Myriophyllum heterophyllum*), anacharis (*Egeria densa*), and cabombas, are planted in a similar way. First, fill the pot with soil and top off with sand or pea gravel. Water the soil thoroughly. Put a hole in the center of the pot about 1½–2 inches deep, and insert five to ten stems. Push the soil back around the stems and submerge in the pond. Some underwater plants may also be grown in a pond by gently tying them to a rock that is placed at the bottom of the pond.

For plants that grow from a main crown, such as *Vallisneria* and *Sagittaria*, select a pot that is wide and shallow. A cat litter tray works well. Fill it slightly more than half full of soil. Set the plant on top of the soil and spread the roots over the soil surface. Cover the roots with sand, taking care not to

Planting stem-cut oxygenators

## PROPAGATION

cover the crown of the plant. If fish dig through the sand, top with some gravel.

Submerged plants are often sold as un-potted bunched stems or clumps. Lead weights are sometimes attached so that the plants may be simply sunk to the bottom of the pond. Some people believe that these lead weights can be a problem in areas with acid water that will dissolve the lead and release it into the water. Some water gardeners prefer not to use lead weights because lead has been associated with lead poisoning, and if lead is being released by the weights then the water should not be used on vegetables. If you purchase a bunch that has been sold with a lead weight, simply remove the weight before pushing the stems into the soil.

Because submerged plants dry out quickly, they should be kept wet, or at least moist and covered with a wet towel or paper. Place out of direct sunlight. When taking them home from the store, we simply place them in watertight plastic bags with a little bit of water and some air. Too much water will cause them to slosh around and break.

Submerged water plants that grow from fleshy central stems are easily propagated from stem cuttings. This includes *Cabomba*, *Egeria densa*, *Myriophyllum*, *Ranunculus*, *Potamogeton*, and any plant that branches above the soil line. This is the norm for aquatic plants. Other plants that grow from a central crown can be divided by taking offshoots or by cutting it up into sod pieces.

Few have given time or attention to the interesting prospect of hybridizing submerged water plants. Generally new introductions are found by accident as sports from propagated stock or collected from the wild. In the water gardening industry, selections are often made from plants introduced for aquariums or other indoor applications.

## PESTS AND DISEASES

Fish are the biggest pests of submerged plants, destroying them in a matter of hours or minutes depending on the fish. Koi are by far the most destructive, and goldfish to a much lesser extent. Generally koi larger than 10 inches long are pretty hard on plants, but goldfish of the same size do little feeding damage. They are more likely to harm plants mechanically during breeding.

Snails can be very damaging, but unfortunately they are usually sold in pet shops for ponds. The most destructive include apple snails, Columbian ram's horn, and tropical trap-door snails. I have seen these eat waterlilies right down to the roots, tuber and all. They turn submerged plants into coleslaw in no time. Trapping these pests is the only answer—use cucumber or cabbage attached to a string so it is retrievable. In addition, recent studies have shown that caffeine kills snails and slugs without harming other wildlife, but this is experimental so treat it with caution. Safe snails are hardy native trap-door snails, small hardy rams horn, and great pond snails.

Crayfish are very destructive, eating the plants off at the root and sending them floating. They are most destructive to sagittarias and vallisnerias, where they eat the crown and roots but let the leaves float. Crayfish can be trapped, or most of the treatments used for anchorworm on fish will also kill crayfish.

Some of the same pests that attack emerged plants will also find submerged plants when they grow too close to, or above, the surface. Aphids can sometimes be seen, but simply adding more water so the plants are submerged is the answer. China mark moth can be a problem when infestations are high. Use Bt (*Bacillus thuringiensis*) to control this pest.

## PLANT PROFILES

*Acorus calamus*, left, and *A. calamus* 'Variegatus', right, frame *Myosotis scorpioides* 'Wisconsin'

## *Cabomba*
### fanwort
### Cabombaceae

*Cabomba* is a member of the family Cabombaceae, which it shares with only one other genus, *Brasenia*. Seven species of *Cabomba* are reported, many of them native to warmer regions of North, South, and Central America. Cabombas have long been a favorite aquarium plant and are naturalized in Europe and Australia. Species are noted for their foliage, which is usually submerged and dissected. It can be very showy in green with purple backs or red to orangey. Cabombas have single, yellow-centered flowers of white, yellow, or pink, which float on the water surface, usually appearing in late spring or early summer.

### *Cabomba caroliniana*

*Cabomba caroliniana* is native to the southeastern U.S. and is the species most often sold in the United States. Most others need more specialized conditions to thrive, such as acidic water. The delicate, finely cut leaves are a dark green on top and dark red or purple underneath. It is winter-hardy in colder regions, rated for Zones 5–11, and can spend the entire winter out of doors, even when the winds are blustery and ice forms on the pond. It benefits from being cut back for the winter to below the freeze line and being protected from fish. In the summer, it grows stems as long as 6 feet that reach to the water surface to display a multitude of small white flowers with bright yellow centers. Each plant spreads about 12 inches wide. *Cabomba caroliniana* grows in 1–10 feet of water in sun or shade and makes a versatile and attractive submerged aquatic in the backyard pond. It propagates from stem cuttings. Here are some other forms to try:

- *C. aquatica* has yellow flowers on green- or orange-red-leafed forms.
- *C. caroliniana* var. *flavida* has yellow new growth and pale yellow flowers.
- *C. caroliniana* 'Silver Green' has white flowers and foliage with a silver sheen.
- *C. furcata* has purple-red leaves and pink flowers.
- *C. palaeformis* has white flowers and green- or bronze-leafed forms.

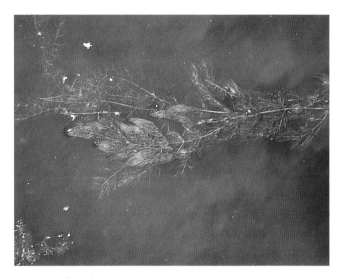

*Ceratophyllum demersum*

## *Ceratophyllum*
### hornwort
### Ceratophyllaceae

The sole member of its family, *Ceratophyllum* is also almost cosmopolitan in its distribution. Hornwort looks something like an underwater juniper bush. The genus includes about a half dozen species, or one species and several subspecies, and like junipers they are hard to tell apart. Hornwort is a many-branched submerged plant with thick, dense, dark green foliage. It grows in a fluffy floating mat with no true roots, and so has no need of pot or soil. It flowers in midsummer with very small white to creamy blooms that look more like pinecone pollen than flowers.

*Ceratophyllum demersum* is often sold commercially in the United States. It is native to North America and offers valuable habitat to fish and other wildlife, particularly in winter when little other foliage is available in the water. It grows 8–10 feet long in sun to part shade in water 1–10 feet deep, spreading 12 inches or more and forming large mats in a single season. It overwinters well in cold climates, being hardy in Zones 5–11. Allow it to sink to the bottom of the pond and protect it from fish for the winter, when it often continues to grow at a reduced level even under ice. It is adaptable to a wide range of water temperatures and is remarkably easy to propagate—just break off a bit and throw it into a new pond. Hornwort is highly resistant to potentially damaging fish and pests.

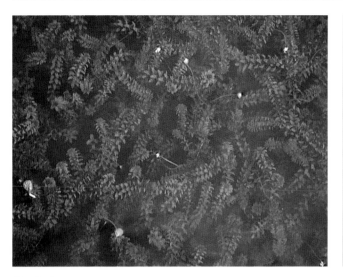

*Egeria densa*

*Egeria densa*

## *Egeria densa*
anacharis
Hydrocharitaceae

A more tender submerged plant native to South America, anacharis has shiny, fleshy leaves that radiate from a central stem. Cheerful and bright green, they resemble a submerged feather duster or feather boa. Three-petaled, white flowers float on the water surface in late summer, a reminder of the plant's presence down in the pond. It grows in sun to shade in water 1–10 feet deep. Its stems reach as long as 6–10 feet, but each plant spreads only about 12 inches. To overwinter anacharis in colder climates, bring in stem cuttings and keep them in an aquarium. They will quickly root and grow indoors and in fact have long been sold as aquarium plants. Anacharis will often overwinter outdoors successfully in Zone 5—cut it back to below the freeze line and protect it from fish. It is very vulnerable to fish and snails. Whether kept in an outdoor pond or an indoor aquarium, it does best potted and appreciates supplemental fertilization during the summer. It is great for removing phosphate from the water.

Because of its aggressive growth habit, *Egeria densa* is listed as a noxious weed in several states and is prohibited from sale or transport in those areas. Use *Elodea* to achieve a similar texture, although it is much smaller.

## *Elodea*
Hydrocharitaceae

Five species of *Elodea* have been identified, growing in and naturalized throughout much of the Americas as well as Europe, Asia, and Australia. *Elodea* grows well in fairly cool water that is on the alkaline side. It does best in fine sand

*Elodea canadensis*

with a small amount of organic matter. It grows in full sun or shade, but becomes much more stringy in shade. It spreads 12 inches and reaches 2 inches to 6 feet tall from the base of the plant. Water depth can be as little as 6 inches or as much as 40 feet, as long as it is clear. Propagate it from stem cuttings and feed it only occasionally. It is suitable for smaller ponds that do not have fish, which like to graze on its foliage and can easily break its brittle stems. *Elodea* is great for the native pond with a few native fish, like sunfish or blue gills, that do not eat plants.

Often mistaken for the dreaded *Hydrilla*, a most pernicious water weed that is illegal to grow, sell, or transport anywhere in the United States, *Elodea* is easily distinguished because it has only three leaves at each segment. *Hydrilla* has

Fontinalis

Hydrilla verticillata

five leaves per segment. *Elodea* is widely available in England because it does so well in the cool pond temperatures. It has female flowers with three small white petals that float on the water surface much like those of *Egeria densa*, a member of the same family. The flowers bloom in late summer, or whenever the stems reach the surface. Male flowers are rarely produced because the male plants themselves are rare. Flowers are not often fertilized and the plant usually spreads by fragments rather than seed production. It is less prone to snail attacks than *Egeria densa*, and much hardier, making it a nuisance in Europe, where it is called the American waterweed. It overwinters as an evergreen and continues to photosynthesize even under ice, albeit at a reduced rate. Hardy in Zones 3–9.

## *Fontinalis*
**willow moss**
**Sphagnaceae**

This is the ultimate spawning media, soft and covered with small scale-like leaves to which eggs easily adhere. Many forms of this non-flowering, worldwide plant exist, from "rooted" ones that grow attached to rocks in the stream or waterfall, to free-floating forms that grow in the pond. They require fairly clean water and are a good indicator of water quality in the pond system. They are difficult to grow if the pond has green water problems or hard water. They thrive in neutral to slightly basic water and do very well in full shade or part sun. They need water just deep enough to keep them covered. Hardy in Zones 3–11, depending on the species, they are evergreen, just slowing their growth in winter. The most available is usually the tropical form for fish tanks,

*Fontinalis antipyretica*. Propagate by tearing off chunks and rubberbanding to rocks or tucking into cracks in the stream or waterfall.

## *Hottonia palustris*
**water violet**

Longtime water gardener and writer Philip Swindells calls this "probably the finest hardy submerged aquatic, but one of the most fickle." He says that it is a "beautiful plant with large whorls of bright green foliage and spikes of whitish or lilac-tinted blossoms. Rarely does this succeed when introduced into a newly established pool. Produces turions of winter buds which ensure its distribution to other parts of the pool where the following season it may reappear unexpectedly. Readily increased from summer stem cuttings" (*The Complete Book of the Water Garden*, 1990, Overlook Press: Woodstock, N.Y.). It requires still, mineral-free, slightly acidic water that is 4–24 inches deep. It spreads to 6 inches, and the flower stems can be up to 9 inches above the water. Grows in sun to part shade. It is hardy in Zones 4–7, but this plant is not often grown in the U.S. because it can be difficult to establish. It is well worth a try. *Hottonia inflata* is a form with white flowers.

## *Hydrilla verticillata*
**Hydrocharitaceae**

A member of the family Hydrocharitaceae along with *Egeria*, *Elodea*, and *Lagarosiphon*, which it closely resembles, the sole species *Hydrilla verticillata* is considered one of the most troublesome submerged weeds in the world. Hydrilla grows from any remnant piece of foliage, stem, or root, no matter how small, and can quickly engulf an entire pond with its thin, extremely brittle foliage. It can spread to cover a half-acre pond in just two seasons. Leaves are thin and pointed, whorled around the central stem in sets of five or six. Flowers float just at the water surface, but are small and inconsequential to the naked eye. It grows in sun to shade in water 4 inches to 10 feet deep. Hardy in Zones 5–11, or possibly as cold as Zone 3, it overwinters as turions or as a green plant. It seems to be impervious to pests, though manatees like it, I hear. If found in a pond or as a remnant piece on a boat, fishing pole, or so on, it should be removed and thrown away. Never grow hydrilla in your pond. Many other underwater plants are more ornamental, less invasive additions to the water garden.

## Lagarosiphon
**Hydrocharitaceae**

Nine species of *Lagarosiphon* are reported growing in Africa and naturalized throughout Europe, North America, and Australasia. It is remarkably similar in appearance to *Egeria* at first glance. On closer inspection, *Lagarosiphon* has alternate leaves, rather than whorled, which grow more closely curled back to the main stem. It has the apearance of a fluffy feather boa. Like *Egeria*, *Lagarosiphon* is a pernicious weed in many parts of the world and is listed as a noxious weed in the United States. Still often sold as *Egeria crispa* or *Elodea crispa* in the pet trade, it has been shipped to me repeatedly as *Egeria densa*. *Lagarosiphon* is readily available in England, where it is one of the best known and most widely planted submerged aquatic plants. Grows in sun to shade in clear water as deep as 10 feet or more and fares well in flowing water. It spreads 12–24 inches and its stems reach to only about 6 feet or so. Once they reach the surface in summer, if the water is not too deep, they send white flowers floating out on the water. Hardy in Zones 5–11, it overwinters as an evergreen below the freeze line. Propagate by stem cuttings. It is a favorite of fish—I cannot grow it in ponds with koi.

## Myriophyllum
**milfoil**
**Haloragaceae**

With about 60 reported species, *Myriophyllum* is virtually cosmopolitan in its distribution. It is part of the family Haloragaceae, and like its relatives, produces both submerged and emerged foliage. One species native to North America and often available in the United States as an underwater plant is *M. heterophyllum*, commonly called fox-

*Lagarosiphon*

tail. A very winter-hardy underwater favorite, it has very thin, wispy leaves that grow from a stout central stem. Foliage is dark reddish brown and fluffy when submerged, not altogether unlike a fox's tail. It produces no noticeable flowers and is valued instead for its fuzzy-textured foliage. The emerged foliage is unsightly and should be removed—small, toothed leaves poke out of the water looking like they have been chewed off. Foxtail grows in sun to shade in water 1–10 feet deep. It spreads to 12 inches and produces stems about 6 feet long. Hardy in Zones 3–11. In all but the coldest climates, it overwinters in the pond with no special care or attention, even freezing solid without suffering any harm. Propagate by stem cuttings.

Two other species are sometimes mentioned in books and sold in stores, but they should be avoided. They are very invasive and hard to get rid of.

*Myriophyllum verticillatum*, or whorled milfoil, is smaller and maybe just a little more dense than *M. spicatum*.

Potamogeton

It has bright green, needle-like foliage carried in dense whorls on long stems. With its rather robust stretchy stem it can make another good plant for spawning fish.

*Myriophyllum spicatum*, either Eurasian or spiked milfoil, is a favorite plant for the fish fancier, with handsome, much divided foliage on long stretchy, slender stems that provide excellent spawning ground for goldfish. The foliage is coppery green in spring, turning bronze as summer progresses. As the stem reaches the surface it pushes up a tiny crimson spike with tiny, tiny yellow flowers. Sounds great, but it can fill an acre pond in two seasons from just a single piece. It grows to the surface and cuts off light and oxygen to the lower levels of the pond, killing everything. It is a noxious weed that is spread from lake to lake by fishermen and recreational boaters. In lined ornamental ponds annual cleaning and constant removal is needed to keep it under control.

*Myriophyllum spicatum* can be distinguished from native North American forms of milfoil because it has 14 or more pairs of leaflets, whereas native forms have fewer, usually 5 to 12 pairs of leaflets. Native forms are not as invasive, generally do not form a canopy, and do not spread so rapidly by stem fragments. Their overall growth is slower. One native form is *M. sibiricum*, called northern or spiked water milfoil, which has feathery foliage and overwinters by rhizomes and winter buds. It grows in water 13–14 feet deep and does not grow well in lakes with reduced water clarity.

Looking similar to *M. spicatum* but behaving much better are three additional species. Look for *M. pinnatum*, *M. humile*, and *M. tuberculatum*.

## *Potamogeton*
### pondweed
### Potamogetonaceae

Almost 100 species are in this cosmopolitan genus. These also crossbreed to produce interspecies hybrids. A relative few are showy and appropriate for the pond—most others are very weedy. Named from the Greek words "potamos," meaning river, and "geiton," neighbor. Several species grow with both submerged and floating foliage, some having so much difference between the two forms of leaf growth that they appear to be entirely separate plants. Flowers are often small, borne on club-like structures that stand out of the water but that are not highly ornamental. Leaves are glossy, leathery, and highly decorative, forming a mat that shades out sunlight and keeps algae at bay. Several species are native to North America and are hardy even in colder climates, overwintering in the pond by forming nutlets or turions that rest at the pond floor until spring returns. All species of *Potamogeton* are easily propagated by stem cuttings, as they root freely from their stems. Some species tolerate brackish waters.

Submerged foliage of *Potamogeton crispus*

Floating foliage of *Potamogeton illinoensis*

*Potamogeton illinoensis*

## *Potamogeton crispus*
### curly pondweed

Leaves of this pondweed are thin and wavy, like crinkly red tin foil at the outer edges. It is very showy, presenting a nice, red look in the pond. Naturalized in North America and native to Europe, it is an important source of food for waterfowl, and the submerged leaves make good spawning ground for fish. Curly pondweed has an odd growth cycle—it grows even in the coldest months of winter, then goes dormant in the hot days of summer. When the water warms in spring, the plant produces a fresh flush of leaves that are wider and have wavy edges. Then in midsummer when the water warms to above 75°F, the plant begins to go dormant. It produces dark brown turions with sharp, jagged edges that can be found among the foliage. The leaves begin to decay and fall away. When the cool waters return in the fall, the turions germinate and grow winter leaves, which are flat, khaki-green, and narrower and more "translucent" than the summer foliage. The winter leaves are wavy, but not so much so as the spring growth. Curly pondweed grows best in waters that will not warm considerably during the summer, or where other submerged plants can take over for the warmer months.

Curly pondweed is very invasive in earth-bottom ponds, so never discard into natural waters. With its running spread, it grows in water 1–10 feet deep, its stems growing 2–6 feet long. It grows in sun to part shade, but needs sun for best color. It sends up a cream-colored flower spike in late spring. Propagate by division, turions, or stem cuttings. Overwinter by keeping below the freeze line. Hardy in Zones 3–11.

Several additional species sold commercially are showy and native to North America—these should be considered

*Ranunculus longirostris*, terrestrial form

*Ranunculus longirostris*, submerged form

for the pond: *Potamogeton amplifolius* (large-leafed pondweed, bass weed, musky weed), *P. illinoensis* (Illinois pondweed), *P. nodosus* (long-leafed pondweed, American pondweed), *P. pulcher*, *P. perfoliatus*, and *P. richardsonii*. They all have larger submerged foliage and larger, stouter stems that are easier to remove, if needed, or to transplant. They can still be invasive in an earth-bottom pond so use common sense.

## *Ranunculus*
### Ranunculaceae

The genus *Ranunculus* includes more than 400 species, about three dozen of which grow in aquatic conditions. Found throughout all temperate and tropical regions of the world, a few are often sold for their underwater ornamental value. These grow well in sun to part shade in water 1–6 feet deep. They spread about 12 inches wide, with stems reaching 6 inches to 4 feet long or more. They flower on the water's surface in late spring or early summer. Hardy in Zones 4–11, they overwinter easily below the freeze line, and propagate readily from stem cuttings. Koi destroy them, however.

## *Ranunculus longirostris*
### white water buttercup, white water crowfoot

White water buttercup has leaves that are very finely cut, open, and airy, almost thread-like. They are borne alternately, radiating from a central stem. Although it resembles fanwort (*Cabomba*), which has opposite leaves, white water buttercup has foliage that is less dense. It also starts growing earlier in the spring and prefers cooler water. White water buttercup has larger flowers that float on the water surface,

and it is more brittle than fanwort, with stems that break easily when handled. White water buttercup grows quickly from leaf nodes and branches very readily. In still or slow moving water, it can form dense stands. This North American native is very ornamental and should find a home in all ponds. It is not invasive. Large stands of it are very beautiful in flower, looking like snow on the water. *Ranunculus trichophyllus* is a hard-to-find species that is just like a small *R. longirostris*, and *R. aquatilis* is the European version of *R. longirostris*.

## *Ranunculus flabellaris*
### yellow water crowfoot

This plant grows just like white water buttercup with all the accompanying needs and likes. The distinction between the two species is the leaf division, which is always flat for *Ranunculus flabellaris*, compared to the more thread-like appearance of *R. longirostris*. This difference is important for botanists but difficult for the layperson to see or appreciate. Easier, and just as significant, is to remember that *R. flabellaris* has yellow flowers and *R. longirostris* has white. This species is also native to North America, but excluding the Gulf states.

## *Sagittaria*
### arrowhead
### Alismataceae

A few species of *Sagittaria* are grown as underwater plants for the pond. Other species are more emergent, and are discussed in Chapter 7. Like their more emergent cousins, underwater sagittarias produce white flowers in summer.

While the plant remains submerged, the flowers float on the water surface. Plants spread by creeping stolons to form sods or colonies. They are great for ponds by offering extra surface area for bacteria to colonize and aid in filtration. They overwinter outdoors in cold ponds without special protection other than ensuring that they stay below the freeze line. They cannot freeze solid.

### Sagittaria natans
### underwater arrowhead

Looking very much like *Vallisneria*, *Sagittaria natans* has a much more plastic look and feel to it. It is less brittle than *Vallisneria* but not quite as easily moved by the water. Because it is sturdier, the North American native holds up better to koi and large goldfish. Wonderfully, it flowers, with the largest blossoms of all the submerged plants listed here. Flowers are up to ½ inch in diameter, white, summer-blooming, and held on the water surface. The plant grows in sun or shade and is very easy. It is one of the first plants up in the spring, and so is a great aid in removing fish waste, thereby reducing the degree of algae bloom in the spring pond. Each plant's foliage can cover 6 inches and spread by creeping slowly and sending up new plants. It is fine in earth-bottom ponds, where it forms a sod to hold the soil together. It grows 12–36 inches tall from the bottom of the pond. Water depth should be 24–36 inches to promote flowering—it will grow in deeper water but may not flower. Propagate by dividing the underground stolons of the offshoots. Hardy in Zones 4–11. Crayfish will destroy it, and China mark moth will damage foliage that reaches the surface.

### Sagittaria subulata
### dwarf sagittaria

Like its larger cousins, dwarf sagittaria produces a single white flower, floating it upon the water surface intermittently throughout the summer. With its diminutive habit of just 4–6 inch foliage and running spread, it forms a submerged sod on the bottom of the pond. It grows in water from 4 inches to 6 feet deep. In water deeper than 12 inches, it may never flower, but the service it provides is invaluable nonetheless. Because it is short, it will not interfere with boat motors in a natural lake. Its shallow roots make it easily removed from an earth-bottom pond, too. If the pond fish dig it up, plant it in a shallow tray of sand and top it off with

*Utricularia*

pea gravel. Dwarf sagittaria is easy to grow, especially in full sun. It may prove to be a weak grower in full shade. Watch for crayfish. Propagate by dividing the underground stolons of the offshoots. Hardy in Zones 4–11. Native to North America. Also try *Sagittaria subulata* var. *kurziana*.

### Utricularia
### bladderwort
### Lentibulariaceae

A member of a carnivorous family, the genus *Utricularia* comprises about 260 species, found naturalized in most of the temperate and tropical climates of the world. Many species are native to North America and provide food and cover for fish. Bladderworts make unusual submerged plants for the pond or the aquarium. Some have very fine foliage, resembling soft hornwort (*Ceratophyllum*). Others are so fine that they look almost like floating green bits of hairnet or string algae. Look closely and you will see nestled among the foliage the tiny "bladders" that trap prey, microscopic creatures that are unwary enough to trigger the bladders' openings only to get sucked in and digested. The foliage grows as floating mats underwater—some species can reach several feet in length and spread. Each stem is usually 2–24 inches or more long and 1–6 inches wide. Their late-summer flowers can be shades of yellow, white, pink, or purple. The dainty blossoms stand above the water surface and resemble small snapdragons. Submerged bladderworts do not produce roots, so no soil or potting is necessary. These are fascinating and great for kids.

When your pond reaches the stage in which bladderworts grow, you have a pond that will grow many plants. Bladderworts do not tolerate new ponds or those high in hardness, but three- or four-year-old ponds should be suitable. Most prefer neutral to acidic water conditions in full sun to part shade. Bladderworts float just below the surface, so the water has to be just deep enough to keep them covered. Hardy in Zones 3–11, they form overwintering buds that should be allowed to sink below the freeze line, or bring plants or buds indoors into a fish tank. Propagate by stem cuttings. The best species to grow submerged are *Utricularia minor*, which is very easy; *U. vulgaris*, which is very large, like hornwort; *U. radiata*; *U. inflata*; and *U. floridana*, which is quite large and showy. All these have yellow flowers. A purple-flowered option is *U. purpurea*.

## *Vallisneria*
## eelgrass
## Hydrocharitaceae

At least four species of *Vallisneria* are reported, all growing naturally in tropical or temperate regions of the world. Each has long, tape-like leaves and female flowers that float just at the water surface. Male flowers are released underwater, each enclosed in an "envelope" containing an air bubble that causes it to float to the surface. As the male flower sails on the water, chance may bring it to a female flower, which it then pollinates. Once fertilized, the female flower falls back beneath the surface. The plants are wonderfully ornamental near the base of a waterfall or in the deep pockets of a stream where the foliage can ripple in the moving water. Vallisnerias grow from underground rhizomes to form sods or large colonies in earthen ponds. They are easily controlled by raking the sods—this dislodges the plants so that they float to the surface to be skimmed off. Geese and coots use a similar method to ravage the vallisnerias in our ponds. Small fish appreciate them because they are excellent cover for hiding from predators.

## *Vallisneria americana*
## tape grass, water celery

This species is the most common in the trade, the true identity of many misnamed forms. It is very versatile and easy to grow, adapting to a wide range of conditions. Foliage is thin, almost transparent, and slightly jagged at the edges. Water celery grows well even in turbid waters and tolerates a wide range of pH variance. It can tolerate brackish water up to approximately 500 parts per million and a high nutrient load. It prefers coarse silt to slightly sandy soil in 1–15 feet of water, depending on the cultivar. It grows in sun to shade with a running spread, its stems generally reaching 24–36 inches long but also up to 6 feet in some selections. It grows hardy rhizomes and tubers and is very important for wildfowl, especially canvasbacks. Muskrats, crayfish, and coots can harm it. Hardy in Zones 4–11, it will overwinter in the pond if placed below the freeze line. Propagate by division from the runners. Recommended forms follow:

'Asiatica'—its green foliage is twisted but the same size as that of 'Crystal'

var. *biwaënsis*—a corkscrew form with green foliage almost ½ inch wide

'Contortionist'—very twisty and large, almost ½ inch wide

'Crystal'—looks like pulled green glass with air bubbles in it

'Giant'—wide leaves, 1 inch or more across, reach up to several feet in length

'Jungle'—broad, green foliage

'Red Jungle'—broad, burgundy foliage ½ inch wide

# CHAPTER 12

# PESTS AND DISEASES

## ANIMALS

Animals are one of the most destructive things that can happen to a water garden. Literally overnight they can destroy a pond—at our nursery we had 1,500 pots chewed up by a baby muskrat in one night. He found the pond in the evening after we closed, and when we opened the next morning we found in the corner a mound of all the plant remains and a tired little muskrat. Two deer used to come and eat all the new flowers every morning at dawn, giving us three weeks of no flowers on 9,000 lilies. A flock of coots once flew into our 60×90-foot display pond and uprooted two dozen lilies, eating them down to nothing. Another time, four geese ate 10,000 plants of *Vallisneria americana* 'Jungle' in the three days that they visited. The results of animal pests can be swift and devastating.

A happy dog with *Persicaria virginiana* 'Painter's Palette' and *Oenanthe sarmentosa* in the foreground

Heron

Swan

Damage from ducks

Dog

## Birds

Herons are a worry for the fish of the pond, but others can do a lot of harm to the plants. Geese, swans, even ducks, although they are fun to see visiting the pond, they love the very same plants you do but for food and nest building. Geese and swans are less damaging to waterlilies than coots, but they love grassy things: sedges, vallisnerias, juncus. Anything grassy-looking is fair game for geese and swans. Ducks tear up plants but seem to do their damage by nesting in the plants rather than really eating them. Coots love to feed on aquatic plants as they migrate, so you need to move them along in their migration.

Harassment is the best we have been able to do for birds. Loud noises, sprays from a garden hose, dogs, picking up their nests—all give birds the idea thay are not welcome. We have had much success with a motion-activated sprinkler. Also, a low fence or string 6–8 inches high helps keep geese out of the pond.

## Cats

Cats are generally there for the fish buffet. They are usually only destructive if they fall in and tear a hole in the pond liner with their claws, but they also can stand on plants as they get to the pond. A quick spray of water and they are gone. A motion-activated sprinkler deters cats too.

## Crayfish

Crayfish move into a pond unbeknownst to the pondkeeper and start eating away at the base of the plants, dislodging them and usually eating the crowns. With a few crayfish in a pond, the submerged plants will be gone in no time, espe-

cially if they are sagittarias or vallisnerias. Crayfish are best controlled with those methods used for parasites on fish. In all-plant ponds, some people have used pesticides on them, such as Dimilin from Aquarium Pharmaceuticals in Chalfont, Pennsylvania.

## Deer

Deer pose a browsing problem, as they do for the rest of the garden. We have found that they often enter the ponds that have broad shelves and can put holes in the liner. We have also noticed that they love waterlily flowers and need to be repelled to prevent the constant loss of flowers. Scarecrow sprinklers have been the most cost effective and easiest solution.

## Dogs

Dogs are a problem when they cannot resist playing in the water. Dogs bred for water are worse, often using the pond as a personal water hole. Training them to stay out or installing a fence may be necessary. A motion-activated spinkler is no help—it just becomes a game.

## Koi

Koi are the colorful fish that give movement and interest to a backyard pond, but they have a dark side. They are the tyrannosaurs of the pond when it comes to plants. They can be great and never touch the plants—then one day you find mud and coleslaw. And koi, when they decide to eat your plants, are far more destructive than goldfish due to the shape and size of the mouth. The koi are not at fault—they

Koi

Koi

are plant eaters and we put our plants directly in harm's way when we add them to the pond. The only way to control their entirely natural tendency to eat plants is by making the plants inaccessible to the fish. Either place them in separate ponds, install underwater net barriers, or keep the plants in the shallower areas of the pond that the fish cannot reach. Oxygenating plants can be grown in cages to protect them much like vegetable gardeners do to keep out rabbits. Koi less than 10 inches are generally well behaved, and keeping just a few large fish in a large pond with lots of plants will generally limit damage.

## Mice and Voles

Voles and mice are generally not a problem for plants until winter, when they use them for food and cover. Reduce this problem by cutting grasses back and cleaning up around the pond. Mice can also chew through the pond liner to make

Damage from fish

nests in the dry comfort underneath. The best control is trapping. I use live traps to monitor who is being caught, then I relocate or destroy them.

## Muskrats

These little guys love to burrow through the pond liner and build tunnels. They also love to collect plants both to build their homes and to eat, so they are doubly destructive. A scarecrow sprinkler does not help too much with them, as it does for raccoons, so catch-and-release becomes the best method of control. Use cage traps and they will be easy to move. Cover the trap to make a cave and put apples inside—they love apples.

## Nutria

Nutria are giant plant-eating rodents imported from South America for the fur trade. They have escaped and natural-ized in some areas of the country and can devastate a pond like muskrats, but on a grander scale. Nutria are not native, so once caught, they become an issue for the local Depart-ment of Natural Resources or Animal Control. Never release these pests back into the wild.

## Raccoons

Though raccoons are more associated with the destruction of pond wildlife, like fish and frogs, they can do a lot of plant damage while foraging for these in your pond. They also seem to love chewing up water hyacinth (*Eichhornia*). They can destroy dozens of the plants in a single night, just chew-ing them up rather than eating them. They will tip over pots and uproot things in search of their prize. A motion-acti-vated sprinkler is great to control these pests—it turns on when anything passes into its range, spraying the beasts with a short blast of water.

## Snails

Snails these can be a blessing or a scourge, depending on type. Snails are sold to eat algae, and they do that in fish tanks with plastic plants, but many sold in pet shops and in pond shops also eat plants. Apple snails and Columbian ram's horn snails are voracious eaters, attacking waterlilies and other plants that are found below the water surface. See Chapter 11 for more information. Hand picking seems to be the only cure. Recent studies show that caffeine can kill them, but more needs to be done.

Aphids

Aphids

## INSECTS

### Aphids

Aphids, whether black, green, or yellow, are all destructive and cause a lot of damage, yellowing leaves and destroying buds and flowers. Their activity usually attracts other insects. My favorite controls are small fish, frequently wash-ing them into the water, or raising the water level to over-flowing and rinsing them out of the pond. Diatomaceous earth has also proven to work when dusted onto the plants. Poking holes in their exoskeletons is also very effective. An herbal control made of thyme and mint oil is made by Aquarium Pharmaceuticals and is safe for fish.

China mark moth

China mark moth and damage

China mark moth

## China Mark Moth

China mark moth is the most prevalent of the water damaging insects. It is also easy to control with a safe organic solution. China mark moth cuts little pieces of plant material to cover itself while it sleeps or feeds. It tends to cut new pieces every day, stripping plants of their leaves. The moths are generally confined to waterlilies and waterlily-like plants, but they will float off to infect other plants. In heavy infestations any plant touching the water surface is attacked. Large infestations make the pond look like it is slowly being chopped into coleslaw. To control this pest *Bacillus thuringiensis* var. *kurstaki* (Btk) has been shown to be effective in control and has proven totally safe for fish and dragonflies. This is the organic pest control used to control cabbage loopers and corn borers.

## Cucumber Beetles

Cucumber beetles are little yellow- and black-striped beetles that do a great job of destroying the flowers of *Gratiola*, *Canna*, and *Butomus*. They are hard to get rid of. Sevin dust—applied out of the pond—helps but new beetles just fly in from the surrounding fields. Vacuuming them up with a Dustbuster helps control them. Diatomaceous earth also is a good control.

## Caddysfly Larvae

Caddysfly larvae do little damage but in high numbers they can be annoying, constantly chewing off bits of plants to add to their protective cases. Fish usually control these pests, but the pesticide Dimilin will also.

Dragonfly, a helper not a pest

Dragonflies mean fewer bugs

Japanese beetles

## Dragonflies

I list dragonflies here to dispel the myth that they harm plants. They eat bugs and are great for a pond—every pond should have them. More dragonflies means fewer bugs. Large fish can eat dragonfly larvae though.

## Japanese Beetles

Japanese beetles damage a lot of plants in my garden and they also damage marginal water plants. Most prone to their attack are water cannas and taros (*Colocasia*). The most resistant seem to be juncus. The big fleshy leaves seem to really appeal to the beetles and they do a lot of damage. I use a Dustbuster to vacuum them up and destroy them. I have found little else that works. Beetle traps help some. A new product called Japanese beetle repellent is made with Neem and has been helpful but needs to be applied often.

## Lotus Borer

Lotus borer often shows up after lotus have been growing in the pond for a few years. The borers are generally not visible, but you can find a small hole on the petiole and frass around the hole. The leaves and flowers often collapse from the compromised petioles or flower stalks. Sometimes the plants

Mealybugs

Weevil damage

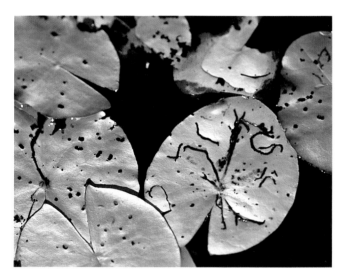

Weevil damage

yellow, but either way they are weakened and flowering is reduced. Lotus borers rarely cause fatalities. They are best controlled by removing affected foliage and cleaning up well at the end of the season. *Bacillus thuringiensis* var. *kurstaki* (Btk) is not that effective because the insect is inside the leaf petiole. Some water gardeners have said injecting Btk into the borer hole is effective, but I have never tried this.

## Mealybugs

Mealybugs can be difficult to combat in the water garden. I have never had a problem with them in an outdoor situation, but indoors while overwintering is another matter. I use houseplant insecticides for tall plants or submerge plants in a bucket with a little soap—two or three drops per gallon

of water—for two to three days. Or, cut plants back severely if you can safely move them outside and into the pond.

## Spider Mites

Spider mites are generally not a problem except in winter storage and in very hot dry summers. If they do show up, then submerging the affected plants for a day or two usually solves the problem. If not, remove the offending plants and spray with a pesticide. Wait a day or two, then rinse the plants and return them to the pond.

## Weevils

I have problems with weevils only on waterlily leaves and hibiscus flowers—if they have been on anything else they have not caused enough damage to mention. The best and

Whiteflies

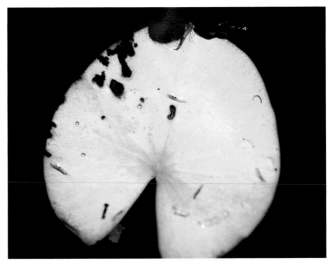

Crown rot

# DISEASES

## Crown Rot

Crown rot is the most devastating disease for waterlilies. It spreads by infected plants being introduced to the pond, and experts say there is no control but destruction of infected plants. This sounds bad, but many waterlily varieties are resistant and show little effect from the infection but those that are susceptible are badly affected. Yellowing leaves in midsummer and no new growth are indicators of the disease as well as the crowns eventually rotting away. If this happens, buy a different variety and go on. If you are a waterlily collector, though, select very small plants of the variety, wash them free of soil, and soak in a fungicide such as Subdue Maxx.

most effective control is removal of the affected plant parts. To prevent the weevils from spreading, freeze any saved hibiscus seed or dust it in diatomaceous earth.

## Whiteflies

Whiteflies usually go for *Hibiscus*, *Gymnocoronis*, *Mentha*, *Mimulus*, and *Ruellia*, but they have shown up on other plants also. Submerge the plants for two or three days, or remove them from the pond and spray with a pesticide. Maverik is also very effective for controlling whiteflies.

## Fusarium

Fusarium is a common soil- or water-borne fungus that affects only a few aquatics, such as *Mimulus guttatus*, *Myosotis scorpioides*, and *Pistia stratiotes*. For control use a fungicide like Subdue out of the pond, or spray affected plants with a 5–10 percent solution of hydrogen peroxide—the stuff you buy at the drugstore works great.

## Rust

Rust is another disease of cannas, but this one is curable. Canna rust will appear as orange dust on the leaves. Cut off and remove affected foliage as you find it. In the fall when the cannas should be dormant, cut the foliage to the ground and remove it from the pond. Spray the remaining crown with a solution of 10 percent bleach. I also remove the top inch of soil from the plant and add new soil. These measures should prevent new infection when the new shoots emerge in the spring.

## Sooty Mold

Sooty mold is accompanied by an insect infestation and is the result of the insects giving off a sugary secretion called honeydew. The fungus feeds on both the honeydew and the plant. I spray with a 5–10 percent solution of hydrogen peroxide.

## Virus

Viruses are everywhere and can affect virtually any plant. The one most often encountered in the pond is canna virus. The plants look burned and never recover. Each new shoot is affected. The only control is to destroy the plant and start over. Canna virus is spread by sucking insects, and in my case Japanese beetles were the vectors.

Virus

# Plants for Special Places and Purposes

## PLANTS TO FILTER POND WATER

These plants are all excellent for filtering algae out of pond water. They provide filtration wherever they are located in the pond, but they are more efficient if planted where there is some water flow. Use them in a stream, waterfall or biological filter, or in a bog that is designed to accommodate water plants.

*Acorus calamus*
*Acorus calamus* 'Variegatus'
*Alternanthera philoxeroides*
*Bacopa lenagera* 'Variegata'
*Cyperus alternifolius*
*Cyperus papyrus*
*Eichhornia azurea*
*Eichhornia crassipes*
*Eleocharis parvula*
*Eleocharis vivipara*
*Glyceria aquatica* 'Variegata'
*Hydrocotyle ranunculoides* 'Ruffles'
*Hydrocotyle umbellata*
*Iris pseudacorus* and cultivars
*Iris versicolor* and cultivars
*Iris virginica* and cultivars
*Juncus balticus* 'Spiralis'
*Juncus effusus* and cultivars
*Juncus inflexus*
*Juncus inflexus* 'Afro'
*Juncus polyanthemus*
*Juncus* spp., African thatching rush
*Ludwigia arcuta*
*Ludwigia arcuta* 'Grandiflora'
*Ludwigia peruviana*
*Mentha aquatica*
*Oenanthe javanica* 'Flamingo'
*Oenanthe sarmentosa*
*Pistia stratiotes*
*Pistia stratiotes* 'Aqua Velvet'
*Sagittaria latifolia*
*Sagittaria sinensis*
*Scirpus*
*Tillaea recurva*
*Typha*

## PLANTS SUITABLE FOR PATIO AND TABLE-TOP PONDS

*Acorus calamus*
*Acorus calamus* 'Variegatus'
*Acorus gramineus* and cultivars
*Alternanthera reineckii*
*Azolla caroliniana*
*Azolla pinnata*
*Bacopa caroliniana*
*Bacopa lenagera* 'Variegata'
*Bacopa monnieri*
*Baldellia ranunculoides* f. *repens*
*Baumea rubiginosa* 'Variegata'
*Carex flacca*
*Carex flacca* 'Bias'
*Carex muskingumensis*
*Carex muskingumensis* 'Oehme'
*Ceratopteris thalictroides*
*Colocasia esculenta* 'Black Magic'
*Cotula coronopifolia*
*Cyperus alternifolius* 'Gracilis'
*Cyperus isocladus*
*Dichromena*
*Echinodorus cordifolius* 'Marble Queen'
*Eichhornia azurea*

*Eichhornia crassipes*
*Eleocharis parvula*
*Eleocharis vivipara*
*Glyceria aquatica* 'Variegata'
*Hydrocleys nymphoides*
*Hydrocotyle bonariensis*
*Hydrocotyle lemnoides*
*Hydrocotyle ranunculoides*
*Hydrocotyle ranunculoides* 'Ruffles'
*Hydrocotyle sibthorpioides* 'Variegata'
*Hydrocotyle verticillata* 'Little Umbrellas'
*Hygrophila corymbosa* 'Stricta'
*Hygrophila difformis* 'Variegata'
*Hymenocallis caribaea* 'Variegata'
*Isolepis prolifer*
*Juncus balticus* 'Spiralis'
*Juncus decipiens* 'Curly-wurly'
*Juncus effusus* 'Cuckoo'
*Juncus effusus* 'Gold Strike'
*Juncus effusus* 'Spiralis'
*Juncus glaucus*
*Juncus inflexus*
*Juncus inflexus* 'Afro'
*Juncus polyanthemus*
*Juncus* spp., African thatching rush
*Laurentia palustris*
*Lemna*
*Limbonium spongeanum*
*Ludwigia peploides*
*Ludwigia repens*
*Lysimachia nummularia* 'Aurea'
*Marsilea drummondii*
*Marsilea mutica*
*Marsilea mutica* 'Micro Mini'
*Marsilea quadrifolia*
*Marsilea schelpiana*
*Mentha pulegium*

*Mimulus guttatus* 'Variegatus'
*Mimulus* 'Lothian Fire'
*Myosotis scorpioides* 'Mermaid'
*Myosotis scorpioides* 'Pinkie'
*Myosotis scorpioides* 'Snowflakes'
*Myosotis scorpioides* 'Wisconsin'
*Neptunia aquatica*
*Nymphoides aquatica*
*Nymphoides crenata*
*Nymphoides cristata*
*Nymphoides geminata*
*Nymphoides indica*
*Oenanthe javanica* 'Flamingo'
*Oenanthe sarmentosa*
*Physostegia leptophylla*
*Pistia stratiotes*
*Pistia stratiotes* 'Aqua Velvet'
*Pontederia cordata* 'Crown Point'
*Pontederia cordata* 'Spoon River'
*Ranunculus flammula*
*Ranunculus flammula* 'Thor'
*Regnellidium diphyllum*
*Rotala rotundifolia*
*Ruellia brittoniana* 'Chi Chi'
*Ruellia brittoniana* 'Katie'
*Ruellia brittoniana* 'Strawberries and Cream'
*Sagittaria* 'Bloomin' Baby'
*Sagittaria latifolia* 'Flore Pleno'
*Sagittaria natans*
*Sagittaria sinensis*
*Salvinia molesta*
*Samolus parviflorus*
*Tillaea recurva*
*Typha minima*
*Veronica americana*
*Veronica beccabunga*
*Wedelia trilobata*

## WATER PLANTS THAT TOLERATE SHADE

Gardeners associate water plants with full sun and sometimes think water plants will not grow in the shade. They overlook many impressive shade-loving water plants, such as the ones in the following list. Shade that is created by trees presents a special challenge to the water gardener. Trees produce leaves, twigs, branches, and seeds. If you want to put a pond where there are a lot of trees, use a netting to reduce the amount of tree debris that will fall in the pond. Another alternative is to invest in a good pond vaccuum and have a regular maintenance schedule to remove leaf debris from the pond. Or, install a skimmer box. The water flows through a weir and into a net, which you can remove at the edge of the pond.

*Acorus calamus*
*Acorus calamus* 'Variegatus'
*Acorus gramineus* 'Ogon'
*Acorus gramineus* 'Variegatus'
*Acrostichum danaeifolium*
*Alisma plantago-aquatica*
*Alternanthera philoxeroides*
*Alternanthera reineckii*
*Apios americana*
*Aponogeton distachyus*
*Azolla caroliniana*
*Azolla pinnata*
*Bacopa caroliniana*
*Bacopa lenagera* 'Variegata'
*Bacopa monnieri*
*Calla palustris*
*Caltha palustris*
*Carex flacca*
*Carex flacca* 'Bias'
*Carex muskingumensis*
*Carex muskingumensis* 'Oehme'
*Ceratopteris thalictroides*
*Colocasia esculenta*
*Colocasia esculenta* 'Black Magic'
*Colocasia esculenta* 'Metallica'
*Colocasia jensii*
*Crinum americanum*
*Cyperus alternifolius* 'Gracilis'
*Dichromena colorata*
*Dulichium arundinaceum*

*Echinodorus cordifolius*
*Eichhornia crassipes*
*Eleocharis parvula*
*Eleocharis vivipara*
*Elodea*
*Epilobium hirsutum*
*Equisetum fluviatile*
*Equisetum hyemale*
*Glyceria aquatica* 'Variegata'
*Gymnocoronis spilanthoides*
*Houttuynia cordata* 'Chameleon'
*Hydrocotyle americana*
*Hydrocotyle ranunculoides*
*Hydrocotyle ranunculoides* 'Ruffles'
*Hydrocotyle sibthorpioides* 'Variegata'
*Hydrocotyle umbellata*
*Hygrophila corymbosa* 'Stricta'
*Hygrophila difformis*
*Hygrophila difformis* 'Variegata'
*Hymenocallis liriosome*
*Ipomoea aquatica*
*Iris pseudacorus*
*Iris pseudacorus* 'Ecru'
*Iris pseudacorus* 'Ivory'
*Iris pseudacorus* 'Sun Cascade'
*Iris versicolor*
*Iris virginica*
*Juncus balticus* 'Spiralis'
*Juncus decipiens* 'Curly-wurly'
*Juncus effusus* 'Cuckoo'
*Juncus effusus* 'Gold Strike'
*Juncus inflexus*
*Juncus inflexus* 'Afro'
*Juncus polyanthemus*
*Juncus* spp., African thatching rush
*Laurentia palustris*
*Lemna*
*Limbonium spongeanum*
*Limnocharis flava*
*Lobelia siphilitica* 'Alba'
*Lobelia* 'Tania'
*Ludwigia arcuta* 'Grandiflora'
*Ludwigia repens*
*Lychnis flos-cuculi*
*Lycopus europaeus*
*Lysimachia ciliata*
*Lysimachia nummularia* 'Aurea'
*Lysimachia thyrsiflora*
*Marsilea drummondii*
*Marsilea mutica*
*Marsilea mutica* 'Micro Mini'
*Marsilea quadrifolia*
*Marsilea rotundifolia*
*Marsilea schelpiana*
*Mentha aquatica*

*Mentha pulegium*
*Menyanthes trifoliata*
*Mimulus alatus* 'Snow Crystal'
*Mimulus ringens*
*Myosotis scorpioides* 'Mermaid'
*Myosotis scorpioides* 'Pinkie'
*Myosotis scorpioides* 'Wisconsin'
*Myriophyllum aquaticum*
*Neptunia aquatica*
*Nymphoides aquatica*
*Nymphoides crenata*
*Nymphoides cristata*
*Nymphoides indica*
*Oenanthe javanica* 'Flamingo'
*Oenanthe sarmentosa*
*Orontium aquaticum*
*Peltandra virginica*
*Petasites hybridus*
*Phyla lanceolata*
*Physostegia leptophylla*
*Pistia stratiotes*
*Pistia stratiotes* 'Aqua Velvet'
*Potamogeton crispus*
*Proserpinaca palustris*
*Ranunculus longirostris*
*Ranunculus repens* 'Buttered Popcorn'
*Rotala rotundifolia*
*Ruellia brittoniana*
*Ruellia brittoniana* 'Chi Chi'
*Sagittaria latifolia* 'Brevifolia'
*Sagittaria latifolia* 'Flore Pleno'
*Sagittaria natans*
*Sagittaria sinensis*
*Salvinia longifolia*
*Samolus parviflorus*
*Saururus cernuus*
*Saururus cernuus* var. *ruminoides*
*Sium suave*
*Sparganium*
*Trapa bicornis*
*Vallisneria*
*Veronica americana*
*Veronica beccabunga*
*Wedelia trilobata*

## ROOTED FLOATERS

Arranging potted plants in the pond so that the pots don't show is sometimes tricky. We recommend using certain plants as under-plantings at the base of taller plants. These smaller plants can be planted with their larger neighbor or kept in their own pots. The following plants are especially favored because their stems float on the water surface but stay rooted in their container, so they won't float around all over the pond.

*Aeschynomene fluitans*
*Alternanthera philoxeroides*
*Bacopa monnieri*
*Calla palustris*
*Eichhornia azurea*
*Hydrocotyle ranunculoides* 'Ruffles'
*Hydrocotyle umbellata*
*Ipomoea aquatica*
*Limnocharis flava*
*Ludwigia arcuta*
*Ludwigia arcuta* 'Grandiflora'
*Marsilea mutica*
*Marsilea rotundifolia*
*Mentha aquatica*
*Menyanthes trifoliata*
*Myriophyllum aquaticum*
*Neptunia aquatica*
*Phyla lanceolata*
*Trapa bicornis*

## PLANTS FOR STREAMS AND WATERFALLS

*Acorus gramineus* and cultivars
*Alternanthera*
*Bacopa*
*Baldellia ranunculoides* f. *repens*
*Carex flacca*
*Carex flacca* 'Bias'
*Carex muskingumensis*
*Carex muskingumensis* 'Oehme'
*Cotula coronopifolia*
*Echinodorus cordifolius*
*Eleocharis acicularis*
*Eleocharis parvula*
*Eleocharis vivipara*
*Glyceria aquatica* 'Variegata'
*Hydrocotyle*
*Hygrophila difformis*
*Hygrophila difformis* 'Variegata'
*Ipomoea aquatica*
*Isolepis prolifer*
*Justicia americana*
*Laurentia palustris*
*Limnocharis flava*
*Ludwigia arcuta* 'Grandiflora'
*Ludwigia repens*
*Lysimachia nummularia* 'Aurea'
*Marsilea*
*Mentha aquatica*
*Mentha pulegium*

*Menyanthes trifoliata*
*Mimulus guttatus* 'Variegatus'
*Myosotis scorpioides* and
    cultivars
*Myriophyllum aquaticum*
*Neptunia aquatica*
*Oenanthe javanica* 'Flamingo'
*Oenanthe sarmentosa*
*Phyla lanceolata*
*Ranunculus*
*Regnellidium diphyllum*
*Rotala rotundifolia*
*Sagittaria subulata*
*Samolus parviflorus*
*Tillaea recurva*
*Veronica*
*Wedelia trilobata*

## PLANTS FOR ATTRACTING BUTTERFLIES

A list for all those pondkeepers who enjoy visits from butterflies. Many of these plants also attract hummingbirds.

*Asclepias incarnata*
*Asclepias incarnata* 'Ice Ballet'
*Canna* 'Endeavor'
*Canna* 'Erebus'
*Canna flaccida*
*Canna* 'Florence Vaughn'
*Canna* 'Intrigue'
*Canna* 'Panache'
*Canna* 'Pretoria'

*Canna* 'Ra'
*Canna* 'Taney'
*Cotula coronopifolia*
*Epilobium hirsutum*
*Gymnocoronis spilanthoides*
*Hygrophila corymbosa* 'Stricta'
*Hygrophila difformis* 'Variegata'
*Iris pseudacorus* and cultivars
*Iris versicolor* and cultivars
*Iris virginica* and cultivars
*Lobelia cardinalis*
*Lobelia cardinalis* 'Red Giant'
*Lobelia fulgens* 'Queen Victoria'
*Lobelia siphilitica*
*Lobelia siphilitica* 'Alba'
*Lobelia* 'Tania'
*Lysimachia ciliata*
*Lysimachia terrestris*

*Mentha aquatica*
*Mentha pulegium*
*Myosotis scorpioides* 'Pinkie'
*Myosotis scorpioides* 'Wisconsin'
*Nelumbo*
*Nymphaea*
*Phyla lanceolata*
*Physostegia leptophylla*
*Pontederia cordata* and cultivars
*Preslia cervina*
*Ranunculus acris*
*Ruellia brittoniana*
*Saururus cernuus*
*Saururus cernuus* var.
    *ruminoides*
*Sium suave*
*Stachys palustris*
*Veronica americana*

# Plants by Flower Color

To help with pond landscape planning, here are lists of water plants grouped according to bloom color and function in the pond.

## WHITE

### Hardy Marginals

*Alisma plantago-aquatica*
*Asclepias incarnata* 'Ice Ballet'
*Calla palustris*
*Cephalanthus occidentalis*
*Echinodorus*
*Hibiscus moscheutos*
*Justicia americana*
*Lobelia siphilitica* 'Alba'
*Lychnis flos-cuculi*
*Lycopus europaeus*
*Menyanthes trifoliata*
*Mimulus alatus* 'Snow Crystal'
*Myosotis scorpioides*
   'Snowflakes'
*Oenanthe javanica* 'Flamingo'
*Petasites hybridus*
*Pontederia cordata* 'Alba'
*Sagittaria* 'Bloomin' Baby'
*Sagittaria latifolia*
*Sagittaria latifolia* 'Brevifolia'
*Sagittaria latifolia* 'Flore Pleno'
*Sagittaria latifolia* 'Leopard
   Spot'
*Sagittaria sinensis*
*Samolus parviflorus*
*Sarracenia leucophylla*
*Saururus cernuus*
*Saururus cernuus* var.
   *ruminoides*

*Saururus chinensis*
*Sium suave*
*Tillaea recurva*

### Tropical Marginals

*Alternanthera philoxeroides*
*Alternanthera reineckii*
*Bacopa monnieri*
*Crinum americanum*
*Dichromena*
*Gymnocoronis spilanthoides*
*Hydrocotyle americana*
*Hymenocallis caribaea*
   'Variegata'
*Hymenocallis liriosome*
*Ipomoea aquatica*
*Sagittaria lancifolia*
*Sagittaria lancifolia*
   f. *ruminoides*
*Sagittaria montevidensis*

### Waterlily-like Plants

*Aponogeton distachyus*
*Nymphoides cristata*
*Nymphoides indica*

### Floating Plants

*Nymphoides aquatica*

### Submerged Plants

*Potamogeton crispus*
*Ranunculus longirostris*

### Hardy Waterlilies

*Nymphaea* 'Alba plenissima'
*Nymphaea* 'Candida'

*Nymphaea* 'Chubby'
*Nymphaea* 'Colossea'
*Nymphaea* 'Gladstone'
*Nymphaea* 'Gonnère'
*Nymphaea* 'Hal Miller'
*Nymphaea* 'Hermine'
*Nymphaea* 'Laura Strawn'
*Nymphaea* 'Laydekeri Alba'
*Nymphaea* 'Marliac Albida'
*Nymphaea* 'Mt Shasta'
*Nymphaea* 'Odorata Dwarf'
*Nymphaea* 'Odorata Gigantea'
*Nymphaea* 'Perry's Double
   White'
*Nymphaea* 'Perry's White
   Wonder'
*Nymphaea* 'Pöstlingberg'
*Nymphaea* 'Queen of Whites'
*Nymphaea* 'Starbright'
*Nymphaea tetragona*
*Nymphaea* 'Venus'
*Nymphaea* 'Virginalis'
*Nymphaea* 'Virginia'
*Nymphaea* 'Walter Pagels'
*Nymphaea* 'White 1000 Petals'
*Nymphaea* 'White Sensation'
*Nymphaea* 'White Sultan'
*Nymphaea* 'Yogiji'

### Tropical Waterlilies

*Nymphaea* 'Alice Tricker'
*Nymphaea* 'Brazo's White'
*Nymphaea* 'Florida Star'
*Nymphaea* 'Janice Wood'
*Nymphaea* 'Josephine'
*Nymphaea* 'Juno'
*Nymphaea* 'Louella G. Uber'
*Nymphaea* 'Marion Strawn'
*Nymphaea* 'Missouri'
*Nymphaea* 'Shirley Ann'

*Nymphaea* 'Sir Galahad'
*Nymphaea* 'Ted Uber'
*Nymphaea* 'Trudy Slocum'
*Nymphaea* 'White Delight'
*Nymphaea* 'White Lightning'
*Nymphaea* 'Wood's White
   Knight'

### Lotus

*Nelumbo* 'Alba Grandiflora'
*Nelumbo* 'Alba Plena'
*Nelumbo* 'Alba Striata'
*Nelumbo* 'Angel Wings'
*Nelumbo* 'Baby Doll'
*Nelumbo* 'Bai Mudan'
*Nelumbo* 'Chawan Basu'
*Nelumbo* 'Chong Shui Hua'
*Nelumbo* 'Crane Head Red'
*Nelumbo* 'Empress'
*Nelumbo* 'Little Green'
*Nelumbo nucifera*
*Nelumbo* 'Shirokunshi'
*Nelumbo* 'Shiroman'
*Nelumbo* 'Versicolor Edge'
*Nelumbo* 'Wan-er Hong'
*Nelumbo* 'Xiamen Bowl'

## YELLOW

### Hardy Marginals

*Caltha palustris*
*Cotula coronopifolia*
*Ludwigia arcuta*
*Ludwigia arcuta* 'Grandiflora'
*Lysimachia ciliata*
*Lysimachia nummularia* 'Aurea'
*Lysimachia terrestris*

*Lysimachia thyrsiflora*
*Mimulus guttatus* 'Variegatus'
*Orontium aquaticum*
*Ranunculus acris*
*Ranunculus flammula*
*Ranunculus flammula* 'Thor'
*Ranunculus repens* 'Buttered
    Popcorn'

## Tropical Marginals

*Canna flaccida*
*Canna* 'Ra'
*Limnocharis flava*
*Ludwigia peploides*
*Ludwigia peruviana*
*Neptunia aquatica*
*Wedelia trilobata*

## Water Irises

*Iris fulva* 'Marvell Gold'
*Iris pseudacorus*
*Iris pseudacorus* 'Beuron'
*Iris pseudacorus* 'Ecru'
*Iris pseudacorus* 'Ivory'
*Iris pseudacorus* 'Sun Cascade'
*Iris pseudacorus* 'Variegata'

## Waterlily-like Plants

*Hydrocleys nymphoides*
*Hydrocleys peruviana*
*Nymphoides crenata*
*Nymphoides geminata*

## Floating Plants

*Aeschynomene fluitans*

## Hardy Waterlilies

*Nymphaea* 'Betsy Sakata'
*Nymphaea* 'Carolina Sunset'
*Nymphaea* 'Chromatella'
*Nymphaea* 'Chrysantha'
*Nymphaea* 'Colonel AJ Welch'
*Nymphaea* 'Denver'
*Nymphaea* 'Gold Medal'
*Nymphaea* 'Helvola'
*Nymphaea* 'Highlight'
*Nymphaea* 'Joey Tomocik'
*Nymphaea* 'Lemon Chiffon'
*Nymphaea* 'Lemon Mist'
*Nymphaea mexicana*
*Nymphaea* 'Moon Dance'
*Nymphaea* 'Moorei'
*Nymphaea* 'Starburst'
*Nymphaea* 'Sulphurea'

*Nymphaea* 'Sulphurea
    Okeechobee'
*Nymphaea* 'Sunrise'
*Nymphaea* 'Texas Dawn'

## Tropical Waterlilies

*Nymphaea* 'Aviator Pring'
*Nymphaea* 'El Dorado'
*Nymphaea* 'Golden West'
*Nymphaea* 'Jamie Lu Skare'
*Nymphaea* 'Key Lime'
*Nymphaea* 'Laura Frase'
*Nymphaea* 'St. Louis Gold'
*Nymphaea* 'Trail Blazer'
*Nymphaea* 'Yellow Dazzler'

## Lotus

*Nelumbo lutea*
*Nelumbo* 'Yellow Bird'

## ORANGE OR PEACH

## Tropical Marginals

*Canna* 'Erebus'
*Canna* 'Florence Vaughn'
*Canna* 'Phasion'
*Canna* 'Pretoria'
*Canna* 'Taney'

## Hardy Waterlilies

*Nymphaea* 'Barbara Davies'
*Nymphaea* 'Barbara Dobbins'
*Nymphaea* 'Berit Strawn'
*Nymphaea* 'Clyde Ikins'
*Nymphaea* 'Colorado'
*Nymphaea* 'Cynthia Ann'
*Nymphaea* 'Florida Sunset'
*Nymphaea* 'Georgia Peach'
*Nymphaea* 'Peaches and Cream'
*Nymphaea* 'Peach Glow'
*Nymphaea* 'Reflected Flame'
*Nymphaea* 'Sunny Pink'
*Nymphaea* 'Thomas O'Brien'

## Tropical Waterlilies

*Nymphaea* 'Peach Blow'

## RED

## Hardy Marginals

*Apios americana*
*Hibiscus moscheutos*
*Lobelia cardinalis*
*Lobelia cardinalis* 'Red Giant'
*Lobelia fulgens* 'Queen Victoria'

## Tropical Marginals

*Canna* 'Endeavor'
*Canna* 'Panache'
*Mimulus* 'Lothian Fire'

## Hardy Waterlilies

*Nymphaea* 'Almost Black'
*Nymphaea* 'Atropurpurea'
*Nymphaea* 'Attraction'
*Nymphaea* 'Black Princess'
*Nymphaea* 'Burgundy Princess'
*Nymphaea* 'Charles de
    Meurville'
*Nymphaea* 'Charlie's Choice'
*Nymphaea* 'Conqueror'
*Nymphaea* 'Ellisiana'
*Nymphaea* 'Escarboucle'
*Nymphaea* 'Fireball'
*Nymphaea* 'Froebelii'
*Nymphaea* 'Gloriosa'
*Nymphaea* 'Gypsy'
*Nymphaea* 'James Brydon'
*Nymphaea* 'Laydekeri Fulgens'
*Nymphaea* 'Laydekeri
    Purpurata'
*Nymphaea* 'Little Champion'
*Nymphaea* 'Low Country'
*Nymphaea* 'Lucida'
*Nymphaea* 'Météor'
*Nymphaea* 'Newton'
*Nymphaea* 'Perry's Baby Red'
*Nymphaea* 'Perry's Black Opal'
*Nymphaea* 'Perry's Dwarf Red'
*Nymphaea* 'Perry's Red
    Sensation'
*Nymphaea* 'Red Queen'
*Nymphaea* 'Rembrandt'
*Nymphaea* 'René Gérard'
*Nymphaea* 'Sirius'
*Nymphaea* 'Steven Strawn'
*Nymphaea* 'Sultan'
*Nymphaea* 'Vésuve'
*Nymphaea* 'Wildfire'
*Nymphaea* 'Wucai'
*Nymphaea* 'Ziyu'

## Tropical Waterlilies

*Nymphaea* 'Antares'
*Nymphaea* 'Emily Grant
    Hutchings'
*Nymphaea* 'Jack Wood'
*Nymphaea* 'Jennifer Rebecca'
*Nymphaea* 'JoAnn'
*Nymphaea* 'Judge Hitchcock'
*Nymphaea* 'Maroon Beauty'
*Nymphaea* 'Mr. Martin E.
    Randig'
*Nymphaea* 'Mrs John Wood'
*Nymphaea* 'Red Cup'
*Nymphaea* 'Red Flare'
*Nymphaea* 'Ruby'

## Lotus

*Nelumbo* 'Ohga'
*Nelumbo* 'Red Bowl'

## PINK

## Hardy Marginals

*Asclepias incarnata*
*Baldellia ranunculoides* f. *repens*
*Butomus umbellatus*
*Epilobium hirsutum*
*Hibiscus moscheutos*
*Hibiscus palustris*
*Lychnis flos-cuculi*
*Mentha aquatica*
*Myosotis scorpioides* 'Pinkie'
*Phyla lanceolata*
*Physostegia leptophylla*
*Pontederia cordata* 'Pink Pons'
*Stachys palustris*

## Tropical Marginals

*Rotala rotundifolia*
*Ruellia brittoniana* 'Chi Chi'

## Water Irises

*Iris virginica* 'Pond Lilac
    Dream'

## Hardy Waterlilies

*Nymphaea* 'Amabilis'
*Nymphaea* 'American Star'
*Nymphaea* 'Anna Epple'
*Nymphaea* 'Appleblossom'
*Nymphaea* 'Arc en Ciel'

*Nymphaea* 'Bleeding Heart'
*Nymphaea* 'Bory de St-Vincent'
*Nymphaea* 'Celebration'
*Nymphaea* 'Fabiola'
*Nymphaea* 'Firecrest'
*Nymphaea* 'Formosa'
*Nymphaea* 'Gloire du Temple-
    sur-Lot'
*Nymphaea* 'Hollandia'
*Nymphaea* 'Improved Firecrest'
*Nymphaea* 'Joanne Pring'
*Nymphaea* 'Laydekeri Rosea'
*Nymphaea* 'Lily Pons'
*Nymphaea* 'Louise Villemarette'
*Nymphaea* 'Marliacea Carnea'
*Nymphaea* 'Martha'
*Nymphaea* 'Mary'
*Nymphaea* 'Masaniello'
*Nymphaea* 'Mayla'
*Nymphaea* 'Mrs CW Thomas'
*Nymphaea* 'Mrs. Richmond'
*Nymphaea* 'Norma Gedye'
*Nymphaea* 'Patio Joe'
*Nymphaea* 'Peace Lily'
*Nymphaea* 'Pearl of the Pool'
*Nymphaea* 'Perry's Crinkled
    Pink'
*Nymphaea* 'Perry's Fire Opal'
*Nymphaea* 'Perry's Rich Rose'
*Nymphaea* 'Perry's Vivid Rose'
*Nymphaea* 'Pink Grapefruit'
*Nymphaea* 'Pink Opal'
*Nymphaea* 'Pink Pumpkin'
*Nymphaea* 'Pink Sensation'
*Nymphaea* 'Pink Sparkle'
*Nymphaea* 'Pink Sunrise'
*Nymphaea* 'Ray Davies'
*Nymphaea* 'Rose Arey'
*Nymphaea* 'Rosennymphe'
*Nymphaea* 'Rosey Morn'
*Nymphaea* 'Somptuosa'
*Nymphaea* 'Splendida'
*Nymphaea* 'Strawberry Pink'
*Nymphaea* 'Wow'
*Nymphaea* 'Yuh Ling'

## Tropical Waterlilies

*Nymphaea* 'Emily Grant
    Hutchings'
*Nymphaea* 'Enchantment'
*Nymphaea* 'Evelyn Randig'
*Nymphaea* 'General Pershing'
*Nymphaea* 'JoAnn'
*Nymphaea* 'Mrs. Geo.
    Hitchcock'
*Nymphaea* 'Pink Capensis'
*Nymphaea* 'Pink Champagne'
*Nymphaea* 'Pink Passion'

*Nymphaea* 'Pink Platter'
*Nymphaea* 'Pink Star'
*Nymphaea* 'Queen of Siam'
*Nymphaea* 'Rosa de Noche'
*Nymphaea* 'Rose Bowl'
*Nymphaea* 'Shirley Bryne'
*Nymphaea* 'Sturtevantii'
*Nymphaea* 'Tammy Sue'
*Nymphaea* 'Texas Shell Pink'

## Lotus

*Nelumbo* 'Beauty'
*Nelumbo* 'Ben Gibson'
*Nelumbo* 'Birthday Peach'
*Nelumbo* 'Blue Girl'
*Nelumbo* 'Carolina Queen'
*Nelumbo* 'Charles Thomas'
*Nelumbo* 'Debbie Gibson'
*Nelumbo* 'Double Pink'
*Nelumbo* 'Drunkard on a Jade
    Tower'
*Nelumbo* 'Glen Gibson'
*Nelumbo* 'Greg Gibson'
*Nelumbo* 'Hindu'
*Nelumbo* 'Linda'
*Nelumbo* 'Maggie Bell Slocum'
*Nelumbo* 'Momo Botan'
*Nelumbo* 'Mrs. Perry D.
    Slocum'
*Nelumbo* 'Nikki Gibson'
*Nelumbo* 'Patricia Garrett'
*Nelumbo* 'Pekinensis Rubra'
*Nelumbo* 'Perry's Super Star'
*Nelumbo* 'Pink Bowl'
*Nelumbo* 'Red Scarf'
*Nelumbo* 'Rosea Plena'
*Nelumbo* 'Sharon'
*Nelumbo* 'Sparks'
*Nelumbo* 'Suzanne'
*Nelumbo* 'Table Lotus'
*Nelumbo* 'The Queen'
*Nelumbo* 'Welcoming'
*Nelumbo* 'Yangzhou Bowl'

## PURPLE

## Hardy Marginals

*Lobelia* 'Tania'
*Thalia dealbata*

## Tropical Marginals

*Canna* 'Intrigue'
*Eichhornia azurea*

## Floating Plants

*Eichhornia crassipes*

## Water Irises

*Iris virginica* 'Purple Fan'

## Tropical Waterlilies

*Nymphaea* 'Dir. Geo. T. Moore'
*Nymphaea* 'Edward D. Uber'
*Nymphaea* 'Hilary'
*Nymphaea* 'Islamorada'
*Nymphaea* 'Midnight'
*Nymphaea* 'Mme. Ganna
    Walska'
*Nymphaea* 'Purple Zanzibar'
*Nymphaea* 'Rhonda Kay'
*Nymphaea* 'William McLane'

## BLUE

## Hardy Marginals

*Laurentia palustris*
*Lobelia siphilitica*
*Mentha pulegium*
*Mimulus ringens*
*Myosotis scorpioides* 'Mermaid'
*Myosotis scorpioides* 'Wisconsin'
*Pontederia cordata*
*Pontederia cordata* 'Crown
    Point'
*Pontederia cordata* 'Spoon
    River'
*Preslia cervina*
*Veronica americana*
*Veronica beccabunga*

## Tropical Marginals

*Bacopa caroliniana*
*Bacopa lenagera* 'Variegata'
*Hygrophila corymbosa* 'Stricta'
*Hygrophila difformis*
*Hygrophila difformis* 'Variegata'
*Ruellia brittoniana*
*Ruellia brittoniana* 'Katie'
*Ruellia brittoniana*
    'Strawberries and Cream'
*Thalia geniculata*
*Thalia geniculata* f. *ruminoides*

## Water Irises

*Iris* 'Gem Dandy'

*Iris* 'Gerald Darby'
*Iris* 'Mountain Brook'
*Iris versicolor*
*Iris virginica*
*Iris virginica* 'Pond Crown
    Point'

## Tropical Waterlilies

*Nymphaea* 'Anne Emmet'
*Nymphaea* 'August Koch'
*Nymphaea* 'Bagdad'
*Nymphaea* 'Blue Beauty'
*Nymphaea* 'Blue Capensis'
*Nymphaea* 'Blue Spider'
*Nymphaea* 'Blue Star'
*Nymphaea caerulea*
*Nymphaea capensis*
*Nymphaea* 'Charles Thomas'
*Nymphaea* 'Clint Bryant'
*Nymphaea* 'Dauben'
*Nymphaea* 'Electra'
*Nymphaea elegans*
*Nymphaea gigantea*
*Nymphaea* 'Green Smoke'
*Nymphaea* 'Hudsonia'
*Nymphaea* 'Leopardess'
*Nymphaea* 'Margaret Mary'
*Nymphaea* 'Margaret Randig'
*Nymphaea* 'Moon Shadow'
*Nymphaea* 'Mrs. Martin E.
    Randig'
*Nymphaea* 'Nora'
*Nymphaea* 'Pamela'
*Nymphaea* 'Paul Stetson'
*Nymphaea* 'Perry's Blue
    Heaven'
*Nymphaea* 'Robert Strawn'
*Nymphaea* 'Silvermist'
*Nymphaea* 'Star of Siam'
*Nymphaea* 'Star of Zanzibar'
*Nymphaea* 'Tina'
*Nymphaea* 'Wood's Blue
    Goddess'

# Native and Rare or Endangered Plants

We are often asked which of our water plants are native to the United States. The following compilation is considerably longer than most people might expect. In fact, even we were a little surprised at just how many water plants listed in our catalog actually originated from our own waters.

Included in this list and shown by an asterisk (*) are those natives that are rare or endangered by loss of habitat. At the end of the natives list, then, is a list of rare or endangered non-natives.

## Hardy Marginals

*Acorus calamus*
*Acorus calamus* 'Variegatus'
*Alisma plantago-aquatica*
* *Apios americana*
*Arundo donax*
*Arundo donax* 'Variegata'
*Asclepias incarnata*
*Asclepias incarnata* 'Ice Ballet'
* *Calla palustris*
*Caltha palustris*
*Carex flacca*
*Carex muskingumensis*
*Carex muskingumensis* 'Oehme'
*Cephalanthus occidentalis*
*Cotula coronopifolia*
*Cyperus fluviatilis*
*Cyperus longus*
*Dulichium arundinaceum*
*Echinodorus cordifolius*
*Echinodorus cordifolius* 'Marble Queen'
*Eleocharis obtusa*
* *Equisetum fluviatile*
*Equisetum hyemale*
*Glyceria aquatica* 'Variegata'

*Hibiscus moscheutos*
*Hibiscus palustris*
*Hydrocotyle ranunculoides* 'Ruffles'
*Juncus effusus*
* *Juncus effusus* 'Cuckoo'
* *Juncus effusus* 'Gold Strike'
*Juncus effusus* 'Spiralis'
*Juncus glaucus*
*Justicia americana*
*Lobelia cardinalis*
*Lobelia cardinalis* 'Red Giant'
*Lobelia siphilitica*
*Lobelia siphilitica* 'Alba'
*Ludwigia arcuta*
*Ludwigia arcuta* 'Grandiflora'
*Ludwigia repens*
*Lysimachia ciliata*
*Lysimachia nummularia* 'Aurea'
*Lysimachia terresis*
*Lysimachia thyrsiflora*
*Mentha aquatica*
*Menyanthes trifoliata*
* *Mimulus alatus* 'Snow Crystal'
*Mimulus ringens*
*Orontium aquaticum*
*Peltandra virginica*
*Penthorum sedoides*
*Phragmites australis*
*Phyla lanceolata*
*Physostegia leptophylla*
*Pontederia cordata*
*Pontederia cordata* 'Alba'
*Pontederia cordata* 'Pink Pons'
*Pontederia cordata* 'Spoon River'
*Sagittaria* 'Bloomin' Baby'
*Sagittaria latifolia*
*Sagittaria latifolia* 'Brevifolia'
*Sagittaria latifolia* 'Leopard Spot'
* *Sarracenia leucophylla*
*Saururus cernuus*

*Saururus cernuus* var. *ruminoides*
*Scirpus americanus*
*Scirpus cyperinus*
*Scirpus validus*
* *Sium suave*
*Sparganium*
* *Stachys palustris*
*Thalia dealbata*
*Thalia dealbata* 'Broad Leafed Form'
*Typha angustifolia*
* *Typha domingensis*
*Typha latifolia*
*Typha laxmannii*
* *Veronica americana*

## Tropical Marginals

*Acrostichum danaeifolium*
*Bacopa caroliniana*
*Bacopa monnieri*
*Canna flaccida*
*Crinum americanum*
*Dichromena colorata*
*Hydrocotyle americana*
* *Hymenocallis liriosome*
*Ruellia brittoniana*
*Ruellia brittoniana* 'Chi Chi'
*Ruellia brittoniana* 'Katie'
*Ruellia brittoniana* 'Strawberries and Cream'
*Sagittaria lancifolia*
*Sagittaria lancifolia* f. *ruminoides*
*Thalia geniculata*
*Thalia geniculata* f. *ruminoides*

## Water Irises

* *Iris fulva* 'Marvell Gold'
*Iris versicolor* and cultivars
*Iris virginica* and cultivars

## Floating Plants

*Azolla caroliniana*
*Ceratopteris thalictroides*
*Lemna*

## Submerged Plants

*Ceratophyllum demersum*
*Potamogeton*
*Proserpinaca palustris*
*Ranunculus longirostris*
*Sagittaria natans*
*Sagittaria subulata*
*Vallisneria*

## Lotus

*Nelumbo lutea*
*Nelumbo* 'Yellow Bird'

---

## RARE OR ENDANGERED PLANTS NOT NATIVE TO THE UNITED STATES

*Aeschynomene fluitans*
*Hygrophila difformis* 'Variegata'
*Isolepis prolifer*
*Laurentia palustris*
*Lobelia* 'Tania'
*Mimulus guttatus* 'Variegatus'
*Salvinia longifolia*
*Saururus chinensis*
*Trapa bicornis*

# Measurement Conversion Charts

| To convert length: | Multiply by: |
|---|---|
| Miles to kilometers | 1.6 |
| Miles to meters | 1609.3 |
| Yards to meters | 0.9 |
| Inches to centimeters | 2.54 |
| Inches to millimeters | 25.4 |
| Feet to centimeters | 30.5 |
| Kilometers to miles | 0.62 |
| Meters to yards | 1.09 |
| Meters to inches | 39.4 |
| Centimeters to inches | 0.39 |
| Millimeters to inches | 0.04 |

## Temperatures

$$^{\circ}C = 5/9 \times (^{\circ}F - 32)$$
$$^{\circ}F = (9/5 \times ^{\circ}C) + 32$$

| To convert area: | Multiply by: |
|---|---|
| Square inches to square centimeters | 6.45 |
| Square feet to square meters | 0.093 |
| Square yards to square meters | 0.836 |
| Acres to hectares | 0.4 |
| Square miles to square kilometers | 2.6 |
| Square centimeters to square inches | 0.155 |
| Square meters to square feet | 10.8 |
| Square meters to square yards | 1.2 |
| Hectare to acres | 2.5 |
| Square kilometers to square miles | 0.386 |

| inches | centimeters |
|---|---|
| ⅛ | 0.3 |
| ⅙ | 0.4 |
| ⅕ | 0.5 |
| ¼ | 0.6 |
| ⅓ | 0.8 |
| ⅜ | 0.9 |
| ⅖ | 1.0 |
| ½ | 1.25 |
| ⅗ | 1.5 |
| ⅝ | 1.6 |
| ⅔ | 1.7 |
| ¾ | 1.9 |
| ⅞ | 2.2 |
| 1 | 2.5 |
| 1¼ | 3.1 |
| 1⅓ | 3.3 |
| 1½ | 3.8 |
| 1¾ | 4.4 |
| 2 | 5.0 |
| 3 | 7.5 |
| 4 | 10 |
| 5 | 12.5 |
| 6 | 15 |
| 7 | 18 |
| 8 | 20 |
| 9 | 23 |
| 10 | 25 |
| 12 | 30 |
| 15 | 38 |
| 18 | 45 |
| 20 | 50 |
| 24 | 60 |
| 30 | 75 |
| 32 | 80 |
| 36 | 90 |

| feet | meters |
|---|---|
| ¼ | 0.08 |
| ⅓ | 0.1 |
| ½ | 0.15 |
| 1 | 0.3 |
| 1½ | 0.5 |
| 2 | 0.6 |
| 2½ | 0.8 |
| 3 | 0.9 |
| 4 | 1.2 |
| 5 | 1.5 |
| 6 | 1.8 |
| 7 | 2.1 |
| 8 | 2.4 |
| 9 | 2.7 |
| 10 | 3.0 |
| 12 | 3.6 |
| 15 | 4.5 |
| 18 | 5.4 |
| 20 | 6.0 |
| 25 | 7.5 |
| 30 | 9.0 |
| 35 | 10.5 |
| 40 | 12 |
| 45 | 13.5 |
| 50 | 15 |
| 60 | 18 |
| 70 | 21 |
| 75 | 22.5 |
| 80 | 24 |
| 90 | 27 |
| 100 | 30 |
| 125 | 37.5 |
| 150 | 45 |
| 175 | 52.5 |
| 200 | 60 |

**USDA Plant Hardiness Zone Map**

AVERAGE ANNUAL MINIMUM TEMPERATURE

| Temperature (°C) | Zone | Temperature (°F) |
|---|---|---|
| -45.6 and Below | 1 | Below -50 |
| -42.8 to -45.5 | 2a | -45 to -50 |
| -40.0 to -42.7 | 2b | -40 to -45 |
| -37.3 to -40.0 | 3a | -35 to -40 |
| -34.5 to -37.2 | 3b | -30 to -35 |
| -31.7 to -34.4 | 4a | -25 to -30 |
| -28.9 to -31.6 | 4b | -20 to -25 |
| -26.2 to -28.8 | 5a | -15 to -20 |
| -23.4 to -26.1 | 5b | -10 to -15 |
| -20.6 to -23.3 | 6a | -5 to -10 |
| -17.8 to -20.5 | 6b | 0 to -5 |
| -15.0 to -17.7 | 7a | 5 to 0 |
| -12.3 to -15.0 | 7b | 10 to 5 |
| -9.5 to -12.2 | 8a | 15 to 10 |
| -6.7 to -9.4 | 8b | 20 to 15 |
| -3.9 to -6.6 | 9a | 25 to 20 |
| -1.2 to -3.8 | 9b | 30 to 25 |
| 1.6 to -1.1 | 10a | 35 to 30 |
| 4.4 to 1.7 | 10b | 40 to 35 |
| 4.5 and Above | 11 | 40 and Above |

# Index